MARKETING

A RESOURCE BOOK

Andy Hutchings

BA, PGCE, DipM, MCIM, M Inst TT

Senior Lecturer in Marketing and International Business
Faculty of Teaching, Professional and Management Studies
The University College of Ripon and York St John

PITMAN
PUBLISHING

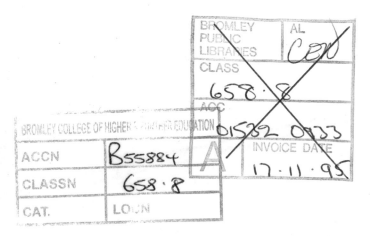
PITMAN PUBLISHING
128 Long Acre, London WC2E 9AN

A Division of Pearson Professional Limited

First published in Great Britain in 1995

© Pearson Professional Limited 1995

ISBN 0 273 60735 9

British Library Cataloguing in Publication Data
A CIP catalogue record for this book can be obtained from the British Library

1 3 5 7 9 10 8 6 4 2

Typeset by PanTek Arts, Maidstone, Kent
Printed and bound in Great Britain by Clays Ltd, St Ives plc

The Publishers' policy is to use paper manufactured from sustainable forests.

MARKETING
A RESOURCE BOOK

..ned on or before
..ast date stamped below.

'7

97

CONTENTS

PREFACE

The idea for this book evolved over a period of time, as a result of my own long-term involvement and interest in the subject matter and appreciation of the types of practical materials currently needed to match the expansion of marketing courses in higher education. It was written in various locations, ranging from Hull, York and Knaresborough to Geneva, Singapore, Venezuela and on the Sepik River in Papua New Guinea.

After an uncertain baptism in which it uncomfortably straddled the disciplines of economics, business studies and the social sciences, marketing has finally emerged in the 1990s as a fully- fledged academic subject in its own right, with a resultant rapid growth in the numbers of people involved in or studying it throughout the world.

Marketing incorporates the study of all facets of products, services and markets, and their relationship with consumers. As such, it is the most dynamic and interactive of the business disciplines but is both changeable and unpredictable. Indeed, its boundaries are constantly being shaped and redefined as the social and commercial worlds evolve and the customer becomes the common denominator in all business decision making. Its growth is reflected by greater company representation and continual professional development, guided by such organisations as the Chartered Institute of Marketing.

The concept of marketing has assumed the role of fundamentally underpinning every business course, owing to the increasingly widespread recognition that the needs of the customer must be fully understood before any product or service can take its position in the market-place.

Many textbooks have covered the theoretical building blocks of marketing, in varying degrees of complexity and for varying levels of educational study. This resource book, however, introduces the core concepts within a practical framework, to promote better understanding and emphasise the fact that marketing in one form or another pervades most of life's nooks and crannies.

As such, it complements the basic texts by providing topical and flexible supplementary material suitable for stimulating ideas or providing a wide variety of seminar or tutorial work, whilst including sample reference, reading and revision information, ideal for examination or assignment preparation. The book is organised in a logical sequence of topics, each containing theoretical and practical sections, and can be used to fit either traditional or unitised/semesterised courses.

It is envisaged that this approach will be appropriate for students pursuing basic business or marketing courses at BTEC, HNC/D or first/second year undergraduate degree levels, and for those following non-business courses containing a marketing element. In addition, the text is designed to be relevant to any personal study of the principles and practices of marketing undertaken for business training or updating purposes, for open or distance learning and for all forms of self-assessment in the subject.

The book attempts to illustrate marketing's dynamism and unpredictability whilst outlining the key theoretical concepts and setting them in a day-to-day context. Above all else, marketing is essentially an indispensable, practical philosophy of business and society relevant to everyone in today's world, and it is this fact which gives it the importance and the significance it has come to assume.

Thanks in particular are due to Susan Green for her skill, professionalism and hard work in typing the text, to Keith Stanley and Pitman Publishing for their interest and encouragement, to the Marketing Interest Group at the University of Humberside for their academic support and personal friendship, and to Pauline for her advice, patience and understanding throughout the project.

Andy Hutchings

Every effort has been made to trace and acknowledge ownership of copyright material in this book. The Publishers will be glad to hear from any copyright holder whom it has not been possible to contact.

1

THE MARKETING PHILOSOPHY

DEFINITIONS

Marketing is the management process responsible for identifying, anticipating and satisfying customer requirements profitably.

CHARTERED INSTITUTE OF MARKETING, UK

Marketing is the process of planning and executing the conception, pricing, promotion and distribution of ideas, goods and services to create exchanges that satisfy individual and organisational goals.

AMERICAN MARKETING ASSOCIATION

INTRODUCTION

Marketing is a term which tends to mean all things to all people. It has frequently been misunderstood, dismissed as a meaningless piece of current business jargon or considered to be a specific function such as selling, advertising or research. In fact, while all of these aspects of business certainly contribute to the overall marketing performance, they do not individually explain what marketing is really all about. The one ingredient often missing in any discussion of marketing is the word *customer* – but without customers, there can be no business activity in the first place.

So marketing is a philosophy and an attitude of mind which puts the customer at the centre of everything the business does. It is *not* just pricing or retailing or promotion, but a combination of many aspects of business which identify and satisfy customer needs and create new ones. Marketing is thus more than a set of techniques and not just the prerogative of marketing managers. Clearly it is the main reason for business' existence and all employees contribute to the effectiveness of their organisation's marketing performance, whether they realise it or not.

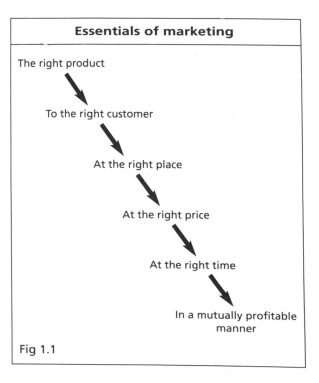

Essentials of marketing

The right product

To the right customer

At the right place

At the right price

At the right time

In a mutually profitable manner

Fig 1.1

In summary, marketing is concerned with trying to create and retain customers. The essentials of this process are illustrated in Figure 1.1. But the key component is the customer. After all, no customers equals no business, so ensuring the total satisfaction of the customer in all respects should become the main priority of any organisation. Certainly, the adoption of a philosophy of customer care will provide the central focus of operations throughout a marketing orientated business.

KEY CONCEPTS

DEVELOPMENT OF MARKETING

Adam Smith first referred to the importance of the customer in his book *The Wealth of Nations*, written over two hundred years ago at the time of the Industrial Revolution. Despite this, most firms continued to adopt a production orientation to business in the knowledge that whatever they could manufacture would be sold and the needs of the end consumer were therefore largely irrelevant.

But the requirement for a more modern approach to ensure business survival became paramount as society changed fundamentally over time. Historical factors such as the improvement in educational, technological and living standards, the removal of distance barriers and the population explosion led to two significant developments:

- increasing numbers of producers competing for limited amounts of business; and
- consumer demand becoming more specific and discriminating as goods and services became more available, the ability to pay for them improved and choice widened.

In turn this has meant that an orientation, first towards the selling function and latterly towards the consumer, now termed 'marketing', has inevitably emerged (see Figure 1.2).

So only comparatively recently have companies started to revise their historical traditions of production and sales orientation and to implement policies which are essentially customer centred. Even then, recent research has shown that many organisations still have no clear marketing strategy or philosophy.

ROLE OF MARKETING

The central importance of the customer in the whole buyer/seller exchange relationship is so fundamental as to make marketing thinking applicable to organisations of all sizes in all spheres of business. Its principles can be applied equally to fast-moving and durable consumer goods, industrial products, the service sector, non-profit concerns and individuals. On most days of our lives we are either involved in a buying and selling transaction or we are marketing ourselves at work, at home or socially. Even traditionally non-business orientated aspects of society, such as religion, the police and charity organisations, are appreciating the need to develop a customer-centred approach to their affairs. For marketing to be truly effective, every person within an organisation should adopt a marketing philosophy, i.e. 'think customer'.

Any application of basic marketing principles involves five broad areas of management:

1. Discovering people's needs or wants.
2. Producing goods or services to fulfil such needs or wants.

The history of marketing

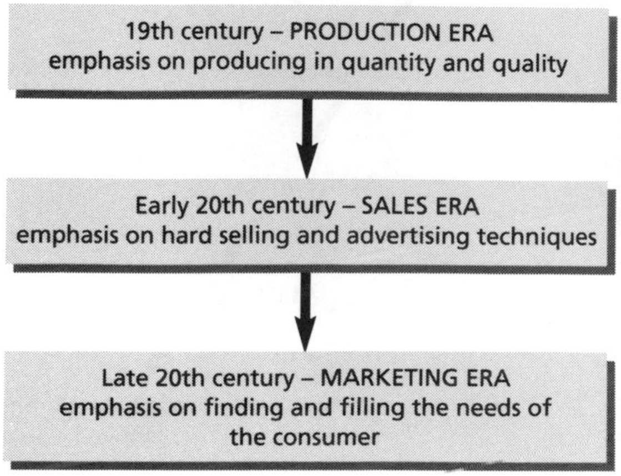

19th century – PRODUCTION ERA
emphasis on producing in quantity and quality

Early 20th century – SALES ERA
emphasis on hard selling and advertising techniques

Late 20th century – MARKETING ERA
emphasis on finding and filling the needs of the consumer

Fig 1.2

3. Using appropriate marketing techniques to sell what has been produced.
4. Ensuring that both buyer and seller will benefit from such exchange relationships.
5. Organising all available resources to achieve the first four objectives.

To ensure that these principles are adhered to, the following key marketing questions need to be asked on a regular basis by any organisation or individual:

To whom can we sell?
What can we sell?
When?
Where?
At what price?
In what quantities?
Why are we doing so?

Such questions involve decision making in many areas of business and several more abstract considerations. Tony McBurnie, former Director of the Chartered Institute of Marketing, believes that effective marketing can only take place following analysis and understanding of the 'Ten Cs':

- Customers
- Choice
- Competition
- Communication
- Culture
- Creativity
- Commitment
- Continuity
- Comprehensiveness
- Compatibility

Each of the 'Ten Cs' is an integral part of an organisation's effectiveness and day-to-day functioning, as well as contributing towards its overall marketing performance.

MARKETING ACTIVITIES

'Marketing' is an umbrella term incorporating many inter-related aspects of business, with customer focus as the common denominator binding them all together. It can therefore be reasonably argued that marketing should be the central element of business on which all other functions depend.

Chronological cycle of marketing activities

Product or service idea
Development and exporting — Research and development
Customer feedback — Design and planning
After-sales service — Market analysis and forecasting
Sales management and analysis — Costing and pricing
Selling — MARKETING — Branding
Merchandising and display — Raw materials and purchasing
Wholesaling and retailing — Production
Physical distribution — Quality control
Test marketing — Packaging
Sales promotion and public relations — Advertising and direct marketing

Fig 1.3

Table 1.1 Marketing and production orientations compared

Business Area	Marketing Orientation	Production Orientation
Advertising	Stresses need-satisfying benefits	Stresses features and production techniques
Customer Credit	A customer service	A necessary evil
Customers	Customer needs determine company plans	Customers depend on the company
Innovation	Exploits new opportunities	Uses technology to cut costs
Inventory levels	Reflect customers' needs and budgets	Reflect production requirements
Management	All customers are different and are targeted as such	Everyone is similar so 'mass marketing' will do
Market needs	External factors more important than internal ones	Inflexibility limits response and change
Marketing research	Determines customer needs and product suitability	Determines customer reaction, if used at all
Packaging	For customer convenience and a selling tool	Provides product protection
Products	Make what can be sold	Sell what can be made
Profit	A critical objective for company and customer	What's left after costs are covered
Sales Force	Helps customers buy if the product fits needs	Sells to customers
Transportation	A customer service	An extension of production and storage

From a basic idea to commercial success, all products and services experience a chronological cycle of business activities related to the marketing function, as indicated in Figure 1.3. The sequence and emphasis of these activities will vary according to the product, service and organisation concerned.

In a marketing orientated organisation, certain key activities will be ever-present throughout the cycle. These include marketing research, customer care, publicity and legal, ethical and other environmental considerations.

However, a production orientated company will only pay lip-service to marketing activities. The differences in outlook between production and customer orientated organisations can best be illustrated by comparing their respective attitudes towards various areas of business incorporated under the marketing umbrella (see Table 1.1).

THE FOUR Ps AND THE MIX

Marketing involves so many business functions that organisations find it necessary to apply all these activities in a systematic way. The most con-

Table 1.2 Marketing activities and the Four Ps

Product	Place	Promotion	Price
Features	Channel of distribution	Personal selling	Short-term strategy
Specifications	Retailing	Sales force	Long-term strategy
Appearance	Wholesaling	Sales analysis	Discounts
Benefits	Agents	Advertising	Allowances
Unique aspects	Franchising	Mass media	Costs
Research and development	Warehousing	Advertising agencies	Levels over time
Quality control	Transportation	Sales promotion	Geographic terms
Life cycle	Market exposure	Public relations	Credit agreements
Warranties/ guarantees	Outlet atmosphere	Corporate Image	Facilities
Accessories	Exporting	Merchandising/ display	Flexibility
Branding		Direct marketing	Consumer elasticity
Packaging			

venient method has proved to be grouping the fundamental principles into the 'Four Ps', an idea originally conceived by Jerome McCarthy.

The Four Ps consist of key concepts which can be defined and linked to the 'Four As' in the following way:

- *Product* – what is being offered to the market and provides ACCEPTABILITY.
- *Place* – how and where the product reaches the market and provides AVAILABILITY.
- *Promotion* – informing the customer about the product and providing AWARENESS.
- *Price* – establishing an exchange value for the product which provides AFFORDABILITY.

Each of these broad areas of marketing decision making contains a number of components, many of which are listed in Table 1.2. An organisation could refer to some or all of these when considering its strategy.

Only a few activities of marketing do not readily fit into this scenario, each of the Four Ps also incorporates specific objectives and strategic considerations. In addition to the Four Ps, there are two other key areas of marketing decision making:

- Marketing research – getting information on all aspects of the company, its customers and products.
- Market selection – identifying and targeting specific sections of the total market.

These are ever-present concerns for any organisation and serve to support all the activities covered by the Four Ps.

The combination of all the marketing tools available to a firm aiming to sell a product or service is called the 'marketing mix', a term first used in 1964 by Neil Borden, illustrated in Figure 1.4.

The marketing activities used and the type of marketing mix selected will depend on many factors, involving the organisation, its resources, environment, products and, of course, customers. Although these decisions are made as scientifically as possible, marketing is essentially a social science in which unpredictable human beings are at the centre. So a product's marketing mix is invariably trial and error, and is subject to constant review and adjustment to ensure a more successful performance.

Fig 1.4

ARTICLES

A1

Communication breakdown makes meaningful performance difficult

AS MARKETING REQUESTED IT.

AS SALES ORDERED IT.

AS ENGINEERING DESIGNED IT.

AS DATA-PROCESSING PROGRAMMED IT.

AS SERVICE INSTALLED IT.

WHAT THE CUSTOMER WANTED...

1 Explain the main reason for the situation depicted. What do you think is the overall message behind the cartoon?

2 Describe the difference between 'marketing' and 'sales' and the relationship between 'marketing' and 'communications'.

3 How could an organisation best avoid the situation illustrated?

4 Outline your ideas for the most effective relationship between the departments of 'engineering', 'data processing', 'service' and 'marketing'.

A2

Marketing – will it help you to survive and prosper in the '80s?
by Mr. H. Jevons of H. Jevons & Partners Ltd., Bradford.

After the 'production' era of the 1950s and the 'selling' predominance of the 1960s came the 'marketing' phase of the 1970s and 1980s. Where is Marketing now, and how does the marketing philosophy stand up in today's business conditions?

Have you heard comments similar to these when Marketing is discussed? "Marketing is all very well in periods of growth, but it doesn't work in periods of decline and recession."

"Marketing may work for large consumer product companies – but it won't work for a small industrial product company like mine."

"When I've costed my raw materials, production and overheads, I can't afford Marketing."

"Isn't Marketing just a fancy word for selling anyway?"

My definition of Marketing "The management function which profitably anticipates and meets customer needs" – will put these comments into perspective.

1 Why do many people believe marketing only works in 'periods of growth'?

2 Explain the validity of adopting a marketing philosophy during a period of economic decline or recession.

3 Are there any organisations, products or services for which a marketing approach would be either unnecessary or ineffective?

4 Put forward an economic argument to convince any company they could and should afford marketing.

 A3

Marketing: the central business function

Peter Blood

During the last few years there has been a remarkable increase of interest in the subject of marketing. This has been reflected both in statements by government ministers and in the calibre of marketing management. I believe that the recession has quite dramatically 'sharpened up' management attitudes and companies are now far more aware of the need to make the marketing function the central activity in the business. What this means, in effect, is that every business must recognise that its first purpose is to secure and keep customers. However, there is still some confusion about the role of marketing and many people use the term to refer to either selling or advertising. What exactly is marketing?

It has been said that marketing is a science and that its practice is an art. Not everyone would agree with this, but one thing is certain: there are too many definitions and descriptions of what marketing is!

Source: The Leeds Journal

1 Why does confusion exist about the definition of marketing?

2 Do you agree that 'marketing is a science'?

3 In what ways is the practice of marketing 'an art'?

4 Describe the role of the customer in a marketing orientated organisation.

 A4

ANITA RODDICK AND MARKETING – DOING WHAT COMES NATURALLY?

Question: *if Anita Roddick doesn't know what a marketing department does – let alone have one – how come The Body Shop made profits of £20 million last year?*

Answer: she doesn't need a marketing department to tell her what to do because she does it instinctively.

The question then really boils down to just another version of that old chestnut: which came first, the chicken or the egg? Marketing theory or common sense?

The fact that Ms Roddick puts her success down to common sense and a series of hunches only goes to show on what sound basic principles the discipline of marketing is founded. Whether she admits it or not, her actions vindicate what the profession has been trying to get across for years.

For example, a company is run by people for people, so it makes sense to ask customers what they think. There are suggestion boxes in every single shop and they are well used. This is the very essence of market research.

In marketing terms, keeping a close eye on the design and decor of all outlets maintains a strong corporate identity. Yet this strategy was born of a sense of aesthetics and the desire to communicate rather than any other more scientific motives.

The only difference between The Body Shop and other successful High Street ventures is this: the company is not afraid to have a soul and make it visible. Yet because human values have almost become The Body Shop's trademark, many commentators assume that they are nothing more than a marketing gimmick.

1 Is it necessary to have a marketing department to practise marketing?

2 Do you believe marketing theory is merely the application of common sense in a business environment?

3 What is the secret behind the success of The Body Shop?

4 How does Anita Roddick's use of communication methods overcome the criticism of marketing as a gimmick?

 A5

Saying 'Yes' puts business in Clover

Reluctance to give customers what they want is still endemic to British business. **Stephen Biscoe** *talks to a manager who sees it as a fatal flaw.*

THE woman was indignant. Her vacuum cleaner, she said on the phone, was just one day old and already it had stopped working, she needed it badly, lived miles from the store and it was most inconvenient. Would they please take it away and send her a new one?

If she had expected opposition, none materialised. The service manager said yes, they would send out a van that very day, and when her returned vacuum cleaner was eventually examined it was found to be full of wet grass – it had been used to vacuum a lawn.

Stuart Sandler, operations director with the Clover division of department stores group Allders, tells the story in spite of his insistence that the customer is always right.

Indeed, so firmly does he believe it that he introduced a customer-care programme in the store he ran which demanded a positive response to whatever customers asked for.

"Saying 'Yes,'" he says, "stretches the imagination. It makes possible what you thought was impossible."

Source: By courtesy of *The Yorkshire Post*, 28 February, 1994

1 According to the Clover division of Allders, what is meant by the term 'customer care'?

2 Is the customer always right?

3 Do you believe that 'reluctance to give customers what they want is still endemic to British business'? If so, why? Compare American and British attitudes towards the customer.

4 Describe examples of organisations that have established their reputation on a customer centred philosophy. Outline situations where the opposite applies.

ISSUES

ERAS OF MARKETING

Three historical phases:

a. Production
b. Sales
c. Marketing

1 Describe the historical reasons for the three eras and the emergence of marketing.

2 In what conditions might the production and sales eras return?

3 Could a new emphasis replace the marketing orientation and become the fourth phase?

A SHORT- OR LONG-TERM CONCEPT?

Marketing has been regarded both as a 'quick fix' solution to business problems and a longer-term consideration.

1 Give examples of organisations using marketing effectively in the short term.

2 In what situations are 'quick fix' marketing solutions justified?

3 How can an organisation best incorporate the marketing philosophy in the long term?

NATURE OF MARKETING

Variously described as an art, a science, a facet of business or a social science.

1 Examine the view that marketing is a social science. Do you agree with this description and if so, why?
2 What aspects of marketing are not business related in origin?
3 Can marketing be justifiably described as a business philosophy?

THE MARKETING MIX

Functions linked into convenient areas of business activity.

1 Do the 'Four Ps' represent a realistic coverage and sorting of the key marketing components? Suggest another division.
2 Describe and assess the usefulness of the 'Ten Cs'. Should they be incorporated into the 'marketing mix' and if so, how?
3 Does any one definition adequately describe what marketing is?

MARKETING'S ROLE IN BUSINESS MANAGEMENT

Referred to as an 'umbrella' area incorporating all other business activities.

1 Discuss the link between marketing and the production function in different organisations.
2 Should the marketing department, if one exists, be referred to at every stage of a product's life?
3 Research and describe an organisation where marketing performs a central, all-embracing role.
4 Explain the reason for the importance of 'customer care', giving examples of organisations in your experience which (a) do and (b) do not practise the philosophy.

RELEVANT IN ALL SITUATIONS?

Marketing is regarded as appropriate for all types and sizes of organisation.

1 Are there any business situations in which marketing is not relevant or is less important?
2 Is marketing more important for large concerns than for small businesses?
3 Can you apply the main principles of marketing to individuals, places and ideas, as well as to organisations? If so, how?
4 Is the marketing concept as relevant to industrial as to consumer markets?

QUESTIONS

1 Give the Chartered Institute of Marketing's definition of marketing.
2 Give another definition of the subject.
3 What is the key element at the centre of marketing?
4 What is meant by 'customer care'?
5 Give two reasons for the growing importance of marketing in recent times.
6 Name the three historical areas of marketing.
7 When and by whom was the term 'marketing' first discussed?
8 Which broad areas of business management are covered by marketing?
9 Which key questions have to be asked by companies adopting the marketing philosophy?
10 List the 'Ten Cs' of marketing.
11 List five characteristics displayed by a typically marketing orientated company.
12 List five characteristics displayed by a typically production orientated organisation.
13 List ten business activities which come under the general umbrella heading of marketing.
14 Give a definition of the marketing mix.
15 What are the 'Four Ps'?
16 Name two other key marketing decision-making areas.
17 Name five business activity areas which are covered by each of the 'Four Ps'.

PROJECTS

1 Consider an organisation of any size with which you are familiar. Are it and its products or services marketing or production orientated? Describe the aspects of business which provide clues to its philosophy and comment on how you think it could change for the better.

2 What is the relative importance of each element of the marketing mix in the sale of the following products or services:

- take-away hamburgers;
- a top restaurant meal;
- tinned spaghetti;
- mineral water;
- machine tools;
- computer software;
- spin-dryers.

3 Marketing has been described as the difference between 'making what you can sell' and 'selling what you can make'. Explain this statement, using examples.

4 'Consumption is the sole end and purpose of all production' – Adam Smith (*An Inquiry into the Wealth of Nations*, 1776). What did Adam Smith mean by this? Why has it taken such a long time for the importance of this statement to be recognised and why do many organisations still not follow it?

5 Does marketing apply equally to different types of organisations of all sizes? Include examples in your answer.

6 Put forward an argument as to why marketing should be a core study area in any business curriculum. Why is it increasingly assuming a wider role in society as a whole?

7 escribe and account for the likely variations in the marketing mix for consumer goods, services and industrial products.

8 Discuss all the ways in which a philosophy of customer care can be put into effect by an organisation.

9 'Marketing is the ability to create and retain customers.' How appropriate a definition do you consider this to be, and why?

10 'The only part of a business that brings in revenue is the customer – anything else is an expense.' Do you agree?

GLOSSARY

Customer the central element on which the marketing philosophy is based.

Customer care a marketing philosophy which focuses on ensuring the total satisfaction of the customer at all times and in all aspects of an organisation's business.

Customer orientation a marketing approach which places the needs and wants of the customer before any other consideration.

Four As the concepts of acceptability, availability, awareness and affordability, which help to define the Four Ps of the marketing mix.

Four Ps a method devised by Jerome McCarthy to group together all the activities of marketing into four broad areas, i.e. the Product, the Place, the Promotion and the Price, to provide for clearer decision making.

Macro-marketing a social process that directs an economy's flow of goods and services from producers to consumers in a way that effectively matches supply and demand and accomplishes the objectives of society.

Market all the potential customers who share common needs and wants and who have the ability and willingness to buy the product or service.

Marketing era the current period of time in which the importance of marketing is recognised and the concept is increasingly playing a central role in the business philosophy of many organisations.

Marketing (exchange) a set of processes stimulating and facilitating exchanges between buyer and seller for the mutual benefit of an organisation and its customers.

Marketing mix a term first used by Neil Borden to describe the combination of controllable variables available to an organisation to aid the process of selling a product or service.

Marketing orientation a philosophy adopted by an organisation which places its resource emphasis on understanding and meeting the needs of its customers.

Marketing philosophy an attitude of mind, pervading every aspect of an organisation, which places the customer at the centre of everything the business does.

Micro-marketing the performance of activities that seek to accomplish an organisation's objectives by anticipating customer or client needs and directing a flow of need-satisfying goods and services from producer to client or customer.

Production era a time when organisations focused their efforts on the production of goods or services rather than on their consumption.

Production orientation a business philosophy which concentrates on production efficiency and product quality rather than the needs and wants of the customer.

Sales era a time when organisations placed emphasis on the personal selling and advertising functions to sell their goods and services regardless of consumers' needs and wants.

Sales orientation a business philosophy which believes that consumer resistance to the purchase of goods or services will be overcome by creative advertising and personal selling rather than by understanding customer needs and wants.

Ten Cs a list of abstract variables suggested by Tony McBurnie which contribute towards the effectiveness of an organisation's marketing performance.

SUGGESTED REFERENCES

VIDEO MATERIAL

The Marketing Mix, No. 1, 'What is marketing?', Yorkshire Television, 1986.

Marketing in the Real World (Rose Toys), BBC, 1988.

The Manager 'Effective Marketing', Open College, 1990.

Winning – with the customer, BBC, 1992.

In Search of Excellence, Tom Peters Lecture Series.

Health and Disease, 'Customer Service', BBC/Open University, 1993.

The Brand New Marketing Mix, series of ten programmes, Yorkshire Television, 1993.

MAGAZINE ARTICLES

Journal of Marketing Management, Vol. 1, No. 1, Summer 1985, p.1 'Has marketing failed or was it never really tried?'; and p.87, 'Marketing and the competitive performance of British industry: Areas for research'.

Journal of Marketing Management, Vol. 1, No. 2, Winter 1985, p.119, 'In search of excellence in the UK'.

Journal of Marketing Management, Vol. 1, No. 3, Spring 1986, p.303, 'Toward a professional concept for marketing'.

Journal of Marketing Management, Vol. 2, No. 1, Summer 1986, p.1, 'The professional marketing manager'; and p.63, 'Reaching the customer: strategies for marketing and customer service'.

Journal of Marketing Management, Vol. 8, No. 4, Oct. 1992, p.351, 'The importance of customer satisfaction in explaining brand and dealer loyalty'.

Journal of Marketing Management, Vol. 9, No. 1, Jan. 1993, p.43, 'The customer wants service: why technology is no longer enough'.

Journal of Marketing Management, Vol. 9, No. 2, April 1993, 'A philosophy for marketing education in small firms'.

Journal of Marketing Management, Vol. 9, No. 3, July 1993, 'Business orientation, cliché or substance?'.

Marketing Business, April 1989, p.15, 'The Japanese art of marketing'.

Marketing Business, June 1989, p.4, 'Professional marketing', and p.14, 'Tying it all together'.

Marketing Business, Aug. 1989, p.20, 'From logistics to competitive advantage'.

Marketing Business, June 1990, p.22, 'Improving marketing orientation'.

Marketing Business, Nov. 1991, p.14, 'Marketing marketing'.

Marketing Business, Dec./Jan. 1991/2, p.24, 'Silent satisfaction'.

Marketing Business, May 1992, p.18, 'The customer comes first'.

Marketing Business, July/Aug. 1992, p.29, 'Back to the future, again'; and p.24, 'Science of marketing'.

Marketing Business, Sept. 1993, p.12, 'Science of marketing'.

Marketing Business, Feb. 1994, p.13, 'New generation marketing'.

FURTHER READING

Adcock, D., Bradford, R., Halborg, A. and Ross, C., *Marketing Principles and Practice* (2nd edn), Pitman, 1995, ch 1.

Baker, M. (Ed.), *The Marketing Book*, Heinemann/C.I.M., 1990, ch. 1.

Boone, L. and Kurtz, D. *Contemporary Marketing*, Dryden, 1989, ch. 1.

Brown, Andrew, *Customer Care Management*, Butterworth-Heinemann, 1991.

Cannon, Tom, *Basic Marketing*, Holt Business Texts, 1980, ch. 1.

Dibb, S., Simkin, L., Pride, W. and Ferrell, O., *Marketing*, Houghton Mifflin, 1994, ch. 1.

Foster, D., *Mastering Marketing*, Macmillan, 1982, ch.1.

Giles, G., *Marketing*, MacDonald and Evans, 1985, ch.1.

Majoro, Simon, *The Essence of Marketing*, Prentice Hall, 1993.

McCarthy, J. and Perreault, W., *Basic Marketing*, Irwin, 1987, chs 1 and 2.

Mercer, D., *Marketing*, Blackwell, 1992, ch. 1.

Oliver, G., *Marketing Today*, Prentice Hall, 1990, ch. 1.

Peters, T., and Waterman, R., *In Search of Excellence*, Harper and Row, 1984.

Acknowledgements

Borden, Neil, 'The Concept of the Marketing Mix', *Journal of Advertising Research*, 1964.

The Leeds Journal

Tony McBurnie (ex-Director, Chartered Institute of Marketing).

Smith, Adam, *An Inquiry into the Wealth of Nations*, 1776.

The Yorkshire Post

2

THE MARKETING ENVIRONMENT

DEFINITIONS

The marketing environment consists of external forces that directly or indirectly influence an organisation's acquisition of inputs and generation of outputs.   DIBB, SIMKIN, PRIDE AND FERRELL

The actors and forces outside marketing that affect marketing management's ability to develop and maintain successful transactions with its target customers.   KOTLER

INTRODUCTION

An organisation is generally in control of its marketing mix and can alter the variable Four Ps as it wishes, depending on its objectives, resources and so on. But before doing this it should consider a number of environmental factors which affect any organisation's decisions. Some of these are internal and thus to a certain extent controllable, the rest are external and largely uncontrollable, as illustrated in Figure 2.1.

Marketing cannot take place in a vacuum and organisations adopting a customer-led philosophy are sensitive to the ways in which the internal and external environments inevitably shape their orientation to business. As a result, they are likely to want to determine the nature of such influences and take the appropriate action.

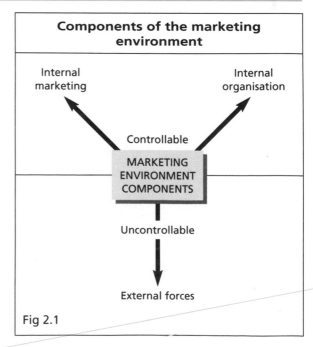

Components of the marketing environment

Internal marketing

Internal organisation

Controllable

MARKETING ENVIRONMENT COMPONENTS

Uncontrollable

External forces

Fig 2.1

KEY CONCEPTS

INTERNAL MARKETING

A fundamental environmental variable is the willingness and ability of the organisation to inculcate the customer-centred philosophy of marketing in all of its employees, whether part-time or full-time, junior or senior in status. Many companies are reluctant to devote resources to this task, preferring to concentrate on external communications, and yet any application of the marketing concept requires the full understanding and support of all employees to be properly effective.

This 'internal marketing' philosophy is described by Dibb, Simkin, Pride and Ferrell as 'the process by which marketing and non-marketing personnel understand and recognise the values of the marketing system and their place in it'. Putting into action such a process requires attention to a number of factors allied to human resource management, including:

- recruitment and retention of appropriate personnel;
- motivation of staff, including incentive schemes and competitions;
- implementing favourable conditions of service and treatment of employees;
- instituting staff training programmes, e.g. in information technology, customer care, communication skills, and so on;
- broadening the internal communications interface between all employees;
- explaining and discussing corporate practices and policies;
- fostering a teamwork approach through sharing of information, provision of social facilities, etc;
- researching, understanding and satisfying staff requirements in the short and the long term.

Successful practice of the above activities and their promotion to employees as part of an organisation's permanent internal management strategy will create a positive and happy business environment, favourable to all. From this solid foundation a co-ordinated and consistent approach can then develop which emphasises the importance of the customer to all personnel throughout the organisation.

An extension of the internal marketing ethos is the development of an appropriate 'organisational culture', or 'way in which things get done' within an organisation. This can be reflected in many ways, for example:

- the way in which people ritually interact, the language and technical jargon they use or the way they dress;
- the norms which govern the way in which work is organised and conducted, e.g. the structure and reporting arrangements;
- the organisation's view of itself, its corporate image and the dominant values it espouses;
- the way in which it treats its customers and its employees;
- the rules for playing the organisational game, i.e. the way in which one 'gets on' in the organisation;
- the organisational climate, as conveyed by its physical layout and general atmosphere.

Several types of organisational culture can emerge, with emphases on features such as power, role, task/achievement or person/support, although a strong, highly resistant culture could become an obstacle to integration.

To be effective therefore, internal marketing must be accepted and its philosophies carried out enthusiastically, which has the combined effect of increasing job satisfaction and improving customer relations. The organisation can then concentrate on how the internal atmosphere it has established is translated into external marketing success.

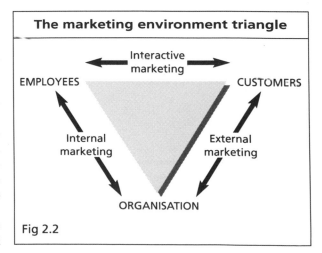

The marketing environment triangle

Interactive marketing

EMPLOYEES

CUSTOMERS

Internal marketing

External marketing

ORGANISATION

Fig 2.2

External marketing includes all the activities discussed in Chapter 1 which enable an organisation to satisfy the needs and wants of the customer. The quality of the interaction between seller and buyer will determine marketing success, but this will often depend upon individual contacts between employees of the organisation and current or prospective customers, or *interactive marketing* as it is known. (The relationships between the internal, external and interactive marketing environments are described in Figure 2.2.)

Customers might soon be lost (or might never be gained in the first place) if such contacts between company and consumer are unproductive, for whatever reason. So a marketing orientated organisation will try to ensure that interactions with customers are appropriate and positive. This does not just apply to sales people – initial contact often involves telephonists or receptionists, whose manner, appearance and skills of communication can either encourage or dissuade a customer seeking further dealings with the company.

While customer-contact staff undoubtedly play a key role, the importance of all other employees adopting the marketing philosophy must not be under-emphasised. The attitude of the caretaker or the delivery driver is just as important as that of the managing director or the team responsible for the production of a high-quality product or service. All communicate with potential customers every day and all contribute directly or indirectly to the overall success of the organisation.

INTERNAL ORGANISATION

So it is not sufficient for only the marketing department of an organisation to practise marketing. All individuals, sections and departments should play the same tune for maximum effectiveness.

However, ensuring that this happens requires the resources of an organisation to be arranged to reflect the marketing focus, and departmental structures to be developed along the same lines.

There are three broad categories of attitude towards marketing which determine the organisation of internal resources: marketing myopia, marketing recognition and marketing commitment.

Marketing Myopia

Theodore Levitt coined this term in 1960 to describe the position of a company which focuses on the production or sales functions rather than the customer and thus suffers from near-sightedness, a failure to appreciate the scope of the business. The marketing function would not exist in the organisation chart of such a company, which would adopt a negative approach and would be unwilling and unable to make any readjustments to its internal structure (see Figure 2.3).

Marketing Recognition

In firms where marketing does play a part, its exact role will generally depend upon the size of the company. Large companies will have correspondingly large marketing departments and employ specialists, while at the other end of the scale the owner/manager of a small business could well double up as marketing manager. The marketing function would feature in an organisation chart as separate from other management functions but with some informal links. Marketing action would

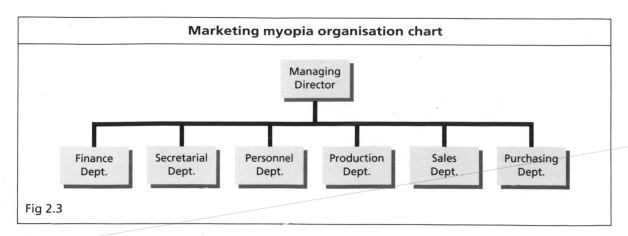

Fig 2.3

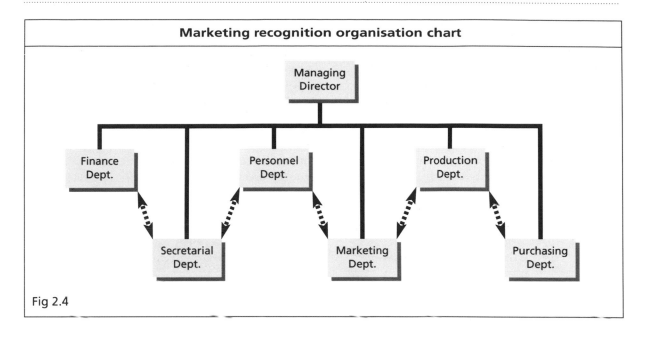

Marketing recognition organisation chart

Fig 2.4

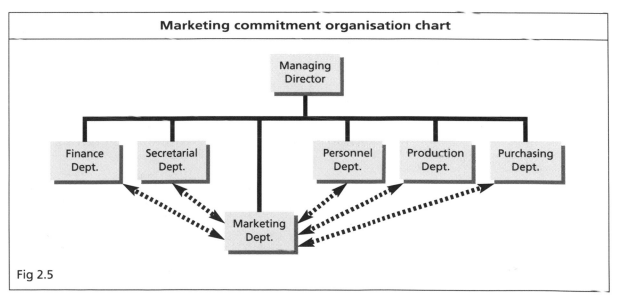

Marketing commitment organisation chart

Fig 2.5

be tactical and short-term in nature, using the tools of marketing as a 'quick-fix' solution (see Figure 2.4).

Marketing Commitment

Companies incorporating a fully developed marketing orientation will exhibit a flexible approach to their organisational structure. Marketing-related activities will predominate within the organisation chart and lines of communication between all sections and departments will be fluid, well developed and regularly reviewed for possible improvement. Marketing action is strategic and long-term in nature (see Figure 2.5).

The attitudes of these three types of company towards their internal organisational environment can also be illustrated by considering how each views the relationship between business functions.

The situation of marketing myopia is usually accompanied by a narrow view of business as a series of separate compartments with barriers between sections and little communication (see Figure 2.6).

Organisations exhibiting marketing recognition see business activities as inter-related and limited communication channels, with marketing viewed as a separate function (see Figure 2.7).

Firms exhibiting marketing commitment illustrate the total system view of an organisation where the marketing function is the common denominator, the concept is fully implemented, internally and externally, and all individuals and departments are led by customer needs and wants, without communication barriers intervening (see Figure 2.8).

Having organised its controllable internal environment and resources to reflect a marketing approach to business, a firm must then consider all the other variable factors which constitute its immediate micro-environment, e.g. its shareholders, the local community and other publics, before it goes on to examine external factors.

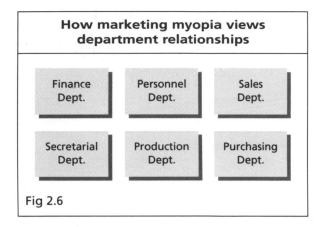

Fig 2.6

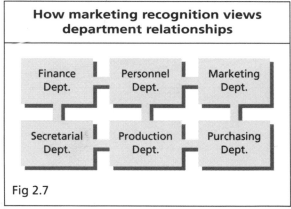

Fig 2.7

Fig 2.8

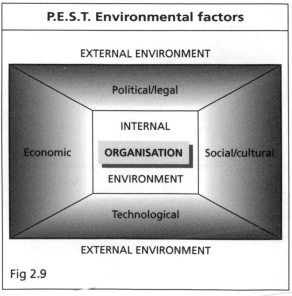

Fig 2.9

PEST EXTERNAL FACTORS

An organisation's *external* or *macro-environment* experiences many influences which the company can seek to understand and utilise or counteract, but not control. For convenience, the PEST acronym is used to identify the key environmental factors – Political/legal, Economic, Social/cultural and Technological. The relationship between the organisation and these external variables is illustrated in Figure 2.9.

Each of these environmental factors contains several aspects, any of which could be particularly significant. The marketing orientated organisation will thus conduct research into all these areas and act upon them where appropriate.

1. *Political/legal environment* – includes:
- central and local government systems;
- political ideologies and pressure groups;
- financing and grants;
- voluntary codes of practice;
- statutory legislation;
- consumer protection measures.

2. *Economic environment* – includes:
- stage of the business cycle – prosperity/recession/depression/recovery;
- rate of inflation;
- unemployment rate;
- resource availability;
- income levels – total/disposable/discretionary;
- interest rates.

3. *Social/cultural environment* – includes:
- demographic (population) and geographic trends;
- socio-economic class groups;
- status and background;
- norms and values;
- lifestyles and habits;
- peer groups and associates;
- specific characteristics, e.g. language and practices.

4. *Technological environment* – includes:
- technology transfer;
- innovation;
- desirable effects – living standards, leisure time;
- undesirable effects – health hazards, unemployment, aesthetic and environmental problems;
- short-term impact;
- long-term application.

In all these key areas there will be local and regional factors and variations to consider; while as the global market rapidly becomes a reality, organisations must take account of the effects of the international environment.

COMPETITIVE ENVIRONMENT

In addition to all the factors mentioned previously, the organisation must be aware of its competition, a key consideration which falls outside the boundaries of the PEST acronym but is nevertheless of vital importance to a company making decisions based on analysis of its environment.

From an economic perspective, an organisation must first understand the nature of the market in which it is operating, i.e. monopoly, duopoly, oligopoly, imperfect or perfect (these are covered in more detail in Chapter 13). Competitors can come in many shapes and sizes at all levels of business. They are usually either 'commodity competitors', where the forces of supply and demand establish the nature and extent of competition, or 'enterprise competitors', where both price and non-price factors come into play.

Another more practical categorisation is to look at the level of competition facing an organisation in terms of specific products and services. Here we can see that four main divisions apply, as illustrated in Figure 2.10.

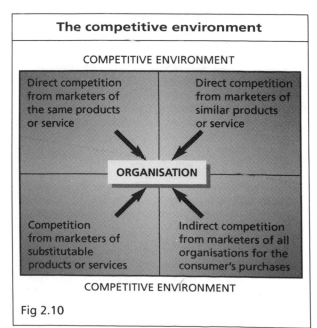

Fig 2.10

Source: Adapted from *Marketing*, Boone and Kurtz, Dryden Press, 1989

Having established the nature of its competitors, the organisation must set about the task of fully understanding those competitors' objectives, strengths, weaknesses and strategies by undertaking detailed research into every relevant aspect of their business.

For example, assessment of the marketing activities of the competition could include the following areas:

- *Product*   – formulation/performance
                        – packaging
                        – pricing
- *Distribution*   – type
                        – scope
                        – method
- *Advertising*   – content
                        – expenditure
                        – media

- *Market position*   – share of market
                           – type of consumer
                           – proportion buying

In fact, organisations committed to marketing will also try to discover the philosophies and ethos of businesses operating in their competitive environment.

Whether or not an organisation is able to gain a distinct competitive advantage as a result of such research will depend on its thoroughness and on its ability to predict the actions of competitors and react speedily and appropriately.

Knowledge of its competitors is thus of paramount and immediate concern to an organisation and, when combined with all the other internal and external environmental variables described earlier, provides a solid background of information on which it can base its marketing decisions.

ARTICLES

A1

Women learn the secrets of internal marketing
By Alex Renton

It wasn't hard to spot the self-assertion consultant. She could only have been the woman power-dressed in a check two-piece who bounced purposefully through the crowd at Women Back To Work '90 exclaiming "You chaps are obviously Press!", while all but grabbing the photographer by his tie.

Georgina Corscadden, managing director of Corscadden Associates, teaches internal marketing. "It's just like external marketing, really, but internal. Getting people to look at themselves as their best market."

A demonstration was needed. Ms Corscadden grinned a self-confident smile, collared Janice Rowe and set about teaching her internal marketing.

Ms Rowe is an administrative assistant with National Power – one of 5,000 who are to lose their jobs because of the company's privatisation. Ms Rowe wants to get into management, Ms Corscadden told her about SWOT – Strengths, Weaknesses, Opportunities, Threats.

After listing her experience and feelings in those categories rather shyly, Ms Rowe was told how to turn even National Power to advantage in interview. "Don't be embarrassed by the public sector, say, 'I've worked for a company four times the size of British Airways.' Turn it round."

"I think I should have seen you a long time ago," Ms Rowe said, and went away with a Corscadden leaflet – "Over 800,000 women want to return to work. Do YOU want to be one of THEM?" Courses start at £50 a day.

In lecture room one a sparse crowd was watching Barbara Jacques, of the Academy of Colour and Style International, show how to mix 'n' match your wardrobe – "making 10 items into 40 different looks". Sue Ash, 40, a former ballet dancer now on a women's management development course, was most impressed by Mrs Jacques's tip for that time when you find that your spare tights and the ones on your legs have got ladders. You cut off the bad leg from each pair and wear both.

Mrs Jacques's advice for women at interview was: "Understate. If you go understated you won't offend anybody. Tights always. No chipped nail polish. And no dangly earrings – they're only fine for arty situations."

Source: The Independent

1 What do you understand by the concept of 'internal marketing' as used by Georgina Corscadden?

2 Devise and justify a possible personal marketing mix for Janice Rowe.

3 Describe all the aspects of company policy Corscadden Associates might advise a client to include when training staff to adopt an internal marketing philosophy.

4 In what ways is internal marketing 'just like external marketing'?

A2

Thorntons' sweet success

Chocolate maker and retailer Thorntons which came up with the "Recessionary Range" to comfort depressed businessmen, announced increased annual profits yesterday.

The Derbyshire-based family company's pretax profits for the year to June 29 rose to £11.9m from £11.3m in the previous year.

Chairman John Thornton said he was confident of solid growth. But he warned: "The economic background remains uncertain and, as a consequence, I must be cautious in the short term."

Seven shops opened during the year and Thorntons plans to open a further 22 by Christmas.

Source: The Northern Echo

1 In what ways can companies like Thorntons try to offset the effects of a recession?

2 Are confectionery products affected any more (or less) than other fast-moving consumer goods by variable factors connected with the economic environment?

3 Describe the competitive environment faced by Thorntons.

4 Construct an organisation chart for Thorntons and explain how it would enable its internal environment to implement fully the marketing philosophy.

A3

New fears at Euro Disney

Auditors yesterday admitted the Euro Disney theme park might go bust if it failed to rework its financing with bankers and parent group Walt Disney by the spring.

But Euro Disney played down the report, saying it had revealed the situation it was facing when it reported a loss of £613m in the last financial year.

The cash-strapped company, which said earlier this year it was facing liquidity problems, is being propped up by its U.S. parent. When this comes to an end in the spring, Euro Disney will need a source of new cash.

"The group will need financial support to face its contractual obligations in the 1994 accounting year," the auditors said.

"If the financial restructuring measures envisaged do not reach a conclusion in sufficient time, the group will have cash problems and will not be able to continue its activities."

The search for new financing could prove difficult, with banks already delaying the start of talks until a separate audit, by KPMG Peat Marwick, has been carried out.

Analysts said banks would have to write-off some debt, which is bound to cause haggling among the 60 institutions involved.

Source: The Northern Echo

1 What cultural factors are important for Walt Disney to consider when building a new theme park outside the USA?

2 Explain the part played by the technological environment in the amusement park industry.

3 What do you believe to be the main international environmental reasons behind the difficulties Euro Disney has experienced?

4 How would you advise Euro Disney to structure its internal organisation chart to improve the chances of economic success for the business?

A4

Reporter **Helen Carroll** goes on the scent of the great perfume debate

THERE'S a bad smell in the air – a bad smell created by the perfume houses who dedicate themselves to making women more desirable to men.

The leading fragrance companies have come up smelling like roses after claims that they were keeping prices of designer perfumes artificially high.

The Monopolies and Mergers Commission investigation into the perfume industry concluded that although a monopoly exists in the industry, it does not operate against the public interest.

Now one thing is very clear – fragrance-lovers will continue to pay through the nose when they splash out on expensive odours.

The MMC investigation was launched after high street discount chain Superdrug complained perfume houses were operating a cartel to keep scent prices artificially high.

Consumers' Association representatives yesterday reacted angrily to the decision.

"The Monopolies and Mergers Commission has swallowed the perfume companies' arguments hook, line and sinker," said CA policy research manager, Philip Cullum. "It is an inconsistent, incoherent, badly-argued report.

"The MMC has given perfume manufacturers carte blanche to charge artificially high prices."

Source: The Northern Echo, 13 November 1993

1 What social factors should perfume companies consider before marketing their products?

2 Explain how a knowledge of demographics is important to an organisation trading in this market.

3 Do you think that the political environment could operate more effectively in this situation? If so, how?

4 What aspects of the legal environment affect the perfume industry directly?

A5

Fostering a greener view from business

Dr Jim Carrick is chairman of a group which aims to promote positive relations between industry and the environment. **David Lee** met him.

LAND reclaimed for industrial use in the heart of industrial Teesside is to be flooded once more as part of an environmental project.

Ironic, perhaps – but good news for migratory birds, which will have better "hotel facilities" when they stop off near Seal Sands as a result of the tidal flooding scheme.

Dr Jim Carrick is delighted with the project, which he highlights as evidence of the growing co-operation between industry and nature on Teesside.

The business technical manager with ICI is the new chairman of Inca (Industry Nature Conservation Association).

Set up four years ago, Inca aims to foster close and productive relations between environmental groups and industry.

"There was a conflict, but perhaps it was more in perception than reality," said Dr Carrick.

"Planning proposals were occasional sources of conflict, but the laying of the Amoco gas pipeline was an example of how we could work together to minimise problems."

Inca, which is also currently involved with environmental improvements near the Enron site at Lazenby, now has more than 30 members, including local authority representatives as well as industrialists and ecologists.

"The aim has always been to seek co-operative outcomes rather than confrontation," said Dr Carrick.

Greenpeace still chooses to attack from the outside, but most other green bodies seem to prefer working within the system.

"There was initial suspicion and perhaps concern from the environmentalists, but now we have the Cleveland Wildlife Trust, English Nature and the RSPB on board," said Dr Carrick.

"I think the growing membership and wide range of projects it has undertaken demonstrates its success."

Inca funds projects by members' subscriptions and is currently monitoring wildlife in the reedbeds at Billingham and seals in the Tees, in addition to the flooding work.

"It is quite a complex environmental project, which involves recreating wetlands. It should be of great help to migratory birds – it's an exciting project and should be finished this year," said Dr Carrick.

"I think these practical examples show that industry is doing its best to positively associate itself with all aspects of the environment in which we operate."

Source: The Northern Echo

1 How does this case illustrate co-operation between industry and the local community?

2 Describe the range of 'green' issues affecting an organisation directly or indirectly.

3 Advise an organisation as to why it should seek to work with the community over environmental matters.

4 Explain the links between the 'green' lobby and the political/legal environments. How might these become stronger in the future?

ISSUES

INTERNAL MARKETING

Means of inculcating the organisation's marketing ethos to all employees.

1 Is it realistic and desirable for a company to expect that every employee can be 'reached' by an internal marketing philosophy?

2 What can an organisation do if it is faced with an employee or employees who resist or question the internal marketing policy? What should an employee do on realising that his or her personal marketing ideas clash with those of the organisation?

3 What do you understand by the term 'organisational culture'? What is the culture of the organisation of which you are a member and what factors help to determine it?

THE ORGANISATIONAL ENVIRONMENT

The way a company arranges its internal structure can affect its ability to respond to market needs.

1 Should marketing assume more importance than other business functions, e.g. personnel? If so, how and why?

2 Should other departments perceive a 'threat' to their existence from the expansion of marketing?

3 Does an organisation chart provide a true indicator as to whether a company is production or marketing orientated?

MARKETING MYOPIA

Many organisations still do not recognise the existence of marketing.

1 What are the main indicators of marketing myopia?

2 Discuss examples of organisations suffering from marketing myopia.

3 What are the main catalysts of change for such an organisation?

4 Is it more likely that industrial marketing companies would suffer from myopia than consumer ones, and if so, why?

EXTERNAL ENVIRONMENT

Provides the crucial supplementary information a company needs.

1 Explain how the external environment can vary depending on its geographic source, e.g. local, regional, national or international.

2 Discuss situations in which the technological environment can have counter-productive effects on the organisation.

3 How can an organisation try to ensure it has current, relevant and detailed environmental information? Refer to the political/legal and social/cultural environments.

4 What areas of marketing activities are affected by national and/or EU laws? Is the increasing significance of the legal environment always advantageous to the organisation and the consumer?

ECONOMIC ENVIRONMENT

Marketing is often the first area of business to be sacrificed in a recession.

1 What are the reasons put forward by organisations for spending less on marketing in difficult economic circumstances?

2 Outline the arguments for an organisation spending more on marketing in a recession.

3 How should a company vary its marketing expenditure in times of depression, recovery and prosperity?

COMPETITIVE ENVIRONMENT

The most volatile environment in which an organisation operates.

1 Is the competitive environment of more immediate importance to marketers than the other external environments?

2 How can an over-emphasis on competitive research become counter-productive or even illegal?

3 How would you advise a company to organise itself internally to reflect the importance of the competitive environment?

QUESTIONS

1 Give a definition of the marketing environment.

2 What are the main components of an organisation's overall marketing environment?

3 What is internal marketing? What is organisational culture?

4 Name four aspects of human resource management which will improve the internal marketing process, if utilised by a firm.

5 Name three ways in which an individual could seek to improve his or her own 'personal' marketing.

6 What is interactive marketing?

7 What are the three broad categories of organisational attitudes towards marketing?

8 What is marketing myopia?

9 What are the main differences in organisational structure displayed by marketing and production orientated companies?

10 What are the main differences between how marketing and production orientated companies view the relationship between business functions?

11 Explain the differences between controllable and uncontrollable environmental factors.

12 Name three political/legal environmental factors.

13 Name three economic environmental influences.

14 Name three aspects of the social/cultural environment.

15 Name three technological environment factors.

16 What are the four main components of an organisation's competitive environment?

17 Give four examples of areas of research which can be undertaken by organisations seeking to assess their competition.

PROJECTS

1 Is the application of internal marketing procedures as important to an organisation as getting its external marketing right? Give reasons for your views and use relevant examples, referring to organisational culture where appropriate.

2 Explain the fundamental differences between the three organisation charts depicted in Figures 2.3, 2.4 and 2.5. Give examples of companies which adopt each philosophy and describe their respective attitudes to business.

3 Choose an example of an organisation in which all employees are encouraged to support the internal environment and to 'think marketing'. Describe its philosophy and how it implements the principles of the marketing mix.

4 Some organisations do not have any executives or departments with the word 'marketing' in their titles. How would you attempt to assess whether or not such a company was successful in marketing terms?

5 Assume the position of a newly-appointed marketing manager of a company manufacturing a consumer or industrial product or service of your choice. You are alarmed to find out that only 2 per cent of the company's financial turnover and personnel is devoted to marketing orientated functions. Describe the main changes you would make to the internal environment and the arguments you would use in a meeting with the board of directors to increase the company's percentage of financial and human resource functions directly related to marketing.

6 In their definition of internal marketing, Dibb *et al.* differentiate between marketing and non-marketing personnel. Is there a difference?

7 'To be successful, a company must adapt its marketing mix to trends and developments in the environment' (Kotler). Compare how organisations marketing (*a*) consumer products, (*b*) services and (*c*) industrial products might accomplish this, referring to PEST factors and the competitive environment.

8 Describe all the marketing actions at each stage which might be taken by (*a*) a consumer and (*b*) an industrial organisation to combat or exploit the effects of the four main phases of the business cycle, i.e. recession, depression, recovery and prosperity.

GLOSSARY

Atmosphere designed environments that create or reinforce the buyer's desire to purchase a product or service.

Business (or trade) cycle changes in the level of business activity over time, ranging from recession and depression to recovery and prosperity.

Commodity competition where supply/demand market forces establish the nature and extent of competition and the prices to apply.

Competition the struggle for customers between companies usually marketing similar or substitutable products or services to the same target market.

Competitive advantage or edge some benefit or value provided by a product or company which gives it superiority in the market-place.

Competitive environment market situation within a company's external environment in which organisations are competing for the consumer's purchasing power.

Cultural environment environment consisting of a complex mixture of values, ideas, attitudes and other meaningful symbols that help people communicate and make purchasing decisions.

Demographics the science of social and population statistics, which provides important information for environmental analysis.

Discretionary income amount of disposable income left over after fixed regular outgoings have been paid. Uncommitted money susceptible to marketing techniques.

Disposable income residue of personal income after statutory deductions at source.

Economic environment factors influencing consumers' buying power and organisational strategy, including stage of business cycle, inflation and interest rates, unemployment situation, income and resource availability.

Enterprise competition where both price and non-price factors play a part in determining the nature and extent of competition.

Environment the world which surrounds an organisation or individual and influences behaviour in a variety of contexts.

External environment environmental factors affecting an organisation from outside its boundaries.

Income flow of payments accruing to an individual or organisation during a period of time (also known as revenue).

Inflation economic situation, contrasting with deflation, where decreasing purchasing power is caused by price rises, usually as a result of too much money chasing too few goods.

Interactive marketing recognition by an organisation that performance in the market-place is greatly affected by the quality of the interaction between buyer and seller.

Internal marketing motivating and training all staff in the organisation's philosophies in order to foster teamwork and provide customer satisfaction.

Legal environment forces arising from the legislation and interpretation of laws which restrain and control marketing decisions and activities.

Macro-environment the larger societal forces that affect the whole micro-environment, including cultural, economic, demographic, legal, political, social, technological and competitive forces.

Marketing environment the forces inside and outside an organisation that affect the ability of marketing management to develop and maintain successful transactions with its target customers.

Marketing myopia term coined by Theodore Levitt to describe a situation applying to organisations lacking any marketing orientation and failing to recognise the broad scope of their businesses.

Mega-marketing the use of various environmental aids or skills to gain the co-operation of influential parties and thus gain access to markets in unreceptive countries (first suggested by Kotler).

Micro-environment forces close to the organisation that affect its ability to serve its customers, e.g. the company, its distribution channels, customer markets, shareholders and publics.

Norms rules and codes of behaviour or conduct pertaining in a particular organisation or society.

Organisational culture the philosophies which are adopted and the ways in which activities are handled within an organisation.

Peer group class or group of people who are equal in social standing, rank, age, etc. and who can affect their associates' behaviour.

PEST analysis survey of the political, economic, social and technological environments, undertaken by organisations to establish the key uncontrollable variable factors affecting them externally.

Political environment forces influencing the economic, legal and political stability of a country which will in turn affect the organisation.

Social environment factors affecting the organisation, which include the family, lifestyles, education, religion and other societal forces.

Technological environment forces of technology, such as business innovation, which influence marketing decisions and activities.

Technology the knowledge of how to accomplish tasks and reach goals.

Values ethical and moral standards of an individual or society which evolve over time through tradition, education, religion and so on.

SUGGESTED REFERENCES

VIDEO MATERIAL

Contemporary Marketing, Video Cases, No. 2 (Mitsubishi Motor Sales of America), Boone, L. and Kurtz, D., Dryden Press, 1989.

Business Studies, 'External environment of the business' (Tyne and Wear Metro), Thames Television, 1990.

MAGAZINE ARTICLES

Journal of Marketing Management, Vol. 1, No. 3, Spring 1986, p.265, 'The role and function of the chief marketing executive and the marketing department'.

Journal of Marketing Management, Vol. 8, No. 2, April 1992, p.117, 'Competitive intelligence'; and p.177, 'Corporate culture: is it really a barrier to marketing planning?'.

Journal of Marketing Management, Vol. 9, No. 3, July 1993, p.219, 'Scope of internal marketing'.

Journal of Marketing Management, Vol. 9, No. 4, Oct. 1993, p.373, 'A cognitive perspective on managers' perceptions of competition'.

Marketing Business, Oct. 1988, p.10, 'How ICL discovered marketing'.

Marketing Business, Sept. 1991, p.24, 'Internally yours'.

Marketing Business, Sept. 1992, p.41, 'Supplementary benefits'.

Marketing Business, Nov. 1993, p.9, 'The transformation of marketing – The challenge of technology'.

Marketing Business, Feb. 1994, p.13, 'New generation marketing'; and p.34, 'Marketing laws – a European flavour'.

Marketing Business, April 1994, p.24, 'Internal affairs'.

FURTHER READING

Adcock, D., Bradford, R., Halborg, A. and Ross, C., *Marketing Principles and Practice* (2nd edn), Pitman, 1995, chs 3, 4 and 7.

Baker, M. (Ed.), *The Marketing Book*, Heinemann/ C.I.M., 1990, chs 2 and 6.

Boone, L. and Kurtz, D., *Contemporary Marketing*, Dryden, 1989, ch. 2.

Cannon, Tom, *Basic Marketing*, Holt Business Texts, 1980, chs 2 and 3.

Dibb, S., Simkin, L., Pride, W. and Ferrell, O., *Marketing*, Houghton Mifflin, 1994, ch. 2.

Kotler, P. and Armstrong, G., *Marketing*, Prentice Hall, 1993, ch. 3.

McCarthy, J. and Perreault, W., *Basic Marketing*, Irwin, 1987, ch. 4.

Mercer, D., *Marketing*, Blackwell, 1992, ch. 4.

Peters, T. and Waterman, R., *In Search of Excellence*, Harper and Row, 1984.

Acknowledgements

The Independent.

Levitt, T., 'Marketing myopia', *Harvard Business Review*, July-August 1960, pp. 45–56.

The Northern Echo.

3

MARKETING RESEARCH

DEFINITIONS

The systematic, objective and exhaustive search for and study of facts relevant to any problem in the field of marketing.

INDUSTRIAL MARKETING RESEARCH ASSOCIATION

The gathering, recording, analysing and reporting of all facts relating to transfer and sale of goods and services. It is usually, but not necessarily, based on statistical probability theory and always uses the scientific method.

AMERICAN JOURNAL OF MARKETING

INTRODUCTION

Gathering information is an essential and permanent feature of any marketing orientated business. Without it, any planning decisions made will lack the background knowledge necessary to be effective.

Research is vital because up-to-date and reliable data is continuously required on all the activities of marketing. It is not a separate component of planning to be treated in isolation, but an integral part of the whole marketing process (see Figure 3.1).

In organisations committed to a marketing philosophy, on-going research is undertaken into every aspect of business, including their internal and external environments – indeed, such organisations will research into the effectiveness of their research methods!

When 'research' is mentioned in the context of marketing, people automatically think of 'market research' rather than the more accurate term 'marketing research'. So at this stage it is important to clarify exactly what is meant by the two expressions.

Market research covers research into all aspects of the specific market under consideration (including population figures, social class statistics, consumer habits, and so on), whereas *marketing research*

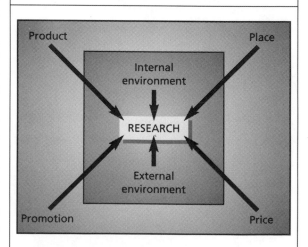

The key role of research

Product   Place

Internal environment

RESEARCH

External environment

Promotion   Price

Fig 3.1

covers research into all aspects of marketing (for example, data relating to advertising, pricing, new product developments, and all the other components of the marketing process).

KEY CONCEPTS

NATURE OF RESEARCH

A comprehensive marketing research campaign thus involves the continuous gathering of information across the full range of an organisation's activities. Some of the more important areas where the provision of accurate market intelligence data is vital include:

- retail audits;
- monitoring market characteristics and changes;
- analysing market share;
- testing the acceptibility of new products/services;
- researching into competitive products/services;
- measuring the effectiveness of promotional methods;
- studying the effects of pricing strategies;
- forecasting short- and long-term business trends.

For the purposes of planning, all the many uses of marketing research can be broadly grouped into three categories, as indicated in Figure 3.2.

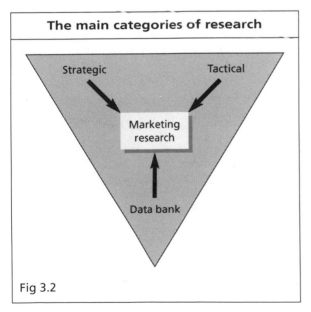

The main categories of research

Fig 3.2

Strategic research includes the knowledge needed to guide decisions which are likely to have long-term implications, such as economic forecasting and resource analysis. This contrasts with *tactical research* which involves information relating to short-term decisions, for example specific actions of competitors or adjustments in prices. *Data-bank research* incorporates all the useful market information which needs constant up-dating, for instance detail on media rates and industrial or commercial trends.

For all three categories, the nature of the information gathered falls into two broad types, quantitative and qualitative.

Quantitative data includes observable and/or recordable facts which are capable of substantiation, such as:

- people's actions, e.g. buying habits;
- demographic and social facts;
- technical and financial requirements.

Using these facts, the characteristics of a small sample are considered to be representative of the larger population. Such information is normally objective, unbiased and reliable and forms the basis of an organisation's research bank.

Qualitative research provides subjective data, seeking people's opinions, attitudes, awareness or impressions, and therefore is dependent upon human response, memory and reaction. It should thus be used by an organisation as a guideline rather than a factual basis for planning. For example, a person's saying they intend to purchase a particular product does not necessarily mean that they will, so the data could be very unreliable.

Qualitative research seeks to elicit information from the potential customer, such as:

- knowledge of a product/service/organisation;
- image or opinions of a product/service/organisation;
- intentions to buy a product or service;
- perceptions, e.g. of advertising or packaging;
- motives for purchasing, whether deliberate or subconscious.

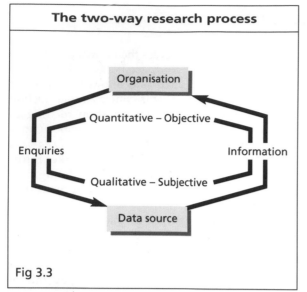

The two-way research process

Organisation

Quantitative – Objective

Enquiries · Information

Qualitative – Subjective

Data source

Fig 3.3

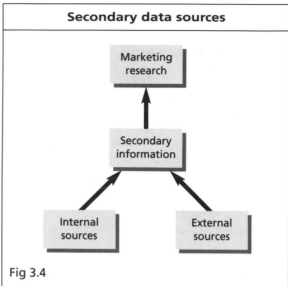

Secondary data sources

Marketing research

Secondary information

Internal sources · External sources

Fig 3.4

Figure 3.3 illustrates that marketing research is a two-way process. To be constantly aware of what the market is demanding at any time and to be able to supply what is required, the producer or service provider must ensure that they are making the appropriate research enquiries and receiving accurate marketing information in return.

So marketing research is not the exclusive domain of the high street interviewer carrying a clipboard, or what results from filling in a mail questionnaire, but a structured and complex operation. Effective research necessitates an understanding of the nature of the information being gathered and utilising it accordingly. There are two main kinds of method used by researchers in their quest for both quantitative and qualitative data, secondary and primary methods.

SECONDARY METHODS

Much of the information sought by organisations already exists in one form or another. Because it is based on data previously collated elsewhere, this kind of research is called *secondary* and is usually the first type to be undertaken as it is generally less expensive than the alternatives. Most secondary data involves reference sources which can be consulted from the comfort of an office desk, hence it is often referred to as *desk research*.

Most organisations already possess valuable marketing information. Such internal sources of important data include:

- records of complaints and enquiries;
- sales records, including prices/geography/orders/customers;
- information gathered by sales representatives;
- client details;
- information on employees;
- management accounts;
- general company statistics.

In addition to internal data, there is an enormous amount of published information available outside the organisation, both official and unofficial (see Figure 3.4). These external sources of research include:

- trade magazines and technical journals/periodicals;
- trade directories, such as the *Kompass* register;
- trade associations;
- company reports/prospectuses;
- reports by chambers of commerce, the Department of Trade and Industry, and business venture groups;
- other Government information, e.g. census surveys, Her Majesty's Stationery Office reports/leaflets;
- yearbooks, such as *Kelly's*;
- world industrial reviews, e.g. *Jane's*;
- *Yellow Pages* and the *Thomson Directory*;
- market and consumer surveys, provided by Mintel (Marketing Intelligence), Target Group Index (British Market Research Bureau), Henley Centre for Forecasting, the Rowntree Trust, and so on;

- newspapers, books, magazines and other library sources;
- consumer reports and articles, e.g. in *Which?* magazine;
- *British Rate and Data* (BRAD) – media rates; commercial market research organisations.

Knowledge of trends in social habits, fashions, buying patterns, demographics and so on can be gained by these methods and could have a significant effect on capital expenditure and future marketing plans.

Secondary research is generally the least expensive method of gathering marketing data and is quicker to locate, collate and use, but the information could be obsolete, incorrect or inappropriately classified.

Desk research is used to gather quantitative data but qualitative information is often required in addition, so secondary methods can help to guide and determine what primary research is necessary.

PRIMARY METHODS

After all secondary methods have been exhausted, where they are unable to provide the required data, or when there is a need for additional support information in conjunction with the same campaign, marketers embark upon *primary research*.

This method of data collection gathers original information by asking people questions or observing their behaviour. As this procedure generally involves obtaining fresh data by direct contact with the population at large, it is often called *field research*, and consists of survey or observation methods.

The main method of gathering primary research data is through a survey, which involves obtaining information from a number of people who are considered to be a representative sample of the particular target population under investigation. The most common types of field survey used by market researchers are illustrated in Figure 3.5.

Personal interviews involve an experienced interviewer gathering in-depth information by putting questions to interviewees, face to face at their home or in shopping malls, and recording the answers.

Postal surveys are conducted by mailing out questionnaires which are completed and returned by respondents from their homes.

Telephone surveys involve an interviewer contacting members of the sample population by tele-

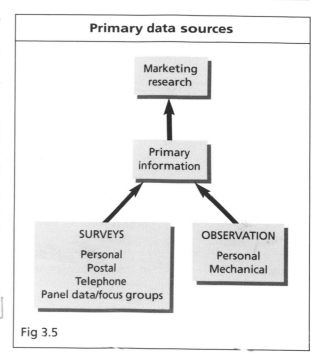

Fig 3.5

phone at work or home, asking them questions and recording the responses.

Focus groups consist of small panels of selected representatives who are either interviewed together (and sometimes recorded or filmed) or asked to keep a factual record of purchases, viewpoints and so on, often receiving gifts or financial incentives for doing so.

One or a combination of these methods can be used in a market research campaign to elicit the essential field data required. Each involves different advantages and disadvantages applicable in varying situations, as described in Table 3.1.

In addition to these methods of primary data collection, researchers can also use *observation* techniques, which can either be:

- *personal* – viewing and recording, for instance noting of retail purchases; or
- *mechanical* – involving some form of machine measurement, such as a supermarket TV camera or checkout recording equipment.
- *anonymous* – where information is gathered secretly to increase the accuracy of results and reduce the likelihood of misleading data, e.g. 'mystery shopping' (written or telephone methods can also be used).

Table 3.1 Research survey methods

Survey method	Advantages	Disadvantages
Personal interview	Questions can be modified In-depth answers possible Much qualitative data from a small sample Flexible – can allow for reaction, visual information Observation improves accuracy Rapport leads to fewer refusals	Professional interviewers expensive Possible interviewer bias Can be slow People often not at home Invasion of privacy Disagreements can arise
Postal survey	No travel expenses, so economic if good return rate No interviewer bias Can be genuinely random Anonymous returns Can be completed at respondent's leisure	Non-response rate high, unless questions are short, simple and not too probing Takes longer Inflexible and no observation Higher postage rates increase costs Difficult and expensive to obtain complete, up-to-date mail lists
Telephone survey	Easy to administer Quick No travel expenses, so cheap if local and in evenings Flexible – can allow for reaction and some in-depth answers Questions can be modified Some anonymity	Professional interviewers expensive Invasion of privacy Telephone charges can be high No observation Hard to develop trust Not genuinely random – sample limited to respondents with telephones and listed numbers Non-response rate high – engaged signal/no answer/refusals
Focus group	Informality and personal rapport encourages accuracy Questions can be modified Can run on a regular basis In-depth answers reliable Observations and recording of answers and reactions Visual detail	Scope and sample limited Might not be treated seriously More costly if incentives are large

Survey data is, however, usually collected by means of *questionnaires* which must be very carefully presented and worded to be effective. The consumer will be more likely to complete a questionnaire fully and accurately if it is:

- brief, simple, precise, logical and attractively presented;
- easy to answer, containing no unfamiliar or ambiguous terms and no jargon;
- acceptable – employing a friendly and informative manner and acknowledging the imposition on the consumer's time;
- well-organised – easy or interesting questions first and more complex ones later on;
- inoffensive – avoiding emotive, confidential/personal, embarrassing or demeaning questions;
- realistic – keeping within the respondent's experiences and not overtaxing memories.

However, for the information to be an accurate basis for planning, the market researcher needs the data to be:

- easily quantifiable;
- unbiased and objective;
- clear of confusion – avoiding leading or ambiguous questions;
- original – no pre-judgement or assessment of the respondent;
- easily identifiable and recordable through names/dates/code numbers etc;
- compatible with computer systems;
- reliable – with control questions included to check the consistency of answers and whether the interviewer is following instructions;
- economic and not wasteful – for example, ensuring the first question is a 'cut-out' to eliminate irrelevant returns at an early stage.

Of course, the quality of a questionnaire depends upon the nature and effectiveness of the questions themselves. A good questionnaire would normally start with simple *dichotomous* questions which require the answer 'yes' or 'no'.

The next and most prevalent type of question, occupying the majority of many questionnaires, would be *multiple-choice*. This style of question offers the respondent a number of alternative answers, with the range of choices being not so wide as to cause confusion but wide enough for a clear distinction to be made between different answers.

Both dichotomous and multiple-choice questions tend to produce data which is quantitative in nature, but *open-ended* questions are likely to produce qualitative information. They are so called because what is being sought is an opinion or a subjective judgement rather than a direct and limited response. There would normally be just one or two such questions, positioned at the end of the questionnaire for maximum return. Often, the key question to which researchers require an accurate answer is hidden in the middle of other 'filler' questions, disguised to avoid bias and increase objectivity.

In some questionnaires a particular type of question predominates; others exhibit a combination of styles, depending upon the nature of the data required. Whichever is chosen, some form of piloting or pre-testing should be undertaken to iron out problems before the questionnaire is used on the sample population.

Another way of ensuring that the results are reliable is by choosing a *representative sample* as scientifically as possible. Samples can be drawn from combinations of people in categories such as:

- sex;
- age;
- marital status;
- qualifications;
- profession;
- ethnic group;
- socio-economic group;
- family background;
- geographical area;
- residential area;
- lifestyle.

To be statistically reliable, a sample should be both large enough to be representative of the total population and proportionate, i.e. the percentages of the various characteristics listed must also be approximately the same in the sample population.

There are two main types of sampling technique, each of which contain variations for appropriate circumstances. These are illustrated in Figure 3.6.

Probability samples give everyone the same chance of being selected. Different methods within this category include:

- *random* – each member of the population has a known and equal chance of being drawn from the total available population;

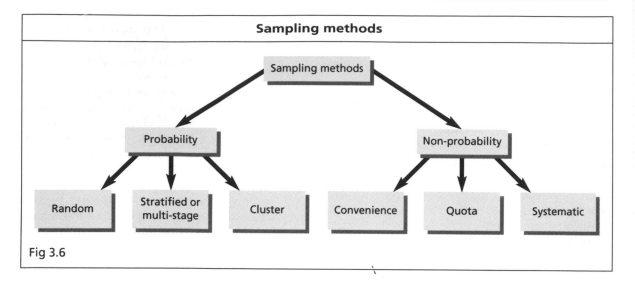

Fig 3.6

● *stratified/multi-stage* – randomly drawn groups are represented in the total (a combination of random and quota methods);
● *cluster* – geographic areas or population clusters are selected as respondents.

Non-probability samples are arbitrary with no standard tests being applied. Examples of this type of sample are:

● *convenience* – selection of people readily available;
● *quota* – contains respondents, segments or groups whose characteristics are pre-determined and roughly in proportion to the total market;
● *systematic* – drawing, say, every tenth member of a population.

In many situations, small-scale surveys which will not yield statistically significant data can still be valuable, e.g. for a small industrial company.

The task of the market researcher is thus to measure the data accurately from whatever source, present it in various meaningful forms (such as tables/graphs/pie-charts/pictograms/bar-charts/histograms, and so on) and make logical deductions based on it.

MANAGEMENT OF RESEARCH

All the activities involved in the marketing research process should be co-ordinated in a chronological sequence, operating along the lines illustrated in Figure 3.7.

Marketing research is a broad term and includes other important marketing activities, such as:

● *Research and development* – the process which an organisation goes through to invent and perfect a new product or service.
● *Test marketing* – researching the viability of a new product or service on a small, representative geographical area or population sample, before deciding whether to conduct a full launch.

Until the late 1960s the little marketing research that was undertaken consisted of simple industrial, behavioural or management statistics conducted on an *ad hoc* basis, i.e. strictly related to specific tasks and problems via random sampling.

However, in the 1970s and 1980s marketing research techniques and systems developed considerably by use of computerised quantitative and consumer-related qualitative methods. Organisations can now monitor their marketing activities and environment on a continuous basis, making use of private and national marketing intelligence systems provided by specialists.

To be of real use, however, the large amounts of information handled must be well organised and easily attainable – part of a structured system, in fact. This is why the *marketing information system* (MIS) plays such a vital role. It can be defined as 'establishing a framework for the day-to-day managing and structuring of information gathered regularly from sources both inside and outside an

The chronological research process

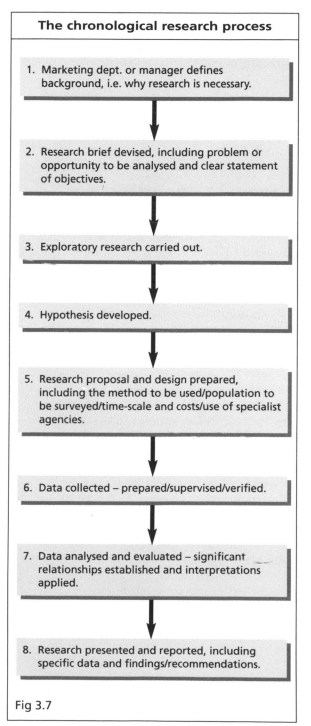

1. Marketing dept. or manager defines background, i.e. why research is necessary.

2. Research brief devised, including problem or opportunity to be analysed and clear statement of objectives.

3. Exploratory research carried out.

4. Hypothesis developed.

5. Research proposal and design prepared, including the method to be used/population to be surveyed/time-scale and costs/use of specialist agencies.

6. Data collected – prepared/supervised/verified.

7. Data analysed and evaluated – significant relationships established and interpretations applied.

8. Research presented and reported, including specific data and findings/recommendations.

Fig 3.7

The marketing information system

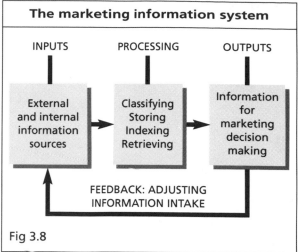

Fig 3.8

Source: Dibb, Sally, Simkin, Lyndon, Pride, William M. and Ferrell, O.C., *Marketing: concepts and strategies,* second European edition. Copyright © 1994 by Houghton Mifflin Company. Reprinted with permission.

organisation' (Dibb, Simkin, Pride and Ferrell). The key components of an organisation's marketing information system are described in Figure 3.8.

The MIS must incorporate and combine the main aspects of marketing research into a centralised management function which will maintain a tight control on research procedures and ensure an accurate data bank of information about customers, products and so on.

As research methods become ever more computerised and sophisticated, an organisation will thus be able to take advantage of developments and design marketing information systems to be increasingly efficient and relevant to future demands, for example in the internationalisation of business and the measurement of more abstract concepts such as branding and advertising effectiveness.

Marketing research is not infallible of course – it costs time and money, tends to lack accountability and can only indicate a course of action. It also suffers from the old adage 'there are lies, damned lies and statistics'. For a company to be ethically correct in its research claims would require an honest statement such as 'we are 90 per cent sure that somewhere between 7 and 9 out of 10 cat owners prefer Brand X.

However, the research function is indispensable in its role of identifying and solving marketing problems and providing the essential evidence upon which business decisions are based. As such, it will play an integral part in the activities of any marketing orientated organisation.

ARTICLES

A1

Getting older – and it shows in spending

BUSINESSMEN who want to get ahead in the 1990s should move into the soft drinks, fruit and vegetables or household insurance markets, according to a report today.

But cobblers and laundry owners could be in trouble, and tobacco products should be avoided altogether.

The forecasts are contained in the 1993 edition of The British Consumer: Patterns of Income and Expenditure, published by market analysts Mintel.

The report, which in previous years was called British Lifestyles, shows the trends set over the last 10 years and predicts changes in the next decade.

'We believe the main growth areas will be educational fees, prepared foods, household insurance, soft drinks, domestic and garden help, and fruit and vegetables,' said Mintel senior analyst Bill Patterson.

But markets in long-term decline included cigars, cigarettes and tobacco products in general, cleaning and laundry, coal, shoes, clothes, furniture repair and meat and fish.

There could also be real decline in the 18-30 holiday market as the structure of British society changes, with an ageing population, fewer marriages, smaller families, more people living alone and a declining workforce, said Mintel.

It predicted a growth of nearly 3pc in the UK population by 2002, but there would be an overall decline in the numbers aged under 30 counterbalanced by 'dramatic growth' in the 30-59 age group.

'These changes will have impacts on many UK markets,' said Mr Patterson.

'Where will all the people be to go on 18-30 holiday packages? Can the health service cope with the growing needs of older people? How will the state pension system cope with the increasing number of pensioners? The examples are endless.'

Other findings in the report included:

● The proportion of women in the workforce was higher than ever before and the number of women in paid employment was falling at a slower rate than for men, partly because many women were in lower paid or part-time positions

● Average annual household disposable income now stood at £18,251 compared with £9,201 in 1982, a growth in real terms of 16%.

Mr Patterson said: 'The proportion of household income derived from salaries has fallen over the last decade, being replaced by increased income from rents, dividends and interest, private pensions and annuities, self-employment and of course social security.'

Source: The Northern Echo, 23 February 1993

1 Describe the main consumer trends indicated in the article.

2 What are the most effective means by which Mintel can obtain information?

3 How reliable are the research findings resulting from such surveys?

4 Explain why these research reports form the backbone of many organisations' research data.

A2

Don't put your shirt on the polls

THERE was a time when it would have been safe to assume that anyone working in market research was gainfully employed in checking out fruit and veg prices. Such uncluttered innocence is a long way behind us.

Nowadays it seems that no organisation, whatever its size or pretensions, can exist without testing public opinion by eliciting answers to generally banal questions line up alongside boxes waiting to be occupied by a tick or a cross.

That the vagaries of life should be reduced to a series of yes/no, sometimes/never options

has always struck me as ridiculous in a gloomy sort of way. 'Well, Mr God, did you create the world in six days because: **a**, it seemed a nice round number; **b**, there was nothing else doing that week; or **c**, you wanted to get the job finished before the weekend.'

Has no one ever stopped to consider that market research did not exist until it was dreamed up by a market researcher? I suspect that the pollster in question leapt from the womb with a pencil and pad to hand, in order to interrogate their mother about how the birth went.

Source: The Yorkshire Evening Press

1 The article implies that the scope of marketing research has increased greatly in recent times. Describe the nature and extent of this change.

2 Can dichotomous and multiple-choice questions really 'test public opinion' effectively? If not, what are the alternatives?

3 What methods can researchers employ to ensure meaningful rather than 'banal' questionnaires?

4 Much scepticism exists about marketing research, as evidenced in the article. Explain why this is so, and put forward a logical argument for the use of such research in business.

A3

Airport asks its customers

A MAJOR passenger survey at Teesside International Airport is starting next month.

A sample of departing passengers will be asked questions, including one on what new services they would like to see operate from the airport.

When the survey is complete in 12 months' time, the information will be used by the air-

port for planning terminal and other facilities.

It will also be used for forecasting air transport demands by local industry, commerce and residents.

John Waiting, marketing and customer services manager at the airport, said: 'This survey will enable us to ensure the services from Teesside meet the demands of our region.'

Source: The Northern Echo, 28 January 1994

1 Should the Teesside International Airport research survey be limited to questioning departing passengers?

2 How large a sample should be taken in order to generate reliable and representative data?

3 Design a questionnaire to fulfil the objectives of the airport campaign.

4 Describe the secondary data available to the airport to back up its field survey.

A4

Sample error is hardly, er, marginal

The chances of an opinion poll being carried out in York looked slim today.

Top pollsters warned it would be a statistical nightmare, since 1987's Tory majority of 147 would mean interviewing up to 10,000 people to balance out the margin of error acceptably.

Most polls are conducted with 1,000-1,500 people.

And even interviewing 10,000 would produce a result accurate only to plus or minus 0.5 per cent. Yet a swing of only 0.1 per cent could be enough to capture the York seat.

Bob Wybrow, polls director for Gallup, said it was possible there had been a large shift to Labour in the city since 1987, meaning it was no longer such a marginal seat.

'But, if York is still marginal at the moment, then to be really accurate we would have to interview virtually all the electors.'

Simon Braunholtz, associate director of MORI, believed a sample of 5,000 would be needed to reduce the margin of error to 0.5 per cent.

'It's highly unlikely that the situation in York is going to be the same as it was in 1987,' he explained, 'given that it's so radically different nationally now.'

Marie Davison, of NOP Market Research, said it was much more difficult to predict election results in marginal seats, and people remembered when the pollsters got it wrong.

She believed that halving the usual margin of error to 1.5 per cent would mean interviewing 4,000 people. And 16,000 people would have to be questioned to halve the margin again.

'It can be done. But it would cost a lot of money.'

Source: The Yorkshire Evening Press

1 Why is such a large sample necessary to produce a reliable opinion poll for York?

2 Would the expenditure required for a poll be justified? If so, why?

3 What sampling methods are used by political opinion polls? Are other methods feasible?

4 Describe the environmental factors which make opinion poll accuracy variable.

A5

Research and development

John Davis

ANNUAL accounts are supposed to give a meaningful picture of how a business is making out. But one important ingredient is often missing - the amount being spent on research and development.

Even among the UK's corporate elite, there is a paucity of information about R&D spending. Yet it is the seed-corn from which tomorrow's growth will come and investors need all the good news they can get, as does the stock market in general.

Of the latest reports from the UK's top 100 companies, only 46 contained meaningful data.

As for the rest, there was either no reference to R&D at all, or a note saying that R&D had been written off.

Even where data were given, the picture painted by the latest set of accounts left much to be desired.

In only a handful of instances did spending on R&D represent more than 1 or 2 per cent of turnover. Leading Japanese and German companies spend three or four times as much, while even businesses in the emerging Far East economies, such as South Korea and Taiwan, are spending around 6 per cent of turnover.

The figures for the biggest 10 spenders among the UK's top 100 added up to £4.1 billion - or only 2.5 per cent of their joint turnover.

The major exceptions were the pharmaceutical companies, notably Glaxo, SmithKline Beecham and Wellcome. They spent £1 billion between them, or 10.9 per cent of their joint turnover of £9.2 billion.

It is perhaps no coincidence that the UK is still strongly placed in pharmaceutical products, nor that the shares of these companies enjoy premium ratings and brokers view their prospects favourably.

That provides some valuable lessons for UK companies in general, and for the Government as well.

For investors, too, there is an important message. They should press for information on R&D spending at every conceivable opportunity.

A company's agm would be a particularly good time to bring up the matter.

Source: The Observer

1 Explain the scope and importance of the research and development function.

2 Why do so many organisations seem to ignore R and D?

3 What is meant by the phrase 'the seed-corn from which tomorrow's growth will come'?

4 Why do you think organisations outside the UK invest more in R and D than their counterparts in the UK, apart from in the pharmaceutical industry?

ISSUES

INVASION OF PRIVACY

Accusations are often made that marketing research intrudes unnecessarily into the lives of consumers.

1 How much of a legal right should the consumer have to withhold information?

2 Are any research methods more 'consumer friendly' than others?

3 How can research be designed to be less intrusive?

UNETHICAL RESEARCH METHODS

Many organisations now indulge in dubious or illegal forms of commercial and industrial espionage.

1 What reasons might companies have for gathering information unethically?

2 What legal procedures exist for preventing these practices?

3 How can organisations try to ensure that their marketing information systems are not infiltrated?

MARKETING RESEARCH AGENCIES

There are now many firms specialising in collecting information and supplying it to organisations on demand.

1 Which types of organisation would be most likely to use a marketing research agency?

2 What advantages does a marketing research specialist possess when gathering information?

3 What are the disadvantages to an organisation of using such an information source?

ACCURACY OF RESEARCH

It is often claimed that research findings are unreliable or biased because of a lack of objectivity or relevance.

1 Which research methods are most likely to suffer from bias and why?

2 How can organisations overcome accusations that their research data is purely subjective and thus flawed?

3 Describe and discuss examples of organisations which have traditionally experienced difficulties in obtaining unbiased or up-to-date information.

USE OF QUESTIONNAIRES

Questionnaire response rates are often extremely low.

1 In what situations would a respondent be less likely to provide accurate information or respond at all?

2 What is the most effective questionnaire design for an organisation of your choice?

3 How can questionnaires be effectively incorporated into a company's marketing information system?

QUANTITATIVE OR QUALITATIVE TECHNIQUES

Organisations often find it difficult to combine factual information sources with more abstract or open-ended ones.

1 Are desk and field methods of gathering data completely separate or mutually interdependent?

2 Describe the situations in which internal data sources can be both primary and secondary in nature.

3 Why do some organisations shy away from panel data sources despite their claim to greater accuracy?

4 Which technique is more appropriate for industrial markets and why?

QUESTIONS

1 Describe the difference between market research and marketing research.

2 List two main reasons for the importance of marketing research within the overall marketing process.

3 Name four areas of an organisation's activities where the provision of accurate research data is vital.

4 What is the difference between strategic, tactical and data bank research?

5 Describe the differences between quantitative and qualitative research, and subjectivity and objectivity.

6 What is secondary or desk research?

7 List six sources of secondary research.

8 What is internal data?

9 Name three sources of internal data.

10 Define primary or field research.

11 What are the four main research survey methods? Give two advantages and two disadvantages of each.

12 What are observation techniques?

13 What are the three different types of question in a questionnaire? Give an example of each.

14 Name three qualities of a good questionnaire.

15 List four characteristics required of a questionnaire by the researching organisations.

16 Name four criteria which could be used for a sample.

17 Name the two main kinds of sample and three examples of each.

18 List three ways in which statistical data can be presented.

19 Define a marketing information system.

20 Describe the key components of an MIS.

21 Describe the stages of the marketing research process.

22 Define research and development.

23 Define test marketing.

PROJECTS

1 Why should an organisation begin a marketing research campaign by gathering secondary data? What types of desk and field research would be most appropriate in a firm with which you are familiar?

2 How would you obtain information on why people buy a particular product or service and why they stop buying and switch to another brand?

3 Describe the sources of information that already exist inside an organisation of your choice and which could be used for marketing decision making, and explain the usefulness of each.

4 What can specialist marketing research organisations offer that a medium-sized company could not provide for itself?

5 Why should an organisation have to think very carefully before selecting the type of survey it uses? Which products and/or services are most applicable to each of the four main survey methods, and why? Use examples to illustrate your answers.

6 Why is the compilation and evaluation of questionnaires considered to have a scientific basis? For a product or service with which you are familiar, devise a questionnaire designed to achieve a stated purpose. Describe and account for the sample population at which it will be aimed.

7 Marketing research can lead to decisions *not* to market a product – for what reasons could this happen?

8 Is marketing research only of relevance to large organisations? What part does it play in small businesses and is it as important in industrial as in consumer marketing?

9 Taking into account all the recent developments in business, society and technology, can an organisation afford not to establish its own marketing information system?

GLOSSARY

Ad hoc research occasional market surveys undertaken as and when required.

Anonymous research the gathering of information by secret means, using either written, spoken or observational techniques to ensure greater authenticity of results.

Area sampling a type of stratified sample where geographic areas are used as the primary sampling criteria.

Attitude research using personal interviews or focus groups to uncover people's attitudes.

Bias research lacking objectivity due to a distortion of the information.

Causal research testing cause-and-effect hypotheses.

Census collection of data from all possible sources in a population or universe.

Classification organisation of data or information in a particular order or category.

Closed-end questions questions that include all the possible answers and require respondents to choose from them.

Cluster sample probability sample where geographical areas or clusters are used as the basis for the research survey.

Continuous research where the same measurements of a particular activity are taken on a regular basis.

Control question survey question which tests the correctness and accuracy of other answers.

Convenience sample non-probability sample based on the selection of readily available respondents.

Data all the statistical information gathered and analysed for research purposes.

Data bank research all research information which requires constant up-dating.

Database collection of data stored in a computer.

Data processing arranging data into a systematic form for easy analysis.

Depth interview detailed, informal and often lengthy personal interview used to uncover motives and viewpoints.

Descriptive research marketing research which is used to define marketing problems or situations clearly.

Desk research the collection and study of information obtained from sources already available, such as internal company records and external published data.

Dichotomous (or yes/no) questions survey questions requiring the answer 'yes' or 'no'.

External data secondary research information originating from sources outside the organisation.

Extrapolation projection of historical data to identify future trends.

Field research primary surveys involving direct or indirect contact with representative samples of the population.

Filler questions survey questions which are not important to the researcher and are used to fill the questionnaire and disguise the key question or questions in order to reduce bias.

Focus group interview or group discussion a means of gathering primary research information by discussion with a small group of people, usually focusing on a specific theme.

Hall test where a representative sample of target consumers is recruited, usually in a shopping centre, and brought into a conveniently located hall to answer questions designed for testing products, advertising, prices, and so on.

Historical trends previous changes indicated by research and used as a basis for future action.

Information data stored by an organisation and used for decision-making.

Internal data secondary research already available within the organisation.

Mail surveys see 'Postal surveys'.

Marketing data bank all the data collected within an organisation's marketing information system.

Marketing information system or MIS an organised way of continually gathering and analysing information from every source relevant to an organisation.

Marketing intelligence information about developments in the marketing environment.

Marketing research gathering information on all the activities of marketing.

Marketing research process organised and chronological application of the scientific methods of marketing research.

Market research gathering information on a particular market for a product or service.

Mintel-Marketing Intelligence, a secondary data source of information about products, services and markets.

Motivational research research into the motives influencing consumer purchasing and other decisions.

Multiple-choice questions survey questions which offer the alternative of several possible stated answers, and require the respondent to indicate which comes closest to their point of view.

Multi-stage sample sample assembled by combining proportionate numbers of respondents of different characteristics represented in a universe, each randomly selected.

Mystery shopping clandestine method of research where a company representative or other professional anonymously contacts the organisation to gather reliable information on the quality of its goods and services or to check the accuracy of data.

Non-probability sample arbitrary sample in which most standard statistical tests cannot be applied to the collected data.

Objectivity a reliable research approach involving honest observation or assessment and no personal bias.

Observation personal or mechanical research technique in which data are collected by means of witnessing or recording the events taking place.

Omnibus survey method of research where different companies each supply a limited number of questions for use in a continuous survey.

Open-ended questions questions that are not limited and allow respondents to answer in their own words.

Opinion research method of research which assesses public opinion on political issues and trends, and current topics of public interest.

Panel volunteer population sample specially recruited to record or provide information, usually opinions or records, for an incentive.

Panel data information provided, often on a regular basis, by members of a panel or focus group.

Personal interview survey face-to-face meeting between two or more people with the purpose of gathering research information.

Pilot survey brief research carried out before the main campaign to test the accuracy and validity of assumptions and method to be used.

Poll public opinion survey, often in connection with political views.

Population (or 'universe') total number in a particular group or geographical area.

Postal check postal method of checking validity of answers to questionnaires, using a percentage of total numbers returned.

Postal survey (or mail survey) questionnaires posted to the selected sample of respondents for completion and return.

Pre-selection interviewees in a sample selected beforehand according to a pre-determined formula.

Primary data information or statistics observed and recorded or collected directly from respondents for the first time during a marketing research study.

Probability sample sample in which every member of the population has an equal chance of being selected.

Qualitative research seeks in-depth, open-ended and unquantifiable information describing opinions, values, and so on, rather than sizes or amounts in numerical form.

Quantitative research seeks structured responses that can be quantified in numerical form rather than general, open-ended information.

Questionnaire research document used in surveys which provides questions and an interview structure and allows room for the answers of respondents.

Quota sample non-probability sample which includes different pre-selected groups representing the known characteristics of the total population.

Random sample probability sample where each member of the research population has an equal chance of being included.

Research and development research undertaken by an organisation when inventing or perfecting a new product or service.

Research mix an organisation's choice of the various research activities available to it for use in a research campaign to achieve the desired objectives.

Research proposal a plan specifying what marketing research information is sought and how it will be obtained.

Response rate the percentage of people contacted in a research sample who complete and return the questionnaire.

Sample a segment of the total population selected for research purposes to represent the whole universe.

Sampling selecting representative units from a total population.

Scientific method approach to research that focuses on objectivity and organisation and employs statistical theories to improve accuracy.

Secondary data information already collected or published and compiled inside or outside the organisation.

Skew the bias or distortion applying to research data, accidentally or deliberately.

Specialist research undertaken to meet the needs of particular sectors of the economy.

Statistical interpretation analysis focusing on what is typical or what deviates from the average, indicating how widely respondents vary and how they are distributed.

Strategic research includes the information necessary to guide decisions which have long-term implications.

Stratified sample method in which randomly selected units are divided into groups according to common characteristics or attributes, a probability sample then being conducted within each group.

Structured interview interview using a questionnaire in which questions are specifically indicated and no diversions allowed.

Subjectivity a research approach involving personal opinion and assessment, and possibly including bias.

Survey research technique involving information gathered from people directly or indirectly through the use of questionnaires.

Systematic sample where, for example, every tenth member of the population is selected for a survey.

Tabulation presentation of data in tables and similar forms for easy understanding and evaluation.

Tactical research collection of information relating to short-term decision making.

Target Group Index or TGI continuous survey of purchasing habits produced by the British Market Research Bureau.

Telephone survey recording by an interviewer of respondents' answers to a questionnaire over the telephone.

Test marketing method of testing a marketing plan cheaply on a limited geographic scale to indicate likely consumer reaction to a full launch. Simulates the factors to be involved in the main campaign and usually carried out in a restricted but representative area.

Thomson Directory list of local/regional business names and addresses produced for advertising purposes and used for compiling secondary research information.

Universe see 'population'.

Unprompted response open or unaided reply by a respondent to a question.

Unstructured interview where the interviewer is not restricted by a particular question or sequence of questioning.

Yellow Pages list of local/regional business names and addresses produced for advertising purposes and used for compiling secondary research information.

Yes/no (or dichotomous) questions questionnaire questions requiring the respondent only to answer 'yes' or 'no'.

SUGGESTED REFERENCES

VIDEO MATERIAL

Electric Avenue, 'Housewives' Choice', BBC, 1988.

The Marketing Mix No. 2, 'Marketing through Research', Yorkshire Television, 1986.

Contemporary Marketing, Video Cases, No. 4 (The Disney Channel), Boone, L. and Kurtz, D., Dryden Press, 1989.

A.G.B. Ltd. – A.G.B. Superpanel, Marketing Video tape, Dibb, S., Simkin, L., Pride, W. and Ferrell, O. Houghton Mifflin, 1991.

Horizon, 'Suggers, fruggers and data-muggers', BBC, 1993.

RADIO MATERIAL

Sampling and Questionnaires (tape–slide), Prismatron Productions, 1975.

Sell, sell, sell, Market Research, BBC Radio Leeds, 1984.

MAGAZINE ARTICLES

Advertiser's Weekly, Special on Test Marketing, Feb. 1968.

Journal of Marketing Management, Vol. 1, No. 3, Spring 1986, p.315, 'Group discussions: a misunderstood technique'.

Journal of Marketing Management, Vol. 3, No. 3, Spring 1988, p.269, 'The market research contribution to new product failure and success'.

Journal of Marketing Management, Vol. 4, No. 1, Summer 1988, p.50, 'Technology and bank marketing systems'.

Journal of Marketing Management, Vol. 8, No. 2, April 1992, p.117, 'Competitive intelligence'.

Quarterly Review of Marketing, Vol. 12, No. 2, Jan. 1987, p.7, 'Interviewing in Industrial Market Research: the state of the art'.

Quarterly Review of Marketing, Vol. 14, No. 3, Spring 1989, p.14, 'A cross-cultural research project – using the mail questionnaire'.

Marketing Business, Oct. 1988, p. 4, 'Information: a key to marketing success'.

Marketing Business, Apr. 1989, p. 6, 'Counting heads – the age-old market problem'.

Marketing Business, Oct. 1989, p.18, 'Thatcher's Society'.

Marketing Business, Feb. 1990, p.18, 'Moving to Market'.

Marketing Business, June 1991, p.35, 'The changing face of desk research'.

Marketing Business, June 1992, p.35, 'Ring my bells'.

Marketing Business, Dec./Jan. 1992/3, p.24, 'Back from the future'; and p.32, 'Leader of the pack'.

Marketing Business, May 1993, p.19, 'A question of quality'.

Marketing Business, Jul./Aug. 1993, p.12, 'Metamorphosis in marketing'.

Marketing Business, Sept. 1993, Special Report, p.29, 'Contact Sport'; p.33, 'Face to interface'; and p.8, 'Vital statistician'.

Marketing Business, Feb. 1994, p.13, 'New Generation Marketing'.

Marketing Business, Mar. 1994, p.6, 'Spies like us'; and p.43, 'Standard practice'.

FURTHER READING

Adcock, D., Bradfield, R., Halborg, A. and Ross, C., *Marketing Principles and Practice* (2nd edn), Pitman, 1995, chs. 7, 8, 21.

Baker, M. (Ed.), *The Marketing Book*, Heinemann/C.I.M., 1990, ch. 11.

Boone, L. and Kurtz, D., *Contemporary Marketing*, Dryden, 1989, ch. 4.

Cannon, Tom, *Basic Marketing*, Holt Business Texts, 1980, ch. 5.

Chisnall, Peter, *The Essence of Marketing Research*, Prentice Hall, 1991.

Crimp, Margaret, *The Marketing Research Process*, Prentice Hall, 1990.

Crouch, Sunny, *Marketing Research for Managers*, Pan, 1985.

Dibb, S., Simkin, L., Pride, W. and Ferrell, O., *Marketing*, Houghton Mifflin, 1994, ch. 6.

Foster, Douglas, *Mastering Marketing*, Macmillan, 1982, ch. 4.

Giles, G.B., *Marketing*, MacDonald and Evans, 1985, ch. 3.

Kotler, P. and Armstrong, G., *Marketing*, Prentice Hall, 1993, ch. 4.

McCarthy, J. and Perreault, W., *Basic Marketing*, Irwin, 1987, chs 5 and 6.

Mercer, D., *Marketing*, Blackwell, 1992, ch. 2.

Acknowledgements

The Northern Echo.
The Observer.
The Yorkshire Evening Press.

4
MARKET SELECTION

DEFINITIONS

Market segmentation involves breaking down the total market into discrete and identifiable sub-groups, each of which may have its own special product or service requirements and each of which is likely to exhibit different habits and characteristics.

WENDELL SMITH, 1956

A targeting strategy concentrates marketing effort on a particular group of consumers or specific segment of the market, reaching them with a tailor-made marketing mix.

Positioning is the place a product or service occupies in a given market, as perceived by the relevant group of customers, or target market segment.

Y. WIND, 1980

INTRODUCTION

In the early days of motor-car manufacturing, Henry Ford stated that 'the customer can have any colour he likes, so long as it is black'. He was speaking at a time when the product was a novel one and in high demand, thus customers could afford to be treated by the producing company as identical parts of a mass market.

However, over the years both competition between producers and customer choice have increased greatly, as discussed in Chapter 1. So nowadays, selling operates best when the customer has been properly identified beforehand. But customers are unique, unpredictable individuals and no two people can be guaranteed to react in the same way. Marketing orientated organisations thus recognise the importance of doing their homework accurately and gaining a thorough understanding of the nature of their markets.

Having used relevant variables to determine its market segments, an organisation must decide which segments it is to focus its marketing ener-

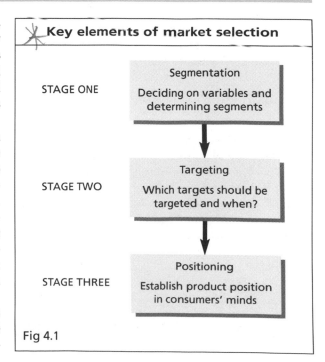

Key elements of market selection

STAGE ONE	Segmentation — Deciding on variables and determining segments
STAGE TWO	Targeting — Which targets should be targeted and when?
STAGE THREE	Positioning — Establish product position in consumers' minds

Fig 4.1

gies upon and what perceptions it wishes consumers to form of its products or services. These three concepts are the main elements of market selection, as illustrated in Figure 4.1.

Only when these strategies are determined in their logical sequence can an organisation design the appropriate marketing mixes for its products or services.

KEY CONCEPTS

MARKET SEGMENTATION

There are two variations in the approach companies can adopt when developing their market selection strategy. They can either:

- group their customers into segments, according to their backgrounds and needs, and aim the product or service at particular segments; or
- differentiate products according to their particular characteristics and market them on this basis.

Most organisations combine these two approaches and seek to modify the product or service to fit customer needs. This philosophy is based upon the notion of the accurate 'rifle shot' being a far more effective marketing weapon than the imprecise 'scatter gun'. Thus the need arises to identify homogeneous market segments within which customers share similar characteristics and purchasing requirements, a process known as *market segmentation* or 'niche' marketing.

This principle can best be appreciated by looking at a practical example. One method of segmenting the UK car market has been by vehicle size, and the way in which two larger manufacturers have used this theory is illustrated in Figure 4.2.

This simple example makes it obvious that each of the four main car segments will attract customers with very different characteristics, and the manufacturers thus have to adapt their marketing strategy to sell to each of these markets.

Of course, this market could be further subdivided to suit the varying needs of customers by using product features such as style, price, engine size, safety features or even colour.

Table 4.1 is a model illustrating the main components of a market segmentation system for the tourism industry. As this research indicates, different categories of customers can be identified and selling operations can therefore be concentrated on

Segmentation in the car industry

Car size \ Company	Ford	Volkswagen
Mini	Fiesta	Polo
Small	Escort	Golf
Large	Sierra	Passat
Family	Granada	Santana

Fig 4.2

Segmentation breakdown for Club 18–30 (now 'The Club')

Main segment - - - - - - - - - - - Holiday tourist

Main sub-segment - - - - - - - Package – fully inclusive

Further sub-segments
Geographical destination - - Mediterranean resorts
Style of holiday - - - - - - - - - - Social
Consumer age - - - - - - - - - - - 18–30
Price of holiday - - - - - - - - - - Middle range
Length of holiday - - - - - - - - Two weeks
Food/accommodation - - - - - Middle range

Fig 4.3

Table 4.1 Segmentation in the tourism industry

Main segments	Main sub-segments
1. Holiday tourist	A. Package – fully inclusive B. Package – partly inclusive C. Independent – travel agent D. Independent – private
2. Business traveller	A. Travel agent B. Employer's travel dept. C. Individual on business D. Individual – inc. short holiday
3. Special or common interest traveller	A. Hobby B. Cultural C. Religious D. Archaeological/historical E. Ethnic/anthropological F. Flora and fauna G. Geographical H. Transport I. Sport J. Outdoor K. Food/wines L. Family visits M. Shopping N. Prestige trips O. Competitions P. Health

Source: Adapted from Foster, Douglas, *Mastering Marketing*, p. 163, Table 6.4, Macmillan Press Ltd, 1982

these separate segments. Some tourism organisations, for example, specialise in marketing holidays purely to the sports sub-division of the special travel segment, offering trips to events such as the Olympics and the soccer World Cup. As a result, they have gradually come to understand both their product and customers intimately and are thus able to respond quickly to changing market needs.

A tourism organisation could further sub-segment its market in order to provide an even more specialist product or service tailor-made to suit an even more specific sub-group identified and understood by the company. A particularly suc-cessful example of this was Club 18–30, as illustrated in Figure 4.3.

Being able to establish a reliable name for a specific product, owing to the build-up of expertise over a long period in its segment, meant that Club 18–30 consistently increased its market share.

Few organisations can hope to enter every market segment and perform well in each. A more successful strategy is usually to concentrate on selling to one sub-segment of the market at first, then when that market has been saturated, or a pre-determined market share percentage achieved, the company can move into another related sub-segment. The objective would then be to attack each sub-segment in turn, before breaking into the other main market segments: a strategy called *market-by-market segmentation*.

Organisations often identify new markets for their products or services, or diversify into related markets, as a result of conducting a paper exercise in market segmentation. By listing the functions performed by their products, the profiles of current customers or the range of goods they could produce, depending on resources and capabilities, it might be revealed that there are other products worthy of research which could feasibly be marketed profitably and which would satisfy related segments.

In order to establish effective market segments, organisations must be able to observe segmentation criteria, such as:

- *measurability* – identifying and quantifying the potential of each segment accurately;

- *accessibility* – reaching every segment with a specific mix and communicating cost-effectively;
- *reliability* – each segment able to be understood, up-dated and not undermined by the competition;
- *viability* – each segment substantial enough to be treated as a separate sub-market.

When such criteria are put into practice, organisations will be able to take advantage of the many benefits of market segmentation, including:

- better understanding of customers and competitors;
- products and services more finely tuned to the needs of the market;
- greater consumer satisfaction;
- focus on sub-markets with greatest potential;
- development of new segments and markets;

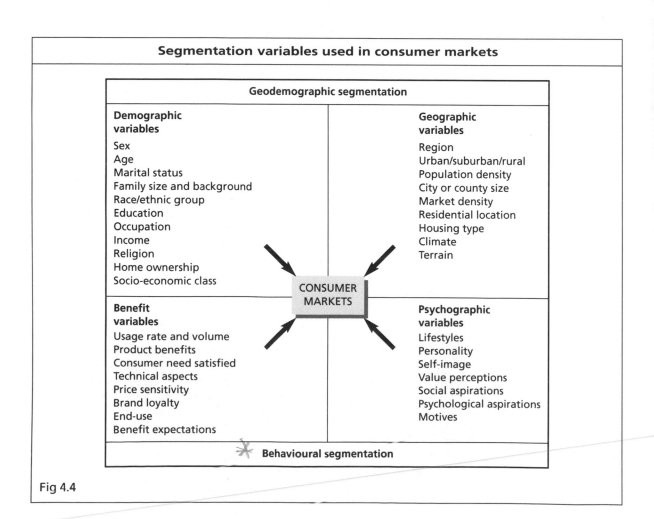

Segmentation variables used in consumer markets

Geodemographic segmentation

Demographic variables

Sex
Age
Marital status
Family size and background
Race/ethnic group
Education
Occupation
Income
Religion
Home ownership
Socio-economic class

Geographic variables

Region
Urban/suburban/rural
Population density
City or county size
Market density
Residential location
Housing type
Climate
Terrain

CONSUMER MARKETS

Benefit variables

Usage rate and volume
Product benefits
Consumer need satisfied
Technical aspects
Price sensitivity
Brand loyalty
End-use
Benefit expectations

Psychographic variables

Lifestyles
Personality
Self-image
Value perceptions
Social aspirations
Psychological aspirations
Motives

Behavioural segmentation

Fig 4.4

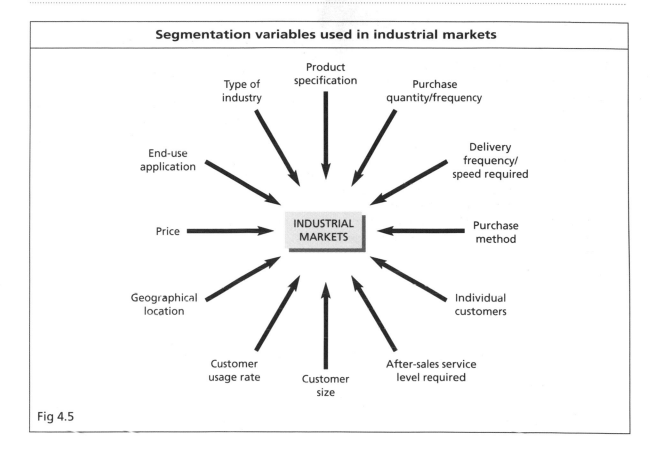

Segmentation variables used in industrial markets

Fig 4.5

- more effective allocation of resources;
- greater sales and profitability;
- more effective short- and long-term market planning.

However, these advantages will only accrue if the company uses appropriate methods to research and compile its market segments.

VARIABLES AND METHODS

The selection of a segmentation method is related to people's needs for, uses of or behaviour towards a product or service. It is influenced by many variables, defined as the dimensions or characteristics of individuals, groups, organisations or products. Organisations must carefully analyse all the possible variables, any one or a combination of which could be proved by research to be the key factor or factors which have to be concentrated upon for success in a market.

The main variables used as bases for segmenting consumer markets can be grouped under four main headings, as illustrated in Figure 4.4.

By contrast, industrial markets are not usually 'mass' in nature, so the main variables used as segmentation bases in these markets are more limited, as described in Figure 4.5.

Organisations need to find as much information as possible about all the customers in their key variable segments. Over the years, various methods have been devised to help collate this information and make the task less random.

The first methods used were demographic, for example socio-economic class, a traditional way of categorising people according to their particular backgrounds, with the assumption that those in the same group will share broadly similar buying habits and spending patterns.

The compilation of these groups takes into account certain environmental criteria which, when combined, theoretically place everyone in a socio-economic class group, or SEG. This is now known as the *Social Grading System*, as illustrated in Table 4.2.

This method of categorisation is now often regarded as rather naïve, limited in scope and inapplicable to current incoming data based on social changes.

A more accurate and detailed classification of consumers was developed in 1978 by CACI, who linked geographic and demographic data to create *A Classification of Residential Neighbourhoods*, now known purely by its acronym *ACORN* (see Table 4.3).

ACORN is a *geodemographic* classification system which relates population characteristics recorded in the Census, including age, sex, socio-economic status and occupation, to the enumeration districts from which the data is collected. Consumers can then be grouped into socio-economic types accord-

ing to the sort of residential area in which they live, on the basis that people living in similar neighbourhoods are likely to have common behavioural, purchasing and lifestyle habits.

The six ACORN categories are divided into 17 groups and further sub-divided into 54 neighbourhood types, each of which can be related to corresponding social grades. Using this kind of cluster analysis, CACI categorises each enumeration district into one of the ACORN types and assigns a type to every postcode.

CACI is now extending its range and using external datasets in combination with census information to produce more specialised classifications, such as Change, Household, Investor, Scottish, Financial and Custom Acorn.

Similarly, CCN has developed the *MOSAIC* database marketing system, which defines 12

Table 4.2 Social Grading System

Social grade	Social status	Chief income earner's occupation
A	Upper middle class	Higher managerial, administrative or professional
B	Middle class	Intermediate managerial, administrative or professional
C1	Lower middle class	Supervisory or clerical and junior managerial, administrative or professional
C2	Skilled working class	Skilled manual workers
D	Working class	Semi-skilled and unskilled manual workers
E	Those at lowest levels of subsistence	State pensioners or widows (no other earner), casual or lowest-grade workers

Source: National Readership Surveys Ltd., London, 1994

Table 4.3 ACORN geodemographic classification

Category	Group	% of population	Corresponding social grade
A Thriving – 19.8%	1. Wealthy achievers, suburban areas 2. Affluent greys, rural communities 3. Prosperous pensioners, retirement areas	15.1 2.3 2.3	A,B,C1 A,B,C2,D A,B,C1
B Expanding – 11.6%	4. Affluent executives, family areas 5. Well-off workers, family areas	3.7 7.8	A,B,C1 A,B,C1,C2
C Rising – 7.5%	6. Affluent urbanites, town and city areas 7. Prosperous professionals, metropolitian areas 8. Better-off executives, inner city areas	2.2 2.1 3.2	A,B,C1 A,B,C1 A,B,C1
D Settling – 24.1%	9. Comfortable middle-agers, mature home-owning areas 10. Skilled workers, home-owning areas	13.4 10.7	A,B,C1 C1,C2,D,E
E Aspiring – 13.7%	11. New home owners, mature communities 12. White-collar workers, better-off multi-ethnic areas	9.8 4.0	C2,D,E C1
F Striving – 22.8%	13. Older people, less prosperous areas 14. Council estate residents, better-off homes 15. Council estate residents, high unemployment 16. Council estate residents, greatest hardship 17. People in multi-ethnic, low-income areas	3.6 11.6 2.7 2.8 2.1	C2,D,E C2,D,E C2,D,E D,E D,E

Source: CACI Ltd., London

major groups and 52 sub-types, based on dimensions of residential area and lifestyle characteristics and linked directly to postcodes (see Fig. 4.4). Specialised versions of this include the Euro-Mosaic and Financial Mosaic classifications, and a profiling system developed specifically for business-to-business markets.

Consumer surveys such as the *Target Group Index* use these classifications to design their sample areas, while organisations purchase ACORN and MOSAIC information to assist in market analysis, credit ratings, direct marketing campaigns and building up customer profile databases, retail site planning and advertising media selection.

Other geodemographic segmentation systems have also been developed, including *TARGET, PINPOINT,* RSL's *SAGACITY,* a life cycle/income/occupation analysis, *CLS* (Consumer Location Systems) and

Table 4.4 MOSAIC lifestyle groupings

Group	Sub-type	%	Group	Sub-type	%
1. High income families 9.9%	Clever capitalists Rising materialists Corporate careerists Ageing professionals Small time business	1.5 1.5 2.4 1.7 2.7	7. Town houses / flats 9.4%	Bijou homemakers Market town mixture Town centre singles	3.5 3.8 2.1
2. Suburban semis 11.0%	Green belt expansion Suburban mock tudor Pebble-dash subtopia	3.4 3.2 4.4	8. Stylish singles 5.2%	Bedsits and shop flats Studio singles College and communal Chattering classes	1.2 1.7 0.5 1.0
3. Blue- collar owners 13.0%	Affluent blue collar 30s Industrial spec Lo-rise right-to-buy Smokestack shiftwork	2.9 3.8 3.3 3.1	9. Independent elders 7.4%	Solo pensioners High spending greys Aged owner occupiers Elderly in own flats	1.9 1.3 2.7 1.5
4. Low-rise council 14.4%	Co-op club and colliery Better off council Low-rise pensioners Low-rise subsistence Problem families	3.4 2.1 3.2 3.5 2.2	10. Mortgaged families 6.2%	Brand new areas Pre-nuptial owners Nestmaking families Maturing mortgagers	1.0 0.8 1.7 2.7
5. Council flats 6.8%	Families in the sky Graffitied ghettos Small town industry Mid rise overspill Flats for the aged Inner city towers	1.3 0.3 1.4 0.7 1.4 1.8	11. Country dwellers 7.0%	Gentrified villages Rural retirement mix Lowland agribusiness Rural disadvantage Tied/tenant farmers Upland and small farms	1.5 0.6 1.8 1.2 0.6 1.3
6. Victorian low status 9.4%	Bohemian melting pot Victorian tenements Rootless renters Sweatshop sharers Depopulated terraces Rejuvenated terraces	2.3 0.1 1.5 1.1 0.8 3.5	12. Institutional areas	Military bases Non-private housing	0.3 0.1

Source: CCN Marketing Ltd., Nottingham

SUPER PROFILES, from CDMS. This growth reflects marketing changes and the need for ever more detailed and sophisticated data.

The information used to compile these systems can also include factors such as household size and composition, car ownership, method of travel to work and amenities available, in addition to the variables listed in Figure 4.4.

However, some segmentation methods relate to specific variables. In this category is CACI's *MONICA* system, which categorises people according to their first names, on the grounds that their age and thus likely purchasing habits can be estimated. Samantha and Ethel, for example, are names which each strongly indicate a probable age band.

Table 4.5 Wells and Gubar life-cycle stages

Category
1. Bachelor stage (young single people not living with parents).
2. Newly married couples without children.
3. Full nest I (youngest child under 6).
4. Full nest II (youngest child 6 or over).
5. Full nest III (older married couple with dependent children).
6. Empty nest I (no children living at home, family head in work).
7. Empty nest II (family head retired).
8. Solitary survivor (in work).
9. Solitary survivor (retired).

Source: Worcester, R. and Downham, J. (Eds), *Consumer Market Research Handbook* (3rd edn), 1986, McGraw-Hill, p.394

Organisations sometimes use this method as a 'fail-safe' for mailshot campaigns generated by computer lists.

In some markets, an understanding of the life cycle stages consumers have reached is an important guide to their spending patterns. Wells and Gubar used this variable to devise the segmentation system outlined in Table 4.5, identifying nine broad life cycle stages.

However, geodemographic information is essentially quantitative and does not take into account consumer attitudes, perceptions and other qualitative factors which help to explain purchasing behaviour.

To introduce this more abstract element into the segmentation equation, recent research has led to the development of behavioural systems based on personality characteristics, buying motives and lifestyles.

One particular strand of this thinking involves *psychographics*, a collection of lifestyle statements which reflect consumers' activities, interests and opinions to create differentiated market segments. For example, research for the President's Commission on American Outdoors identified five main sub-divisions of their market:

- Excitement-seeking competitives.
- Get-away activities.
- The fitness-driven.
- Health-conscious sociables.
- The un-stressed and un-motivated.

The Stanford Research Institute developed the *VALS* (Values and Life-Styles) system, which differentiates eight market categories, as illustrated in Figure 4.6.

OUTLOOK is another psychographic market breakdown which identifies six consumer groups with similar characteristics, namely:

- Trendies.
- Pleasure-seekers.
- The indifferent.
- Working-class puritans.
- Social spenders.
- Moralists.

Organisations seeking more qualitative information about their markets have used these systems, and some have developed their own. For example, the main segments of Esso's typology of motorists' attitudes include the Uninvolved, the Enthusiast, the Professional, the Tinkerer and the Trading-Stamp Collector.

Values and life-styles				
Actualisers	Principle-oriented	Status-oriented	Action-oriented	Strugglers
	Fulfilleds	Achievers	Experiencers	
	Believers	Strivers	Makers	

Fig 4.6

Table 4.6 MONITOR groups applied to the tourism industry

Category		Tourism characteristics
General	**Specific**	
Inner directed	1. Self-explorers	Avoid package holidays and mass sporting activities. Prefer adventure holidays.
	2. Social resisters	Likely to take unadventurous holidays. Entertainment often at home.
	3. Experimen-talists	Holiday in exotic locations. Willing to try new products.
Outer directed	4. Conspicuous Consumers / achievers	Likely to visit currently popular resorts and prefer well-known entertainments and new activities.
	5. Belongers	Holiday with the family, including camping/self-catering/theme parks/ leisure centres.
Sustenance driven	6. Survivors	Prefer holiday camps, Spanish beaches and seaside resorts, spectating at mass sports and eating out at fast food restaurants.
	7. Aimless	Very few holidays or leisure activities. Avoid paying money.

Source: Adapted from Stone, Merlin, *Leisure Services Marketing*, Croner Publications, 1990

Where goods and services are particularly sensitive to consumer lifestyles, values and opinions, the use of psychographic data becomes imperative. Tourism products come into this category, and Table 4.6 illustrates how the industry uses *MONITOR*, Taylor-Nelson's system of seven clusters which is founded on the link between shared social values, attitudes and beliefs, and behaviour patterns.

With this information, players in the tourism industry can accurately identify their main market segments and sub-segments, together with their needs and characteristics, and design the appropriate marketing mixes.

However, psychographic and behavioural data are difficult to measure or prove and can thus be unreliable. Organisations will therefore also endeavour to use geodemographic information to support their research and decision making.

TARGETING

Once a market has been segmented along relevant dimensions, an organisation must make its market target decision. The range of choice available to it can be narrowed down to three broad alternatives, which reflect its attitude towards marketing as discussed in Chapter 2, and the difference between the 'rifle shot' and 'scatter gun' approaches mentioned previously.

The first option involves targeting the whole market, ignoring individual segments and offering the same marketing mix to everyone. This one-dimensional approach is indicative of limited resources and objectives and is termed *undifferentiated marketing* (see Fig. 4.7).

This approach leaves little scope for flexibility and is symptomatic of an organisation with a marketing myopia philosophy and little appreciation of market characteristics and variations.

The main feature of the second option is that market segments are recognised but only one is targeted, using one marketing mix. The main objective of this two-dimensional strategy is a larger market share, with resources focused on excellence in a limited market. Figure 4.8 illustrates this *concentrated marketing* approach.

This form of specialisation offers the opportunity for an organisation to analyse the characteristics and needs of a distinct group of customers carefully and focus its efforts on satisfying them, enabling companies with restricted resources to compete with larger organisations.

Undifferentiated marketing

Organisation → Single marketing mix → Target market → Age under 20 | Age 20 – 40 | Age over 40

One dimension

Fig 4.7

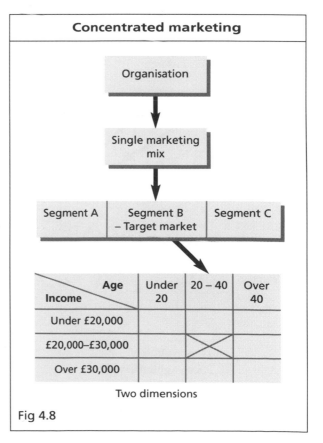

Concentrated marketing

Organisation → Single marketing mix → Segment A | Segment B – Target market | Segment C

Income \ Age	Under 20	20 – 40	Over 40
Under £20,000			
£20,000–£30,000		X	
Over £30,000			

Two dimensions

Fig 4.8

However, if sales depend on a single segment which subsequently declines or provides a limited life span or marginal returns, then concentrated marketing can prove to be a dangerous strategy.

The third option involves targeting two or more segments of a wide market with many variables and offering a unique marketing mix to each segment. Such a three-dimensional approach focuses resources and objectives on growth in several markets and is termed *differentiated marketing* (see Fig. 4.9).

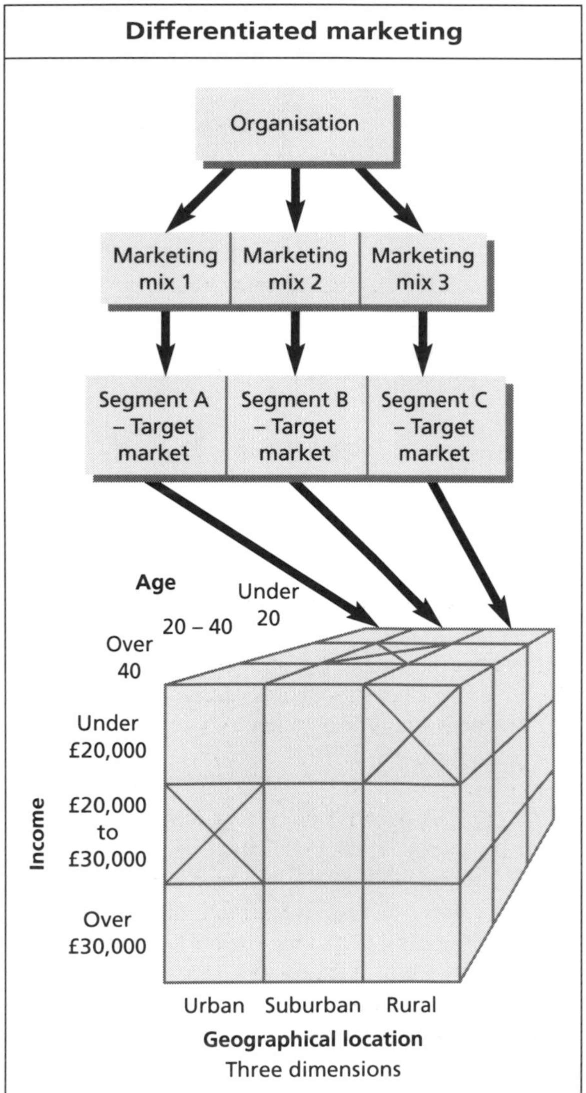

By adopting this strategy, organisations can benefit from the overall increase in sales which often arises from a wide range of marketing mixes, and the sale of products or services to additional segments could help to absorb any excess production capacity.

The disadvantages of such an approach are mainly financial. Differentiated marketing demands a greater number of production processes, materials and people, and together with the associated management and administrative functions, higher costs are incurred.

Choice of targeting strategy is a key aspect of an organisation's marketing management. The final selection will be affected or determined by a number of factors, of which the main ones are:

- objectives of the organisation;
- organisational resources;
- market characteristics and needs;
- nature of the products or services;
- scope of the competition;
- market share of the product/service or company;
- nature of the local, national and international economy.

POSITIONING

Having segmented the market and decided on a targeting strategy, an organisation has one more piece of the jigsaw to complete before it is able to identify and select its markets with confidence. It must endeavour to create and maintain a clear and appropriate positive image of the product or service in the minds of customers. This process of *positioning* involves a number of considerations and can take a long time to perfect, or to change.

The position of a product or service is often expressed in relation to the market leader and its rivals in general, so product positioning can be said to be the manner in which similar products differ and stand out from their main competitors. Establishing this differentiation usually involves an organisation in emphasising a particular product or service attribute, such as:

- quality;
- price and value;
- technical advancement;
- size or duration;
- familiar brand name or logo;
- other benefits or unique selling points.

Differentiated marketing

Organisation

Marketing mix 1 | Marketing mix 2 | Marketing mix 3

Segment A – Target market | Segment B – Target market | Segment C – Target market

Age
Under 20
20 – 40
Over 40

Income
Under £20,000
£20,000 to £30,000
Over £30,000

Urban   Suburban   Rural
Geographical location
Three dimensions

Fig 4.9

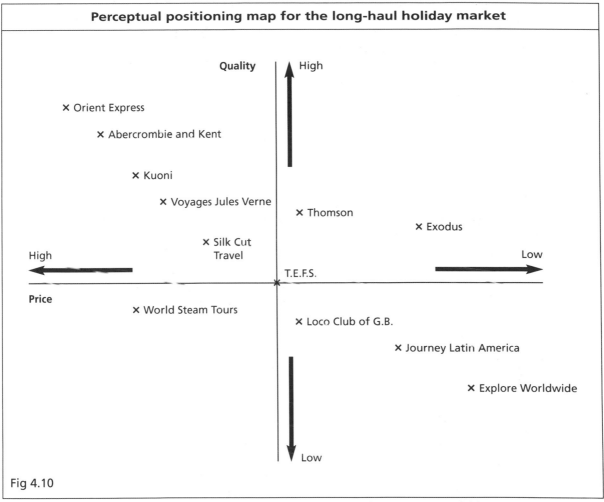

Perceptual positioning map for the long-haul holiday market

Fig 4.10

Source: Adapted from Hutchings, A., 'Tourism Marketing in China', European Case Clearing-House, Cranfield University, 1993

From a consumer's point of view, a product's position is the sum of those attributes normally ascribed to it, which could be tangible or intangible. For example, the perceptions of a target market could be influenced by such product or service characteristics as specific features, the type of people who use it, strengths, weaknesses, what it represents and any other unusual or memorable qualities it exhibits. They could also be affected by the image of the organisation and its other products or services, but the overall effect is to establish the product clearly in consumers' 'collective imaginations'.

An organisation will be able to confirm such perceptions through extensive marketing research before concentrating on a policy of reinforcement or re-positioning.

It is generally easier for organisations to visualise a product's position graphically by means of a *perceptual map*, on which each axis represents a key measurable criterion. The position of a particular company or brand can then be plotted on the scatter diagram along with its competitors, in order for an organisation to assess its situation and prioritise its strategy. Figure 4.10 illustrates a perceptual map for the growing long-haul package holiday market.

Markets are rarely constant and such a scatter diagram serves as a snapshot at a given point in time, depicting consumer perceptions and brand attributes and guiding organisations towards possible courses of action, by suggesting potential market segment gaps or indicating the need for re-positioning.

Organisations thus use perceptual mapping as a means of keeping product positioning under constant review, whilst identifying and validating market segments, developing marketing mixes and determining targeting strategies. The market selection process is then complete, although eventual success will depend upon the actions of the fickle consumer.

ARTICLES

A1

Name that age – salesmen discover your last secret

If your name's Pamela, Heather, Pauline or Ann, then you're a 25–44-year-old married mum who's inundated with junk mail on tumble driers and hatchbacks. So say those who send you persuasive literature through the post. They've decided fashions in first names make a reliable guide to a person's age – and an important pointer in deciding what sort of unsolicited post interests most.

Marketing analysts CACI fed 43 million names into a computer to divide the UK into four age bands. As a result, Tracys, Sharons and Clares (under 25s) should stand by for nightclub info; Joyces, Eileens and Jeans (45–60) for private health care, and Ethel, Hilda and Alice (60+) for young-at-heart hols. Surprisingly, 85% of names fit their age breakdown. Only Mary transcends the eras of fashionableness.

1 In what circumstances could this segmentation system be used?

2 Do you consider first names to be a reliable guide as to age and likely purchasing behaviour?

3 How might the essential research data for this classification system be gathered?

4 Conduct a survey of your friends and family and the 'junk' mail they receive. Is there a relationship with the CACI system described in the article?

A2

Yaks and ewes drive out Yuppies

YUPPIES are no more – they have been replaced by Yaks, a new way of categorising consumers.

The credit-card company Access today announced six categories drawn from the animal kingdom after monitoring the spending trends of its 10 million customers.

YAKS are Young, Adventurous, Keen and Single. They are 18–24, wear designer clothes, drive expensive cars and go on holidays to faraway sun-drenched islands and chic skiing resorts.

They love eating out and clubbing, but take their health seriously.

EWES are Experts With Expensive Style. They are career-minded couples, 25–34, who enjoy two incomes and have a first mortgage but no children.

BATS are the 25–34 group, where Babies Add The Sparkle. They are married or have a partner, and most of their money goes on the mortgaged house and the children. Holidays are spent camping in France or at a friend's cottage in the West Country or Norfolk.

CLAMS are 35–44 and Carefully Look At Most Spending. Some are going through a midlife crisis, and although they have high incomes they have hefty mortgages and high living expenses.

MICE have no such worries as Money Is Coming Easier. They are 45–54, the children have started leaving home, and the mortgage is nearly paid.

OWLS are Older With Less Stress. They are 55 and over, and many have moved into smaller homes and have few overheads.

Source: By courtesy of *The Yorkshire Post*

1 What type of segmentation system is outlined in the article and upon what sort of research information does it depend?

2 How accurate and useful do you consider this classification of consumers to be in marketing terms? Give examples of people you know who fit these categories.

3 Suggest examples of products and services which are suited to this system and explain why.

4 Why should Access segment their market in this way? Is the method appropriate for all financial institutions?

 A3

The holiday huntress

NO LONGER content with lazing on a sun-kissed beach, a growing number of European women are seeking adrenaline-pumping action holidays. Survival training in the jungles of South America and motor-sleigh safaris in Lapland are popular alternatives being snapped up this week.

German, French and British women of all ages are leading this new search for adventure and an increasing amount of firms are catering for their needs.

'Many women are married and want to experience something unusual on their own,' said Ulrike Niemann from the Berlin-based travel agency Women on Travel. 'It is a wish come true for most who book a trip with us.'

This summer, the agency is offering a three-week trip to China for women where they can learn self-defence, or a voyage of similar length into the heart of the French Guyanan jungle.

'For this trip, the women need to be in very good physical condition,' said Niemann. A professional female guide leads them into the jungle where they are taught to find their way by compass and maps. 'They eat the produce they find in the jungle,' she said.

Women on Travel opened in 1984 by offering sport trips such as sailing, surfing and canoeing. 'These offers are still very popular, but people are demanding increasingly outrageous destinations,' said Niemann.

Another Berlin-based travel agency is offering women-only reindeer and motor-sleigh tours of up to three weeks into the heart of Lapland for the first time this year. 'We have had so many requests for women-only trips that it seemed a good idea,' said Sirpon Schettler from Special Finn Journey, who began offering sleigh adventures four years ago for both men and women.

Travel agencies in Britain and France, with exotic names such as Tiger Travel and Marco Polo, are also cashing in on Europe's adventure women by offering white-water rafting in Nepal and hiking in the Himalayas.

'It is not like a package holiday,' said June Campbell from Edinburgh's Women's Adventure Trekking, who charges £700 (Ecu872) for a two-week trip to Nepal. 'We also make sure we visit women's projects and meet local people.'

Mainstream travel agencies are also jumping on the bandwagon by opening new divisions catering exclusively for women.

Source: The European

1 Explain the targeting strategy adopted by travel agencies operating in the market described in the article.

2 What segmentation variables would be most appropriate for an organisation researching into this tourism sector?

3 What positioning strategy might be adopted by a new entrant into this market?

4 Suggest a range of sub-segments of the market into which an organisation might research and expand in the future.

The House of Hermès

Hermès, the £1 billion purveyor of luxury goods, has successfully targeted the world's 'brat pack'. Stella Shamoon reports.

JEAN-Louis Dumas-Hermès, head of the House of Hermès, is a seriously rich person who possesses a peasant's instinct to plough every penny of profit back into the luxury goods maker and retailer that has borne his name for five generations and is still 90 per cent family controlled.

Under his 12-year stewardship, Hermès has emerged from its traditional strength, in somewhat staid silk scarves and ties and hardly affordable handbags, into an exciting emporium of luxury goods which embraces fashion for him and her, leather goods, footwear, watches, crystal, porcelain and, of course, perfume with such classic fragrances as Caleche (1951) and Amazone (1974). *Pour monsieur*: Bel Ami (1986).

Dumas-Hermès repositioned the business by way of a radical change in marketing strategy. Out went complacency along with low-spend advertising directed at the French bourgeoisie which, habitually, proffered predictable presents housed in Hermès' distinctive burnt orange boxes.

He was prepared, if necessary, to jettison the ladies of Paris's 16th *arrondissement* – who owned a vast collection of his *carrés* – in favour of the world's newly-rich brat pack. What Dumas-Hermès was intent on capturing was a stake in the luxury consumer goods boom of the Eighties. High-spend advertising – currently running at some 10 per cent of world-wide sales of FFr2.5 billion (£270 million) – was brought into play and, in the space of seven years, turnover has risen five-fold.

The same instinct that ploughs funds back into the business prevents Dumas-Hermès from discussing profits. All the same, it is no secret that Hermès achieves a pre-tax profit of more than 20 per cent on annual sales.

Hermès breakthrough ads in 1978 featured a girl in denim shirt and jeans with a £120 Hermès *carré* knotted nonchalantly at the neck. In such a way was frump transformed into throwaway chic – at *ooh la la* prices which served to preserve Hermès' cachet as something rather special.

A three-month waiting list for the Kelly – a handmade Hermès handbag favoured by the late Princess Grace of Monaco – bears witness to Hermès' marketing sizzle.

Source: The Observer, 20 May 1990

1 Describe the market segment being targeted by Dumas-Hermès. How much of a risk is the company taking by confining itself to this market?

2 How did the company seek to reposition the business and why did it consider it necessary to do so?

3 Is it more important for Dumas-Hermès to clearly position the company *or* its product range in the minds of the target market?

4 What part does price play in the company's targeting and positioning strategy?

A5

Chocs away for campaign

YORK chocolate maker Terry's is spending millions of pounds on a nationwide advertising campaign for two of its products.

Senior brand manager Ben Clarke said the marketing campaign for Moments and Pyramint started in the last few days and would continue for about a month.

Terry's, whose manufacturing base is in Bishopthorpe Road, launched the original hazel and caramel-flavoured mild chocolate Moments bar about a year ago.

It exceeded the company's own forecasts by notching up sales worth £9.5 million in its first year.

A second variation, with hazelnut truffle and white chocolate, has now been launched to build on the success of the original.

Mr Clarke said the new campaign would also cover Pyramint, which was relaunched last September in the form of a milk chocolate bar with four mint-filled pyramid-shaped sections.

He declined to state exactly how much Terry's was spending, but confirmed that it was a multi-million pound heavy-weight national campaign.

'We are going for the quality end of the market by making things with the richest possible ingredients.'

He said Moments and Pyramint were competing with established favourites such as Cadbury's Flake; Bounty by Mars; and Aero, made by rival York firm Nestle Rowntree.

Source: The Yorkshire Evening Press, 6 February 1992

1 What are the key segmentation variables used by companies in the chocolate bar market, and why?

2 How is it possible for organisations to differentiate and position their brands in such a crowded market?

3 Suggest the possible differences in targeting strategy which Terry's could adopt for Moments and Pyramint.

4 Construct a scatter diagram, using appropriate criteria for the axes, which plots the perceptual position in the minds of customers of the chocolate products mentioned in the article.

ISSUES

MARKET SEGMENTATION

Sometimes regarded as too uncertain to justify a large allocation of resources.

1 How can organisations best avoid a 'hit and miss' approach to market selection?

2 Argue the cases for and against structured market segmentation.

3 What role should marketing research play in determining the selection of markets?

SOCIAL GRADING

Socio-economic class grouping is considered by many organisations to provide a generalised view of markets inappropriate for current social trends.

1 For what products or services could social grading provide an adequate market picture?

2 List all the criteria which could be used to assess a person's socio-economic class group and discuss the relative importance of each.

3 What are the main limitations of the social grading system?

GEODEMOGRAPHIC SEGMENTATION

Based on statistics and groupings which can soon be obsolete.

1 What methods could organisations adopt to ensure the relative accuracy of their systems?

2 Estimate your ACORN and MOSAIC sub-group classification. How true to life do you consider them to be?

3 Which products and services are most suited to geodemographic market selection systems?

4 What are the main reasons for geodemographic data becoming obsolete?

LIFESTYLE AND PSYCHOGRAPHICS

The unpredictability of human beings renders these methods questionable.

1 Is accurate measurement of activities, opinions and interests possible? Can both consumer and industrial markets be measured in this way?

2 What is the relationship between lifestyle variables and purchasing behaviour?

3 Using examples with which you are familiar, apply the MONITOR categories to consumer or industrial products/services and describe their effectiveness.

TARGETING STRATEGIES

Pursuing rigid target markets could lead to inflexibility.

1 Discuss the relative merits and de-merits of undifferentiated, concentrated and differentiated targeting.

2 Which of these strategies is most likely to be used by organisations marketing industrial products or services? What segmentation methods would be most appropriate for these companies?

3 Discuss examples of organisations adopting each of the three methods of targeting.

POSITIONING

Too abstract a concept to be of practical business use?

1 What specific marketing tools can be used to help position a product or service in the consumer's imagination and that of the market as a whole?

2 Can an organisation accurately measure consumer reaction to positioning strategy? What environmental factors could affect their perceptions?

3 Argue the cases for and against scatter diagrams providing an accurate 'snapshot' of the perceptual position of products and services, giving examples.

QUESTIONS

1 Provide a definition of market segmentation.

2 Why is the concept of segmentation an important element in many organisations' marketing strategy?

3 Explain what is meant by the 'rifle shot' and 'scatter gun' approaches to segmentation.

4 What is meant by 'market-by-market segmentation'?

5 Name the four key criteria necessary for effective segmentation.

6 List four benefits accruing to organisations as a result of market segmentation.

7 Name six variable factors used as bases for segmenting consumer markets.

8 List four variable factors used as bases for segmenting industrial markets.

9 Describe the social grading demographic segmentation system.

10 What are geodemographic classifications and when are they used?

11 Explain the ACORN system.

12 Describe the MOSAIC classification.

13 List the Wells and Gubar consumer life cycle stages.

14 What are psychographics?

15 Explain the VALS system.

16 Describe the MONITOR classification.

17 Provide a definition of targeting.

18 What is undifferentiated marketing?

19 Explain concentrated marketing.

20 What is differentiated marketing?

21 List four factors affecting choice of targeting strategy.

22 Provide a definition of positioning.

23 Name four attributes which can be emphasised to differentiate a product or service and create market position.

24 What is a perceptual positioning map?

PROJECTS

1 Suggest appropriate ways of segmenting the markets for the following products or services:

- rail travel;
- ballpoint pens;
- shampoo;
- banks;
- refrigerators;
- ball bearings.

2 What variables could be used to segment the market for beers and lagers? Select two brands from this market and compare and contrast the segments towards which each is targeted and their resulting marketing mixes.

3 Choose an organisation or brand and describe its market selection strategy, referring to the approach adopted towards market segmentation, targeting and positioning.

4 Describe the range of marketing uses to which geodemographic segmentation systems, such as ACORN and MOSAIC, can be put. Give specific examples.

5 Explain the growth of psychographic segmentation and describe the ways in which selected organisations have used systems such as VALS and MONITOR.

6 In what conditions might an organisation vary its targeting strategy and what risks would it run in doing so? Use consumer or industrial examples in your answer.

7 Select an organisation which has attempted to re-position itself or its products in recent times, such as Woolworths or British Airways. Describe the procedures it went through and the problems it faced.

8 'A product's position is the sum of those tangible or intangible attributes normally ascribed to it.' Discuss this definition with reference to (a) the hi-fi market, (b) higher education and (c) telecommunications cable and wiring equipment.

9 Analyse consumer perceptions of (a) the national daily and (b) the Sunday newspaper markets. Using axis measurement criteria based on price and style, construct scatter diagrams which accurately represent the positioning of products in each market.

10 'Positioning is a battle for the consumers' minds and collective imaginations.' Assess this viewpoint, using examples.

GLOSSARY

ACORN a geodemographic market segmentation system developed by CACI which classifies consumers according to the type of residential area in which they live (originally an acronym standing for 'A Classification of Residential Neighbourhoods').

AIO a psychographic segmentation method which involves the collection of lifestyle statements on consumers' activities, interests and opinions.

Baby boomers the post-war birth increase segment, now in middle age and a significant target market.

Behaviour segmentation sub-dividing a market into homogeneous groups based on consumer knowledge, attitude, use or response to product or service.

Benefit segmentation sub-dividing a market into homogeneous groups based on the different benefits of the product or service sought by the buyer.

CLS Consumer Location System, a geodemographic segmentation method.

Combined target market approach combining two or more sub-market segments into one larger target market as a basis for one strategy.

Concentrated marketing a targeting strategy in which an organisation recognises different segments but chooses to direct its resources towards a single market segment using one marketing mix.

Demographic segmentation sub-dividing a market into homogeneous groups based on population characteristics such as age, sex, income and education.

Differential advantage the situation an organisation strives to achieve where it or its products or services contain beneficial characteristics which give it a head over its competitors.

Differentiated marketing a targeting strategy in which organisations direct their resources towards several market segments using a variety of marketing mixes. Also known as 'multi-segment marketing' or 'multi-target marketing'.

DINKS acronym for a market segment where consumers share the characteristic of being couples with 'dual income, no kids'.

Empty-nesters segment of consumers whose children are grown up and who are therefore now able to spend their money in other ways.

End-use application segmentation method of sub-dividing an industrial market into homogeneous groups on the basis of how the product will ultimately be used.

Full-nesters segment of consumers with children who will play an important part in determining their expenditure patterns.

Geodemographic segmentation sub-dividing a market into homogeneous groups based on a combination of geographic and demographic factors.

Geographic segmentation sub-dividing a market into homogeneous groups according to geographical location.

Heterogeneity nature of a market in which all consumers or groups possess different characteristics and wants/needs.

Homogeneity nature of a market in which all consumers or groups possess similar characteristics and wants/needs.

Income segmentation sub-dividing a market into homogeneous groups based on different levels of income.

life cycle and age segmentation sub-dividing a market into homogeneous groups according to their ages and life cycle characteristics.

Lifestyle a person's living pattern, including family, job, social activities and consumer decisions.

Lifestyle segmentation sub-dividing a market into homogeneous groups based on their lifestyles, as measured by activities, opinions, interests and values.

Market segment a homogeneous group of consumers sharing similar characteristics and needs who will be likely to respond to a marketing mix in a similar way.

Market segmentation sub-dividing the total market into homogeneous groups possessing similar characteristics and needs, then using this classification to reach each group or 'niche' with a different marketing mix. Also known as 'niche marketing'.

Market-by-market segmentation a strategy involving maximising potential in one market segment then moving on to another one, and so on.

Monica demographic segmentation system developed by CACI which classifies consumers according to their first names.

MONITOR psychographic segmentation system developed by Taylor-Nelson which identifies seven categories, based on the link between shared social values, attitudes and beliefs, and behaviour patterns.

MOSAIC a geodemographic market segmentation system developed by CCN which classifies consumers according to residential area and lifestyle characteristics and which is linked directly to postcodes.

Multi-segment marketing see 'Differentiated marketing'.

Multi-variable segmentation sub-dividing the market by the use of more than one variable characteristic in order to provide more information.

Multi-target marketing see 'Differentiated marketing'.

Niche marketing see 'Market segmentation'.

Occasion segmentation sub-dividing the market into homogeneous groups according to the occasions when consumers decide to buy, actually make the purchase or use the bought item.

Perceptual mapping using a scatter diagram or 'map' to plot and visually depict consumers' perceptions of products or services relative to the competition, in order to consider strategic marketing options.

Pinpoint a geodemographic segmentation system.

Positioning developing a marketing strategy aimed at creating and maintaining a desired concept and image for a product or service in the consumer's mind.

Product position the way a product or service is perceived by consumers and the place it occupies in prospective customers' minds relative to the competition.

Product segmentation sub-dividing the market for an industrial product into homogeneous groups on the basis of product specifications identified by industrial buyers.

Profiling building up and understanding the characteristics of consumer markets.

Psychographics the technique of measuring lifestyles and developing behavioural profile classifications from the analysis of AIO dimensions, in order to segment consumer markets.

Psychographic segmentation sub-dividing the market into homogeneous groups according to personality, lifestyle and behavioural characteristics.

Rifle shot using market segmentation methods to target specific individuals or groups of consumers.

SAGACITY geodemographic segmentation system devised by RSL.

Scatter diagram used as a 'map' to plot a product or service's perceptual position in the minds of customers relative to the competition, in order to assess possible marketing strategies.

Scatter gun ignoring market segmentation methods and targeting the market as a whole.

Segmentation variable a dimension or variable characteristic of individuals, groups or organisations that is used to divide a total market into segments.

Single-variable segmentation basic form of segmenting a market by using only one variable characteristic.

Social class a division of society containing groups of people who share similar values, interests and behaviour and an approximately equal social position, as viewed by others in the society, which makes them likely to share similar product needs.

Social grading socio-economic class grouping, a demographic segmentation system.

Socio-economic class group segmentation sub-dividing the market into homogeneous segments according to their social class group, as measured by various characteristics such as professional occupation.

Superprofiles a geodemographic segmentation system devised by CDMS.

TARGET a geodemographic segmentation system.

Targeting (or target marketing) evaluating the market segments, selecting those at which to direct marketing resources and developing an appropriate marketing mix or mixes for them.

Target market a selected group of homogeneous customers for whom an organisation creates and maintains a marketing mix designed to satisfy their specific needs and preferences.

Undifferentiated marketing a targeting strategy in which organisations ignore market segment differences, treat all consumers as being homogeneous and direct a single marketing mix for a product or service at a whole market.

VALS Values and Life-Styles, a psychographic segmentation system devised by the Stanford Research Institute.

Wells and Gubar life cycles a life cycle segmentation system.

Yuppies young urban professionals, a homogeneous sub-division of customers within one of the early lifestyle segmentation systems.

SUGGESTED REFERENCES

VIDEO MATERIAL

Marketing in Action, 'Principles for Men', Open University, 1985.

Electric Avenue, 'Housewives' Choice', BBC, 1988.

How to Survive Lifestyle, Channel Four, 1989.

Contemporary Marketing, Video Cases, No. 7 (The Irvine Company), Boone, L. and Kurtz, D., Dryden Press, 1989.

Class by Class, Ray Gosling, Channel Four, 1990.

MAGAZINE ARTICLES

Journal of Marketing Management, Vol. 1, No. 1, Summer 1985, p.75, 'The Methuselah Market'.

Journal of Marketing Management, Vol. 1, No. 2, Winter 1985, p.223, 'The Methuselah Market, Part 2 – decision-making and the older consumer'.

Journal of Marketing Management, Vol. 4, No. 4, Summer 1988, p.13, 'The family life cycle – a demographic analysis'.

Journal of Marketing Management, Vol. 8, No. 4, October 1992, p.303, 'Market and technological shifts in the 1990s: market fragmentation and mass customisation'.

Marketing Business, Oct. 1988, p.16, 'What makes high tech. products sell?'

Marketing Business, Apr. 1990, p.20, 'The Greys are coming'.

Marketing Business, Oct. 1990, p.14, 'A niche for high performance'.

Marketing Business, Nov. 1991, p.48, 'Briefly'.

Marketing Business, Apr. 1992, p.36, 'Pinpoint accuracy'.

Marketing Business, May 1992, p.32, 'Niche marketing'.

Marketing Business, Feb. 1993, p.10, 'Golden oldies'.

Quarterly Review of Marketing, Autumn 1987, Vol. 13, No.1, p. 7, 'Context marketing – the "Honey Pot" approach to segmentation strategy'.

Quarterly Review of Marketing, Winter 1988, Vol. 13, No. 2, p.5, 'A Sales Force approach to industrial market segmentation'.

FURTHER READING

Adcock, D., Bradfield, R., Halborg, A. and Ross, C., *Marketing Principles and Practice*, Pitman, 1995, ch. 7.

Baker, M. (Ed.), *The Marketing Book*, Heinemann C.I.M., 1990, chs 2 and 12.

Boone, L. and Kurtz, D., *Contemporary Marketing*, Dryden, 1989, ch. 7.

Cannon, Tom, *Basic Marketing*, Holt Business Texts, 1980, ch. 6.

Dibb, S., Simkin, L., Pride, W. and Ferrell, O., *Marketing*, Houghton Mifflin, 1994, ch. 3.

Foster, D., *Mastering Marketing*, Macmillan, 1982, ch. 6.

Kotler, P. and Armstrong, G., *Marketing*, Prentice Hall, 1993, ch. 7.

McCarthy, J. and Perreault, W., *Basic Marketing*, Irwin, 1987, ch. 3.

Mercer, D., *Marketing*, Blackwell, 1992, ch. 6.

Acknowledgements

CACI Information Services, London – The 'ACORN' User Guide.

CCN Marketing Ltd., Nottingham – 'MOSAIC' classification system.

CDMS Company, London – 'Superprofiles' system.

The Northern Echo.

The Yorkshire Post.

The European.

The Observer.

The Yorkshire Evening Press.

5

THE CUSTOMER

DEFINITIONS

Consumer buying behaviour incorporates the acts of individuals directly involved in obtaining and using products or services and the decision processes preceding and determining these acts.

Organisational buying behaviour is the decision making process by which producers, resellers and institutions establish the need for purchased products or services and identify, evaluate and choose among alternative brands and suppliers.

INTRODUCTION

Even employing a sophisticated and scientifically based strategy of market selection, companies still find marketing their products or services an unpre-

dictable business. The problem is that customers are either individuals, organisations or other combinations of people or groups forming deci-

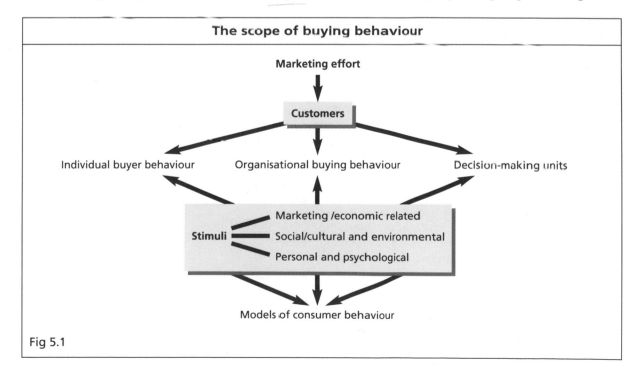

Fig 5.1

sion-making units. All three categories are affected by a wide range of different stimuli and various theories have been put forward to try to make logical patterns from these and create models to explain buying behaviour (see Figure 5.1).

Human behaviour is an intricate process which is almost impossible to define or simulate because many complex variables affect personal and organisational motivation. However, attempting to explain the actions of consumers is a vital research objective because marketing strategies can be based on the reasons behind purchasing decisions, and an understanding of motivating factors means that the selling job can be more scientifically undertaken.

Nevertheless, buying behaviour can never be fully accounted for and organisations must invariably generalise to explain the actions of their customers.

KEY CONCEPTS

INFLUENCES ON CONSUMER BEHAVIOUR

The most straightforward explanation of consumer purchasing actions involves direct responses to *marketing* and *economic related* stimuli provided by the organisation. These include:

- the product itself, and its usefulness and/or benefits;
- the packaging, design, colour, name or other brand attributes;
- the place at which the product is available;
- the channels through which the product is distributed;
- promotional and advertising methods employed;
- corporate image and reputation of the manufacturing organisation;
- after-sales service and other facilities available;
- the economic nature of the product, e.g. luxury or necessity;
- the price of the product in relation to competitors;
- media editorial content.

Any of these or other related factors could lead directly to a purchase. One example is the instant 'impulse purchase' decision made at the point of sale, usually involving relatively cheap consumer products with no economic anxiety attached, and affected predominantly by marketing stimuli.

Other types of buying decisions are based more on inter-personal determinants – social, cultural and environmental. Amongst the many important *social* and *cultural* factors are:

- occupation – products/services associated with employment;
- local, regional and national cultural background and values, e.g. being brought up to think you need something;
- social class group perceptions – the epitome of social influence is the 'status symbol' product which is purchased mainly for the social standing which the ownership of that product brings (cars, yachts, hi-fi systems and colour televisions have all filled this role in the past);
- life cycle and lifestyle developments;
- the 'keeping up with the Jones's' syndrome;
- reference group norms and role behaviour, for example the influences and limitations imposed by others, particularly superiors or status figures (see Figure 5.2);
- past learning experiences and future consequences of actions;
- marital status and income factors – Engel's Laws suggest a correlation between family income and purchasing behaviour (see Figure 5.3);
- family role structures – relationships and established patterns of dominance can determine purchasing decisions (see Figure 5.4);
- viewpoints of opinion leaders.

Additionally, there are certain *environmental* variables which can influence consumer behaviour, including:

- demographic and geographic factors, such as the location, concentration and spread of the market, the age and sex distribution of potential purchasers and the urban/rural nature of the environment;

Reference group influences

Group influence of product class

		Weak	Strong
Group influence on brand type	Strong	Public necessities: Clothing Furniture Soaps Clocks and watches	Public luxuries: Cars Tobacco Wine Restaurant meals Holidays
	Weak	Private necessities: Beds Detergents Bread and milk Roof insulation Soft drinks	Private luxuries: Microwave ovens Video recorders Television games Instant coffee

Fig 5.2

Source: Bearden, W.O. and Etzel, M. J., 'Reference Group influence on product and brand purchase decisions', *Journal of Consumer Research,* Vol. 9, Sept. 1982. Published by the University of Chicago Press and reproduced with permission

- political and legal decision making;
- economic factors, for example the measurable earnings and disposable income of an individual or household, and the price of the product or service and its competition;
- technical aspects, including the specific characteristics products must exhibit to be considered for purchase, particularly applicable in the sale of the more complex consumer goods.

Personal and psychological stimuli also help to explain consumer purchasing actions. Amongst the many *personal* determinants are:

- different idiosyncrasies and peculiarities of mind or character;
- ability and knowledge;
- individual needs and wants;
- the level of involvement and interest a person exhibits in a particular product or service;
- other external and situational circumstances which could reinforce, delay or alter consumer choice.

In recent times considerable research has been undertaken into the numerous explanations of buyer behaviour which are *psychological* in nature. These include:

- subconscious motivations, as suggested by the psychologist Sigmund Freud;

- attitudes, beliefs and perceptions;
- consumer self-image;
- personality traits, such as frustration, aggression, passivity, fantasy, apathy, identification, and so on;
- other motivating factors, such as the psychological characteristics and attributes projected by products or services – e.g. consumers are not encouraged to buy toothpaste but to purchase fresh breath, a nice smile, social attraction, sound teeth or a host of other benefits.

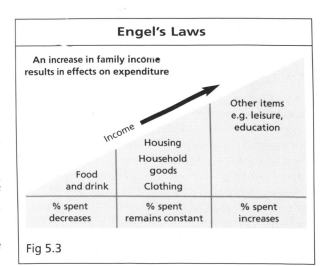

Engel's Laws

An increase in family income results in effects on expenditure

% spent decreases	% spent remains constant	% spent increases
Food and drink	Household goods / Clothing	Other items e.g. leisure, education

Fig 5.3

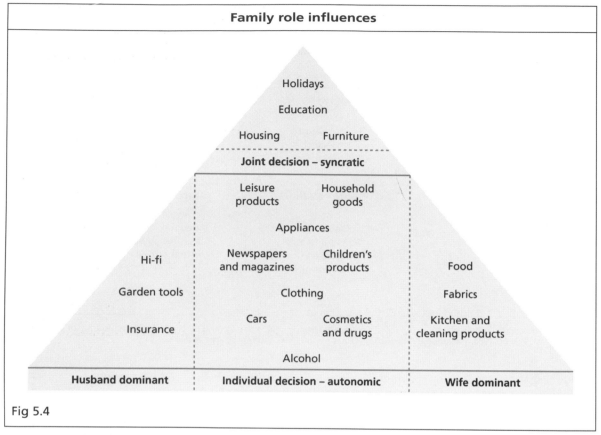

Family role influences

Holidays

Education

Housing   Furniture

Joint decision – syncratic

Leisure   Household
products   goods

Appliances

Hi-fi   Newspapers   Children's   Food
              and magazines   products

Garden tools   Clothing   Fabrics

Insurance   Cars   Cosmetics   Kitchen and
                                and drugs   cleaning products

Alcohol

Husband dominant   **Individual decision – autonomic**   **Wife dominant**

Fig 5.4

Source: Adapted from Davies, H. L. and Rigaux, B. P., 'Perceptions of marital roles in decision processes', *Journal of Consumer Research,* Vol. 1, July 1974. Published by the University of Chicago Press and reproduced with permission

The most established classification of personal and psychological purchasing motivations was originally proposed by Abraham Maslow.

Maslow identified five layers of needs which he felt motivated people's behaviour and ranked them into a series of steps. According to this 'hierarchy of needs' analysis, when the vital lower-order needs are fulfilled, we lose interest in them and concentrate on satisfying needs at the next level up. So marketing practitioners can match consumers' needs by targeting products or services at specific hierarchical levels, as illustrated in Figure 5.5.

Organisations can also use this motivational theory to devise a different promotional campaign for a product, depending on which level of the needs hierarchy is being targeted. For a fast-moving consumer good such as biscuits, Maslow's stages could be matched by appropriate advertising messages, as indicated in Figure 5.6.

All marketing activities are based on buyer behaviour but in practice there is no simple way to predict a customer's actions or analyse the many factors which can stimulate a purchase. Consumer behaviour usually results from the interaction of some or all of these variables.

PROBLEMS AND DECISIONS

When considering the possible purchase of a product or service, consumers have many problems to solve and decisions to make. These can be conscious or subconscious and, as we have seen, are affected by numerous factors.

Consumer problem solving necessitates varying degrees of information gathering and processing before a decision can be made. The information process sequence is illustrated in Figure 5.7.

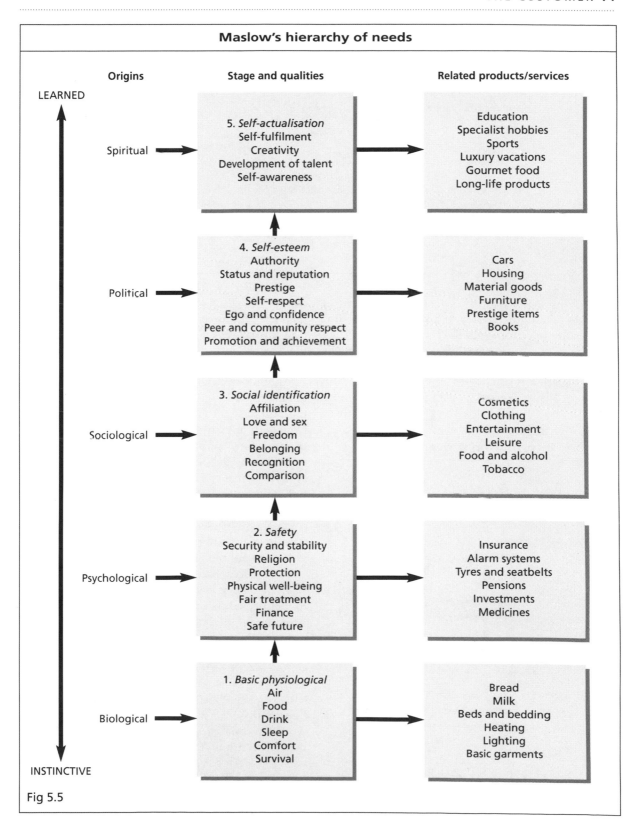

Maslow's hierarchy of needs

Origins	Stage and qualities	Related products/services

LEARNED

Spiritual →
5. *Self-actualisation*
Self-fulfilment
Creativity
Development of talent
Self-awareness

→ Education
Specialist hobbies
Sports
Luxury vacations
Gourmet food
Long-life products

Political →
4. *Self-esteem*
Authority
Status and reputation
Prestige
Self-respect
Ego and confidence
Peer and community respect
Promotion and achievement

→ Cars
Housing
Material goods
Furniture
Prestige items
Books

Sociological →
3. *Social identification*
Affiliation
Love and sex
Freedom
Belonging
Recognition
Comparison

→ Cosmetics
Clothing
Entertainment
Leisure
Food and alcohol
Tobacco

Psychological →
2. *Safety*
Security and stability
Religion
Protection
Physical well-being
Fair treatment
Finance
Safe future

→ Insurance
Alarm systems
Tyres and seatbelts
Pensions
Investments
Medicines

Biological →
1. *Basic physiological*
Air
Food
Drink
Sleep
Comfort
Survival

→ Bread
Milk
Beds and bedding
Heating
Lighting
Basic garments

INSTINCTIVE

Fig 5.5

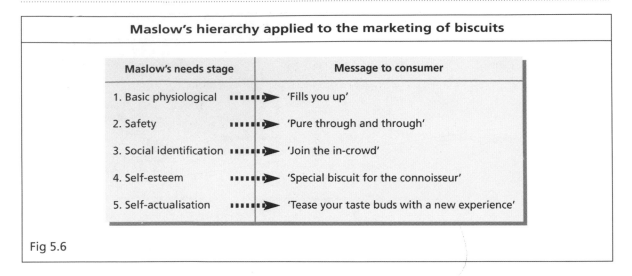

Maslow's hierarchy applied to the marketing of biscuits

Maslow's needs stage	Message to consumer
1. Basic physiological	'Fills you up'
2. Safety	'Pure through and through'
3. Social identification	'Join the in-crowd'
4. Self-esteem	'Special biscuit for the connoisseur'
5. Self-actualisation	'Tease your taste buds with a new experience'

Fig 5.6

One of the key variables affecting the extent of problem solving necessary in any purchasing situation is the importance to the buyer of the product being sought. To simplify this concept, three levels of activity can be identified on a broad continuum.

As Figure 5.8 illustrates, the problem-solving stages a consumer passes through will be far more complex in situations of extensive decision making than for routine response behaviour. The information search will normally be far more thorough, many alternatives will be considered and the actual purchase could require much thought.

Another feature of extensive decision making is the likelihood of a period of evaluation, following the purchase, in which actions are re-considered. Doubts or anxieties could be aroused by the emergence of new information in the form of opinions expressed by people or the media, late awareness of better or cheaper alternatives, or unfavourable initial experience with the product. This process of re-appraisal is known as *cognitive dissonance*, and some organisations seek to suppress it and reassure consumers by after-sales service such as follow-up visits, promotional literature or video material.

Of course, whatever the route taken to the eventual outcome, it is vital for marketing organisations to identify who exactly is responsible in any given situation for the purchase decision.

In consumer markets, the *decision-making unit*, or DMU, is usually relatively straightforward, consisting of an individual, small group or family. Marketing research is necessary to determine the balance of purchasing decision influences within a family. In some markets the DMU could be the woman alone, in others the man alone and in many situations it could be a combination, while children often have no direct say but much influence and must thus be treated as part of the decision-making unit.

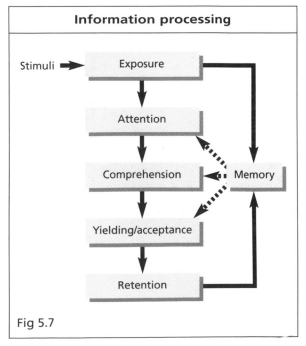

Information processing

Stimuli → Exposure → Attention → Comprehension ⇄ Memory

Comprehension → Yielding/acceptance → Retention

Fig 5.7

Source: Engel, J., Blackwell, R. and Miniard, P., *Consumer Behaviour* (5th edn), © 1986 by the Dryden Press. Reproduced by permission of the publisher

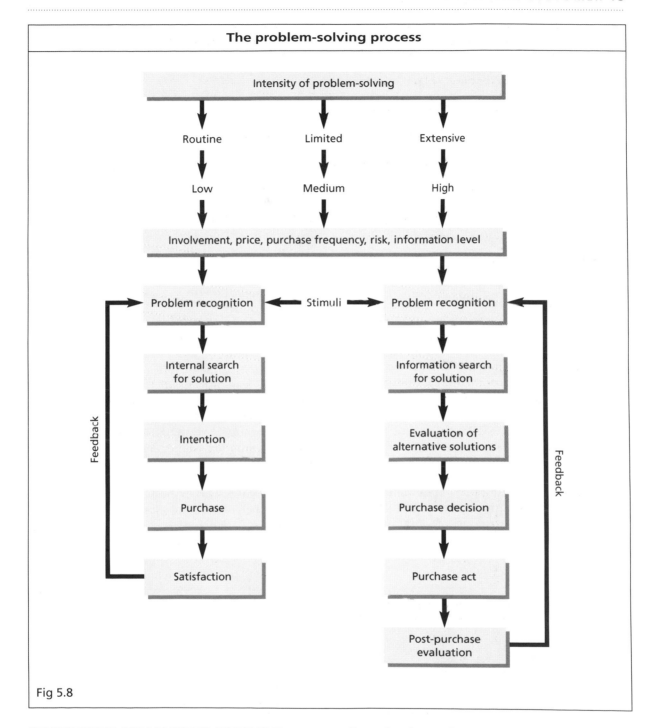

The problem-solving process

Fig 5.8

CONSUMER BEHAVIOUR MODELS

Various models have been proposed by theorists to try to explain consumer behaviour but, as we have already seen, the complexity of influencing factors makes this a very difficult task.

One simple analysis commonly used is the AIDA acronym, a traditional model which suggests that consumers move through four main stages, in response to promotional stimuli, *en route* to making a product or service purchase:

- *Attention* – the initial phase, where customers are fed information to create awareness of a product or service.
- *Interest* – the secondary stage, in which a customer's curiosity about the product or service is aroused and knowledge is heightened.
- *Desire* – the third phase, where the customer's interest hardens into a conviction to buy the product or service.
- *Action* – the last stage, in which the customer is finally persuaded to buy the product or service.

Another limited, traditional view of consumer behaviour is the motivational model, which categorises buying decisions into five distinct groups:

- *Primary* – including basic purchases which are automatic and require no analysis.
- *Selective* – where various stimuli are important in the choice between alternatives.
- *Emotional* – involves decision-making around factors which are intangible and unpredictable.
- *Rational* – including situations where the variable influences on buyer behaviour are clearly identifiable.
- *Patronage* – involving buying decisions where brand loyalty and repeat purchases are the common denominators.

Some models focus on specific aspects of the consumer decision-making process to try to explain buyer behaviour. One method classifies consumers into five groups, depending on their willingness to purchase a new product. Understanding the characteristics of these 'product adopter categories' should then lead to marketing strategies designed to speed up the acceptance process (see Figure 5.9).

The product adopter model suggests that a small number of innovators are the risk-takers who pave the way for everyone else. Then come a larger group of opinion leaders who buy the product in its early stages, followed by the bulk of the normal market, half of whom are more sceptical and only purchase after some delay and consideration. Finally come the suspicious traditionalists, who are the last group to make their decision and buy the product.

In an attempt to understand consumer behaviour and provide an overview of the whole purchasing process, some researchers have incorporated motivational stimuli, problem-solving stages and response variables into one all-encompassing model, such as that constructed by Howard and Sheth (see Figure 5.10).

The Howard-Sheth and other similar models seek to explain the relationship between a multiplicity of factors but are still an over-generalised version of reality. However, they can certainly assist an organisation in predicting and explaining consumer behaviour, thus enabling it to select the appropriate marketing strategies.

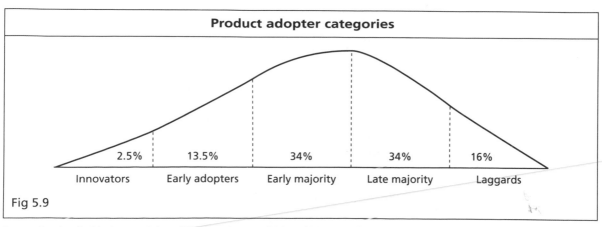

Product adopter categories

| 2.5% | 13.5% | 34% | 34% | 16% |
| Innovators | Early adopters | Early majority | Late majority | Laggards |

Fig 5.9

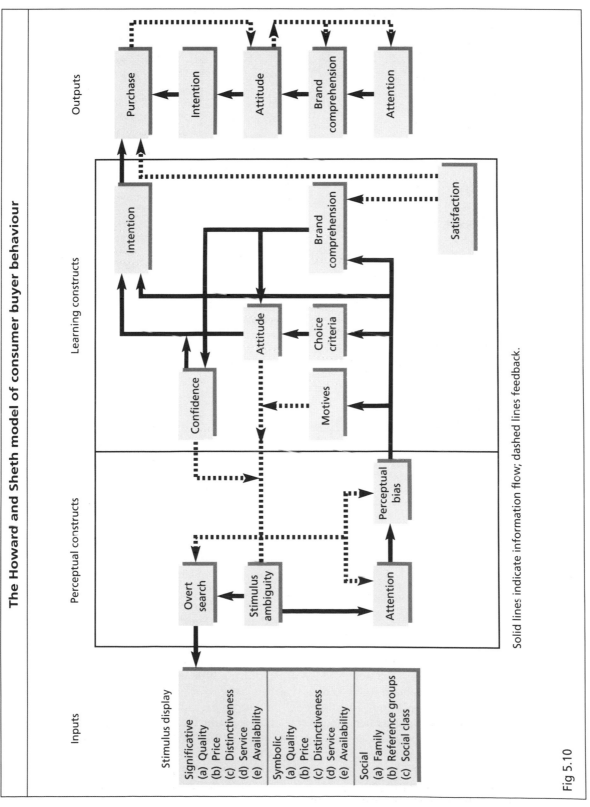

The Howard and Sheth model of consumer buyer behaviour

Inputs

Stimulus display

Significative
(a) Quality
(b) Price
(c) Distinctiveness
(d) Service
(e) Availability

Symbolic
(a) Quality
(b) Price
(c) Distinctiveness
(d) Service
(e) Availability

Social
(a) Family
(b) Reference groups
(c) Social class

Perceptual constructs

Overt search

Stimulus ambiguity

Attention

Perceptual bias

Learning constructs

Intention

Confidence

Attitude

Choice criteria

Motives

Brand comprehension

Satisfaction

Outputs

Purchase

Intention

Attitude

Brand comprehension

Attention

Solid lines indicate information flow; dashed lines feedback.

Source: Howard, J. and Sheth, J., *The Theory of Buyer Behaviour*, John Wiley, New York, 1969. Reprinted by permission of John Wiley & Sons, Inc.

Fig 5.10

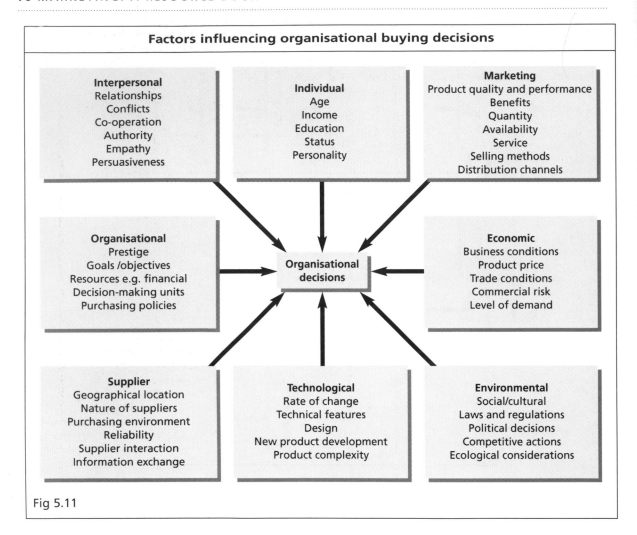

Factors influencing organisational buying decisions

Interpersonal
Relationships
Conflicts
Co-operation
Authority
Empathy
Persuasiveness

Individual
Age
Income
Education
Status
Personality

Marketing
Product quality and performance
Benefits
Quantity
Availability
Service
Selling methods
Distribution channels

Organisational
Prestige
Goals /objectives
Resources e.g. financial
Decision-making units
Purchasing policies

Organisational decisions

Economic
Business conditions
Product price
Trade conditions
Commercial risk
Level of demand

Supplier
Geographical location
Nature of suppliers
Purchasing environment
Reliability
Supplier interaction
Information exchange

Technological
Rate of change
Technical features
Design
New product development
Product complexity

Environmental
Social/cultural
Laws and regulations
Political decisions
Competitive actions
Ecological considerations

Fig 5.11

ORGANISATIONAL BUYING BEHAVIOUR

The industrial or organisational purchaser is affected by rather different factors than the consumer buyer and will thus behave in correspondingly different ways when faced with a purchase problem. Whereas consumer behaviour is often based upon irrational, spontaneous decisions in markets characterised by small quantities and relatively cheap items, industrial buying tends to feature large quantities, expensive items and rational, organised behaviour.

Again, consumer markets consist mainly of individuals, small groups or families, whereas organisational or industrial markets are much more complex. They include a wide range of commercial enterprises, manufacturers and resellers, along with government and other institutional bodies, and tend to be small in number but large in size.

Four broad organisational buying situations can be identified. These are:

- the *straight rebuy*, which equates to the routine consumer purchase and is a regular transaction requiring little information or time;
- the *modified rebuy*, where an alternative source needs to be found for an established product, necessitating a review of the buying situation;
- *new-task buying*, when a firm has a new need and sets about a long process of creating a decision-making unit to gather information and review suppliers, taking into account multiple influences;

● *systems buying*, where an organisation decides to benefit from economies of scale (see Chapter 13) by purchasing whole assemblies rather than individual parts, and thus requires more information and time for the process to be undertaken.

One important characteristic of an organisation is the complexity of its decision-making units. While it is still true that people and not organisations make purchasing decisions, nevertheless it is often very difficult for a marketing company to gather accurate information and discover exactly who is responsible for the ultimate decisions within the target organisation, what their levels of influence are and what evaluation criteria they use.

The organisational decision-making unit could be made up of any one or a combination of the following:

● an individual, such as a general purchasing manager;
● a group or team of people;
● an organisational department, e.g. financial;
● a person responsible for the specific piece of equipment to be purchased;
● a user or operator of the equipment;
● other interested internal parties;
● external influences, e.g. customers;
● a final arbiter, with power of veto.

The DMU could be formal or informal in nature and more than one could be party to any organisational purchasing decision. Webster and Wind define the DMU or buying centre as 'all those individuals and groups who participate in the purchasing decision-making process, who share some common goals and the risks arising from the decisions.'

The factors which influence the purchasing behaviour of the organisational decision-making unit are wide-ranging in nature, as illustrated in Figure 5.11.

Sometimes emotional factors more usually associated with consumer markets, such as packaging, colour and promotional stimuli, play a part in the organisational buying decision, but purchases are usually based upon more quantifiable, visible aspects of business.

Having recognised a need and assessed these mainly tangible influences, organisations will normally follow a logical sequence of stages leading to a purchase, while constantly monitoring the effects of buying decisions, as indicated in Figure 5.12.

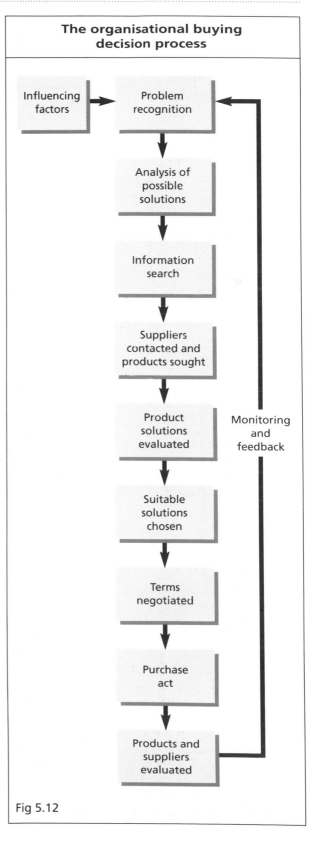

Fig 5.12

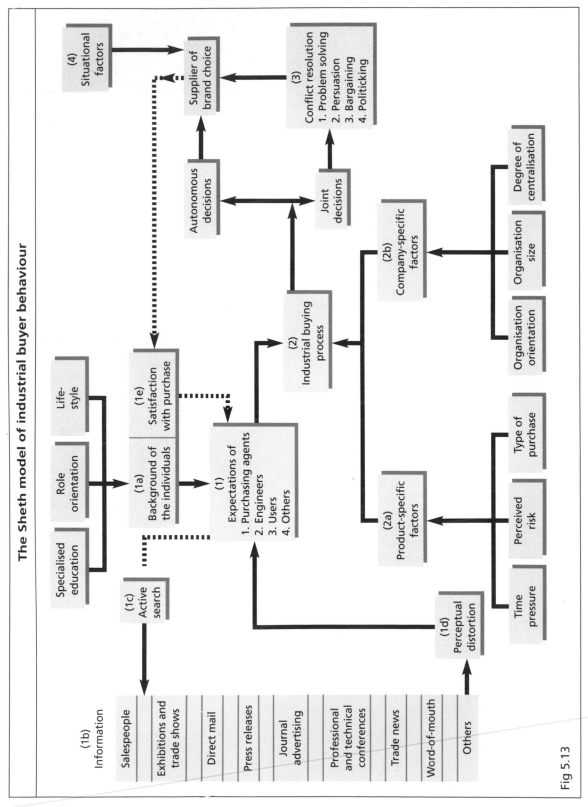

The Sheth model of industrial buyer behaviour

Fig 5.13

Source: Sheth, J., 'A model of industrial buyer behaviour', *Journal of Marketing*, Vol. 37, No. 4, 1973. Permission to reproduce by courtesy of the American Marketing Association

Some organisations will see advantages in concentrating their business on one supplier, known as *sole sourcing*, whereas others will spread their trade more widely.

Just as with consumer markets, researchers have attempted to construct umbrella models, incorporating all the relevant influences and variable factors, to explain industrial and organisational purchasing behaviour (see Figure 5.13).

Again, the Sheth model cannot accurately predict or explain organisational buying patterns, but it does give valuable clues as to the main processes involved in industrial purchases and thus provides important pointers for a company involved in selling to these markets.

ARTICLES

A1

Lifestyle shake-up for the 1990s men as roles change and jobs dwindle

THE lifestyle and role of men in 1990s Britain is changing, new research shows.

According to the Mintel International Group report about a quarter of men are single and 11 per cent live entirely alone.

And although men are more likely than women to remain single, more men remarry after divorce.

Men are also marrying later, going into their first marriage at an average age of 27.

Lone fathers are still rare, with only one per cent of all families headed by a man on his own.

The survey showed current economic conditions favour female employment, and male unemployment has steadily risen since the 1970s, especially for those over 50.

With the death of the idea that a job is for life, Mintel said men will increasingly have to come to terms with periods of unemployment.

But some traditional pastimes of men have not changed. Women have less free time than men, who prefer to take part or read about sport, as well as spending time in that old favourite, the pub.

Men have a high level of financial confidence; the report shows only 16 per cent are not confident in dealing with household budgeting while 15 per cent are not very confident about making long-term financial decisions.

Today's male no longer believes women should stay at home but some traditions are harder to break, the survey shows.

Eighty-three per cent believe married women should be able to work, and even more agree the whole family can benefit from the mother working.

Fewer than a quarter think the wife should stay at home and care for the family while the man goes out to earn the money.

But the older the man, the more likely he is to stick to the old traditions, and half the over-65s believe men should be earning money while wives keep house.

But men are less keen to help out with the household chores; up to 50 per cent admit they are 'sloths', leaving all such tasks to their partners.

Mintel's consumer research manager Angela Hughes said: 'It's tempting to conclude that it may be more a case of men wanting the financial advantages of a working wife than having an idealistic belief in the equality of the sexes.

'While they are reluctant to say the woman's place is in the home, it's clear they still expect her to do the housework.'

Mintel predicts that with more men likely to be on their own in the future there will be a boom in home services, convenience foods and gadgets which make household chores easier.

One in four men are 'happy cookers' who tend to prefer entertaining and experimenting with new recipes rather than doing the everyday meals.

But when it comes to shopping, men enjoy using specialist shops such as off-licence and audio-visual specialists, and are also more influenced by brands than women, the survey found.

Mintel asked 1,576 men and women how they divided up the everyday chores, and 18 per cent of the men qualified as 'newish man' – defined as one responsible for at least one such task.

But Ms Hughes said: 'It seems some may have the role thrust upon them by circumstances.

'The largest group are found among those who are not working or are retired.'

Source: By courtesy of *The Yorkshire Post*, 21 February 1994

1 Identify the likely effects on male consumer behaviour of the social changes mentioned in the article.

2 Outline the probable influences on female consumer behaviour of the Mintel research report findings.

3 Describe the consumer decision-making units operating in the product and service markets referred to.

4 Select products covered in the Mintel report which correspond to the different levels of Maslow's needs hierarchy.

A2

Chocolate bars do all sorts of strange and sensuous things to the female imagination. Or so it would seem judging by a discussion in **Food For Thought** (Channel 4).

A market researcher was questioning a group of women about their different reactions to Cadbury's Flake and Rowntree Mackintosh's Yorkie bar. One woman said she preferred the chunky, 'masculine looking' Yorkie because she fancied the lorry driver in the television advertisements.

Another woman said that her husband was turned on whenever she ate a Cadbury's Flake.

Millions of pounds are spent on advertising by food manufacturers. Their aim is to create images, and to sell more of their products.

Unfortunately their aims are not always compatible with the aim of achieving a healthy national diet.

Source: The Yorkshire Evening Press

1 Which variable factors are the main influences on consumer behaviour in the chocolate bar market?

2 Describe the main stimuli affecting your personal purchase choice in this market.

3 How important are the subconscious motivation theories of Sigmund Freud for this kind of consumer product?

4 Describe how an organisation such as Cadbury or Nestlé Rowntree might use the AIDA model to influence consumer purchase decisions.

A3

The essence of appeal

THE mystery of why particular fragrances appeal to certain people is all to do with the interaction of perfumes with the natural oils and odours we each produce.

Fragrance consultant Arthur Burnham claims much can be told about a woman by the smells which appeal to her and therefore the perfume she is likely to wear.

Amirage by Givenchy is an extremely rich, lingering perfume for the modern woman, whereas the light, fresh fragrance of Anaïs Anaïs by Cacherel would tend to appeal to women who thrive on spring and summertime and the sweet smell of the outdoors.

'Different fragrances perform differently on different people, which is all down to skin types, colouring and individual smells.

'As a result something which smells wonderful on one person will not necessarily on another,' said Mr Burnham.

Contrary to popular belief, however, perfumes which become great classics, like Chanel No.5 and Paris by Yves Saint-Laurent, stand out from the crowd because they have special qualities.

According to Mr Burnham, price tags are often governed by the cost of the raw materials which go to make a particular perfume.

However, he admits that the more a manufacturer spends on advertising and promotion, the more people are likely to turn out in droves to buy the product.

'If all perfumes were cheap then a lot of people would be very disappointed because they really feel that they want to be given a little bit of magic.'

Source: The Northern Echo, 13 November 1993

1 How much importance do you attach to 'a little bit of magic' as a determinant of consumer action in the perfume market?

2 Is price a key influence on consumer behaviour in this market?

3 The article suggests that 'the more a manufacturer spends on advertising and promotion, the more people are likely to turn out in droves to buy the product.' Why? Is this true for all cosmetics?

4 In what circumstances could consumers exhibit (a) routine, (b) limited or (c) extensive behaviour when purchasing perfume? Describe the problem-solving process associated with each level of involvement.

A4

Generous grannies, a telephone jungle and credit card companies with their backs to the wall. ROBIN MORGAN, Business Correspondent, reports in a Letter from America.

AMERICA is still the land of opportunities – and the newest opening for making a million is the booming 'granny' market.

Doting grandparents are promising to become the boom business of the 1990s as they clamour to indulge their offspring's offspring – and entrepreneurs are starting to answer this very profitable need.

Like Britain, the US demographic curve is leading to an increasing population of older people.

Between 1980 and 1990, the over-50s increased by eight per cent – from 59 million to 63 million – and the US Census Bureau says this will grow by 75 per cent to 112 million by the year 2020.

Today, a third of American adults are grandparents and recent statistics show that in a typical month 47 per cent of them buy their grandchild a gift, 26 per cent go shopping with the child, 10 per cent take a holiday with them and 61 per cent talk on the telephone with them.

It is an enormous market of potential gift givers. Those alert to the potential have opened their 'granny' shops. One upmarket speciality toy chain FAO Schwarz, has Grandma's Shops in New York, Boston and San Francisco.

The toy group, Mattel, has done test marketing among grandparents. 'We are in the process of evaluating that effort and looking at how we can refine it,' said the company.

A Maryland travel agency is promoting 16 exotic trips for grandparents and their grandchildren, taking in an African safari and an excursion into the Alaskan wilderness, while the American Association of Retired Persons, with 32 million members, is offering a package for grandparents to take their grandchildren to the Euro-Disney park.

The president of the US National Tour Association, Mr John Stachnik, said: 'As with any emerging market, it is still very small, but it has captured the imagination of people.'

The statisticians have sized up the scope.

American grandparents now harbour 43 per cent of that nation's $139bn discretionary spending power.

Grandparents with one or two grandchildren will spend more per child on them than if they have six or eight – obviously – but the dwindling birth rate is now producing smaller families.

Add to this the fact that the 55–64 age group is at the peak of its earning powers, that it will probably enter the doting grandparent stage during that period and you can hear the cash registers ringing to a crescendo.

How soon before British entrepreneurs latch on to this one?

Source: By courtesy of *The Yorkshire Post*, 25 November 1991

1 Are social and cultural factors, such as family values and reference groups, still relevant in determining buyer behaviour amongst older consumers?

2 How might companies like Mattel seek to understand the behaviour of consumers in their markets?

3 How applicable is Maslow's hierarchy of needs as an indicator of consumer behaviour in the 'granny' market?

4 Which product adopter category is likely to include the growing, older consumer market? Is this true for all products and services? How might this analysis help organisations to plan their marketing strategies?

 A5

Davy wins furnace deal in China

STOCKTON-based engineers Davy International has clinched a £75m contract to design and supply a blast furnace in Taiwan.

The new furnace forms the first stage of China Steel Corporation's fourth phase expansion plan.

Davy, part of Trafalgar House, bagged the contract from under the noses of German and Japanese competitors after more than two years of discussions with China Steel.

According to Roy Tazzyman, chief executive of Davy International, the company's track record in the Far East helped secure the order.

Between 1987 and 1992 the business supplied five blast furnaces in Korea.

Source: The Northern Echo, 9 March 1994

1 What do you consider will be the main factors affecting Davy International's choice of suppliers for the China contract?

2 What issues are likely to have dominated the two years of discussions between Davy and China Steel?

3 As a potential supplier for Davy, how would you plan your business campaign?

4 Describe the process of organisational buying Davy might adopt to choose suppliers and the elements likely to constitute their decision-making unit.

ISSUES

CONSUMER BUYING BEHAVIOUR

Purchasing actions are complex, individual and entirely unpredictable

1 How do organisations try to make sense out of people's unpredictable buying habits?

2 Discuss the factors most likely to confound expectations of buyer behaviour in (a) consumer and (b) industrial markets.

3 Can you suggest any products or services for which consumer purchasing actions are more predictable? Explain the reasons for this.

IMPULSE PURCHASING

Spontaneous buying decisions apply only to a very limited group of products

1 Compile a list of products and services that you have purchased on impulse, and explain your reasons for doing so.

2 In what ways might organisations encourage customers to make instant purchases? Is it always beneficial for them to do so?

3 In what circumstances could there be an element of post-purchase evaluation or cognitive dissonance after an impulse buy?

MASLOW'S HIERARCHY OF NEEDS

An out-moded and restricted way of examining consumer behaviour?

1 Does Maslow's hierarchy accurately represent the life stages through which a person progresses, in your opinion?

2 Is it realistic to relate levels of need to specific types of purchase? Give examples from your own experience.

3 Describe how organisations of your choice have used Maslow's theory to market their products or services.

CONSUMER PROBLEM SOLVING

A rational, sequential but unrealistic framework to explain the consumer behaviour process?

1 For what types of products or services (if any) have you moved through the chronological stages of decision making?

2 Describe your personal experiences of cognitive dissonance. What were the products involved and what factors caused the re-appraisal?

3 Is it always in the best interests of organisations to move the consumer quickly through the problem-solving stages towards a purchase? What are its main weapons when doing so?

MODELS OF CONSUMER BEHAVIOUR

Behavioural models are interesting academic research exercises but do not provide pragmatic business solutions.

1 In what circumstances could the identification of adopter categories enable an organisation to market its products more effectively? What disadvantages might come from using this method?

2 What aspects of consumer behaviour are emphasised by the Howard and Sheth model? How can a firm incorporate these into its marketing strategies?

3 Does the AIDA model tell a firm enough about how its customers behave? Can any behavioural model do so?

ORGANISATIONAL BUYING BEHAVIOUR

So many factors are involved in industrial buying that the true nature of the purchaser is often unknown.

1 In what circumstances could emotional and psychological factors explain industrial purchasing decisions? Give some examples.

2 Do you consider that the processes of organisational buying and the models explaining them are a more accurate reflection of buyer behaviour than those applying to consumer markets? If so, why?

3 What are the main stumbling blocks to the identification of organisational decision-making units? Are small DMUs more effective than larger ones?

4 Why do organisations occasionally adopt a policy of sole sourcing? What are the disadvantages of such buyer behaviour?

QUESTIONS

1 Define consumer buying behaviour.

2 Name five marketing and economic stimuli affecting consumer behaviour.

3 What is an impulse purchase?

4 List six social or cultural factors determining consumer behaviour.

5 What role do reference groups play in purchasing actions?

6 What are Engel's Laws?

7 Describe the influence of family roles in buyer behaviour.

8 Name two environmental determinants of purchase decisions.

9 List three personal influences on consumer behaviour.

10 Name three psychological factors affecting buyer actions.

11 What is Maslow's hierarchy of needs?

12 Describe the five stages of Maslow's hierarchy and relate each to associated products and services.

13 What are the stages of information processing experienced by customers?

14 Name the three levels of intensity of problem solving.

15 List the stages customers pass through in the problem-solving process.

16 What is cognitive dissonance?

17 What is a decision-making unit, or DMU?

18 Describe the AIDA model of consumer behaviour.

19 What is the motivational model of consumer behaviour?

20 Describe the product adopter categories model.

21 What is the Howard and Sheth model of consumer behaviour?

22 What are the main differences between consumer and industrial markets regarding customers?

23 What are the four organisational buying situations?

24 Name four examples of an organisational decision-making unit.

25 List six factors influencing organisational buying decisions.

26 Describe the main stages of the organisational buying decision process.

27 What aspects of organisational and industrial behaviour are emphasised by the Sheth Model?

28 What is 'sole sourcing'?

PROJECTS

1 Outline and discuss the social and demographic changes which will affect consumer purchasing decisions in the next decade.

2 How important are family role influences in determining consumer purchasing decisions? Refer to specific examples of products and/or services in your answer.

3 Describe the stages of the consumer buying decision process for the following products or services:

- a higher education course;
- a new high-performance car;
- an airline ticket to the USA;
- a second-hand washing machine;
- a can of soup;
- a consignment of sheet metal;
- a wedding dress.

4 Compare and contrast the buyer behaviour exhibited in (a) consumer markets and (b) organisational markets, giving examples of

each. Refer to the decision-making units operating in each type of market.

5 'Maslow's hierarchy provides an interesting insight into levels of consumer need but does not offer any clues as to how these needs might be translated into purchases.' Discuss this statement, with reference to specific cases where relevant.

6 How can behavioural models help organisations to understand their customers? Referring to models such as Howard and Sheth, and Sheth, consider both the consumer and the industrial markets in your answer.

GLOSSARY

AIDA a traditional mnemonic denoting Attention, Interest, Desire and Action; the progressive steps organisations aim to persuade consumers to take before making a purchase decision.

Attitude customer's state of mind reflecting a viewpoint about a product or service.

Autonomic type of purchase behaviour in which an individual makes the decision without any family influences.

Buyer behaviour the decision processes and acts of individuals or organisations involved in buying and using products or services.

Buygrid framework industrial buying model which identifies phases of organisational buying and types of general purchase, devised to focus attention on the product decision (what to buy) and the vendor or supplier decision (from whom to buy).

Buying centre all the people who participate in or influence a purchase decision.

Cocooning current consumer behaviour trend which emphasises convenience and household comforts.

Cognitions an individual's knowledge, beliefs and attitudes about products or events.

Cognitive dissonance consumer discomfort or anxiety caused by post-purchase analysis and conflict.

Consumer buying behaviour the buying habits or behaviour patterns of individuals or households purchasing products and services for personal consumption.

Cue environmental effect determining the nature of consumer response to a drive.

Culture complex of values, ideas, attitudes and other meaningful symbols which influence consumer buying behaviour.

Decision-making unit (DMU) group of people who together contribute to, or influence, a purchase decision.

Drive strong stimulus impelling consumer action.

Emotional behaviour purchase decisions made as a result of feeling rather than rationality or logic.

Engel's Laws three general statements about the effects of an increase in family income on spending behaviour.

Extensive problem solving the type of decision making involved when a need is new, costly, or important to a consumer and much effort is taken to decide how to satisfy it.

Freud, Sigmund psychologist who first proposed and investigated the subconscious motivations of consumers.

Howard and Sheth American researchers who devised models of consumer and organisational buyer behaviour.

Impulse goods products or services for which the consumer spends little time in conscious deliberation before making a purchase decision.

Impulse purchase a purchase made without careful prior consideration or on the spur of the moment often without rational justification.

Industrial buying behaviour see 'Organisational buying behaviour'.

Information search the stage of the buyer decision process in which the consumer is aroused to discover more about a potential purchase.

Innovators the first group of consumers to adopt new products or services.

Laggards consumers who take a long time to adopt new products and tend by nature to be traditional and suspicious regarding innovations.

Late majority group of consumers who are cautious about new ideas.

Lifestyle see Chapter 4.

Limited decision making where products are purchased occasionally and the buyer needs to acquire information about unfamiliar brands, often in a familiar product category.

Maslow's hierarchy of needs a traditional consumer behaviour model, proposed by Abraham Maslow, which identifies five levels of needs, each stage of which has relevant products or services associated with it.

Modified rebuy an industrial buying situation in which the purchaser reviews the product and seeks an alternative source for it.

Multiple buying influence a situation in which the buyer shares the purchasing decision with several people.

Needs the basic forces that motivate a person to behave in a particular way towards purchases of products and services.

New task buying when an organisation has a new need and the buyer or buying group requires a great deal of information.

Opinion leader a consumer who influences others regarding the purchase of products or services.

Organisational buying behaviour the decision-making processes and purchasing habits of producers, re-sellers, government units and institutions.

Patronage habitual use of particular sources of supply, influenced by various motives.

Perception manner in which an individual interprets a stimulus.

Perceptual distortion an individual's understanding of an object or concept which is inaccurate or confused.

Physiological needs basic biological needs outlined in Maslow's hierarchy, such as food, drink and rest.

Post-purchase behaviour the stage of the buyer decision process after a purchase when consumers take further action based on satisfaction or dissatisfaction

Pre-purchase behaviour actions and considerations of the consumer before a purchase is made.

Problem recognition initial stage of the buying decision process in which a problem or need is identified and a solution sought.

Problem-solving process stages of decision making experienced by a consumer or organisation considering a purchase.

Product adopter categories model of buyer behaviour which measures consumers' responses to new products or services.

Proposal solicitation stage of the organisational buying process in which the buyer invites qualified suppliers to submit proposals.

Purchase action stage of the buying process in which a consumer or organisation actually purchases the product or service.

Purchase decision stage of the buying process in which an individual or organisation makes a decision to purchase the product or service.

Rational behaviour consumer buying behaviour which exhibits logical decision making.

Reference groups people or groups who influence a consumer's purchasing behaviour or attitudes.

Reinforcement occurs in the learning process when an appropriate consumer response is followed by satisfaction and a reduction in drive.

Routine response behaviour mechanical decision-making used by a consumer when buying cheap, frequently purchased products or services that require little search or thought.

Safety needs psychological needs outlined in Maslow's hierarchy, such as security and physical well-being.

Selective distortion tendency of people to adapt information to personal meanings.

Selective exposure tendency of consumers to seek out and notice only the information that interests them.

Selective perception tendency of people to screen out or modify information that conflicts with previously learned values.

Selective retention tendency of consumers to remember only what they want to remember, reflecting their attitudes and beliefs.

Self-actualisation highest level of Maslow's hierarchy of needs, a stage where consumers seek self-fulfilment and other spiritual objectives.

Self-concept self-image, or the complex mental pictures people have of themselves and the way others see them.

Self-esteem political needs outlined in Maslow's hierarchy, such as status and self-respect.

Social identification sociological needs outlined in Maslow's hierarchy, such as love and affiliation.

Sole sourcing organisational buying situation, where all of an item or range is purchased from the same supplier.

Straight rebuy industrial buying behaviour, in which the purchaser routinely re-orders goods without any modifications.

Strategic business unit (SBU) an organisational unit within a company which makes its own purchasing decisions.

Syncratic type of purchase behaviour in which two people participate in a joint family decision.

Systems buying where an organisation purchases whole assemblies in bulk to avoid making separate buying decisions.

Wants 'needs' that are learned during a person's life and applied to consumer products and services.

Willingness to spend consumer behaviour in which anticipated product satisfaction, combined with the ability to buy and persuasive environmental forces, leads to probable purchase of a product or service.

SUGGESTED REFERENCES

VIDEO MATERIAL

Contemporary Marketing Video Cases, No. 5 (Kawasaki Motor Corporation) and No. 6 (Skyfox Corporation), Boone, L. and Kurtz, D., Dryden Press, 1989.

MAGAZINE ARTICLES

Journal of Marketing, Vol. 37, No. 4, 1973, 'A model of industrial buyer behaviour', J. Sheth.

Journal of Consumer Research, Vol. 1, July 1974, 'Perceptions of marital roles in decision processes', H.L. Davies, and B.P. Rigaux.

Journal of Consumer Research, Vol. 9, Sept. 1982, 'Reference Group influence on product and brand purchase decisions', W.O. Bearden and M.J. Etzel.

Journal of Marketing Management, Vol. 1, No. 1, Summer 1985, p.87, 'Marketing and the competitive performance of British industry: areas for research'; and p.99, 'The practice of systems marketing in the French packaging industry'.

Journal of Marketing Management, Vol. 1, No. 3, Spring 1986, p.265, 'The role and function of the Chief Marketing Executive and the Marketing department'.

Journal of Marketing Management, Vol. 3, No. 2, Winter 1987, p.173, 'Attitudes, structure and behaviour in a successful company'; and p.205 'Successful implementation of new market strategies – a corporate culture perspective.'

Journal of Marketing Management, Vol. 4, No. 1, Summer 1988, p.33, 'Information seeking, external search and "shopping" behaviour. Preliminary evidence from a planned shopping centre'.

Journal of Marketing Management, Vol.8, No.2, April 1992, p.167, 'The effect of experience on the decision-making of expert and novice buyers'.

Marketing Business, July 1988, p.18, 'Marketing's change masters'.

Marketing Business, May 1993, p.48, 'Briefly'.

Marketing Business, July/Aug. 1993, p.12, 'Metamorphosis in Marketing'.

Marketing Business, Feb. 1994, p.13, 'New generation marketing', and p.48, 'Briefly'.

Quarterly Review of Marketing, Vol. 12, No. 2, Jan. 1987, p.12, 'Industrial buyer behaviour applied to imports'.

Quarterly Review of Marketing, Vol. 13, No. 3, Spring 1988, p.18, 'Is there a need for the Product Manager?'

Quarterly Review of Marketing, Vol. 8, No. 4, Oct. 1992, p.315, 'A risk analysis of industrial buyers: the case of mid-range computers'.

FURTHER READING

Adcock, D., Bradford, R., Halborg, A. and Ross, C. *Marketing Principles and Practice*, Pitman, 1995, ch. 5.

Baker, M. (Ed.), *The Marketing Book*, Heinemann/ C.I.M., 1990, chs 7 and 8.

Boone, L., and Kurtz, D., *Contemporary Marketing*, Dryden, 1989, chs 5 and 6.

Cannon, Tom, *Basic Marketing*, Holt Business Texts, 1980, ch. 6.

Dibb, S., Simkin, L., Pride, W. and Ferrell, O., *Marketing*, Houghton Mifflin, 1994, chs 4 and 5.

Engel, J., Blackwell, R. and Miniard, P., *Consumer Behaviour*, Dryden, 1986.

Giles, G., *Marketing*, MacDonald and Evans, 1985, ch. 2.

Howard, J. and Sheth, J., *The Theory of Buyer Behaviour*, John Wiley, New York, 1969.

Kotler, P. and Armstrong, G., *Marketing*, Prentice Hall, 1993, chs 5 and 6.

McCarthy J. and Perreault, W., *Basic Marketing*, Irwin, 1987, chs 7 and 8.

Mercer, D., *Marketing*, Blackwell, 1992, ch. 3.

Webster, F. and Wind, Y., *Organisational Buying Behaviour*, Prentice Hall, 1972.

Acknowledgements

The Northern Echo.

The Yorkshire Evening Press.

The Yorkshire Post.

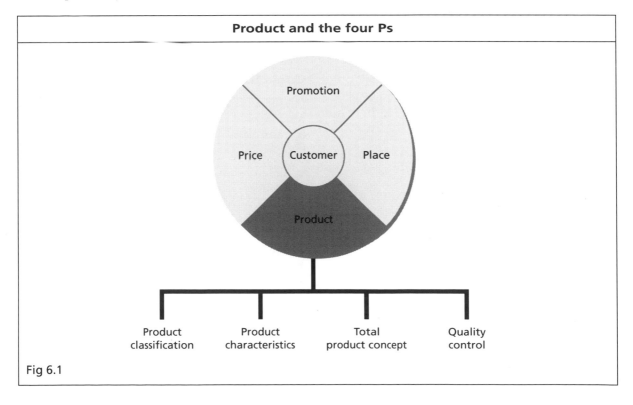

6
PRODUCT DECISIONS

DEFINITIONS

Without a good product you have nothing.

AN OLD MARKETING AXIOM

A product is an idea, a service, a good, or any combination of these three. It is everything that one receives in an exchange – a complexity of tangible and intangible attributes including functional, social and psychological utilities or benefits.

DIBB, SIMKIN, PRIDE AND FERRELL

INTRODUCTION

To be able to enter into business in the first place an organisation needs a product or service to market, preferably an item or items in which it has particular interest and expertise.

Establishing itself in the market-place requires that an organisation makes a number of fundamen-

Product and the four Ps

Promotion

Price Customer Place

Product

Product classification | Product characteristics | Total product concept | Quality control

Fig 6.1

tal decisions relating to the nature of the products it is marketing and their specific characteristics.

To maximise the chances of market success, these characteristics should be collectively developed into a package on offer to, and clearly understood by, the customer target group. The other essential area of decision making involves monitoring the quality of the product and ensuring eventual customer satisfaction.

All these elements together emphasise the importance of the product in an organisation's marketing mix (see Figure 6.1).

KEY CONCEPTS

CLASSIFYING PRODUCTS

The ways in which products are marketed depend on their nature and the categories into which they fall. It is therefore important to establish a broad framework of product types, in order to be able to examine the differences in marketing approach required for each type.

Products can be consumer or industrial in nature as a simple rule, but any classification system must to a certain extent be arbitrary because some items, such as paint, rolls of carpet or electricity, fall into both categories and could be sold in more than one type of market, using varying marketing techniques.

These two main classifications may be broken down into sub-divisions, as indicated in Figure 6.2.

Consumer products can be divided into three main categories which are discussed below.

General consumer products

These form our basic requirements and cover a wide range of goods, from toys to clothing and food to flowers. They possess certain distinctive characteristics and are:

- standardised;
- relatively cheap;
- frequently purchased, hence the term fmcg or fast-moving consumer goods;
- usually bought by cash;
- purchased generally with little consideration;
- frequently bought on impulse;
- available from a wide range of outlets;
- relatively simple in nature;
- widely demanded by a large number of consumers.

For these sorts of goods distribution can be a complicated operation, especially when the product is one which the consumer expects to be able to buy anywhere. Apart from a small number of examples such as Avon cosmetics and Betterware household products, general consumer products are not sold direct to consumers. Instead, the sales force is concerned with ensuring that the goods are stocked and displayed at the appropriate points of sale.

General consumer products normally have a short life and a high fashion content and thus tend to be promoted through the mass media and consumer offers, with an emphasis on packaging. The sale of this class of goods is not seriously hit by credit squeezes or recessions, as the level of expenditure on individual items may drop but consumption usually continues.

Consumer durables

These are more significant purchases and again cover a wide range of goods, such as cookers, cars, furniture and video recorders. The characteristics they exhibit are also distinctive and they tend to be:

- more specialised;
- relatively expensive;
- less frequently purchased;
- usually bought by cheque or credit card and often on hire purchase;
- purchased only after considerable thought;
- available from a limited number of outlets;
- relatively complex in nature;
- demanded only occasionally by a small number of consumers.

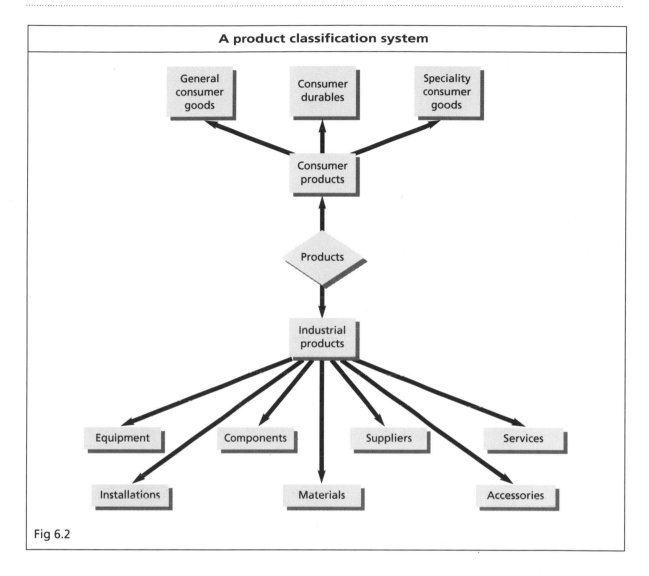

A product classification system

Fig 6.2

Consumer durable goods require attention to servicing and meeting guarantee and warranty agreements, and a sales organisation is generally needed to demonstrate and sell to consumers at the outlets, as well as 'selling in' to the retailer. Direct selling methods are used only rarely, for example double glazing, conservatories and Kirby vacuum cleaners.

Consumer durables have a fairly long life and tend to be promoted through limited media advertising and personal communication methods, although emotional appeals sometimes play a part. Trade-ins often feature as part of the 'deal' price. This class of goods is especially vulnerable to eco-nomic legislation such as credit limitation and reduction of consumer spending.

Speciality consumer products

These are usually luxury goods, prestigious in nature and limited in number, ranging from hand-made shirts and exclusive perfumes to caviar and high performance cars. Speciality products are:

- highly specialised;
- very expensive;
- infrequently purchased;
- usually bought by cheque, special account, credit card or retail card;

- purchased generally after some thought;
- available from very few outlets which provide a prestige atmosphere or a quality image, e.g. Harrods;
- demanded by an exclusive group of customers.

Speciality products vary in life span and can be simple or complex in nature. Their distribution is limited, because of price, exclusiveness or reputation, and is therefore simpler. As the market is a narrow one, speciality goods are liable to changes in fashion or taste, therefore market trends are monitored and the prestige image is usually emphasised to establish customer loyalty.

This type of product can sometimes be sold direct and is often promoted through the quality media, emphasising features such as packaging. It is sometimes vulnerable to changes in the social and economic environment but brand loyalty can often avert real crises in this sector.

Industrial products can be divided into a number of categories which all have slightly different characteristics, as follows:

- equipment – includes buildings, plant and machinery;
- installations – complete purpose-built structures, such as oil drilling rigs or electricity/gas/telephone systems;
- components – specific parts incorporated into the final product, such as spark plugs;
- materials – goods used in production or purchased for re-sale, e.g. paint, adhesives, or natural agricultural products;
- supplies – goods used in production and consumed in the process, including lubricants or replacement parts for repair, operation or maintenance;
- accessories – additional items needed in the manufacturing process, often associated with other product categories;
- services – back-up facilities necessary for improving production and marketing efficiency, such as transportation, storage and advisory services.

Typically, industrial products are sold to intermediate as opposed to ultimate users and are purchased as solutions to particular business problems. The demand for such goods is usually narrow and derived (i.e. the demand for house bricks is derived from the demand for new houses) and the products themselves tend to be relatively specialised and complex in nature.

The industrial good is infrequently purchased and usually has a long life span. This durability means that replacement can be postponed and the existing product can continue to be used at a less efficient level if conditions are not favourable for repurchase.

Other features of industrial products include relatively long manufacturing cycles, which can lead to stock problems and long lead times between demand and supply, limited availability and high costs and prices. The customer tends to order in advance; purchase only after much deliberation in the decision-making unit of rational motives such as fitness for purpose, delivery, service, reputation and price; and pay by trade credit, with leasing and guarantee arrangements. Buying mistakes can be very costly in these markets.

Manufacturing companies usually buy industrial products directly from other industrial organisations, often purchasing for stock purposes and sometimes using wholesalers or distributors. Because of the technical nature of many industrial goods and the knowledge of buyers, transactions tend to feature high-level negotiations and direct buyer/seller contact with technically orientated industrial sales people discussing specific details with customers. Buyers and sellers are also brought together through direct marketing, the use of trade magazines, exhibitions and public relations.

Because of all these distinguishing features, industrial products tend to be more volatile than most consumer products and more sensitive to the prevailing economic climate.

PRODUCT CHARACTERISTICS

Whatever the nature and category of a product, the organisation must ask itself an important question – when customers purchase a product, what exactly are they paying for? Only when the answer has been accurately revealed can the relevant marketing approach be applied.

Although the basic functions and features of the product are obviously important, it is known that customers do not generally buy on a purely functional level. So the organisation must emphasise those characteristics of the product which are perceived by consumers as being important. These could be linked to the customer's technological, social, emotional, psychological, aesthetic or other needs, or to more basic economic considerations.

Product characteristics can be viewed on three broad levels and certain qualities offered to customers to maximise marketing impact at each stage. In ascending importance these levels are:

1. *Features* – the most basic description of the product, i.e. what it is or what it possesses, the essential information required by customers. In marketing terms, however, features are generally better expressed as benefits.
2. *Benefits* – the clearly explained ways in which the product will satisfy aspirations or improve a person's situation, i.e. what it will do for the customer, who will thus be far more likely to respond to a product which offers distinct personal advantages. Examples of this 'what's in it for me?' factor include benefits which make or save money, save time or effort, provide security or safety, impress others, give pleasure, generate self-improvement or satisfy the need to belong.
3. *Unique selling proposition (USP)* – a feature or benefit to the consumer which is unique to that particular item, is not offered by anyone else and thus enables the product to stand out clearly from the competition.

In practice, marketing orientated organisations strive to offer their customers clearly perceived benefits rather than just features. So they will promote the comfort and health advantages of a particular make of chair, for example, rather than the wood, metal and leather of which it is made; and the satisfaction of a top hi-fi sound quality as opposed to the switches and dials on the outer casing. Comparing a product's features and benefits helps an organisation to define its marketing approach. A *feature/benefit analysis* on motor cars is illustrated in Table 6.1 and includes some of the main characteristics which most commonly apply to this consumer durable product.

Similarly, we can take the example of toothpaste referred to in the previous chapter and observe that people are very unlikely to purchase this fast moving consumer product for the actual creamy substance found inside the tube. They will be far more likely to respond to the range of personal benefits resulting from clean teeth, fresh breath, lack of plaque and tooth decay, pleasant taste, a nice smile and sex appeal, and to attractive package design, a cheap price and all the other advantages emphasised by manufacturers of toothpaste.

So an organisation should establish what benefits it hopes to sell for any item in its product range and adjust its message accordingly. It is these benefits which the buyer needs and will buy, not the actual product itself. Preferably, the product will contain one distinctive feature or customer benefit which the organisation can stress because it is only available in that particular brand.

A very small number of products contain such a USP naturally, for instance certain medications, and some develop USPs from innovations which

Table 6.1 Feature/benefit analysis on motor cars

Feature	Benefit
Low price	Saves customer money to be spent elsewhere
Power-assisted steering	Easier to park
Fully adjustable seats	More comfortable to drive
Reinforced bodywork	Safer and could save lives
Latest style and design	Gives status, pride or pleasure
In-built alarm system	Deters thieves and prevents loss and inconvenience

are then patented, an example being Percy Shaw's cat's-eyes, invented to improve road visibility.

Most USPs, however, are created as a result of an organisation focusing on one feature or benefit and developing an original angle to it to differentiate the product from those of competitors, such as clothes with a designer label or a video recorder which eliminates advertisements. Referring to the two examples used previously, a motor car manufacturer might concentrate on establishing a USP from a new shape developed by computer-aided design, while a toothpaste producer might create a brand with a particular coloured stripe down the middle or a type of tube not used before.

When organisations are marketing products which do not possess an obvious USP, are not new or are not essential for survival, they may seek to promote one aspect of the product strongly in order to create a perception of uniqueness in the minds of customers. Their focus of attention could be the packaging, design, taste, flexibility, colour or numerous other aspects of the overall product offering. Whichever is chosen, the aim will be to convince the consumer of the worthiness, attractiveness and, if possible, the indispensability of the product and thereby satisfy the perceived needs of a targeted market segment.

THE TOTAL PRODUCT CONCEPT

To maximise marketing opportunities it is thus vital for an organisation to establish a product's features, benefits and unique selling points clearly in the minds of customers. But a product contains much more than these characteristics. In reality it is a combination of many tangible, intangible and service factors which an organisation seeks to develop and mould into the *total product concept*, eventually presented as a market offering to consumers. Some of the main ingredients of the total product concept are included in Figure 6.3.

Many of the characteristics illustrated in Figure 6.3 are fundamental aspects of marketing and, as such, are covered elsewhere in this book. However, some aspects of the total product concept tend often to be glossed over but in fact play important roles within the product mix.

One such is *design*, an essential feature of any innovative product which is both an integral part of the marketing mix and a separate business element. The purpose of design is to produce an item that will fulfil a particular function efficiently and be attractive to consumers while keeping within specifications and financial restrictions and being practical.

Product design is concerned with shape and dimensions, materials and parts, finish and function, and must satisfy customers in terms of:

- appearance;
- performance;
- durability;
- simplicity;
- cheapness;
- ease of carriage;
- reliability;
- safety.

In some innovative organisations, such as IBM, Sony and BMW design is viewed as the most efficient and effective product differentiator. In these organisations, the design role would be represented permanently on the marketing team and regarded as a 'major corporate resource', which is the view taken by motor manufacturers Ford. At Sony the Design Division is at the core of the total marketing activity, with responsibility for marketing research, corporate identity, product planning and development, and packaging and display.

Design orientated organisations recognise the important role played by design in certain key areas where commercial marketing functions, including research and development, interface with practical feasibility considerations such as production quantity and quality, technology and finance. They would also acknowledge that an element of originality and surprise is essential to good design and enables consumer inertia to be overcome, but only when designers are liberated from traditional constraints and empowered from the highest corporate level.

Another important product decision which is often underplayed concerns *colour*. A basic knowledge of colours and their effects on people helps marketers to select the shades and schemes most likely to attract customers and influence their product-buying behaviour.

Colour psychologically conveys ideas about products and provokes an emotional response in people which can play an important part in the purchase decision. So the selection of colour or combinations of colours tends to stimulate associations and create favourable or unfavourable

The total product concept

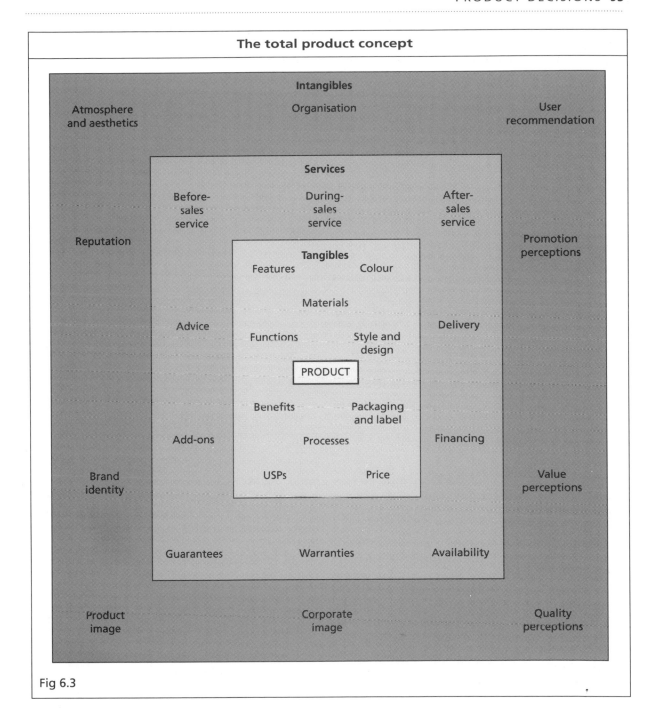

Intangibles

Atmosphere and aesthetics

Organisation

User recommendation

Services

Before-sales service

During-sales service

After-sales service

Reputation

Promotion perceptions

Tangibles

Features   Colour

Materials

Advice

Functions   Style and design

Delivery

PRODUCT

Benefits   Packaging and label

Add-ons

Processes

Financing

USPs   Price

Brand identity

Value perceptions

Guarantees   Warranties   Availability

Product image

Corporate image

Quality perceptions

Fig 6.3

product images. Some of the most clearly established links between colour as a marketing tool and product association are listed in Table 6.2.

Organisations use different shades of colour to emphasise or soften the product idea conveyed to customers. Combinations such as orange and black can be highly sensuous, while green and blue together tend to indicate modesty, intelligence and dynamism in the western world. Of course, different ethnic groups and cultures interpret the

Table 6.2 Colour and product symbolism

Colour	Image/association
White	Purity, cleanliness, honesty
Black	Strong, dark, death
Blue	Cool, distinctive, distance (air, sky, water), space, calm, authority, conservation
Brown	Utility, comfort, basics
Gold	Royal, rich, prestigious
Green	Quiet, relaxation, nature, legality, environment, reliability, casual, passive
Orange	Warmth, movement, vitality
Purple	Lush, extravagant, mysterious, serious
Red	Heat, excitement, danger, arousal, emotion
Yellow	Sunshine, heat, well-being, hygiene, life

meaning and symbolism of marketing tools such as colour and language very differently, a fact that has obvious implications for organisations involved in international markets.

Colour can be used to convey the desired product message via a number of mechanisms, the most important of which is *packaging*, a very big industry in its own right and an increasingly important component of the total product concept, particularly in the field of consumer goods. The only USP many products offer is a distinctive and memorable pack.

Recent technological innovations and greater availability of materials, together with the growth of self-service stores and the requirement for promotional sophistication, have led to an increasing demand for packaging. Its role has thus developed from the basics of protection and identification to a far more complex area of decision making for all types of product. Packaging must now meet various demands and perform many tasks for the manufacturer, the re-seller, the consumer and the wider environment in general (see Figure 6.4), utilising more flexible materials, functional designs, new printing methods, product visibility and quick conversion of adaptable cartons or outers into display units.

The most important of the numerous roles played by packaging are:

- basic protection, ensuring preservation and durability against damage or wear and tear in the store, the home and in transit;
- security and safety against pilferage, contamination, extremes of temperature, flavour loss, leakage, mould, insects, handling injury, corrosion and other chemical change, and so on;
- convenience and compactness, both in use and for handling, storage and transportation;
- environmental flexibility, emphasising returnable and recyclable materials rather than pollutants such as aerosols and plastics, and minimising packaging waste;
- legality, addressing the need to conform to increasingly stringent regulations concerning

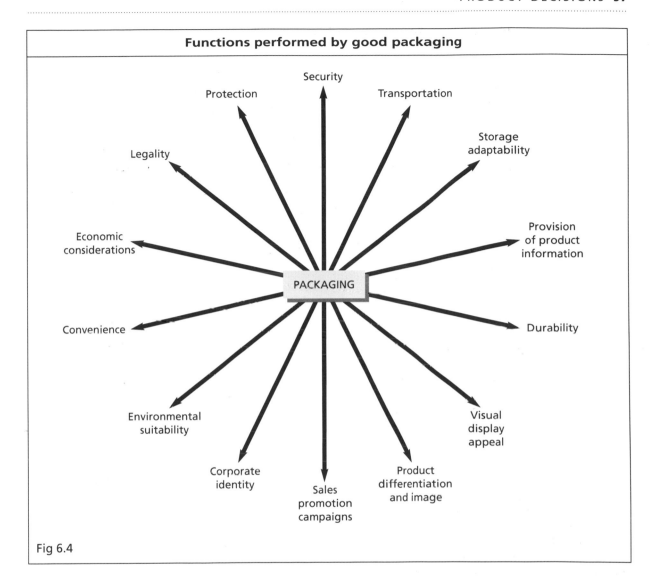

Functions performed by good packaging

Security
Protection
Transportation
Storage adaptability
Legality
Provision of product information
Economic considerations
PACKAGING
Convenience
Durability
Environmental suitability
Visual display appeal
Corporate identity
Product differentiation and image
Sales promotion campaigns

Fig 6.4

accurate identification of contents, ingredients, weights, price, production and sell-by dates and manufacturer details;

- promotion, including the communication of product information, the use of shape, design and colour to stimulate visual appeal and product differentiation, the incorporation of specific sales promotion campaigns such as special offers and coupons, and utilising logos and slogans to make brand statements, create a favourable product image, reinforce corporate identity and support media advertising;

- economic viability, taking into account research and material costs and the need for different layers of packaging to satisfy protection, promotion and transportation requirements.

These ingredients of packaging are essential for a product to gain retail display or shelf space initially and then to compete effectively in the market by clearly standing out from the competition. In this way, packaging can be used as a promotional tool designed to extend the life cycle of the product, and improved storage capacity can lead to greater scope for seasonal variations.

Customer brand loyalty created over time through familiarity with a pack design should also not be under-estimated, as the Coca-Cola company discovered to their cost when they tried to change the traditional Coke bottle and were faced with waves of public protest. Packaging thus tends to evolve gradually in order not to jeopardise brand loyalty, but it can often be a significant contributory factor to product success in the long term: for instance, the Toblerone chocolate bar and Terry's Pyramint and Chocolate Orange, tomato ketchup in squeezy containers, grandly packaged wedding presents such as glasses or cutlery sets, and some cosmetics which sell on their appearance on the dressing table.

So packaging is an important method of communication between an organisation and its customers and plays a key role in the total product concept on offer. In a marketing orientated firm, financial resources are committed to packaging design and research, always taking into account influences exerted by the cultural, social and political environments.

Packaging gives the customer an opportunity to become involved with the brand at the moment of decision and could cause an impulse purchase. At the point of sale it is the pack which often tips the scales in favour of the product, or otherwise, and so it is sometimes referred to as 'the silent salesman'.

QUALITY CONTROL

Before a customer makes the purchase decision there is a need to monitor the product or service to ascertain that its quality meets the required standard. This process of *quality control* originally involved the random inspection of goods as they came off the production line.

However, in recent times the enforcement of quality control procedures has assumed far greater importance as standards demanded by consumers, industry and national and international regulations become progressively more stringent.

As a result, many countries have established their own equivalent of the kitemark of quality assurance for a wide range of products and services. In the United Kingdom, these measurements of quality are incorporated into a scheme known as BS (British Standard) 5750, while its international equivalent is ISO 9000.

BS 5750 represents an easily understood, systematic approach to quality in which the onus is on the company to meet the required standards and be registered accordingly, thus proving that it or its products/services has achieved the acceptable quality threshold and can be relied upon as a trading partner. Clients can monitor quality by dealing only with suppliers who hold the BS 5750 registration. Companies without such a recognised label of quality assurance will therefore be at a competitive disadvantage, as customers look for organisations which attach sufficient priority to quality before purchasing any product or service.

But even this development is regarded by some quality-conscious organisations as not going far enough, concentrating more on standards than on quality and aiming purely to pass the audit and maintain certification. Such companies regard BS 5750 registration as just the first step down the road towards *Total Quality Management (TQM)*, which is closely linked with marketing through one main common denominator, i.e. both try to define what the customer wants and satisfy those wants.

TQM pursues this marketing philosophy right through to delivery. It concerns quality from the organisation and product/service focus, developing a quality culture which is people led and management organised and which concentrates on the pursuit of continuous quality improvement. TQM is fundamental to all aspects of the product or service offering, as evidenced in companies such as BP Chemicals and Elida Gibbs.

A total integrated marketing approach to quality involves the entire company: all people, all functions and all external organisations, such as suppliers. The several facets of TQM include:

- recognising customers and discovering their needs;
- setting standards which are consistent with customer requirements;
- controlling processes and improving their capability;
- establishing systems for quality;
- management's responsibility for setting quality policy, providing motivation through leadership and equipping people to achieve quality;
- empowerment of people at all levels in the organisation to act for quality improvement.

The task of implementing TQM is daunting and involves establishing policies and procedures within the organisation which are understood and accepted by all. The key components of such a model are outlined in Figure 6.5.

At the heart of the TQM model is the essential identification of customer/supplier relationships

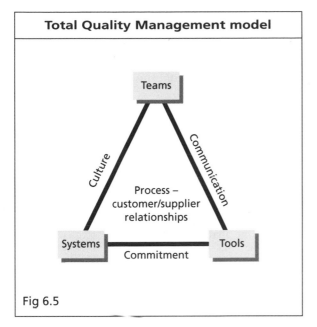

Total Quality Management model

Teams

Culture

Communication

Process –
customer/supplier
relationships

Systems

Tools

Commitment

Fig 6.5

and the management of the processes necessary to convert inputs to outputs. Other key variables are changing the culture to a 'right first time', zero errors and defects philosophy, improving communications and teamwork, establishing models of 'best practice' and instilling long-term commitment.

Additionally, a TQM model of operation requires some more tangible management activities, for example, the institution of systems (international standards such as ISO 9000), teams (quality committees, quality improvement groups, quality circles, 'corrective action departments', and so on) and tools (for analysis, correlation, and predictions for action or continuous improvement to be taken).

A simple summary of the new initiative on quality designed to gain and retain customers could be 'deliver what the customer wants first time, every time'. For this reason, quality control and marketing are two interactive and closely related cultures, both essential to business success.

ARTICLES

A1

Northern chocoholics

ARE you a nibbler, a sucker, a chunky eater, a sensuous female or a street-wise male?

This is not some rude questionnaire but part of a serious chocolate profile.

Experts say you can tell a lot about a person by the way he or she eats a Cadbury's Creme Egg.

If you are a Nibbler you nibble the chocolate around, a Sucker bites the top off and sucks the centre out but a Chunky Eater can demolish it in one go.

If you eat Flake or Galaxy you are likely to be a sensuous female who knows how to spoil herself while Mars and Snickers are bought by young, street-wise males.

Sales of chocolate in Britain soared last year and people in the North-East are the biggest chocolate munchers. We eat 13pc more than the national average, just behind the Scots, but way above people in the North-West.

Each person spends an average 98p a week on chocolate. That amounts to an annual average of 120 chocolate bars, ten bags of chocolate and 3.5 Cadbury's Creme Eggs – which is a lot of cocoa beans.

Cadbury's Chocolate Market Review says sales of chocolate have boomed even in the recession as it 'offers reassurance in an uncertain world'.

John Taylor, marketing director at Cadbury, said: 'During difficult economic times, the British appear to turn to the products they know and trust.

'People associate chocolate with good times like birthdays, anniversaries or Christmas. It represents an ideal gift or treat or purely as a little self indulgence.

'While many other businesses have suffered the effects of people spending less money, the British appetite for chocolate remains high.'

Regional differences are hard to pinpoint but some say North-East people eat more chocolate because of the colder climate or the fact we tend to snack more.

Simon Goodman, from Cadbury's said: 'People in the North-East tend to go for more solid chocolate bars like Boost. When Boost was launched we tested it in the North-East to see how it would sell.'

The Top Five best-sellers are Kit Kat, Mars bar, Twix, Snickers, and Cadbury's Creme Egg.

People either buy chocolate on impulse or to store at home in the kitchen cupboard. Women buy two-thirds of chocolate but eat only 40pc, men eat about 29pc and the remainder is eaten by children.

Cadbury's have identified types of people who buy chocolate. You are either a self-eater, who scoffs the bar all on your own, a family sharer, who dishes the chocolate out among people, or a multi-pack buyer, who stores them in the cupboard.

Cadbury's say people buy chocolate because it is linked to childhood values like fun, togetherness, caring and warmth.

But the whole question of caring and warmth goes out the window when it comes to a packet of Rolos. After all who would you give your last Rolo to?

Source: The Northern Echo

1 List the main features offered by products in the various chocolate markets.

2 Using the examples provided in the article, outline the benefits accruing to the purchaser of chocolate products.

3 Suggest one or more USPs a manufacturer could focus on in this market.

4 What qualities of chocolate bars could turn them into products the customer knows and trusts? How long might this process take?

A2

With designs on industry

BACK in the high spending Eighties British consumers put a high price on good design.

They were willing to shell out extravagant sums on designer labels and were easily wooed by the undue emphasis placed on design by glossy 'style' magazines.

However, the Designer Decade is now a memory and we now live in a more practical age tempered by prevailing worries about the economy.

Nevertheless good design still holds sway and never more so among British manufacturers struggling to win a slice of an increasingly competitive market.

As design expert Bill Morrison insists: 'Good design can improve business performance.'

As design adviser at the Newcastle office of the Design Council Morrison has a vested interest in the design gospel. Nevertheless he makes a convincing commercial argument for investing in research and development and quality design.

The argument goes thus: Successful companies are using the latest development in design management to compress market lead times, reduce product introduction costs, improve customer satisfaction and increase profits.

And Morrison insists that it is during a recession that companies can benefit most from good design strategies.

He claims good design can prove 20 times more effective an investment than investing in, say, production methods.

'The design process moves down from the raw materials a company buys in, to the actual process of making a product that people want to buy – it streamlines the manufacturing process,' says Morrison.

'What I'm interested in is producing products that have differentiation – products that, whether they be clothing or heavy engineering equipment, stand apart from the run of the mill. That's how you make money.'

According to the Design Council research shows that virtually all on-going design projects in small and medium-sized companies make a profit, with an average payback of 15 months from product launch.

'One of my missions,' says Morrison, 'is to try to improve the quality of the products coming out of British manufacturing industry.

'If we expect to export to foreign countries, we have to beat them on quality and design, because the customer's 'desire to purchase' is determined by this.'

The danger now exists, however, that the recession has been so deep and so long that manufacturing is simply surviving from day to day with little thought for anything else.

'What it should be doing,' claims Morrison, 'is spending money on developing new products and ideas. Only by doing this will they be competitive enough to take advantage of the upturn.'

The DTI enterprise initiative is currently spreading the design gospel but so far few companies have heard the call.

For several years now the Design Council's efforts have largely been devoted to educating the British consumer about the importance of design. Now the council, which is funded with a £7m grant from the DTI, is moving onto the factory floor and is helping companies develop design strategies which could eventually add something to British industry's bottom line.

Morrison is often invited onto the factory floor to offer help and advice at companies throughout the region which are willing to develop their design and research strategies. 'I act as a troubleshooter,' he says. 'Most of my contacts come from cold calls but often companies actively seek our advice and we can draw on a great deal of expertise covering a wide range of industries.'

In the past the Design Council has done work with Nissan at Washington, Bridon Ropes on Tyneside, Typhoon at Redcar and Cleveland Action Team.

But Morrison stresses that the important thing is not glossy brochures and high-blown sales talk. 'Effectively the design process isn't about a beginning and an end. It's an on-going process. It has to be because that's how companies keep ahead of the competition.

Source: The Northern Echo

1 Why do you think the 'designer decade' is now a memory?
2 Describe and explain the 'design gospel' as perceived by the Design Council.
3 Give examples of products where the USP lies in the design. How does their design affect you?
4 What part is played by design in the total product concept for (a) consumer, (b) industrial and (c) service goods? Give examples of each.

A3

Colour 'key to selling car'

THE colour of a used car is far more important to a prospective buyer than an on-board computer.

That is the wisdom from motor industry price handbook *Glass's Guide*. Managing editor Leslie Allen warned those about to buy a brand new car that they should not think optional extras would add greatly to its resale value.

'Our intelligence gathered from auctions and dealers and the industry is that the colour of the paintwork is far more important than a catalytic converter, a CD player or £1,000 worth of leather seats,' he said yesterday.

'The first signs are coming through that the used car customer is backing off too much new technology.'

While new car sales in 1994 are predicted to reach just under two million, Mr Allen forecasts the secondhand market will top seven million – half being sold privately and half through the trade.

Source: By courtesy of *The Yorkshire Post*, 4 April 1994

1 How important a part would colour play in your choice of car?
2 What images are conveyed by different colours of car?
3 Describe other consumer durable goods which place an emphasis on colour within the total product offering.
4 Would motor car manufacturers be justified in identifying market segments purely by colour? In what circumstances might this happen?

A4

Kit Kat gets a crisper look

HAVE a break – with tradition.

Kit Kat wrappers have been redesigned for the first time in 20 years.

But changes in the look of Britain's best-selling chocolate snack – six million are eaten every day – are subtle. The backs of all wrappers, both four finger and two finger, now also bear the famous 30-year-old slogan 'Have a Break Have a Kit Kat'.

And the Kit Kat logo has been given a crisper look with a slightly different oval and the use of a different typeface, while retaining the distinctive 'K' capital letters.

The changes, which took months of research by in-house designers at Nestlé, come as plans are in place to open an extra £28 million Kit Kat plant in York to increase production.

The white keyline surrounding the oval and white background were introduced back in 1973, but the logo itself has not been altered since the 1950s.

Source: The Northern Echo

1 Do you consider packaging to be mainly a protective method or a promotional tool in the marketing of chocolate snacks?

2 How could the Kit Kat wrapper influence the customer at the point of sale?

3 What functions have to be performed by the Kit Kat pack at retail outlets?

4 In this market do you feel the packaging emphasis should be on traditional designs or a constantly evolving approach to reflect changes in society?

A5

The gospel according to the evangelist of quality

DOCTOR Rosabeth Moss Kanter was billed in advance as 'the most sought after speaker on management in the world.'

Given that nearly 700 business leaders last week paid in excess of £150 to hear the Harvard Business School professor speak at a Quality North conference she could possibly also lay claim to being among the most expensive.

The event marked the high point of the Northern Development Company's year of Quality projects. A full house at Newcastle Playhouse and another capacity audience at Wynyard Hall on Teesside, linked by video, meant Dr Kanter lived up to her publicity.

Central to her presentation were the '4 fs'. Companies, she argued, need to become focused, fast, flexible and friendly. And, of course, they have to take the Quality concept to heart.

'But who could not like Quality? It's unpatriotic not to salute at the flag of Quality,' she asserted.

Her particular form of business evangelism discards a lot of the rather dry and jargon-ridden language of Quality which is the norm in many companies.

Not once did she make reference to 'the price of non-conformity', 'corrective action teams', or 'corrective action requests'.

She did, however, wheel out the touchstone of the Quality fanatics. 'The aim of all companies must be to delight the customer.'

And her own '4f' concept, outlined in ten books, numerous Harvard Business School Review articles and complementary videos, was also given an airing.

'Companies should be focused. They should take a few manageable goals and aim to fulfil them. You can't be all things to all people. Pick those areas in which you are willing to devote resources and concentrate on them,' she advised.

'To achieve the second 'f' – fastness – a company needs speed of innovation and speed of service.

'Most of all, though, it should be flexible. Customers have more options than ever before and they will exercise that choice if not catered for.

'And the fourth 'f' – friendliness – can be gained through internal and external joint ventures and partnerships,' she said.

Dr Kanter also added a fifth 'f'. 'The final 'f' is for fun. If it's not fun in a company the rest cannot apply.'

With such a structure in place she added a stern rider that companies can then only win in the 'game of management' by adopting new management techniques.

'No top-down chain of command. No rules and precedents. How many customers want to wait before you say 'I have to check with my boss'? We need change in the way we think about organisations. And the Quality revolution is providing that.'

Source: The Northern Echo, 25 November 1991

1 Outline Dr Kanter's '4fs' concept of quality. Do you consider these criteria to be comprehensive?

2 How might an organisation implement and monitor the '4fs' to control quality provision?

3 Describe a consumer, industrial or service product where quality is carefully defined and enforced.

4 Do you believe that the main reason for the recent introduction of quality thresholds such as BS 5750 is to 'delight the customer'?

ISSUES

FEATURES, BENEFITS AND USPs

In the real world a consumer purchases a product which can do the job and suits the pocket.

1 Are benefits really taken consciously into account by consumers? If so, for what types of products?

2 In what markets might manufacturers concentrate purely on product features?

3 Is there any such thing as a genuine USP? Discuss this question and give examples.

TOTAL PRODUCT CONCEPT

A confusing piece of marketing jargon?

1 Are certain classifications of products more suited to an integrated marketing campaign than others?

2 Argue the case for a customer being more susceptible to such an approach, giving examples.

3 Make a list of all the characteristics of a product which could be incorporated into its total concept.

DESIGN IN MARKETING

The realm of artists and boffins, not the concern of marketing people?

1 Discuss examples of products you consider to be well designed and those which are not.

2 What does the role of design in marketing imply for management and organisational structures?

3 What do you think are the main design factors in the process of creating an innovative product of quality?

COLOUR IN MARKETING

Is colour a promotional tool or an arbitrary product feature?

1 Make a list of consumer and/or industrial products which use colour as a strong promotional weapon.

2 Make a list of product categories for which the choice of colour is largely irrelevant.

3 Select and discuss products which in your opinion use colour (a) effectively and (b) ineffectively as a promotional tool.

PACKAGING

Does packaging sell goods or merely protect them?

1 Select and describe three products where you feel the packaging plays a major part in the selling process.

2 Select and describe three products for which the packaging is, in your opinion, inappropriate or ineffective. Outline alternative designs.

3 List the main qualities a good pack should contain in the marketing of (a) consumer and (b) industrial products.

QUALITY CONTROL

Are conformity standards such as BS 5750 genuine methods of raising product quality or just handy marketing tools?

1 Do you consider that the imposition of formal quality procedures is always beneficial to the customer in the long term?

2 Discuss the advantages and disadvantages accruing to the organisation when it adopts a philosophy of full quality measurement and control.

3 Research and present your findings on an organisation which (a) does and (b) does not believe in the implementation of the quality ethos.

QUESTIONS

1 Give three characteristics of general consumer products.

2 Give three characteristics of consumer durable products.

3 Give three characteristics of speciality consumer products.

4 List four types of industrial products.

5 Give three characteristics of industrial goods.

6 What are product features?

7 What are product benefits?

8 What is a feature/benefit analysis?

9 What is a unique selling proposition?

10 Name three product features or benefits typically used as USPs.

11 What is the total product concept?

12 Name four characteristics of effective design.

13 Select three colours and the images associated with them for marketing purposes.

14 Name three of the reasons for the growth in importance of packaging.

15 List four of the functions fulfilled by packaging.

16 Give three ways in which packaging can promote the product.

17 What is meant by quality control?

18 What is BS 5750?

19 What is Total Quality Management?

20 Name three functions of TQM.

PROJECTS

1 Examine the differences and similarities between consumer and industrial products. What implications does this have for devising a marketing campaign for each?

2 Undertake a full feature/benefit analysis of the toothpaste example mentioned in the chapter, or a product of your choice. How can such an analysis assist the marketer?

3 A product has been referred to as a 'psychological bundle of satisfactions'. Discuss the appropriateness of this definition, giving examples and mentioning the total product concept.

4 Why has good design come to the forefront in the quest for successful competitive product advantage in the 1990s? Discuss the types of product for which it is most essential, suggesting examples.

5 The packaging industry has increased dramatically in the last 10 years. Why should this be so and in what sectors is effective packaging most important? Give examples.

6 Examine the contention that colour is a key component of the total product offering for all classifications of goods.

7 'Quality is an intrinsic part of a good product and cannot be added on at a later stage.' Discuss this viewpoint with reference to the philosophy of Total Quality Management.

GLOSSARY

Accessories short-lived capital items not part of the final product, such as tools and equipment used in production or in the office.

After-, before- or during-sales service advice on or assistance with the purchase and use of a product given to customers at any stage of their relationship with the organisation and thus part of the total product offering.

Benefit characteristic of a product which offers a tangible or intangible advantage to the consumer and which is therefore developed and focused on by an organisation.

Best practice models of excellence in all areas of business, established by organisations focusing on total quality management and a customer-orientated philosophy of marketing.

Colour part of the total product concept and an important decision-making area for an organisation.

Component a finished product which is used in the manufacture of another, larger item.

Consumer durable goods those consumer goods which last for and are used over an extended period of time.

Convenience goods see 'General consumer goods'.

Deceptive differential a unique selling point created for a non-essential product.

Derived demand consumers buying certain products, often industrial, as a direct result of the purchase of another good (e.g. the demand for house bricks is derived from the demand for new houses).

Design creativity applied to the aesthetic aspects of product shape, function, packaging, and so on. Part of the total product concept.

Durables see 'Consumer durable goods'.

Family packaging where a range of products all use similar packaging with the same design characteristics.

Fast-moving consumer goods (fmcgs) repeat selling, low unit value goods normally attracting a high level of demand.

Feature specific basic aspect or characteristic of a product.

Forward ordering method of purchase and distribution used for industrial products to ensure regular deliveries of bulk items.

General consumer goods goods purchased frequently by consumers with a minimum of effort, and available in many outlets.

Generic name brand name that has become a generally descriptive term for a product.

Generic product food or household item characterised by a plain label, little or no advertising, and no brand name.

Good a tangible product.

Industrial market market involving the buying and selling of products for re-sale or for further production use.

Industrial marketing marketing activities between organisations (not involving end consumers) and dealing with products for re-sale or further production use.

Industrial products goods purchased for use directly or indirectly in the production of other goods for re-sale.

Installations complete purpose-built industrial structures.

Labelling descriptive part of a product package, including brand name, manufacturer details and product information and instructions, conforming to legal requirements.

Materials goods used in production or purchased for re-sale.

Natural products products occurring in nature, such as minerals, fish and wood.

Non-durable goods consumer goods normally consumed in one or a few uses.

Packaging designing and producing a product's wrapping or container to fulfil objectives of promotion and protection and contribute to the total product concept.

Prestige good a product with an expensive, top quality, up-market image.

Product the total combination of features and characteristics a consumer receives in an exchange, including tangible goods and intangible services, places or ideas.

Product classification grouping of products into discrete categories, such as consumer, durable, industrial and service.

Quality circles small, autonomous groups of employees in an organisation, formed to spontaneously think of, discuss and assist each other in carrying out improvements in the quality of all aspects of the organisation's business.

Quality control establishing a system of close and regular monitoring of products to ensure they are in perfect condition when reaching the customer.

Raw materials component goods, either natural or industrial, used in the production of final products.

Shopping product products that a customer feels are worth the time and effort to compare with other brands before final selection.

Speciality goods consumer products that the customer really wants and is prepared to make a special effort to find.

Standard Industrial Classification (SIC) a system of code numbers for categorising the industrial market-place into detailed segments, based on what organisations produce or serve.

Style modification modification directed at changing the sensory appeal of a product by altering one or more of its characteristics, such as design, colour, taste, smell or sound.

Substitutes products that can be used in place of something else, thus offering the consumer a choice.

Supplies items that contribute towards an organisation's production and operations, but do not become part of the finished product.

Total product concept combination of all the tangible and intangible features and advantages which an organisation selects and offers to customers as part of a completely integrated package.

Total Quality Management (TQM) organisational philosophy concentrating on setting, monitoring and upholding quality standards throughout the firm, and its products and customer relationships.

Unique selling proposition (USP) particular characteristic of a product which is unique to that item in the eyes of the consumer and is thus clearly differentiated from rival products.

Unsought products products that potential customers do not yet want or know they can purchase.

White goods term used for consumer durable household appliances traditionally white in colour, such as refrigerators and washing machines.

SUGGESTED REFERENCES

VIDEO MATERIAL

Design Matters, 'Where and why do you buy?', Channel 4, Malachite Ltd., 1983.

The Marketing Mix No. 3, 'Product decisions', Yorkshire Television, 1986.

Business of Excellence series, The Open College, Channel 4, 1986.

Technology Design, BBC2, 1986.

Design Classics, Coca-Cola Bottle, BBC, 1987.

Design and Innovation – Images and Innovation, Open University, BBC, 1988.

Managing Design – Suite Dreams, Open Business School, BBC, 1988.

Contemporary Marketing, Video Cases, No. 8 (Carushka), Boone, L. and Kurtz, D., Dryden Press, 1989.

The Manager, 'A question of quality ...', Open College, Channel 4, 1990.

The Colour Eye, 'Rainbow For Sale', BBC, 1991.

Equinox, 'Zen on Wheels', Channel 4, 1992.

Winning – with quality, BBC, 1992.

Business Matters, 'Get better or get beaten', BBC, 1993.

BBC Design Awards 1994 – Products and Graphics', BBC, 1994.

RADIO MATERIAL

Sell, sell, sell, 'Packaging', BBC Radio Leeds, 1984.

MAGAZINE ARTICLES

Journal of Marketing Management, Vol. 1, No. 2, Winter 1985, p.119, 'In search of excellence in the UK'.

Journal of Marketing Management, Vol. 3, No. 2, Winter 1987, p.133, 'Designing a quality product'.

Journal of Marketing Management, Vol. 3, No. 2, Spring 1988, p.372, 'Re-innovation and robust designs: producer and user benefits'.

Journal of Marketing Management, Vol. 8, No. 3, July 1992, p.259, 'Product classifications and marketing strategy'.

Marketing Business, April 1989, p.4, 'The quality of marketing – Rank Xerox'.

Marketing Business, June 1989, p.14, 'Tying it all together'.

Marketing Business, Dec. 1989, p,12, 'The quality of marketing'.

Marketing Business, Aug. 1990, p.4, 'Balancing the brand'.

Marketing Business, Oct. 1991, p.48, 'Briefly'.

Marketing Business, Nov. 1991, p.30, 'Standard bearers'.

Marketing Business, Dec./Jan. 1991/92, p.14, 'Quest for quality'.

Marketing Business, April 1992, p.41, 'It's a wrap'.

Marketing Business, May 1992, p.10, 'Hallmark of success'.

Marketing Business, Feb. 1993, p.32, 'Wrap it up'.

Marketing Business, July/Aug. 1993, p.29, 'Called to account'.

Marketing Business, Oct. 1993, p.29, 'Design'.

Quarterly Review of Marketing, Vol. 14, No. 3, April 1989, p.6, 'Managing design to improve international competitiveness'.

FURTHER READING

Adcock, D., Bradfield, R., Halborg, A., and Ross, C., *Marketing Principles and Practice* (2nd edn), Pitman, 1995, chs 2 and 11.

Boone, L. and Kurtz, D., *Contemporary Marketing*, Dryden, 1989, ch. 8.

Cannon, Tom, *Basic Marketing*, Holt Business Texts, 1980, ch. 4.

Dibb, S., Simkin, L., Pride, W. and Ferrell, O., *Marketing*, Houghton Mifflin, 1994, chs 7 and 8.

Foster, Douglas, *Mastering Marketing*, Macmillan, 1982, ch. 5.

Giles, G., *Marketing*, MacDonald and Evans, 1985, ch. 4.

Kotler, P. and Armstrong, G., *Marketing*, Prentice Hall, 1993, ch. 8.

Lorenz, Christopher, *The Design Dimension*, Blackwell, 1990.

McCarthy, J. and Perreault, W., *Basic Marketing*, Irwin, 1987, ch. 9.

Mercer, D., *Marketing*, Blackwell, 1992, ch. 7.

Opie, Robert, *Packaging Source-book*, MacDonald Orbis, 1989.

Smith, P.R., *Marketing Communications*, Kogan Page, 1993, ch. 18.

Acknowledgements

The Northern Echo.
The Yorkshire Evening Press.
The Yorkshire Post.

7
PRODUCT DEVELOPMENT

DEFINITIONS

A brand is the unique sum of a product's taste and texture, flavour and smell, appearance and associations. A successful brand reassures, gives confidence and, like an old friend, promises the certainty of pleasure. From all this comes the probability of long-term profits.

KENNETH DIXON, FORMER CHAIRMAN OF ROWNTREE MACKINTOSH, NOW PART OF NESTLÉ

In our experience, the key to successful marketing is superior product performance.

CHAIRMAN, PROCTER & GAMBLE

The Product Mix is the composite or total group of products that an organisation makes available to customers.

DIBB, SIMKIN, PRIDE AND FERRELL

INTRODUCTION

Whatever their classification, products are not guaranteed to be successful because they happen to exhibit certain characteristics, offer the consumer benefits or unique selling points, are part of a total concept approach or are closely monitored along quality guidelines.

Profitability and permanence in the market instead depend on how the organisation develops and manages all these factors in combination, a process illustrated in Figure 7.1.

So product success can only be achieved as a result of a long-term organisational strategy which commits resources to the research and development of new products, the creation of distinctive product personalities or brands, the constant monitoring of the life cycle stage each product is in, and the overall management of the mix of products at the organisation's disposal.

The product development and management process

PRODUCT DEVELOPMENT

↓

1. Establishing new products

↓

2. Branding

↓

3. Monitoring product life cycles

↓

4. Managing the product mix

Fig 7.1

KEY CONCEPTS

ESTABLISHING NEW PRODUCTS

In order to ensure its profitable existence, an organisation needs to introduce new products or services periodically to add to a range, keep ahead of the competition or replace unfashionable or technically obsolete items. Additionally, as the increasing boredom factor of society affects consumer purchases, there is an ever-growing need for new product development to be strongly represented within company strategy.

Organisations with a genuine commitment to such a strategy will devote considerable resources to research and development, a process referred to in Chapter 3. Depending on the size of the company, this work could be undertaken by various means, including:

● a new product committee;
● a new product department;
● a venture team set up for the purpose;
● a product manager or manageress;
● a specialist external agency.

The first task of the person or team responsible will be to define the intended nature of their new product offering. It could, for example, involve any of the following characteristics:

● totally new;
● a new product line;
● additions;
● improvements;
● repositionings;
● cost reductions;
● strategic considerations;
● defensive considerations.

Having established the guidelines for action, an organisation can embark on the chronological phases of new product development illustrated in Figure 7.2.

Each phase involves consideration of several important management decision-making areas:

● *Generation of ideas* – achieved through various means, such as brainstorming, 'think tanks', employee suggestions, technological discoveries, customers, competitors or the use of independent specialists.

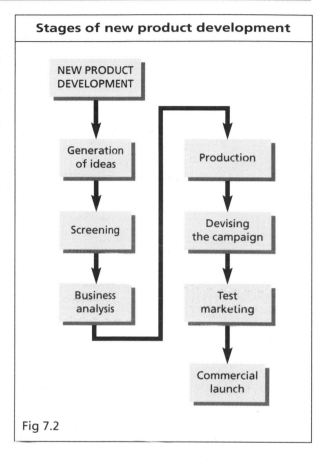

Stages of new product development

Fig 7.2

● *Screening* – analysing basic suitability in terms of the expertise and experience in the company, financial resources required, market demand in the short and long term, likely return on investment (or ROI), availability of raw materials, legal aspects such as patents, and company objectives, policies and overall strategy.
● *Business analysis* – detailed evaluation of the idea, including further testing of concept and ROI, marketing research, competition comparisons, full analysis of resource and production requirements and the general risk factor.
● *Production* – complete research and development, make models/prototypes and revise if necessary.
● *Devising the campaign* – marketing planning, production scheduling, financial calculations, final product market research.

- *Test marketing* – introduction of the product on a limited scale to one particular segment or region representative of the total potential market (referred to in Chapter 3) as the final insurance policy against failure.
- *Commercial launch* – finalisation of product, ROI and marketing plan, production and marketing plan commence, product introduced into the total market on a market-by-market basis or nationally, supported by sales effort, promotion and distribution channels.

The resources and time required to establish a new product by this means can be considerable. The Rowntree company, for example, committed huge resources and two years of research and development before the Yorkie chocolate bar was perfected and launched nationally. They had previously tested and rejected several other alternative names, such as O'Hara, Rations, Jones, Smithy, Carter and Trek. The Yorkie image was bold and chunky but clean-cut, enhanced by an advertising campaign featuring a 'macho' truck driver, and this contributed greatly to the brand's success.

Of every 100 ideas, it has been estimated that only five arrive at the launch stage and of these only one will be successful, giving a failure rate of 99 per cent. The extremely low success rate for new product ideas means that at each phase of the development process an organisation will be conscious of the need to ensure that only the products with the highest probability of success are allowed to progress, and the ones more likely to fail are dropped before too much time and effort is devoted to them. This ruthless approach is necessary for a company to reduce the risk factor to a minimum in a competitive business world.

Nevertheless, organisations still experience considerable difficulty in convincing re-sellers to stock new products, and research by KAE Surveys suggests that the main reasons for this are, in order of importance:

1. No product advantage.
2. No shelf space.
3. Declining market.
4. Poor quality.
5. Little advertising support.
6. No introductory bonus.
7. Product from a small company.

One way of ensuring that a new product has the best chance of being accepted is the careful creation and nurturing of a distinctive personality or brand, which has the effect of giving it a visible product advantage.

However, good ideas and apparently sound products are rarely certain of being converted into marketing success and there are many examples of missed opportunities. The Invicta plastics company, for example, turned down the chance of manufacturing and marketing the eventually hugely successful Rubik's Cube.

BRANDING

There are a huge number of branded goods currently available but relatively few are purchased on a regular basis by the typical household. The Media Register lists over 32,500 advertised brands but, according to Winston Fletcher in *A Glittering Haze*, only 9,500 command a budget of over £50,000 a year (and are thus heavily advertised) and of these, few consumers are likely to buy more than 400, or 4 per cent of the total, in any one year.

On the subject of how to measure whether a product brand is successful or not, A.J. O'Reilly, Chairman of the H.J. Heinz Company, once said, 'my acid test on the issue is if a housewife intending to buy Heinz Tomato Ketchup in a store, finding it to be out of stock, will walk out of the store to buy it elsewhere or switch to an alternative product.'

If the consumer exhibits *brand loyalty* by making the effort to stick with the product and buy it elsewhere, the likelihood is that it will have been strongly branded. A brand adds value to a product, service, person or place by investing it with an image and bestowing a distinctive identity which differentiates it from competitors.

These added brand values have the effect of creating beliefs within customers that the product is reliable and the best, and a feeling that you will be happier with it rather than a rival product, a particular city is your kind of place or that 'X' is more your type of person. These beliefs and feelings are based on impressions of the organisation or brand relative to others, and perceptions of the company's authority and reputation.

Specifically, an organisation endeavours to instil the brand image concept by offering a product which satisfies consumers' physical and emotional needs and contains a rational benefit or USP, while all elements of its marketing mix are perceived as compatible, believable and relevant. Pursuing this type of policy provides a sound platform for ensuring repeat purchases.

Research into successful brands has revealed that consumers describe such products in terms normally associated with people, for example warm or friendly, cold or modern, old-fashioned, romantic, practical, sophisticated, stylish, and so on. References to a brand's persona, image and reputation reinforce this aura and serve to illustrate that brands, like people, possess a 'personality' of one kind or another.

But like the strongest individuals, the strongest brands have more than just personality. They also have a dynamic 'character', perceived by consumers as containing more depth and integrity and standing out from the crowd. So despite increasing competition and costs, static markets and converging technological parity amongst manufacturers, organisations still try to develop powerful and enduring brand characters based on superior product quality. Such a policy stimulates brand loyalty amongst consumers and distributors, reduces a product's elasticity of demand (see Chapter 13) and makes a company less vulnerable in the market-place.

The main problem facing an organisation concerned with developing a successful brand is to decide what characteristics, when applied to the product, will best stimulate and maintain demand and create the required brand identity which will be favourably perceived by the target market segment of consumers. Many product features are at a company's disposal and can be utilised individually or in combination to achieve the desired objectives (see Figure 7.3).

Each of these factors in turn involves a considerable amount of decision making and takes much care to perfect. A good brand name, for example, usually contains certain characteristics:

- short and simple but interesting and/or exciting;
- easy to spell, read and pronounce (in all languages);
- easy to recognise and remember;
- cannot be mistaken or misunderstood;
- suggestive of product benefits;
- adaptable to packaging and labelling needs;
- not offensive or negative;
- does not date;
- adaptable to any advertising medium;
- legally available for use;

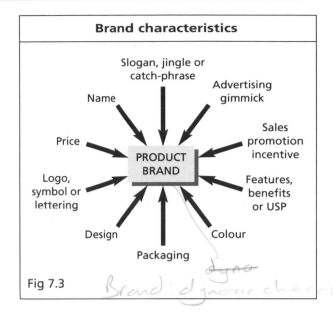

Fig 7.3

- appropriate to product image;
- instantly conveying product offering, e.g. Gas-Miser, Wonderbra or Slim-Fast.

Even then, an effective brand name cannot usually ensure product success on its own. It generally requires the backing of other brand characteristics to project the desired identity, as the Ford Edsel, Nissan Infiniti, Sinclair C5 and Co-op found to their cost.

It is useful here to distinguish between a brand name, which refers strictly to letters, words or groups of words which can be spoken, and a trademark, which is a legal term covering words and symbols that can be registered and protected. Both terms have the effect of differentiating one organisation's goods or services from that of another.

By one or more of these methods of branding, an organisation will aim to convey the image of a product to consumers over a period of time, gradually drawing them through progressive stages of brand familiarity, as illustrated in Figure 7.6 on page 115.

Recently there has been a trend towards organisations developing their own brand image as well as, or instead of, that of their products. Some firms have invested incorporate as opposed to product branding as a means of being seen to be responsible citizens (this will be referred to further in Chapter 12), while others have put the emphasis on the corporate brand but attached a product identification.

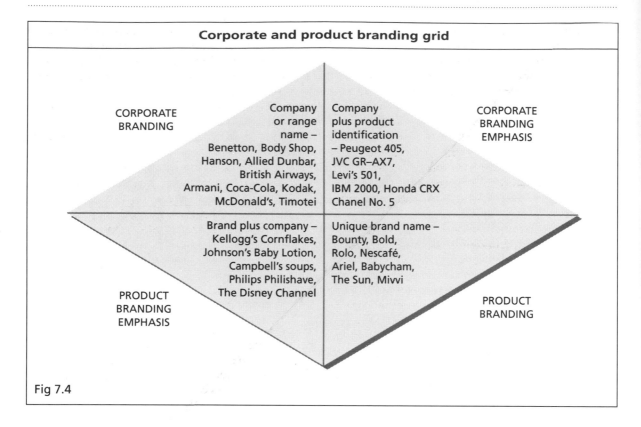

Corporate and product branding grid

CORPORATE BRANDING

Company or range name – Benetton, Body Shop, Hanson, Allied Dunbar, British Airways, Armani, Coca-Cola, Kodak, McDonald's, Timotei

Company plus product identification – Peugeot 405, JVC GR–AX7, Levi's 501, IBM 2000, Honda CRX Chanel No. 5

CORPORATE BRANDING EMPHASIS

Brand plus company – Kellogg's Cornflakes, Johnson's Baby Lotion, Campbell's soups, Philips Philishave, The Disney Channel

Unique brand name – Bounty, Bold, Rolo, Nescafé, Ariel, Babycham, The Sun, Mivvi

PRODUCT BRANDING EMPHASIS

PRODUCT BRANDING

Fig 7.4

Again, certain firms either work on making their own image harmonise with that of their branded products or concentrate solely on their brands to the exclusion of any corporate reference. These four approaches towards branding are illustrated in Figure 7.4, together with examples of organisations within each category.

Which route is chosen towards a sustainable competitive advantage will depend on a multiplicity of organisational, market and environmental factors.

Branding can be a powerful and all-pervasive marketing tool. The Hamlet, Midland Bank and Gold Blend advertising campaigns defined the brands and ensured the long-term memorability of the products, while the Mars Bar has almost become part of our way of life. Occasionally the image portrayed becomes so strong that the brand name enters everyday language, replacing the original product description. To illustrate this effect, we now 'Hoover' a room rather than vacuum clean it, use Tipp-ex rather than correction fluid and refer to the generic term J.C.B. to represent any form of mechanical digging machine.

Tampax, Sellotape and Brillo Pads are other examples of the power of product branding. Often a successfully established 'umbrella' brand name is used by an organisation for related products to take advantage of easy identification.

But like other assets, brands depreciate without continual nurturing and investment. Singer sewing machines and MG cars were examples of products suffering from such a lack of attention over time. Again, some brands can be overshadowed by the power of the imagery used. By common consensus, the humorous Cinzano advertising campaign did a lot for the careers of Joan Collins and Leonard Rossiter, the actors featuring in the commercials, but not a lot for the brand identity or eventual sales of the product.

Brand loyalty is thus usually gained only at a cost and over the long term, such as the insurance sales person who nurtures a relationship with clients throughout their lives. It generally requires the specialist attentions of a brand manager to plan and follow through on every aspect of the marketing performance of their particular product or service, whilst liaising closely with all other relevant departments of the organisation (in multi-brand firms, product or brand managers can find themselves competing against each other). And even then, some products are historically less susceptible to the attempts of marketers to create a loyal consumer following. Research has shown that mayonnaise, toothpaste, coffee, detergent and automobile brands, for instance, attract a higher percentage of regular purchasers than do jeans, batteries, tyres, televisions or athletic shoes, which are thus more likely to experience 'brand switching', where consumers show no particular allegiance to one specific product.

A common feature in the retailing world is the '*own-label*' brand, whereby firms introduce products under their own store name, for example Tesco's coffee and Sainsbury's wines, or that of the company brand, such as Marks and Spencer's St Michael label. In the past the tendency for these to cost less contributed to a down-market image, but today the twin demands of quality and competition have led to own-label products often being viewed by consumers as on a par or superior to manufacturers' brands. Indeed, own-label brands now account for two-thirds of Sainsbury's total sales.

Own-label brands are usually marketed by wholesalers and retailers that do not manufacture themselves but are supplied by companies which do, then add their labels, packaging and other identifying marks. Marks and Spencer lay down very precise specifications and exercise rigid quality control over manufacturers that supply 'St Michael' products.

Organisations are attracted to own-brand marketing mainly because they want to limit the control exercised by manufacturers of traditionally strongly branded products and bring more competition into the market-place. Own-label brands also have the effect of creating company or store identity, and hence consumer loyalty, and of introducing greater price variations.

In addition to increasing customer recognition and loyalty, competitive advantage, sales and profitability, the effort put into branding secures a number of other important benefits for organisations, such as:

- a more ready acceptance of the product by wholesalers and retailers and thus the easier granting of special promotions and display space;

- elimination of the importance of price differentials;
- easier introduction of associated brands (n.b. the opposite would be true if the brand were to fail);
- assistance with directing the firm's marketing communication campaigns;
- enabling consumers to self-select easily in stores;
- reducing the amount of personal selling necessary;
- making market segmentation easier, as specialist brands are developed to meet the needs of specific consumer categories;
- giving a manufacturer potentially greater control over marketing strategy and channels of distribution.

Where a product has few competitors in a particular market and thus customers would buy it whether or not it were branded, intense branding is less likely to occur. This is also the case where the costs of brand advertising and promotion are prohibitive, when it is more difficult to control quality, or where products are not difficult to evaluate objectively – for example, industrial rather than consumer goods.

But increasingly branding is an indispensable aspect of business for many organisations, particularly now that international markets are becoming far more attainable (the implications of global branding will be discussed in Chapter 15). Company policy has to be considered carefully each time a brand is introduced onto the market to ensure the right balance is maintained between new products and the established brands, with others being withdrawn as and when necessary. However, competitive pressures, changing consumer attitudes and behaviour, and the variable political, economic and technological environments mean that no organisation can assume that any current or future brands are ever assured of success.

PRODUCT LIFE CYCLES

In a changing market, one method used by organisations to chart the development and progress of their brands is the *product life cycle*, (PLC). All products and services have a distinct life span from their introduction until final withdrawal from the market. This pattern tends to be measured in terms of a chronological history of sales which companies try to predict in order to make product

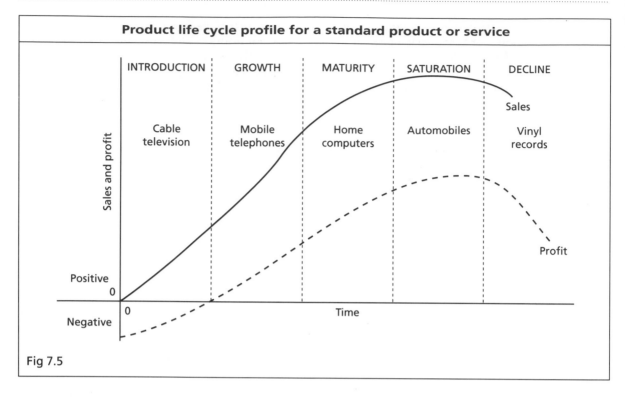

Product life cycle profile for a standard product or service

INTRODUCTION | GROWTH | MATURITY | SATURATION | DECLINE

Sales

Cable television | Mobile telephones | Home computers | Automobiles | Vinyl records

Sales and profit

Positive
0

Negative

0

Time

Profit

Fig 7.5

decisions based more on experience and research than arbitrary guesswork.

Obviously the length of life and sales volume vary according to the type and relative success of the product or service. For example, an issue of a daily newspaper has a life span of less than a day, that of a fad or fashion product could be months, whilst the lives of some food products can be measured in years or even centuries. However, individual brands will tend to have a much shorter life cycle than that of the product type. A typical life cycle pattern is illustrated in Figure 7.5, together with current products typifying each phase.

Each stage of the life cycle for a typical product or service exhibits certain characteristics which enable an organisation to identify it easily and relate it to their brands. Chronologically, there are five such phases.

Introduction

As we have seen, it can take a long time for a product or service to complete the gestation period and be launched into the market. At this stage it is the aim of the company, having decided on an initial marketing mix, to move potential consumers along the continuum described in Figure 7.6.

Sales tend to be slow at first as the new offering gradually gains acceptance and information about it has to be widely disseminated by advertising, publicity and word of mouth from the early adopters, the most reliable and credible information source.

For a given product or service, some potential customers move along this continuum faster than others, and some never progress beyond a particular stage (the different categories of product adoption by consumers were discussed in Chapter 5). Would-be purchasers are then further encouraged by company promotions, the efforts of sales representatives, independent reports and other recommendations.

At the introduction stage, organisations tend to monitor the product closely and indulge in fine tuning but are reluctant to make significant alterations too soon while the market adjusts to the newcomer. Having penetrated the early users, more and more consumers reach the trial stage of the continuum and sales improve. The product will now enter the next stage of its life cycle.

Growth

As social acceptance is gained, competition is now attracted from other companies who imitate the

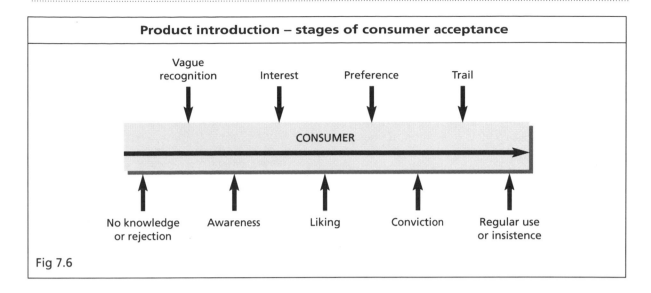

Product introduction – stages of consumer acceptance

Fig 7.6

successful product and perhaps add further features or benefits. The brand should now be satisfying market needs and growing stronger all the time, building market share and earning profits for the organisation as original costs are recouped. Costs will still be incurred, however, mainly as a result of the company employing promotional activities and general resources in an effort to build up the brand.

At this stage, an organisation should be more aware of its market and prepared to cope with higher levels of demand whilst modifying price to take account of increased competitive activity, wider distribution, increasing usage and lower unit costs. It should also be prepared for further fine tuning and consolidation of outlets and merchandising, if necessary. By the end of the growth stage all potential customers should have considered the product for purchase.

Maturity

During this phase sales growth will flatten out and any further growth will result from replacement demand or an increase in the total market rather than the brand share. Although efforts will be made to defend by differentiation and retain existing market share through promotional campaigns, energies will start to be channelled into other products at earlier stages of the PLC curve. This is normally the longest life cycle phase and some famous brands are still in the maturity stage after 30 years or more, e.g. Cadbury's Dairy Milk, Oxo, and Tate & Lyle's Golden Syrup.

Saturation

At this stage, sales growth slows down eventually to zero because customers know all about the product or service and have begun to seek substitutes or stop purchasing altogether. Up to this point, however, profits are still accumulating as costs are reduced, but sales rely on repeat purchases so the firm will start to consider and implement new strategies.

Decline

Most products or services eventually enter this phase, which is marked by a fall in sales. Competitors could take advantage of this, but some customers might still be brand loyal and not sensitive to price, thus delaying the decline. Others could be traditional in nature, with a tendency to prefer old-fashioned products.

An organisation has to choose from a number of strategies available to it at the decline stage. It might:

- leave the product to die of its own accord;
- make price adjustments in an attempt to prolong the PLC;
- try to revive the product with an advertising campaign or special promotion;
- bring more youthful products to maturity as quickly as possible to act as replacements;

- alter the distribution channels or other marketing mix elements;
- re-define the product or market in preparation for a re-launch and re-positioning;
- withdraw it rapidly, or phase it out, to cut losses.

It is obviously important for an organisation to recognise when its products or services are becoming obsolete, so that alternative strategies can be developed. Some companies phase out products early in their life cycle to take advantage of new innovations; but this can incur consumer displeasure, of which reaction to the discontinuance of the 'Aztec' chocolate bar is one example.

Other companies, such as the Japanese hi-fi and radio manufacturers, deliberately design their products to last for a specific time before being withdrawn and replaced by the next model. This policy is known as *planned obsolescence* and ensures that a product range will remain up to date whilst the market for it stays vibrant, with some consumers keen to purchase the latest innovation and others obliged to replace their redundant model. The increasing rate of technological advancement is another factor contributing to the gradual shortening of product life cycles.

The product life cycle concept is thus a flexible organisational device to aid in the understanding and management of products and services. However, in practice it is often difficult to identify life cycle stages, except in retrospect, or to measure cumulative profit.

MANAGING THE PRODUCT MIX

Few companies manufacture a single item for a single market. A balance of products at various stages of their life cycles is usually preferred as a means of ensuring that a sufficient cash flow from established brands is maintained to finance the development of new ones.

Larger organisations often deal with more than one product line, each of which contains several brands. The total assortment of products a company offers to consumers is known as the *product mix* and can be expressed in terms of its width and depth, as illustrated in Figure 7.7.

In its total range of assorted products, a new or established company may offer a wide variety of items differing in aspects such as size, power, shape, function, quality, price or style. It could

The product mix

Width of range

	Product line A	Product line B	Product line C
Depth of range	Brand 1 Brand 2 Brand 3 Brand 4	Brand 5 Brand 6 Brand 7 Brand 8 Brand 9	Brand 10 Brand 11 Brand 12

Fig 7.7

The Ansoff matrix

Products or services	Markets: Existing	Markets: New
Existing	1. Market Penetration Plans	2. Market Development Plans
New	3. Product Development Plans	4. Total Diversification Plans

Fig 7.8

Source: Adapted from Ansoff, H.I., *The New Corporate Strategy*, John Wiley, New York, 1988. Reprinted by permission of John Wiley & Sons Inc.

extend its product mix by modifying or improving any of these features, developing associated brands or producing completely new items in response to customer needs in existing, larger or new markets.

The main product development strategies available to an organisation are summarised in the model illustrated in Figure 7.8.

The Ansoff matrix enables a company to identify or choose between four key areas of marketing activity:

1. *Market penetration or operating plans* – the continuation of existing products in their present form,

sold to existing markets with the aim of increasing market share and extending the customer base.

2. *Market development plans* – the conscious entry into new markets for the existing product range, building on known strengths and seeking to exploit new market opportunities and ideas. For example, Horlicks was sold purely as a baby food until research showed that more adults than babies consumed it.

3. *Product development plans* – seeking to capitalise on existing market knowledge or connections by identifying and launching new products into a familiar market, such as that for computers or motor cars.

4. *Total diversification plans* – focusing on a completely new product line in a new market if the other options do not offer potential for development or growth. A risky option requiring considerable financial commitment, but giving protection against the possible failure of other lines. More likely to be successful if a joint effort, or *synergy*, can be made to maximise the organisation's strengths in terms of technology, skills, investment or markets.

An organisation contemplating general expansion of its product lines has to take account of the advantages and disadvantages of such an action. On the positive side, an extension of its range could lead to beneficial effects such as:

● winning new dealers;
● gaining more satisfied customers;
● enabling a move into new outlets for all items;
● reducing costs such as transportation;
● smoothing out seasonal fluctuations;
● giving more opportunities to the sales force.

Conversely, there could also be negative results, including:

● over-stocking;
● more capital tied up;
● sales effort spread too thinly;
● lower quality on new lines dragging down the whole range;
● problems to be resolved in areas such as production planning and financing.

Whether an organisation lays its emphasis on launching new items, deleting or altering old ones, combining two products into one or adapting to the competition, it will need to monitor its overall situation closely.

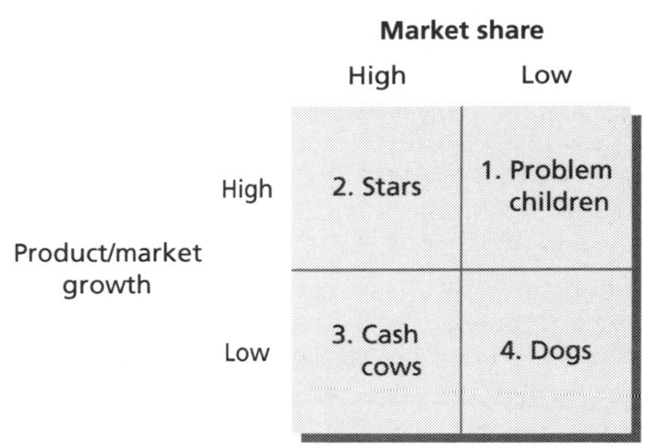

Fig 7.9

One method of doing this was developed by the Boston Consulting Group and involves an organisation in charting its product portfolio in terms of profitability and contribution to the company at different stages of the life cycle. Strategic decisions can then be made based on the result (see Figure 7.9).

The Boston box suggests that there are four main product groupings within a matrix of market growth and market share. These are:

1. *Problem children or question marks* – products at the introductory stage of the PLC experiencing rapid growth but, attracting low profits and using up resources heavily, e.g. city light railway and tram systems. Strategies could include penetration of a market niche, considerable investment, or abandonment following constant review.

2. *Stars* – these are fast-growing market leaders, making large profits but requiring high levels of investment, e.g. mountain bikes. Organisations could consider maintaining or increasing market share, extending the product range, or looking for improvements in the particular brand.

3. *Cash cows* – profitable products reaching the maturity and saturation stage and generating more cash than is needed to maintain market share, e.g. Paramount's Star Trek films and TV series. Strategies might be to maintain market dominance, try to develop the product or market further, or use the excess cash to support research and growth for new products.

4. *Dogs* – these are products in declining markets with little new business, therefore operating at a cost disadvantage with few opportunities for

growth, e.g. engineering courses in Higher Education. Here an organisation might consider focusing on a specialised market segment, cutting back financial support, taking measures for alteration or adjustment, thus aiming for revival, or opting for deletion.

Any organisation using one or more of these methods to monitor the performance of its portfolio of products in the market-place is in a sound position to adjust or respond to the demands of the marketing environment and to make the right strategic decisions on the development of its product range.

ARTICLES

A1

Take a brand new look...

So you're in the supermarket looking for instant coffee. You always buy Nescafe – the one with the picture of coffee beans and a red mug. You pick one up with that label and take it home.

Only when the coffee tastes a bit strange, you look more closely at the label and discover that it wasn't Nescafe at all, but Sainsbury's own instant coffee, with a remarkably similar label.

Does it matter?

Yes. It matters to you, because you don't always get what you thought you were buying.

And it matters desperately to the manufacturers. They spend tens of millions of pounds developing new products and the packaging to go with them. Just when, for instance, Head and Shoulders has made its own distinctive mark on the shelves, along comes a supermarket with a similar shampoo in a similar bottle in a similar colour scheme.

Well, you can see manufacturers are not going to be best pleased. Especially when own-label brands now account for a third of supermarket sales and are growing rapidly.

Manufacturers are now trying to treat packaging as part of the trademark. They want the law changed – to what it is in many other countries – so that it's not just the name that's protected, but the whole package, literally.

Supermarkets say that there is no confusion really, that their name is always clearly on display on any packaging, so people know what they're buying.

Source: The Northern Echo

1 Why should products such as milk and bread have a considerably larger percentage of own-label brands than toothpaste or washing-up liquid?

2 Do you buy own-label brands? If so, which ones and why? Which ones would you never consider purchasing, and why?

3 Describe the business and ethical conflicts which could arise between manufacturers and retailers in the marketing of own-label brands.

4 Discuss the factors which you think might contribute to an own-label product becoming a household brand name.

A2

New product from York

YORK Trailers yesterday announced plans to move back into the refrigerated semi-trailer market.

The firm has collaborated with Danish-group Norfrig on body panel design for the new product, currently being built at the Northallerton plant.

'1994 is the right time to move back into the sector and we have made our plans accordingly,' said York managing director David Steel.

'We have evaluated all the methods and materials in use in the UK and Europe.'

Source: The Northern Echo, 1 March 1994

1 Describe the stages of new product development which you think apply to York Trailers in this market.

2 Can a product such as a refrigerated semi-trailer be branded in the same way as a fast-moving consumer good? If so, how?

3 What is the likely product life cycle of an industrial good such as that illustrated in the article?

4 What aspects of the marketing environment will affect York Trailers as it launches the new semi-trailer?

A3

Firm launches new brand for choc lovers

A CONFECTIONERY firm is spending £1.5m to tempt the taste-buds of chocolate lovers with the launch of their latest product.

And they are hoping their Vice Versas will have the same soaraway success as brands like Kit Kat and Smarties – which have been selling in their millions for years.

York-based Rowntree Mackintosh – part of the Swiss Nestlé group – is initially launching the new sweets in the Tyne-Tees, Yorkshire and South-West TV regions.

And they claim that Vice Versas, the product of two years of secret research, will offer their customers a unique new taste.

They are made of white chocolate surrounded by a crisp brown sugar shell and milk chocolate in a crisp white sugar shell – hence the name.

Brand manager Dominic Box predicted: 'The white chocolate is the point of difference that will ensure the new brand's success.

'It has broad appeal and combines deliciously with milk chocolate to produce the ultimate product for chocolate lovers.'

He said they had identified the possibility for the brand some years ago and had spent the time refining it until they were sure they had just the right combination.

'Long-term we expect it to grow into a brand worth the equivalent of £20m a year in consumer value.'

Source: The Northern Echo

1 What do you think are the key characteristics of the new product which the company will focus on to create a lasting brand?

2 Why have Nestlé/Rowntree chosen a limited geographical launch initially? Can you suggest what may be the reasons for their selection of the three test market regions?

3 Do you think 'Vice Versas' is an effective brand name? Give your reasons.

4 The company has taken two years to reach the launch stage for this product. Describe the main aspects of research, market identification and refinement they might have undertaken to obtain 'just the right combination', and suggest the shape their product life-cycle curve might take in the long term.

A4

Brand new ideas to help adapt to a fast-changing marketplace

Andrew Beven

IT HAS become something of a cliché that the British are great at inventing things but leave the exploitation of ideas to foreign competitors.

The very opposite of the white-coated boffin beavering away in his backroom on some technological innovation, is the specialist new product development agency. These are hired by manufacturers or, increasingly, companies purveying financial or other services, to identify a 'consumer need' and devise a product to satisfy it.

This may involve creating a new brand, but the expense of that has made companies look more carefully at their existing brand properties.

Alternatives include seeking a complementary product area in which a successful brandname can be exploited, such as the recently launched Mars range of ice creams or Persil's move into dish-washing liquid. On the other hand, they can overhaul a brand that is ailing; Lucozade was taken out of the sickroom and repositioned as a drink for athletes, for example.

NPD's establishment as a separate industry dates from 1970 when two of its oldest players –

KAE Development and Craton Lodge and Knight – were founded. Pam Robertson, aged 48, has been involved since then, becoming chief executive of KAE before resigning over its 'relentless desire for expansion at all costs'. In 1989, she founded Redwood Associates, which has just seven employees, although freelance researchers and analysts are used on specific projects, 'which does limit growth because we can only sell our time'. She understands that companies like hers which typically employ only a handful of people are viewed as a cottage industry, but sees their importance as far greater than staff numbers suggest.

'Marketing managers are essentially juggling and reacting. It's hard for them to take a long view. Too often they think a brand that's big will always be big.' Manufacturers, she believes, can have too fixed an idea of their own strengths and weaknesses or will apologise for constraints such as under-used plant when these are really the starting point for a development strategy.

Source: The Guardian, 2 June 1992

1 What are the advantages to an organisation of hiring a specialist new product development agency?

2 List some of the disadvantages which might accrue.

3 What does Pam Robertson mean when she says that marketing managers are 'essentially juggling and reacting'?

4 The article describes how new products have been created out of complementary and repositioned brands. Why have Mars ice-creams, Persil washing-up liquid and new Lucozade been successful in the market-place? Think of other examples and consider whether they have worked or not.

A5

Unilever clears brand shelf

Andrew Lorenz

UNILEVER plans a worldwide cull of its lesser brands in a move that could shed one-fifth of its vast product portfolio. The Anglo-Dutch leviathan is streamlining to focus on its leading brands, including Persil, Wall's and Birds Eye, *writes Andrew Lorenz*.

Unilever's rationalisation drive – affecting some brands that it has owned for decades – is a landmark in the history of the consumer-products industry. The brand owners are facing an unprecedented combination of margin pressures, including low inflation and intense competition from both rival brands and big retailers' private labels.

Niall Fitzgerald, head of Unilever's detergents business and heir-apparent to Sir Michael Perry, chairman of Unilever's British side, told The Sunday Times the group would progressively shed between 10% and 20% of its products.

'We will look very aggressively at our brand tail,' Fitzgerald said. 'We don't make much money out of it and it complicates the whole business process: it slows down the speed at which we can bring anything to market.'

The products that go will be those without either a multinational presence or a strong local niche. 'We will make sure that we avoid the dead middle ground,' Fitzgerald said. 'The more we do that, the more we strengthen our key brands and the less vulnerable we are to a retailer because he does not have this tail to pick off piece by piece.'

Analysts say Unilever will either sell the lesser brands – estimated to represent between 5% and 10% of near-£25 billion annual sales – or let them fade away. One to go is John West, the canned food business, which is up for sale at £50m.

Michael Birkin, chief executive of the brand consultancy group Interbrand, said: 'There is a weeding-out process going on for weaker products.'

Unilever will next month start what will be Britain's biggest new grocery product campaign this year: the £25m marketing launch of a super-concentrated Persil range.

Source: The Sunday Times, 3 April 1994. Copyright © Times Newspapers Ltd. 1994

1 Why is Unilever planning to rationalise its product portfolio? Will it be the width or depth of its product mix which is more affected?

2 Discuss Unilever's product strategies using the Ansoff matrix and Boston box theoretical models.

3 Explain the company's strategy of shedding its 'brand tail'.

4 What do you consider to be the main features and characteristics of the household name brands mentioned in the article? Why do you think they have attracted strong brand loyalty during their life cycles?

ISSUES

NEW PRODUCT DEVELOPMENT

Only 2 per cent of a company's turnover, on average, is dedicated to new product development.

1 Argue the case for more organisational resources being devoted to the development of new products or services.

2 What type of products do you think benefit most from on-going research and development? Are there any product categories which do not require attention of this sort?

3 What part do you consider luck plays in the development and success of a new product or service?

BRANDING

Can a product really be ascribed a personality of its own?

1 Discuss the differences between a product and a brand, identifying and comparing the main characteristics of each.

2 What constitutes a successful brand? Select five well-known brands, indicating what qualities you associate with them and what factors have led to their success.

3 Draw up a list of products to which you are brand loyal. Analyse the reasons for this. What would induce you to move to a competitive brand?

PRODUCT LIFE CYCLES

The PLC curve is only a monitoring facility, not a strategic weapon.

1 Can you think of any situations in which following the product life cycle philosophy could be detrimental for a company?

2 Plot the likely PLC curve for a fad or fashion product, such as a skateboard, a soccer shirt or the Rubik's Cube, and a prestige good, such as a Porsche car, champagne or a Rolex watch.

3 Discuss what stages of the product life cycle have been reached by (*a*) satellite TV, (*b*) leaded petrol, (*c*) personal computers and (*d*) typewriters. What strategies might organisations pursue for each of these products?

OWN-LABEL BRANDS

Provide healthy market competition or no substitute for the real thing?

1 Discuss the advantages and disadvantages which might be experienced by organisations diversifying into own-label brands.

2 Why do many people view these brands as being inferior in quality to the established products?

3 Is the wider choice created for consumers by own-label brands always beneficial?

THE PRODUCT MIX

A broad portfolio of products is preferable to narrow concentration?

1 Compile and discuss the arguments for a company maintaining a wide range of products.

2 Compare the approach and relative success of (*a*) an organisation concentrating on depth in one product line with (*b*) a company focusing on product range width.

3 When should an organisation add depth to its product lines rather than width to its product range? Give examples.

PRODUCT STRATEGIES

Are models of product strategy reliable decision-making tools or merely methods of monitoring the progress of a brand?

1 Discuss the product and market circumstances in which an organisation would adopt each of the four Ansoff matrix strategies.

2 How do a typical company's profits change as a product moves through the stages of the Boston box?

3 Argue the case for and against test marketing in the launch of a new product.

QUESTIONS

1 Name three methods of undertaking research and development into new products.

2 What is the success rate for new products?

3 Name two ways in which the risk factor for new products is reduced.

4 List the main stages of new product development.

5 Name four sources of new product ideas.

6 Describe three methods used in the screening process.

7 What is test marketing?

8 Give four reasons for the resistance of re-sellers to stocking new products.

9 Give a definition of 'branding'.

10 Explain the term 'brand loyalty'.

11 List six characteristics of a brand.

12 List six characteristics of an effective brand name.

13 What is the difference between a brand name and a trademark?

14 What is 'corporate branding'? Give three examples of organisations practising it.

15 Give three examples of successfully branded products.

16 What are own-label brands? Give two examples.

17 List four benefits to a company of branding.

18 Describe the five stages of the product life-cycle.

19 Give an example of a product at each phase of the PLC.

20 List the main strategies available to a firm at each PLC stage.

21 Give four strategies a firm might adopt when faced with product decline.

22 List four of the stages of consumer acceptance of a new product, just launched.

23 What is 'planned obsolescence'?

24 Define the product mix, product line depth and range width.

25 Describe the Ansoff matrix and its four key 'situations'.

26 Give three advantages and three disadvantages of product range extension.

27 Describe the four stages of the market share, product/market growth matrix.

28 Give two reasons for an organisation using the Boston box.

PROJECTS

1 A product has been referred to as a 'psychological bundle of satisfactions'. Is this a good definition? Give your reasons, referring to the theory of branding.

2 A leading manufacturer of beauty products has stated that 'in the factory we sell cosmetics, in the store we sell hope.' How can an organisation convert its product offering from a physical good to a desirable, intangible image?

3 Consider the practical implications of product life cycle analysis for an organisation with which you are familiar. Do any items in the portfolio owe more to the past than the future, and do any cash cows or dogs offer potential for rejuvenation? Which Ansoff matrix strategy is likely to be adopted and why?

4 Selecting an organisation, consider whether it caters for all its new product development needs and if so, how? In what circumstances might it use an external specialist to do the job and how might one be appointed?

5 Many products fail, some of them spectacularly. Choose an example, such as the Sinclair C5, and account for its lack of success with reference to the stages of new product development.

6 How might a small organisation, lacking the resources of larger companies, set about developing a favourable brand identity for itself and/or its products?

GLOSSARY

Ansoff matrix a method of monitoring an organisation's growth opportunities, devised by Igor Ansoff, which identifies four possible strategies based on market and product analysis.

Assortment an organisation's mix of offerings measured in terms of product range width and line depth.

Boston box a product portfolio matrix developed by the Boston Consulting Group that enables an organisation to classify its products and services into four main segments, based on market share and market growth relative to the competition.

Brand a product containing individual characteristics which are designed to appeal to consumers, differentiate it from competitors and establish it in the market-place.

Brand awareness or recognition a measure of the consumer's knowledge of a product and ability to identify it, as a preliminary stage before purchase.

Brand extension a new or modified product launched under an already established brand name.

Brand identity or image the collection of beliefs, viewpoints and evaluations consumers hold about a product which contribute to its perceived position in the market.

Branding attributing specific characteristics to a product so that consumers can readily identify with and therefore purchase it.

Brand insistence where a consumer will not accept alternatives and will search extensively for a particular product.

Brand leader a product with the greatest share of the market.

Brand loyalty regular consumer support, often subjective or subconscious, for a particular product in preference to rival brands.

Brand manager person assigned to manage a specific product or brand.

Brand mark part of the brand, such as a symbol, design, colour or lettering, which can be identified but not uttered.

Brand name distinctive, utterable name by which a product or a range of products is identified.

Brand preference where the customer will select one specific product in preference to any rivals.

Brand rejection situation in which customers will not buy a product unless its image is changed.

Brand switching where consumers change preference and buy an alternative branded product or service, which offers a greater perceived benefit or benefits than the previous purchase.

Built-in obsolescence see 'planned obsolescence'.

Business analysis detailed screening and evaluation of a new product idea.

Cash cows mature products generating cash but requiring little financial support, low in growth and with a high market share.

Coarse screening an initial rough check, at an early stage, on the viability of a new product idea.

Commercialisation new product development phase where the decision has been made to go ahead and launch onto the market.

Concept testing checking the possible acceptability of a new product idea before manufacture.

Corporate branding developing recognisable characteristics and a positive identity for an organisation rather than any of its products or services.

Dealer brands brands created, manufactured and marketed by distributors or intermediaries.

Decline stage of the product life cycle during which a product's sales and market share decline.

Deletion elimination of a product that no longer appeals to the market or contributes to the profitability of an organisation.

Diffusion process associated with the market acceptance of new products or innovations.

Diversification strategy new to an organisation involving the introduction of new products or services into new markets.

Dogs declining products with low growth, low market share, poor prospects and a high likelihood of deletion.

Dual branding where an organisation adopts two branding positions for one basic product or service.

Evoked set small group of brands considered by the buyer as potential purchases.

Fads fashion products with abbreviated life cycles, such as some types of clothes or popular music.

Family brands a brand name that is used by an organisation for several products.

Fashions accepted or popular style products often with a limited life cycle.

Flanker brands new products introduced into markets in which the organisation is already established in order to increase overall market share.

Flagship brand the main branded product upon which an organisation depends or for which it is most well known.

Generic brand original or established brand name which indicates the product category rather than its identifying features or company name.

Growth product life cycle stage in which sales rise rapidly and profits increase.

Idea generation the search by organisations for new concepts, images, designs or products to help them achieve their objectives.

Individual branding branding policy in which each product is named differently.

Introduction early stage of the product life cycle in which a product has just been launched and is still to be accepted by consumers, thus it is not yet earning profits.

Line extension new product that is closely related to other products in the firm's existing product line.

Manufacturers' brands brands created, produced and marketed by their manufacturers.

Market development growth strategy which concentrates on finding new markets for existing products.

Market leader organisation or brand with the largest market share.

Market penetration a strategy for obtaining growth by increasing market share with the same product and target market.

Market share/market growth matrix see 'Boston box'.

Maturity stage of the life cycle at which a product has 'peaked' in terms of sales and growth, but is still earning profits.

Multi-brand strategy where an organisation has several brands within the same product category.

Multi-product brand the use of the same brand name for several product categories.

New product a product that is new in any way for the organisation concerned and its customers.

New product development the introduction of original or innovatory products, product improvements or modifications and new brands, through an organisation's research and development efforts.

Operating plans strategy adopted by an organisation where existing products are offered to existing markets in order to increase market share.

Own-label or private label brands brands owned and controlled by the retailer to compete with manufacturers' brands and often very similar to them.

Pilot launch a trial run to investigate problems before a national launch; an important part of test marketing.

Planned obsolescence (or built-in obsolescence) where products are not built to last a lifetime but to wear out in a relatively short time so a strong replacement demand exists. Usually involves frequent product re-styling to encourage consumers to 'move with the times' and buy the latest version of the product as it becomes available.

Private brand brand created and owned by a wholesaler, retailer or other re-seller of the product or service.

Problem children or question marks products in their introductory phase, using up resources but not yet profitable and with an uncertain future.

Product branding see 'Branding'.

Product deletion see 'Deletion'.

Product depth the average number of different products in the product mix offered to buyers in an organisation's product line.

Product development growth strategy based on the introduction of new products into existing or established markets.

Product launch stage of product development where a new or established product is first made available to the market.

Product life cycle the stages a new product idea goes through from launch to eventual withdrawal.

Product line a set of individual products that are closely related and marketed by the same organisation.

Product management, or brand management where the marketing function is centred around individual products, brands or product portfolios.

Product mix assortment of product line depth, range width and individual offerings that an organisation makes available to the consumer.

Product obsolescence where a product becomes out of date and is withdrawn.

Product portfolio approach which manages the product mix so as to balance short-term gains with long-term profitability, aided by the use of theoretical models such as the Boston box and Ansoff matrix.

Product portfolio analysis where an organisation concentrates on a product's market growth rate and relative market share in order to determine marketing strategy.

Product strategy marketing activities involved in developing the right product or service for the organisation's target customers, including elements of the total product concept, product life-cycles, portfolio analysis and new product development.

Product width the number of product lines an organisation offers as part of its product mix.

Pseudo brands 'copy cat' products which mimic established brands, e.g. retailers' own labels, Virgin Cola, etc.

Question-marks see 'Problem children'.

Repeat purchases products bought again by consumers after the initial purchase.

Saturation stage of the product life cycle where a product's sales and profitability have slowed to zero, before declining.

Screening process whereby new or modified products are evaluated on many criteria as to their potential for success.

Simultaneous product development new product development approach where company departments work together to speed up the process and increase effectiveness.

Stars successful, high market share products requiring heavy investment to finance their rapid growth.

Synergy where the combined effect of two or more courses of action is greater than the sum of the individual parts, as in the overall effectiveness achieved through the co-ordinated operation of the many elements of the marketing mix.

Trademark brand that has been given legally protected status exclusive to the organisation which owns it.

Umbrella branding where an organisation markets a number of products under one collective or corporate brand name, often that of the company.

SUGGESTED REFERENCES

VIDEO MATERIAL

The Marketing Mix, No. 9, 'What is a Brand?', Yorkshire Television, 1986.

Casebook Scotland – developing new products, BBC Scotland, 1986.

Business Matters, 'Sloan's Rangers', BBC, 1988.

Contemporary Marketing, Video Cases, No. 9 (Robert Mondavi), Boone, L. and Kurtz, D., Dryden Press, 1989.

Equinox, 'A brush with the Greens', Channel 4, 1990.

Product development and consumer design – vacuum cleaners and CDs, Open University, BBC, 1991.

France Means Business, 'Birth of a Yoghurt', BBC, 1993.

Q.E.D., 'Craig's Boot', BBC, 1994.

RADIO MATERIAL

Sell, sell, sell, 'Research and Development', BBC Radio Leeds, 1984.

MAGAZINE ARTICLES

Journal of Marketing Management, Vol. 1, No. 1, Summer 1985, p.27, 'New product development – proactive or reactive?'.

Journal of Marketing Management, Vol. 1, No. 2, Winter 1985, p.213, 'Market development in practice: a case-study of user-initiated product innovation'.

Journal of Marketing Management, Vol. 1, No. 3, Spring 1986, p.291, 'Substance v. trappings in new product management'.

Journal of Marketing Management, Vol. 2, No. 1, Summer 1986, p.73, 'New product adoption by pharmacists'.

Journal of Marketing Management, Vol. 3, No. 3, Spring 1988, Special Issue, 'Marketing and Innovation: research and practice'.

Journal of Marketing Management, Vol. 8, No. 2, April 1992, p.127, 'The sourcing of retailer brand food production by a UK retailer'.

Journal of Marketing Management, Vol. 8, No. 4, Oct. 1992, p.351, 'The importance of customer satisfaction in explaining brand and dealer loyalty'.

Journal of Marketing Management, Vol. 9, No. 1, Jan. 1993, p.23, 'Dimensions of success in New Product Development: an exploratory investigation' .

Journal of Marketing Management, Vol. 9, No. 2, April 1993, p.173, 'Categorising brands: evolutionary processes underpinned by two key dimensions'.

Journal of Marketing Management, Vol. 9, No. 4, Oct.

1993, p.405, 'Does head office involvement matter in product development?'.

Marketing Business, June 1989, p.20, 'Product life cycle – need for re-definition and re-launch'.

Marketing Business, April 1990, p.14, 'Putting a brand on British Airways'; and p.23, 'Brand management – culture, values and change'.

Marketing Business, Aug. 1990, p.12, 'Burmese ways after the oil rush'.

Marketing Business, July/Aug. 1991, p.24, 'Making your mark'.

Marketing Business, Sept. 1992, p.28, 'Science of marketing'.

Marketing Business, Feb. 1993, p.18, 'Science of marketing'.

Marketing Business, April 1993, p.15, 'Born again brands'.

Marketing Business, May 1993, p.30, 'Science of marketing'.

Marketing Business, June 1993, p.48, 'Briefly'.

Marketing Business, Oct. 1993, p.36, 'Brands across the border'.

Marketing Business, April 1994, p.41, 'Launching pad'.

Quarterly Review of Marketing, Vol. 11, No. 1, Autumn 1985, p.1, 'The marketing practice of innovation theory'; and p.7, 'Integrating marketing variables in the early stages of the new product process'.

Quarterly Review of Marketing, Vol. 11, No. 4, Summer 1986, p.13, 'The diffusion of innovations and their attributes: a critical review'; and p.7, 'Own labels: problem child or infant prodigy?'.

Quarterly Review of Marketing, Vol. 13, No. 3, Spring 1988, p.18, 'Is there a need for the Product Manager?'.

Quarterly Review of Marketing, Vol. 13, No. 4, Summer 1988, p.1, 'Clarifying the difference between Manufacturers' Brands and Distributors' Brands'.

Quarterly Review of Marketing, Vol. 14, No. 3, Spring 1989, p.10, 'New product development – a literature review'.

FURTHER READING

Adcock, D., Bradford, R., Halborg, A. and Ross, C., *Marketing Principles and Practice* (2nd edn), Pitman, 1995, chs 11 and 20.

Baker, M. (Ed.), *The Marketing Book*, Heinemann/C.I.M, 1990, ch. 13.

Boone, L. and Kurtz, D., *Contemporary Marketing*, Dryden, 1989, ch. 9.

Cannon, Tom, *Basic Marketing*, Holt Business Texts, 1980, ch. 12.

Dibb, S., Simkin, L., Pride, W. and Ferrell, O., *Marketing*, Houghton Mifflin, 1994, chs 7, 8 and 9.

Fletcher, Winston, *A Glittering Haze*, N.T.C. Publications, 1992.

Giles, G., *Marketing*, MacDonald and Evans, 1985, ch. 4.

Kotler, P. and Armstrong, G., *Marketing*, Prentice Hall, 1993, chs 8 and 9.

McCarthy, J. and Perreault, W., *Basic Marketing*, Irwin, 1987, chs 9 and 10.

Mercer, D., *Marketing*, Blackwell, 1992, chs 7 and 8.

Acknowledgements

The Guardian.
The Northern Echo.
The Sunday Times.

8

SERVICE MARKETING

DEFINITIONS

Services are activities, benefits or satisfactions which are offered for sale or are provided in connection with the sale of goods.

AMERICAN MARKETING ASSOCIATION

The pivotal difference between goods businesses and services is that goods businesses sell things and service businesses sell performance.

(LEONARD BERRY, 'BIG IDEAS IN SERVICE MARKETING',
JOURNAL OF SERVICES MARKETING, VOL. 1, SUMMER 1987)

INTRODUCTION

The general concept of marketing revolves around tangible products, such as fast-moving consumer goods. But marketing underpins many sectors of business and increasingly includes non-profit and voluntary organisations, activities such as pressure groups, public facilities and politics, and even more abstract concepts such as people, places and ideas. The biggest business growth area in recent times has been the service sector, which covers a wide range of public and private activities. All of these aspects of life encompass many different types of 'product'.

By its very nature, a service tends to focus on the customer and is thus inextricably intertwined with the philosophy of marketing. But to understand fully the often subtle differences between product and service marketing it is necessary first to appreciate the scope and nature of the service sector, and the characteristics possessed by services, then to analyse the unique marketing mix applying to them and how it can best be managed to ensure a profitable outcome for both the organisation and its customers (see Figure 8.1).

Components of service marketing

SERVICE MARKETING

↓

The service sector

↓

Characteristics of services

↓

The service mix

↓

Management of services

Fig 8.1

KEY CONCEPTS

THE SERVICE SECTOR

In all European Union countries service activities easily outstrip the commercial, industrial and agricultural sectors as the leading employer and income generator. The service sector covers a wide range of employment activities, including the following:

- *Financial services* – banks, building societies, accountants, stockbrokers, insurance agents, actuaries.
- *Professional services* – estate agents, architects, designers, solicitors, lawyers, consultants, surveyors, valuers, management, personnel.
- *Marketing services* – advertising agencies, marketing research, public relations, sales agents.
- *Catering* – hotels, hospitality, restaurants, fast food and take-aways.
- *Leisure and recreation* – sports clubs, theme parks, zoos and wildlife parks, national parks and National Trust properties, tourism organisations, amusement centres, libraries, museums, the arts, cinemas, theatres, musical entertainment.
- *Other services* – painting and decorating, cleaning, repairs, health and social services, education and training, travel and transport, postal services, police, public utilities, telecommunications, hairdressing.

Of course the sector also encompasses the full range of services a customer expects from an organisation before, during and after a commercial or industrial sales transaction.

All these activities can be further understood by placing them in distinctive categories, each exhibiting different characteristics and thus requiring a separate marketing approach. For example, services could be classified according to:

- Type of market, such as consumer (legal advice and repairs) or industrial (consulting and installation services).
- Degree of labour intensiveness, whether labour based (education and hairdressing) or equipment based (telecommunications and public utilities).
- Level of customer contact, ranging from high (as in restaurants and air travel) to low (postal services and estate agents).

- Skill of the service provider, which could be mainly professional (lawyers and teachers) or non-professional (cleaners and public transport).
- Goal of the service provider, at one end of the scale profit based (banking and hotels) and at the other end non-profit orientated (police and some leisure/recreation services).

The rapid increase in importance of all the activities mentioned and many other service businesses, and their need to adopt a marketing approach, is due to a variety of reasons, such as:

- general economic prosperity and growth in various markets;
- lifestyle changes, e.g. use of technology, women in the workforce, popularity of fitness and leisure, need for wider experiences and avoidance of specialist tasks such as cleaning, financial management and meal preparation;
- extended leisure time, leading to greater service opportunities and elimination of seasons;
- move to the private sector, for example education, health and transport;
- demographic movements, such as a decrease in employment, early retirement and an increasingly older population;
- increase in ownership of goods, leading to an increase in the repair services and maintenance sectors;
- increase in consumer and business competition, leading to an increase in demand for personnel and consultancy services, leasing and caretaking, marketing and advertising, and so on;
- diversification into the services sector by retailers, for instance in the areas of optical, travel and tourism, and financial services;
- other factors, such as the increase in commercial and industrial services as a result of pressures for quality standards.

In order to sustain the rapid growth rate in the services sector it has become vital for the concept and tools of marketing to be applied and managed effectively. This can only happen if the organisation understands the nature and characteristics of those services it is offering to consumers.

CHARACTERISTICS OF SERVICES

Unlike products, services are essentially people based and thus dependent on factors such as quality of customer care, recruitment, training, motivation, management and control processes. They are usually supplied by third parties and consumed away from home, while customers tend to be very sensitive to images of the service and its supplier. Again, the customer's perception of a service is often affected by the particular context of its consumption. For example, if you are choosing a holiday you will have expectations of the type of people you will meet, the climate, the surroundings and the general ambience. Clearly, services are characterised by many factors that distinguish them from products and influence the ways in which they are marketed. For clarity, these characteristics are generally grouped into five main areas, as illustrated in Table 8.1.

These key characteristics possessed by services imply many potential problems for marketers. The element of intangibility, for example, means that services tend to be hard to grasp mentally and the customer thus becomes sensitive instead to images perceived of the product and the supplier. This makes accurate research and effective branding and promotion more difficult to attain.

The inseparability factor also places pressures on the producer to be present at the 'sale' of the product, and the scale of its operations is thus more limited. Dental services offer a good example

Table 8.1 Main characteristics of services

Characteristics	Distinguishing features
Intangibility	Cannot be tested, seen, heard, touched or smelled before purchase. Judgement therefore based on opinion, attitude, feeling, perception and experience, e.g. education provision.
Inseparability	Production and consumption are inseparable, creation/performance/consumption are often identical and distribution roles integrated. The product cannot usually exist without the customer, e.g. restaurant service.
Heterogeneity	Standardisation of output is generally difficult, units differ in price, quality and conformity, and judgement is difficult in advance of purchase, e.g. tourism products.
Perishability	Services are perishable and cannot be stored, while short capacity is lost forever with fluctuations in demand, e.g. in transport and travel.
Ownership	Customers only have access to, or use of, a service, rather than ownership. There are thus no ownership transfers, patents or inventories and payment is for hire or temporary use, e.g. leisure facilities.

Source: Adapted from Cowell, Donald, *The Marketing of Services*, Butterworth-Heinemann, 1991

of this, although energy provision by its nature does not contain this requirement.

Under the heterogeneity heading the standard of a service depends on who provides it and when it is provided. This will vary enormously for any one service, thus making it very difficult to assure quality and consistency throughout, so this characteristic is often known as 'variability'.

The perishability and ownership aspects also place obvious pressures and limitations on services. We will look at some of the possible marketing solutions to all these problems later in this chapter.

While all service organisations generally exhibit most of these common characteristics they do so in differing degrees and combinations, depending on the exact nature of the service product offered, and this has to be taken carefully into account in any marketing decision making. For example, although both are services, education provision embodies certain different characteristics from a fast food take-away. These differences can be clearly seen by using the intangibility variable to construct a continuum of goods and services (see Figure 8.2).

The measurement of degrees of tangibility helps to position a product or service accurately and determine the appropriate marketing approach to be taken. Physical goods tend to be tangible in nature, whereas services are predominantly intangible, although there are many shades of emphasis in between. Fast food outlets, for instance, are a mixture of goods and services and therefore contain both tangible and intangible elements. Again, some services incorporate products as an integral part of their total offering to consumers, such as sports centre exercise equipment, videos in hotels and educational textbooks.

THE SERVICE MIX

Because the nature and characteristics of services differ so much from those of products, it will be apparent that the normal marketing mix for products, described in Chapter 1, needs to be revised and extended for services to encompass their wider emphases.

The Four Ps will still apply in varying degrees to services, particularly those with a strong prod-

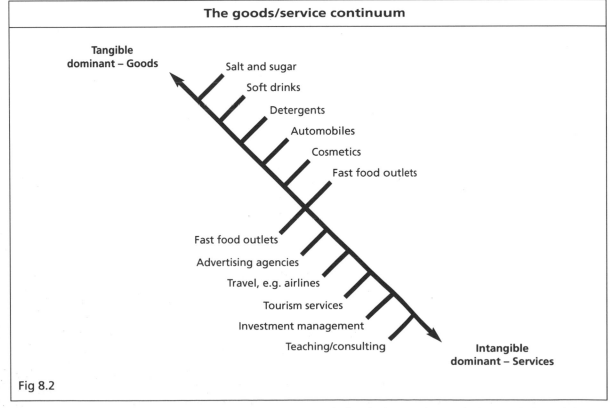

The goods/service continuum

Tangible dominant – Goods

Salt and sugar
Soft drinks
Detergents
Automobiles
Cosmetics
Fast food outlets

Fast food outlets
Advertising agencies
Travel, e.g. airlines
Tourism services
Investment management
Teaching/consulting

Intangible dominant – Services

Fig 8.2

Source: Shostack, G. Lynn, 'Breaking free from product marketing', *Journal of Marketing,* American Marketing Association, Vol. 41, No. 2, April 1977

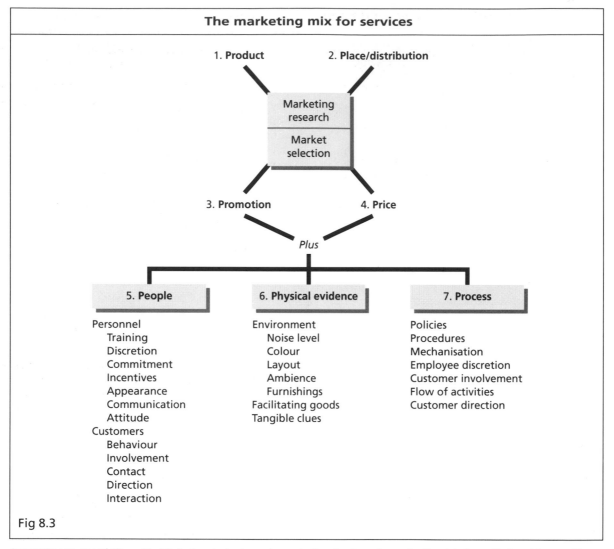

The marketing mix for services

1. **Product**   2. **Place/distribution**

Marketing research

Market selection

3. **Promotion**   4. **Price**

Plus

5. **People**	6. **Physical evidence**	7. **Process**
Personnel	Environment	Policies
Training	Noise level	Procedures
Discretion	Colour	Mechanisation
Commitment	Layout	Employee discretion
Incentives	Ambience	Customer involvement
Appearance	Furnishings	Flow of activities
Communication	Facilitating goods	Customer direction
Attitude	Tangible clues	
Customers		
Behaviour		
Involvement		
Contact		
Direction		
Interaction		

Fig 8.3

Source: Booms, B. and Bitner, M., 'Marketing strategies and organisation structures for service firms', in Donnelly, J. and George, W. (Eds), *Marketing of Services,* American Marketing Association, 1981

uct element. However, three extra Ps are often added to the marketing mix for services to enable marketers to cater for the more abstract and communication-based nature of the service sector (see Figure 8.3).

An analysis of all the factors incorporated in the three additional Ps, together with the standard Four Ps, will provide a far more accurate picture of a service and enable a more appropriate marketing mix to be selected and implemented as part of an overall marketing strategy.

The kind of analysis necessary can be illustrated for restaurant service. While the food itself is obviously an important component of the total product offering, an examination of the more abstract dimensions of the meal experience will be essential for the most appropriate marketing mix to be devised. Some of the potentially important features are listed in Table 8.2.

An audit of consumer satisfaction and dissatisfaction measured over key variable aspects of the meal experience will provide a check-list of viewpoints which can be used as a basis for marketing planning.

Similarly, detailed analysis of the service on offer and its main characteristics should provide clues as to where the marketing emphasis could lie. For example, an organisation might select the

Table 8.2 Dimensions of the customer meal experience

Aspect	Examples of consumer satisfaction	Examples of consumer dissatisfaction
Physiological	Correctly prepared steaks Comfortable seats	Overcooked food Static from nylon carpet
Social	Enjoyable company Helpful table service	Rowdy customers Waiter language difficulties
Psychological	Secure, intimate environment Enhanced self-esteem	Understanding French menu or wine list Smoky atmosphere
Economic	Good value food Restaurant accessibility	Unacceptable credit card High-priced entrées

Source: Adapted from Buttle, Francis, 'Unserviceable concepts in service marketing', *Quarterly Review of Marketing*, Vol. 11, No. 3, Spring 1986, p. 8

people element of the service mix as its key variable and try to examine the exact role it plays in the final product offering and whether this role can be improved in any way (see Figure 8.4).

By locating its personnel on a grid of contact and visibility, an organisation is more able to assess whether a marketing strategy based on more or less contact with clients and more or less visibility to clients is the best way to proceed for the eventual success of the service.

Role of people in the service marketing mix

Contact Visibility	Contact with client	Non-contact with client
Visible to client	Waitress Service engineer	Cook in steak house Computer operator
Non-visible to client	Telephone operator Airline	Maintenance worker Accountant

Fig 8.4

Source: Cowell, Donald, *The Marketing of Services*, Butterworth-Heinemann, 1991

MANAGEMENT OF SERVICES

Decisions on how best to manage the marketing of services are fraught with difficulties because of the special characteristics of services, their unpredictable nature and the problems associated with them, as already described.

However, certain strategies can still be pursued by organisations in an attempt to overcome these inherent problems. Some of the potential solutions for each main service characteristic are outlined in Table 8.3.

One strategic issue which needs to be resolved concerns positioning. Whereas physical goods such as automobiles are tangible dominant and thus tend to emphasise abstract aspects such as image, services often exhibit the opposite tendency. So an airline, top-heavy in intangible elements, will tend to focus on the more tangible, physical evidence as a way of balancing its marketing mix.

Table 8.3 Marketing solutions to service constraints

Service characteristics	Possible marketing solutions
Intangibility	Increase tangibility and physical representation. Focus on benefits/reputations/brand names/personalities, to pinpoint the 'product'. Use physical evidence where available. Develop internal/external research programme.
Inseparability	Emphasise service aspects. Re-organise work schedules. Train service providers.
Heterogeneity	Careful personnel selection and training. Monitoring of standards/quality control. Pre-packaging of services. Emphasise tailor-made features and units.
Perishability	Better match between supply and demand. Short-term, tactical policies – e.g. off-peak price reductions, promotional campaigns, etc.
Ownership	Stress advantages of non-ownership, e.g. easier payment systems, less risk, spontaneity and surprise.

Source: Cowell, Donald, *The Marketing of Services*, Butterworth-Heinemann, 1991

Examining the wider range of service industries, many technical and strategic possibilities exist for satisfying the perceived outcomes sought by consumers. Table 8.4 outlines some of these solutions for selected services.

Development of new services can be monitored through theoretical devices such as the product life cycle curve. These new services usually arise from a need to counter obsolescence or meet the competition, to fill spare capacity or even out seasonal fluctuations, to reduce the risk resulting from a narrow service portfolio, or to exploit opportunities arising from the need for improved performance or economics.

But ideally several pre-conditions should exist when new services are being introduced and an overall service marketing strategy is being developed. These pre-conditions (adapted from Dibb, Simkin, Pride and Ferrell) include:

● marketing occurring at all levels, from the marketing department to the point where the service is provided;
● flexibility allowed in providing the service, particularly when direct interaction with the customer is involved;
● successful service organisations differentiated by high-quality personnel;

Table 8.4 Service marketing strategies

Service industry	Outcome sought by buyer	Technical possibilities	Strategic possibilities
Higher education	Educational attainment	Tutoring Staff development	Higher entrance demands Pre-entry courses
Hospitals	Health	Instruct patients to manage problems and prevent others	Market preventive medicine services, e.g. stress reduction/weight loss
Banks	Prosperity	Money management courses Small business management assistance	Market financial expertise by industrial specialisation
Plumbing repairs	Free-flowing pipes	Provide consumers with instructions and supplies to prevent further blockages	Diversify, e.g. home water-purification systems

Source: Adapted from Gelb, Betsy, 'How marketers of intangibles can raise the odds for consumer satisfaction', *Journal of Service Marketing*, Summer 1987. Reproduced with the permission of MCB University Press Ltd.

- marketing to existing customers to increase their use of the service or create loyalty to the service provider;
- problems quickly resolved in providing the service, to maintain an organisation's reputation for quality;
- high technology used to provide improved services at a lower cost;
- continual evaluation to customise service to each consumer's unique needs and wants;
- service branded to distinguish from the competition;
- recognition of the importance of the time dimension for services, e.g. the creation of pleasure is usually for a particular time span and not continuous;
- company-wide acceptance and application of the key determinants of service quality, i.e. factors such as access, communication, competence, courtesy, credibility, reliability, responsiveness, security and understanding.

In an attempt to incorporate all the elements of service marketing into one central framework similar to the total product concept, David Ballantyne has proposed a total systems view of the management of services, as illustrated in Figure 8.5.

In this model, all the elements are inter-related and any action or development with one is likely to influence the actions or developments in another. So the marketing of services is thus perceived as being organic rather than mechanistic, emphasising service quality and the 'on-going sale'

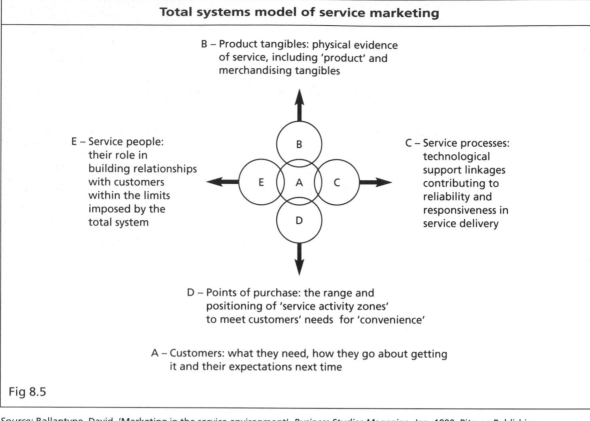

Total systems model of service marketing

B – Product tangibles: physical evidence of service, including 'product' and merchandising tangibles

E – Service people: their role in building relationships with customers within the limits imposed by the total system

C – Service processes: technological support linkages contributing to reliability and responsiveness in service delivery

D – Points of purchase: the range and positioning of 'service activity zones' to meet customers' needs for 'convenience'

A – Customers: what they need, how they go about getting it and their expectations next time

Fig 8.5

Source: Ballantyne, David, 'Marketing in the service environment', *Business Studies Magazine,* Jan. 1990, Pitman Publishing

and envisaged as a continuous time-based process.

This type of approach reinforces the intrinsic differences between physical goods and intangible services, whilst emphasising the essential requirement for organisations to understand their service offerings, create successful marketing strategies for their customers, and establish the appropriate internal and external relationships for these processes to take place.

ARTICLES

A1

Co-op opens video bank

THE Co-operative Bank yesterday stole a march on its larger high street rivals with the official launch of a revolutionary unmanned branch linked to a cashier by video phone.

Its Bankpoint kiosk is the ninth self-service centre opened in recent months, but the first to offer face-to-face contact with a member of staff.

Like its predecessors, the latest octagonal Bankpoint – measuring just 120 square feet – can be used by customers of more than 40 other banks and building societies at no extra charge.

The Co-operative Bank hopes that by offering the cash and deposit service 24 hours a day, seven days a week, it might tempt users from other institutions to switch their accounts.

Source: The Northern Echo

1 How important do you consider 'face-to-face contact' to be in the marketing of financial services?

2 Make a list of the tangible and intangible products the Co-operative Bank offers to its customers.

3 Which do you think are the most important elements of the marketing mix for banking organisations such as the Co-op?

4 Do you feel that the new Bankpoint kiosk constitutes a unique selling proposition for the Co-operative Bank?

A2

Well done, Middlesbrough

FOOTBALL clubs generally are not renowned for the tremendous service they provide their fans, on or off the pitch. Sub-standard catering, uncomfortable surroundings and toilet facilities straight out of the Hammer House of Horrors.

There are signs, however, that things are changing. Sunderland FC is known as the caring club and has made great efforts to give supporters a decent deal in recent years.

And now there is a major national award for Middlesbrough FC for the standard of care and facilities they provide for their disabled followers.

We congratulate the Boro staff on their award; it is well deserved for the efforts they have made in recent years. Now, perhaps, other clubs will follow their lead.

Source: The Northern Echo

1 Describe the marketing approach adopted by a football club or other service organisation of your choice. Suggest an appropriate service mix it could utilise.

2 What services do Middlesbrough and Sunderland Football Clubs offer to their customers? What else should they provide?

3 What are the main differences, if any, between leisure services (as mentioned in the article) and commercial services such as, for example, hairdressing or insurance? Will these differences affect the marketing emphasis selected by the organisation?

4 What aspects of the marketing environment will affect Middlesbrough and Sunderland Football Clubs and how can they best deal with them?

A3

School's classic bid for pupils

A NORTH YORKSHIRE school has started a national radio advertising campaign to boost applications for places.

Queen Ethelburga's College has taken to the national airwaves – probably the first school ever to make such a move.

After a survey showed 31 per cent of parents of children at independent schools listen to Classic FM, the image-makers felt they had found the medium they wanted.

In the advert, one of the school's 300 children, the bursar's 12-year-old daughter, has thirty seconds to sell the school to the nation.

She says: 'Its warm, comfortable and the food is good.'

The response to the advert, broadcast 26 times last week, has been 'far higher than we could have imagined,' Governors' chairman Brian Martin said today.

'Well in excess of 100 people have contacted us,' he said, 'And a boarding taster planned for next weekend is so over-subscribed that we have had to turn people away and look to organising another one.'

Out of those who visit the 82-year-old boarding school, about 95 per cent finally send their child there.

Now they want to spread their net as far and wide as possible.

Queen Ethelburga's recently moved from Harrogate to Thorpe Underwood Hall and has spent some £6 million on new buildings and technical facilities, including more than £2 million on boarding.

With boarding numbers falling sharply, the school has bucked the national trend and doubled its figures in three years, largely due to the move.

But more pupils are needed, and they are looking to double those figures again.

Source: The Yorkshire Evening Press, 1 March 1994

1 What do you think are the main elements of the educational product?

2 Who are the customers of a school such as Queen Ethelburga's College? Describe the range of services offered to them.

3 Why should the school have chosen a national radio advertising campaign to promote themselves and their services? What were the possible alternatives?

4 Suggest an appropriate service marketing mix for Queen Ethelburga's College and give reasons for your choice.

A4

Hotel guests on a winner should the world end

IT WAS inevitable that the year, in the world of hotels, should end with a gimmick.

The St George's Hotel at Harrogate, North Yorkshire, decided to slash its prices between Boxing Day and today to mark the declaration by 16th century Yorkshire prophetess Mother Shipton that the world would end in 1991.

End of the World cocktails have been on offer but the biggest enticement has been that guests won't have to pay if old Ma Shipton proves right.

The offer is an example of the growing number of gimmicks used by hotels to weather the recession.

At the Redworth Hall Hotel, near Shildon in County Durham, manager Brian Philpotts has devised a bewildering variety of events to tempt punters to the country house hotel.

These have varied from a weekend for shaving enthusiasts to a money back insurance policy for any guests who may be disturbed by ghosts in the allegedly haunted hotel. Strange groans and bumps in the night all count.

Mr Philpotts also dreamed up a Telly Break weekend, where guests who stayed two days without watching any television were given a television to smash up as a reward.

But such a curious marketing strategy is not as weird as it may seem.

Tim Rodgers, who has the task of attracting tourists to Cleveland said: 'The county council works with the hotels when they are promoting an area but some of them are just done for publicity.'

Cleveland is keen for hotels to develop the industrial heritage theme of the area, said Mr Rodgers.

'There's the Captain Cook theme in the Whitby area but we want to develop something people will identify with Teesside,' he said.

In the New Year, Cleveland's tourism department is co-operating with the Parkmore Hotel, Eaglescliffe, to give guests an environmentally friendly stay.

Organic wine and food will be part of the deal with 'green' soap, toilet paper and shampoo supplied to each room.

However, while such breaks are all the rage it does not follow that the more outrageous ideas get the biggest response.

The Esplanade Hotel in Scarborough had to cancel a Life Drawing weekend complete with nude model because there were no takers.

Jacqui Maloney, deputy manager of the St Nicholas Hotel, Scarborough, has devised a £125-a-head weekend where guests take part in a music hall variety performance. Scripts and costumes are provided – all the visitors have to do is make fools of themselves.

These quirks and gimmicks are not unique to the North-East. In Bristol, a hotel invites business colleagues to fight each other, with boxing and wrestling bouts provided.

Getting away from it all no longer seems to have the power to keep hotel rooms full out of season.

At the Three Tuns Hotel, in Durham City, guests can share their bed with a skeleton as part of the hotel's Horror Holiday. The appropriately named manager Andrew Gore also provides books on torture at each bedside.

Seasonal offerings vary from shopping breaks to Black Christmas at the Swallow Chase Hotel, in York.

Guests who hate Christmas can enjoy a solitary cold, Christmas dinner while sipping Ebenezer cocktails. For their £50 staff shout 'Bah, humbug' at them – and there is no electricity in the rooms.

Meanwhile, at St George's Hotel, the hours are ticking away ...

Source: The Northern Echo

1 Do you agree that the 'quirks and gimmicks' described in the article represent a 'curious marketing strategy'?

2 How much of the hotel business is a tangible product and how much is an intangible service?

3 Suggest other themes which could be used as the basis of a promotion for a hotel holiday break.

4 As a holidaymaker, what do you expect from hotel and other tourism services?

A5

ON THE MOVE

Buying a house is the biggest purchase most people will ever make, but if it all goes wrong in the first year you can't tear round to the seller's new address and demand your money back.

Even with a full survey – and only 2-3pc opt for one – there isn't a guarantee that the central heating will keep you cosy through the winter.

Or that the water will flow freely every time you turn on your taps. Or that the tumble drier you take on from the last occupant won't grumble to a halt the day after you arrive.

In America they don't grin and bear this kind of thing. Since the 1970s estate agents there have operated a scheme whereby sellers pay to insure the heating and plumbing for a year after the sale.

This year the home warranty scheme came to Britain. Michael Jones, Lloyds broker and now director of the Home Guarantee Corporation, had been waiting for 12 years for the right time to start it. The right time, he said, had to be when the market was 'pretty duff'. In 1988 nobody was looking for extra reassurance.

His organisation's Home Warranty scheme began in February and is now selling at a rate of eight to ten a day. He plans to target the North-East early next year.

For a fee of £300 the seller can cover all the working parts of his or her house for six months before the sale and a year after it is sold.

It means buyers can move in, confident that if the plumbing seizes up or the wiring fizzles out they will not have to meet the bill for repairs.

The warranty covers plumbing, central heating, electric wiring and any domestic appliances the seller leaves in the house. Buyers taking on the former owner's fitted kitchen could find themselves with a year free of worry over a whole range of white goods.

Traditionally the first 12 months after moving into a new home is a time when people are at their most hard up and any spare cash is likely to be directed towards new carpets, curtains or furniture.

At the same time £300 is not an inconsiderable amount of money to have to find when you are moving house.

Michael Jones believes sellers will be happy to pay for the marketing edge the warranty can give.

'From the vendor's point of view it's a considerable marketing tool. If there are a lot of similar houses for sale in the same street and his has the warranty, then it's an advantage,' he said.

'It's of benefit to the purchaser because it's giving him free cover. It could be worth a couple of grand to him if the central heating goes in that first year.'

The seller only has to pay up when the sale is completed and if he decides to take his house off the market, then there is no premium to pay.

Even so, for six months he will have free cover on the operating parts of his house. Mr Jones does not think people will abuse the system by putting their homes on the market when they suspect the washing machine is about to go on the blink – then taking down the board as soon as it is fixed.

'If we believed it was a problem obviously we and our underwriters wouldn't have taken it on.'

HAZEL DOLAN

Source: The Northern Echo, 31 October, 1992

1 Describe the range of services offered to customers by an estate agent.

2 Do you believe the Home Warranty scheme mentioned in the article constitutes a unique selling proposition? Explain how it could give the estate agent a 'marketing edge'.

3 What do you think are the other main 'marketing tools' at the disposal of an estate agent?

4 In many markets, after-sales service is considered a crucial part of the marketing mix. Why should this be so, and how important do you think it is for the housing market?

ISSUES

THE EXTENT OF SERVICES

Eventually the business environment will be dominated by services.

1 Discuss the reasons for the growth of the service sector.

2 Where do you think the main growth areas within the service sector will be in the future, and why?

3 What are the main beneficial effects of the growth in services? Are there any detrimental effects on society?

GOODS AND SERVICES

There are no real differences between goods and services – both aim to make a profit, however this is achieved.

1 Is profit always the main goal of a service organisation? If not, consider other possible objectives.

2 Discuss whether a restaurant sells a meal or a service.

3 Explain what you consider a customer requires from the following services – building societies, architects, doctors, the police, dry-cleaning, music concerts, national parks, cinemas, taxis, a golfing holiday, electricity, museums and art galleries.

4 Debate the accuracy of the five main characteristics of services as opposed to goods, outlined in Table 8.1. Are there any services which do not fit these criteria, or goods which do?

THE SERVICE MIX

Services require a totally different approach to marketing than that for tangible products.

1 What are the main differences in approach and are they relevant for all services?

2 Do you consider that the three extra Ps of the service mix are more important than the four original Ps for products?

3 Select and discuss examples of service organisations which use (a) people, (b) physical evidence and (c) process as the key component of their marketing mix.

THE ROLE OF PEOPLE IN SERVICES

People play the key role in an organisation's service offering.

1 Do you agree with the above statement? Are there any situations in the marketing of services where people are not important?

2 It has been said that service marketers are 'selling long-term relationships'. What does this mean? Discuss examples of service organisations which (a) do and (b) do not follow this philosophy.

3 What do you think are the essential elements of the role of people in service marketing? Discuss qualities such as personal touch, contact, dialogue and visibility.

TOTAL SYSTEMS VIEW

The marketing of services requires an interaction between several components in an overall system.

1 What do you understand by 'the total systems view of service marketing opportunities'?

2 What are the main differences between the total product concept of marketing and the total systems view of services?

3 Choose any business within the service sector and debate how it might adopt a total systems approach. What might be the outcome if it does not do so?

AFTER-SALES SERVICE

A marketing campaign is not complete without after-sales service.

1 Discuss the full range of after-sales services which could be provided by a consumer business of your choice.

2 What types of after-sales service might be put into effect by an industrial organisation? Describe examples.

3 Are there any circumstances in which after-sales service is not necessary?

QUESTIONS

1 List ten examples of business activities in the service sector.

2 Give five reasons for the growth of services.

3 List three ways in which the service sector could be classified.

4 What are the five main characteristics of services?

5 Define each of the five service characteristics.

6 What is the goods/services continuum?

7 What are the seven Ps of the service marketing mix?

8 Define the three extra Ps of the service marketing mix and give four examples of each.

9 Give two possible marketing solutions for the problems deriving from each of the five service characteristics.

10 List five of the pre-conditions which should exist before an organisation introduces new services.

11 Define the 'total systems' model of service marketing.

12 List the five key components of the total systems view of service marketing.

PROJECTS

1 Using examples, describe the differences between goods and services in terms of factors such as frequency of purchase, duration of the decision-making process, novelty value and customer interaction with the source of the product.

2 Is the dimension of time important in the marketing of a service? Using examples in your answer, compare services which are instant with those that take place over a long period.

3 'The service systems which make it easy for a customer to leave a car for service and collect it at some agreed time; which make it easy for a busy executive to pick up a hire car at an airport; which give reliable and prompt service in a restaurant; which allow customers to book a holiday or a hairdressing appointment with little effort; all these systems will have advantages over competitive systems which do not run to time, impose excessive demands on customers, break down while operating or simply do not deliver what they promise.' Using Donald Cowell's definition and examples of your own, discuss the role of Process in the seven Ps of the service marketing mix.

4 Do you consider that the creation and delivery of a degree of pleasure is always essential in the marketing of services?

5 What are the main differences between the marketing of services connected with tangible goods, such as consumer durables and industrial products, and pure services, such as cleaning, tourism and postal deliveries?

6 Select a service, such as a sports club, theatre, solicitor or travel facility. Outline any marketing problems it might face as a result of its key characteristics, e.g. intangibility, inseparability, heterogeneity, perishability and ownership. Identify the possible marketing solutions it might use to overcome these disadvantages.

7 'The three dimensions of service convenience are location, time and speed.' Do you agree with Francis Buttle's assessment?

8 The higher education service is increasingly concerned with marketing considerations. Referring to your own college or university, consider the environmental factors which affect it and their implications, and then discuss:

(a) what products and services it should be offering;

(b) how it should research and segment its market;

(c) what methods of promotion are most appropriate for it;

(d) what pricing strategies it should be adopting.

GLOSSARY

After-, before- and during-sales service see Glossary, Chapter 6.

Consumer services services operating in consumer product markets.

Financial services the range of activities incorporated in the financial business sector.

Goods/services continuum a method by which all products and services can be compared according to their degree of tangibility, from pure tangible goods to pure intangible services.

Heterogeneity or variability characteristic of services whereby no two offerings are the same – services are usually performed by people and will thus all vary in nature, however small the variation.

Industrial services services operating in markets for industrial products.

Inseparability characteristic of services whereby production and consumption normally occur at the same time and the consumer is often involved in the production process.

Intangibility characteristic of services whereby the product is a performance and cannot be seen, touched, smelled, heard or tested before purchase.

Leisure services the range of activities incorporated within the leisure and recreation business sector.

Mental intangibility condition in which a service is difficult for the consumer to grasp or understand mentally.

Non-business marketing situation sometimes present in the services sector whereby there are other reasons for being in business than purely those of finance and profit.

Ownership characteristic of services whereby customers only have access to, or use of, the 'product' and there is no transfer of ownership title present in the transaction.

Palpable intangibility condition in which a service cannot be touched, a pre-requisite for service products.

People the human side of services, one of the three extra Ps in the marketing mix for services.

Perishability characteristic of services whereby the product cannot be stored and used later because of the simultaneous nature of production and consumption.

Physical evidence ambience, environmental proof and tangible clues as to the nature of a service, one of the three extra Ps in the marketing mix for services.

Process the systems involved in the production of services, one of the three extra Ps in the marketing mix for services.

Professional services the specialist sector of services which require a high degree of skill, such as surveyors or designers.

Service an intangible performance, benefit or activity offered by an individual or organisation to a customer who does not claim ownership of anything as a result.

Service department section of an organisation concerned with handling complaints, providing before-, during- and after-sales service and ensuring goodwill is maintained and improved between the company and its customers.

Service industry an area of business involved with intangible performance, help and advice rather than physical manufacturing.

Service marketing mix the marketing mix for a service product, selected by an organisation from the Seven Ps: the traditional Four Ps for physical goods together with the three extra Ps for services – people, physical evidence and process.

Service organisation company involved with service products and marketing them to target customers.

Service providers persons in a service organisation who communicate directly with customers and provide the actual service product.

Seven Ps extension of the traditional Four Ps for physical products to incorporate three extra Ps deemed appropriate for services, namely people, physical evidence and process.

Tangibility physical aspect of products not possessed by services.

Total systems model (of service marketing) method of marketing services based on five key interrelated elements – the customers, product tangibles, service processes, points of purchase and service people.

Variability see 'Heterogeneity'.

SUGGESTED REFERENCES

VIDEO MATERIAL

Diamonds in the Sky, 'Travelling for Fun', BBC, 1979.

Commercial breaks, 'Off the Beaten Track', BBC, 1984.

Marketing in Action, 'If the customer's happy', Open University, 1985.

Marketing the Arts: Foundation for Success, Office of Arts and Libraries/Arts Council, 1988.

The Marketing Mix – Social Variety, No. 1 (The Promotion of Health); No. 2 (Organisations in the Face of Change); and No. 4 (Product Decisions in the Face of Change), Yorkshire Television, 1988.

T.V. Advertising Clinic for Travel and Tourism, Chartered Institute of Marketing Travel Industry Group and Yorkshire Television, 1988.

The Small Business Programme, 'The Successful Seven', BBC, Open University, 1989.

Contemporary Marketing, Video Cases, No. 20 (Azure Seas), Boone, L. and Kurtz, D., Dryden Press, 1989.

Federal Express – setting the pace for the '90's, Marketing Videotape, Dibb, S., Simkin, L., Pride, W. and Ferrell, O., Houghton Mifflin 1991.

Business Matters, 'Front Line Manager' and 'Under the Knife', BBC, 1990; and 'At your Service', BBC, 1991.

Walk the Talk, No. 6 (Dr. Cruikshank's Casebook); No. 8 (Pride and Privilege); and No. 10 (Confidence à la Carte), BBC, 1991.

Business Studies series, Channel 4, 1991.

More than a game series, BBC, 1992.

High Interest, 'Sick as a Parrot'; and 'On the Buses', Channel 4, 1993.

France Means Business, 'Selling a City', BBC, 1993.

Forty Minutes, 'A case of corporate murder', BBC, 1994.

RADIO MATERIAL

Market Forces, No. 3 (Packaging the Professions), BBC Radio, 1984.

MAGAZINE ARTICLES

Business Studies Magazine, Jan. 1990, 'Marketing in the services environment'.

Cornell Hotel and Restaurant Administration Quarterly, May 1981, 'The positioning statement for hotels'.

Cornell Hotel and Restaurant Administration Quarterly, May 1986, 'Finding the heart of your restaurant's markets'.

European Journal of Marketing, Vol. 17, No. 6, 1983, p.57, 'Problems in marketing services: the case of incoming tourism'.

Journal of Marketing (American Marketing Association), Vol. 41, No. 2, Apr. 1977, 'Breaking free from product marketing'.

Journal of Marketing Management, Vol. 3, No. 3, Spring 1988, Special Issue, p.296, 'New Service Development'.

Journal of Marketing Management, Vol. 9, No. 3, July 1993, p.287, 'Strategy analysis in the health service'.

Journal of Services Marketing, Vol. 1, Summer 1987, 'Big ideas in services marketing'; and 'How marketers of intangibles can raise the odds for consumer satisfaction'.

Marketing Business, Feb. 1990, p.24, 'Hotel marketing: more than filling rooms'.

Marketing Business, April 1990, p.2, 'Branding by rail'; and p.4, 'Marketing travel in the 1990's'.

Marketing Business, June 1990, p.4, 'Rough waters for P. and O.'.

Marketing Business, Sept. 1991, p.40, 'At the end of the day Brian'.

Marketing Business, Oct. 1991, p.8, 'Swings and Roundabouts'; and p.40, 'Balancing act'.

Marketing Business, Mar. 1992, p.10 , 'Shining example'; and p.29, 'Consumer speak'.

Marketing Business, April 1992, p.30, 'Marketing solutions – the cat's whiskers'; and p.33, 'Flights of fancy'.

Marketing Business, June 1992, p.10, 'Tunnel vision'.

Marketing Business, July/Aug. 1992, p.15, 'Troubles aside'; p.30, 'Marketing solutions – Bridgework'; p.32, 'Science of Marketing – the art and science of service'; and p.41, 'Duty calls'.

Marketing Business, Oct. 1992, p.18, 'Marketing solutions – teamwork'; and p.42, 'Grave undertakings'.

Marketing Business, Nov. 1992, p.30, 'Home comforts'.

Marketing Business, Feb. 1993, p.42, 'Travelling light'.

Marketing Business, May 1993, p.28, 'Marketing solutions – prime target'.

Marketing Business, Sept. 1993, p.22, 'Can marketing save the unions?'.

Marketing Business, Oct. 1993, p.19, 'Marketing Services guide'.

Marketing Business, Mar. 1994, p.11, 'Accidental tourist'.

Marketing Business, June 1994, p.24, 'The Marketing prescription'.

Marketing Magazine, Aug. 1984, 'Britain's tourist class'.

Quarterly Review of Marketing, Vol. 11, No. 3, Spring 1986, p.8, 'Unserviceable concepts in service marketing'.

Quarterly Review of Marketing, Vol. 13, No. 1, Autumn 1987, p.16, 'How far can marketing be applied within the Further Education sector?'.

Quarterly Review of Marketing, Vol. 14, No. 3, April 1989, p.1, 'Once more on "goods" and "services": a way out of the conceptual jungle'.

FURTHER READING

Baker, M. (Ed.), *The Marketing Book*, Heinemann/C.I.M., 1990, ch. 21.

Bateson, John, *Managing Services Marketing*, Dryden, 1992.

Boone, L. and Kurtz, D., *Contemporary Marketing*, Dryden, 1989, ch. 20.

Buttle, Francis, *Hotel and Food Service Marketing*, Holt, Rhinehart and Winston, 1986.

Cannon, Tom, *Basic Marketing*, Holt Business Texts, 1980, ch. 9.

Cowell, Donald, *The Marketing of Services*, Butterworth-Heinemann, 1991.

Dibb, S., Simkin, L., Pride, W. and Ferrell, O., *Marketing*, Houghton Mifflin, 1994, ch. 24.

Diggle, Keith, *Guide to Arts Marketing*, Rhinegold Publishing, 1984.

Donnelly, J. and George, W. (Eds), *Marketing of Services*, American Marketing Association, 1981.

Foster, D., *Mastering Marketing*, Macmillan, 1982, ch. 9.

Holloway, J.C. and Plant, R.V., *Marketing for Tourism*, Pitman, 1993.

Kotler, P. and Armstrong, G., *Marketing*, Prentice Hall, 1993, ch. 18.Leadley, P., *Leisure Marketing*, Longman, 1992.

Mercer, D., *Marketing*, Blackwell, 1992, ch. 7.

Payne, Adrian, *The Essence of Services Marketing*, Prentice Hall, 1993.

Stone, Merlin, *Leisure Services Marketing*, Croner, 1990.

Surprenant, Carol (Ed.), *Add Value to Your Service*, American Marketing Association, 1987.

Wood, Malcolm, *Tourism Marketing*, English Tourist Board, 1980.

Acknowledgements

The Northern Echo.
The Yorkshire Evening Press.

9

PLACE DECISIONS

DEFINITIONS

A marketing channel is a channel of distribution, or group of inter-related intermediaries who direct products to consumers.

DIBB, SIMKIN, PRIDE AND FERRELL

Distribution is the most neglected element of the marketing mix. This may reflect the complexity of decisions which have to be made regarding distribution strategy and on-going channel management, but it is also a function of the way in which firms organise their overall marketing effort.

COLIN EGAN, WARWICK UNIVERSITY BUSINESS SCHOOL

INTRODUCTION

A customer cannot buy, and the producer cannot sell, unless the product or service is available at the right time and in the right place. For this reason, considerations revolving around where and when the customer makes a purchase form a vital part of marketing mix decision making (see Figure 9.1).

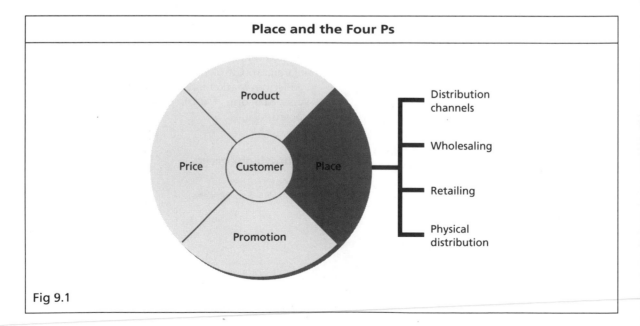

Place and the Four Ps

Fig 9.1

Place decisions involve all aspects of the ways in which products are distributed from manufacturer to consumer. In fact, the words 'place' and 'distribution' are often used synonymously to describe this area of marketing activity.

Within the sphere of place, or distribution, organisations must consider several elements, as illustrated in Table 1.2. However, the four central areas of decision making concern the selection of appropriate channels of distribution, whether to use wholesalers, the role of retailing and the ways in which products will be physically distributed. The strategies adopted in these key areas will constitute an organisation's place or distribution mix.

KEY CONCEPTS

DISTRIBUTION CHANNELS

The most important place decision taken by the marketer usually concerns the distribution channel or route taken by goods as they move from producer to final customer or industrial user, and the functions performed at each stage.

The simplest form of distribution is direct from manufacturer to consumer. This method is often adopted with products which require demonstration or after-sales service or are custom-made to particular client requirements, computer systems being an obvious example. Such products generally have a limited number of buyers and are usually of a high unit value, as otherwise it would prove very expensive for company sales representatives to deal with each customer individually. Nevertheless, there are a number of examples of successful direct distribution of cheaper goods such as the Avon cosmetics and Betterware household products door-to-door operations, service organisations, Tupperware parties, market gardening, double-glazing and insurance direct selling, and many mail order and industrial products.

The main advantage of the direct method is that the channel of distribution is totally within the control of the organisation with no intermediaries present. However, most companies do not sell directly to consumers, for the following main reasons:

- lack of skills and resources to do so;
- a consumer may wish to inspect before ordering, thus display facilities would be required on a national basis;
- customers now often require a large variety of products to be available in a single place;
- the national distribution of people geographically tends to separate producer from consumer;
- the tendency for manufacturers to concentrate

on producing goods rather than selling them;
- the growth of specialist intermediaries, such as retailers and wholesalers.

All these factors militate against direct distribution, but the most important argument is that using a middle person is usually a far more efficient way to reach customers, as illustrated in Figure 9.2.

Intermediaries come in various forms but the main types available to an organisation are wholesalers, retailers and agents or brokers.

Wholesalers are most commonly used for consumer products where the breaking of bulk into smaller quantities is necessary before the goods make further progress down the channel to retailer or end-user. Retailers also break bulk and provide a range of different but often related products made by various manufacturers, usually on display, to give customers a wider choice than if they dealt directly with the producer. Agents, brokers and factors are specialist intermediaries offering a more personal service at any stage of the distribution network, for example in the motor-car retailing market.

By using middle persons, some of the manufacturer's control of its distribution channels and thus the fate of its products is inevitably lost and a certain amount of potential income forgone. However, this option utilises the specialist knowledge and experience of intermediaries, reduces the extent of involvement and risk, and allows the manufacturer more time to concentrate on considerations such as production and finance.

Many criteria will affect the firm's choice of channel, but the key determinant is whether the goods and customers involved are consumer or industrial in nature. The alternative distribution

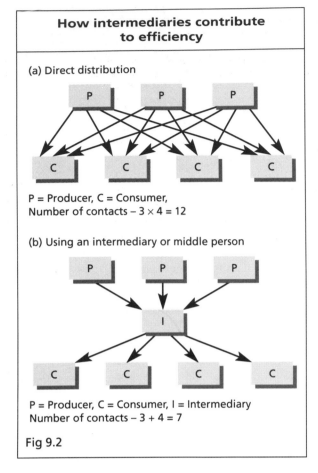

How intermediaries contribute to efficiency

(a) Direct distribution

P = Producer, C = Consumer,
Number of contacts – 3 × 4 = 12

(b) Using an intermediary or middle person

P = Producer, C = Consumer, I = Intermediary
Number of contacts – 3 + 4 = 7

Fig 9.2

- consumer behaviour, e.g. purchasing and demand habits;
- the nature of the competition and other environmental forces;
- the merits and demerits of available intermediaries and their suitability for the tasks to be undertaken;
- geographical dispersal of producer, channel members and customers.

Whichever channel system an organisation selects, trade discounts operate to enable each stage in the chain to cover its costs and make a profit. For industrial products, a more direct distribution pattern usually exists as the requirements are generally more individual and the scale of purchase justifies this more costly approach. As a rule, channel routes tend to be shorter when the product is perishable, has a high unit value or large physical dimensions, and has to meet technical or other specifications.

The role of the intermediary has traditionally been concerned with handling the exchange process between manufacturer and consumer and ensuring an effective overall distribution policy through the fulfilment of basic marketing processes:

- bringing buyers and sellers into close contact;
- supplying a choice of goods to gain interest and meet buyers' needs;
- physically distributing the goods;
- encouraging a favourable attitude from consumers;
- maintaining acceptable price levels;
- ensuring an on-going flow of sales;
- providing appropriate services, such as advice and repairs.

channels utilised by each of these are outlined in Figure 9.3, while services by their very nature tend to be performed direct to the consumer or conveyed by an agent.

In reality, these seemingly simple channel networks are usually more complex in nature and often involve a pyramid of regional wholesalers and local retailers, particularly where large volumes of goods are being distributed.

A number of factors will influence an organisation's selection of the appropriate channel which minimises selling costs and maximises sales:

- financial considerations;
- the characteristics of the particular market, including type, size and concentration;
- producer factors, such as size, output, objectives, resources and background;
- product attributes, promotion, image, value and perishability;

Increasingly, however, channel members are becoming involved in or assuming responsibility for other marketing management activities such as advertising, sales promotion and marketing research.

Another development has been for producer or intermediary organisations with appropriate resources to forge formal or informal relationships with other members of their channel of distribution, to acquire them or to develop their own. The ultimate situation, where an organisation owns every stage of the channel system from production to final distribution to the consumer, is known as *vertical integration* (see Figure 9.4).

Distribution channels for consumer and industrial goods

Type of product	Channel method	Producer	Agent or broker	Wholesaler or industrial distributor	Retailer	Consumer or industrial buyer
Consumer products	1	X	X	X	X	X
	2	X		X	X	X
	3	X			X	X
	4	X				X
Industrial products	1	X	X	X		X
	2	X	X			X
	3	X		X		X
	4	X				X

Fig 9.3

Vertical integration in distribution

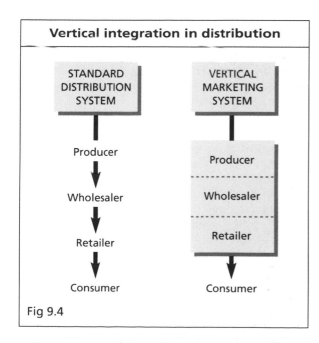

Fig 9.4

In such a vertical marketing system, each level is planned and interdependent with the others and the organisation assumes responsibility for all the many distribution functions which need to be addressed. It will thus gain from all the advantages of enjoying complete control over the product, but this is a costly strategy which accepts all the associated risks and does not utilise external specialist experiences.

Examples of vertical marketing systems are professional services and some of the larger brewery companies, while other organisations like Benetton, Marks and Spencer and McDonald's exercise a large degree of control over their products without being truly vertically integrated. Both Boots and W.H. Smith have diversified and manufacture many of their own products as well as selling them.

Overall, some organisations will favour a distribution channel system where the marketing tasks are dominated by the manufacturer, while others prefer the intermediary to take on more of the responsibility. Before completing its place mix, an organisation must tackle another important area of strategic decision making, namely the level of exposure it deems suitable for the products being marketed. Here there are three broad options open to it, whether it is operating on a local, regional, national or international basis:

1. *Intensive distribution* making the product available as widely as possible, either to all outlets of a specific type or to every outlet. This level of exposure is usually appropriate for cheap products in mass markets using many channel routes, for example fast-moving consumer goods such as chocolate or toothpaste.
2. *Selective distribution* limiting product availability to certain areas or outlets, in order to create a more favourable image or allow for special servicing requirements. This method normally involves more expensive products with fewer customers and more limited channel routes, e.g. certain cosmetics and consumer durables such as television sets.
3. *Exclusive distribution* ensuring that only a very small number of outlets (perhaps only one) are guaranteed handling and selling rights. This strategy would generally apply to expensive products with few customers and just one channel route. It often involves the use of wholesalers rather than retailers in specific geographic areas, such as exclusive car dealerships; can include arrangements for land, buildings and equipment, as in petrol station agreements; and is used for the creation and marketing of prestige goods.

Distribution channel routes are becoming ever more varied as organisations seek new ways to reach their customers. Some are complex – paperback books, for example, are channelled through a multiplicity of wholesalers and retailers – while others are direct and relatively straightforward. Whichever routes are chosen, it is imperative that the strategy is logical and well considered beforehand and that the roles of the channel members are agreed by all parties and fit for the task of marketing the product concerned.

WHOLESALING

Wholesaling is concerned with the activities of organisations selling products to retailers and other industrial, institutional and commercial users rather than to final consumers, and includes all transactions in which goods are to be re-sold or used in making other products.

Wholesalers help to provide economies of distribution by ensuring that the right stocks reach the right customers at the right place and time.

They are often used by manufacturers who cannot afford the high costs of an extensive distribution network and a large sales force, and in the UK for instance, about 40 per cent of foodstuffs are distributed by wholesalers.

The wholesaling function originates from the Middle Ages when associations of traders, or merchant guilds, purchased bulk supplies from outside their particular town and allowed their retailer members to take advantage of better priced, quality goods. Specialist wholesalers emerged in the agricultural and industrial revolutions, often growing up alongside large firms, new industries and ports, and taking over the distribution of goods from the manufacturer to final seller for a percentage of the selling price.

Nowadays, wholesalers operate either nationally with a large capital outlay, distributing goods all over the country and holding large amounts of stock, often including their own brands, or on a local or regional scale, offering a more restricted service within easy range of the warehouse bases. They may specialise in a certain product or carry a wide range of different goods, and in some situations more than one wholesaler may be required to complete the task of delivery to the retailer.

The wholesaler usually, but not always, handles the merchandise in which it deals or processes it in some way, as is mainly the case with agricultural products. However, sometimes the job involves merely providing a link between the source of supply and the demand for it, for example Stock Exchange brokers.

Wholesalers can be manufacturer or retailer owned, but generally they are divided into two clear types, merchants and agents. *Merchants* buy from the manufacturers and thus own the products they sell and take on the associated risks, whereas *Agents* (including brokers and factors) do not. There are numerous variations of each of these categories.

Some merchant wholesalers provide the complete range of functions and are known as *full-service wholesalers*. These usually come in one of four forms:

- *general merchandisers*, which carry a wide variety of non-perishable items serving many kinds of retail stores;
- *single-line operators*, handling, for example, only groceries or industrial supplies;
- *specialists*, carrying a very narrow line of prod-

ucts, such as only oriental foods instead of general groceries;

- *marketing boards*, government run operations buying from producers and guaranteeing to sell on to other distributors or retailers, for example agricultural goods such as milk.

Other merchant wholesalers function on a more limited basis and are known as *limited-service wholesalers*. These include:

- *cash-and-carry outlets*, wholesale supermarkets offering low prices but no credit facilities or delivery services and used wherever the commodity has a high stock turnover, such as in the food trade;
- *drop shippers*, who obtain orders for products and pass these to producers, but do not handle, stock or deliver the goods despite owning them. The products are then shipped direct to the customer;
- *rack jobbers*, who collect from producers and deliver direct to retailers without storing. They may take over responsibility for maintaining stocks and displays in some areas and tend to specialise in non-food items sold in grocery stores and supermarkets, e.g. a display of paperback books;
- *truck wholesalers*, delivering products stocked in their own trucks, such as perishables that normal wholesalers prefer not to carry. These are mainly found in the USA where greater distances are involved.
- *mail-order wholesalers*, who sell out of catalogues distributed widely to smaller customers or retailers;
- *producers' co-operatives*, operating as wholesalers and existing to serve local co-operatives and retailers whilst assisting with the provision of capital. Profits go to their customer–members and local co-op shops receive dividends on purchases. Some brand and promote their own products and others have expanded into retailing, for example sponsored voluntary group chains such as Spar and Mace and Viva.

Agents and brokers act for a principal and take a commission for the service of negotiating exchanges between buyers and sellers. *Agents* normally represent either the purchaser or the vendor on a permanent basis and come in several forms:

- *manufacturers' agents*, self-employed sales representatives, often selling similar products for several non-competing producers on a commission or service fee arrangement. They are usually given sole rights and work in limited geographical areas, enabling the manufacturer to benefit from people with local knowledge and thus not have to open up new branches – for example, in automobile or textile distribution;
- *selling agents*, who perform the whole range of marketing activities in addition to the selling function, leaving the manufacturer to concentrate on production. They might also provide working capital;
- *commission merchants*, handling products or samples sent by sellers, sometimes working on credit, completing the sale and sending the money (less commission) to the vendor;
- *factors*, who work for the seller and provide wholesaling facilities, usually where there are many small producers and few large central markets, e.g. in agriculture;
- *auction houses*, which sell goods to the highest bidder and take commission from the vendor after the transaction has been completed, for example Christie's and Sotheby's.

Brokers bring buyers and sellers together on a temporary basis by negotiation and gain their profit from commissions or fees. Their 'product' is information about what buyers need and what supplies are available, and they tend to operate in narrow markets, such as sugar, tea, insurance or real estate.

As illustrated in Figure 9.5, it is possible for the wholesaler to provide some or all of the key marketing activities, from storage, security and financing to research, promotion and management. But the main reason for wholesalers' continued existence is the range of advantages they offer to both the producer and the retailer. For the manufacturer, wholesalers may:

- simplify the distribution process by breaking the bulk, buying in large quantities from producers and selling in smaller quantities to retailers. The manufacturer thus only has to make one large delivery to the wholesaler rather than many smaller and more expensive deliveries to shops;

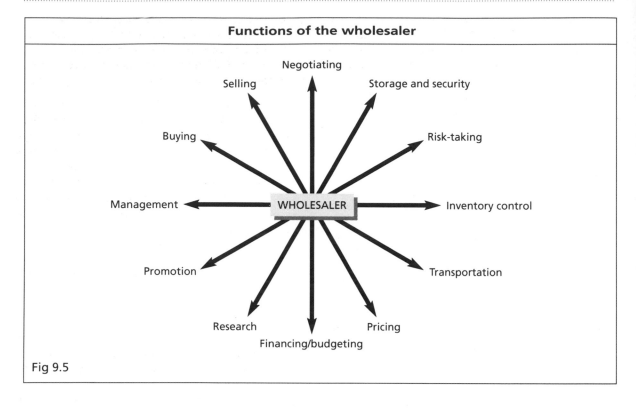

Functions of the wholesaler

Negotiating
Selling
Storage and security
Buying
Risk-taking
Management
WHOLESALER
Inventory control
Promotion
Transportation
Research
Pricing
Financing/budgeting

Fig 9.5

- provide information on the state of the market and help the manufacturer to anticipate demand;
- help to create and expand markets by utilising their experience and the services of their sales staff;
- relieve them of products quickly and, by carrying out the warehousing function, make it possible for manufacturers to produce ahead of demand and use their buildings for production, not storage;
- normally pay promptly by cash for purchases to enable the manufacturer to regain capital for continued production;
- take over or share many transportation, promotion and administration problems and expenses, thus relieving manufacturers of all or some of the burdens and risks involved, including finance, pilferage and spoilage;
- complete all or some of the finishing operations, for example, blending, sorting, grading, packaging and merchandising;
- help to preserve stable prices for the product by varying supply and stockholding.

For the retailer, wholesalers may:

- supply the products of many manufacturers regularly and promptly, giving retailers a choice from a variety of goods;
- provide a service conveniently located geographically for the retailer;
- sell in small quantities according to retailer requirements;
- carry stock, thus enabling the retailer to economise on storage space, minimise losses from unsold goods and reduce the risk of tax deductions;
- allow long periods of credit so the retailer may sell most of the goods before repayment;
- grade, pre-pack and price the goods ready for sale, and test for quality;
- keep prices more stable than if the retailer had to buy from the manufacturer;
- offer special price concessions, discounts and credit facilities, plus guarantees and the like;
- ensure an up-to-date flow of information and trends and give expert advice based on experience, knowledge and research.

Of course, there are also disadvantages of using wholesalers for the producer or retailer to consider, not the least financial, as profit margins will be lower for both and the customer will eventually pay for the service offered by such intermediaries. Again, new products might not receive the type of promotion manufacturers or retailers would prefer, and the producer might have little control over which retailers will stock the goods or key aspects such as stock levels, price, display and merchandising.

The wholesaling function, as with all marketing activities, is constantly undergoing changes owing to the globalisation of markets, the advent of computer technology, and so on. The industry has been consolidated by greater specialisation, increased pricing power over producers, larger retailers offering opportunities through expanded product lines and wider ranges, and mergers and acquisitions which have led to increased size and greater efficiency. The future of all types of wholesaler will depend on their ability to delineate markets and furnish the desired level of service.

RETAILING

A retailer is a person or organisation selling goods to the final consumer, usually through a retail outlet such as a shop or store, and generally dealing in products for personal, family or household purposes. Retailing is the final link in the chain of distribution for consumer products. Its main function is to ensure that goods are available when and where the customer wants them for maximum convenience and to pass on product information to customers and back to producers, so that effective channels are maintained and a change in ownership is brought about.

Retail outlets come in a great variety of shapes and sizes and can be classified according to the services they provide, the product lines they offer, their location, the nature of their ownership or the amount of effort expended by customers in using them. For instance, if retailers are categorised by ownership they can be identified as independent, owned by the manufacturer, franchised from the main operator, or part of a corporate or voluntary chain or co-operative association.

Probably the most logical way to classify retail outlets is to delineate them in terms of a combination of the products and services they offer and their location. In this way, two main categories can

be identified, retail stores and non-store retailing.

Retail stores are usually fixed-site establishments and all reach the customer over the counter, but they can be divided into various types according to their distinctive characteristics:

- *Independents or 'convenience' stores* – small traditional corner shops, general stores or specialists, such as grocers, offering a conventional single or limited-line choice and employing few people. Usually owned by the shopkeeper, they provide a convenient, local and personal service but are declining through competition, so are combining or joining voluntary chains and copying multiple trading methods, such as bulk-buying and self-service.
- *Manufacturers' or factory shops* – direct selling by producers, possibly on their own premises but often including goods other than those made by the manufacturer. Used when trading is on a large scale and can require a big capital outlay, but reduces organisational problems, can increase sales if well promoted and can lead to opportunities of entry into high street markets or other outlets.
- *Franchise* – where a parent company, or 'franchiser', grants a smaller, individual organisation, or 'franchisee', the right or privilege through a licensing agreement to do retail business in a prescribed manner over a certain period of time in a specified place. The franchisee will usually invest in the business and use the franchiser's methods, trademarks, symbols or architecture, examples being various car dealerships, Holiday Inn, Dyno-rod, Sketchley dry-cleaning, Budget Rent-a-Car and fast food operations such as Kentucky Fried Chicken and Wimpy.

An extension of the franchising system is *multi-level marketing*, otherwise known as network marketing or pyramid selling, a distribution and trading scheme for selling goods or services which operates on a number of levels. Participants join up by investing in products and selling them whilst recruiting other members further down the chain, who in turn recruit more distributors, and so on. This network of self-employed sales people provides members with discounts based on the amount of stock purchased, and income from sales to distributors together with a percentage commission from the sales of participants recruited lower in the pyramid. The system gained a bad reputation through the disillusionment of members facing losses and through its image of 'corporate evangelism'. It tends to be more directed towards selling interests in the pyramid structure itself than to selling goods, to favour those higher in status within the system, and to create too many participants chasing too little business. It is not illegal but is now controlled by strict legislation, and includes organisations such as Amway, from the USA.

- *Speciality stores* – traditional retailers selling only one product, such as bookstores, or limited lines, for example clothing or furniture, and offering various degrees of service and price advantages and considerable depth in the chosen product area.
- *Department or 'shopping' stores* – really a series of specialist shops arranged as departments under one roof, carrying a broad assortment of product lines with a medium depth in each. Traditionally in city centres, such as Harrods, Lewis's, Debenhams, Selfridges and House of Fraser, and providing a full service based on bulk-buying and heavy promotion. Appealing to the older age ranges and losing market share without the younger, more affluent customers, but addressing the situation by including self-selection and open display and utilising centralised buying and own-label brands.
- *Co-operative societies* – retail units involving voluntary ownership by consumers or employees, based on purchase dividends or trading stamps, and linked to manufacturing plants and the wholesale movement. A traditional method of retailing which declined due to fragmented structure and poor promotion, emphasis on book-keeping, lack of membership involvement, investment and dynamism, and a forbidding environment. It is now righting some of these problems and undergoing a revival, led by organisations such as Co-operative Wholesale Society (CWS).

Superseding all these traditional retailers in the so-called historical 'wheel of retailing' are the *mass merchandisers*, including:

1. *Multiple shops and chain or variety stores*, concentrating on one type of product (Next for clothes), more than one (Boots and Marks and Spencer), or

several (Woolworths). Usually defined as retail enterprises with 10 or more outlets, taking advantage of bulk buying and so on, and can be local, regional or national, sometimes run by manufacturers. Products sold are generally universal and in regular demand, achieving rapid turnover and offering quality and competitive pricing, and varying degrees of service.
2. *One-stop shops* – provide a wide range and full facilities by licensing departments to outside organisations, for example Woolco (Woolworths).
3. *Supermarkets* – self-service outlets, such as Tesco, Safeway and Sainsbury's, originally specialising in groceries and foods and then diversifying into a range of household items. Developed because of the cost of good sales people, the need for convenience and fast service and the growth of pre-packed foodstuffs. Benefit from rapid turnover, low labour costs and computerisation and offer low prices and selection freedom, but provide little direct service and profit margins can be low.
4. *Superstores* – large supermarkets offering the same advantages but a larger number and wider range of products.
5. *Hypermarkets* – huge self-service supermarkets, such as Costco and Carrefour, usually on the outskirts of cities and offering parking, a very wide range of products and an opportunity for customers to take advantage of low prices and infrequent shopping trips. Expanding now to include warehouse and wholesale clubs, where membership is required, such as Matalan (clothes).
6. *Warehouse and catalogue showrooms*, e.g. Argos – offer low prices, through reduced costs, for various goods listed in the company's catalogue and stored in a warehouse, although a limited number of products are visible in the showroom. Catalogues are available in the store or mailed out.
7. *Discount houses* – offer standard goods at very low prices on a self-selection basis, with little service, often in fierce competition with other outlets. They tend to deal in a wide breadth of products but a limited selection of each type, e.g. Kwik Save, Poundstretcher, Netto and the Reject Shops.

Each type of outlet offers its own advantages, but the retail store is not always the best solution for consumers wishing to obtain products.

Non-store retailing is not usually limited to a fixed site and does not generally take place over the counter but direct to the customer. There are several examples of this method of purchasing goods, most of which offer added convenience and higher profit margins but a reduced assortment of products. The main types of non-store retailing are:

- *Mail order* – a rapidly growing section of the retail trade as consumers increasingly wish to 'shop' within their own homes after viewing a catalogue, press advertisement or television screen listings of available goods. Costs are high and customer contact limited, but the method provides for leisurely self-selection of branded goods, delivery to the home, targeted markets, credit and instalment terms offered, goods sent on approval or return and glossy catalogues. Many products are retailed this way, for example clothes.
- *Door-to-door and telemarketing* – direct selling methods including doorstep and telephone selling, both practised by various companies, e.g. Everest double-glazing. Their services are limited and costs are high, but such operations provide strong control over the market.
- *Home selling or home shopping* – usually involves tests or demonstrations to families or groups of people, such as cosmetics, pottery and fashion shows, Tupperware parties or dedicated interactive TV such as QVC (the satellite 'shopping channel'). Benefits from the informal atmosphere and often involves commissions for hosts or hostesses and free gifts as incentives. Sometimes known as 'direct response marketing'.
- *Market stalls* – operated by market traders and allowing for a social climate of curiosity and browsing. Small outlets offering cheap goods and having minimal overheads.
- *Mobile shops* – selling from adapted vans and offering convenience but a limited range of products, e.g. books, fast food, ice-cream.
- *Automatic vending machines* – began with the early confectionery venders on railway stations and so on. Now more sophisticated and include a wide range of hot and cold foods and other goods. Offer self-service and convenience but can be expensive in order to cover costs.

The retail world is never constant and the tendency is for new types of outlet to become higher-price operations, at the same time leaving room for cheaper outlets to gain entry at the lower end of the market. Thus the more traditional general and department stores have been gradually replaced by discount stores and supermarkets which are themselves being superseded by hypermarkets and home shopping. This effect is known as the *wheel of retailing* and can also be monitored by reference to the product life cycle concept (see Figure 9.6).

Retail strategy involves many elements of marketing, the end result designed to ensure that the maximum number of products are sold at the minimum cost. Retailers of all types must address various problems and make 'retail mix' decisions, of which the following are the most crucial:

- appropriateness for target markets;
- product and service decisions;
- retail pricing strategy;
- physical distribution decisions;
- retail image and promotional strategy;
- merchandising decisions, such as location and nature of point-of-sale advertising, display and sales promotional material, inclusion of relevant literature, incorporation of house style, and store layout strategy, designed to maximise traffic flow, convenience and sales;
- financial aspects, such as credit, and so on;
- service levels, e.g. delivery, demonstrations, after-sales service, flexibility of access and opening hours, availability of additional services such as canteens and banking facilities;
- ambience and atmosphere;
- location – the selection of prime sites, taking into account convenience for customers, ease of parking, access to transportation, nature of the catchment area, cost of buildings or rental, government policies and local planning regulations;
- purchasing decisions – larger retail units often purchase directly from the manufacturer while smaller ones tend to buy from a wholesaler.

Retailing has seen many dramatic changes in recent years and will undoubtedly continue to exhibit the same pattern in the future. From the supplier's perspective, the main features of the 'retail revolution' have been:

- rapid growth of the strategically located multiples and other large operators, to the detriment of the independents and co-operatives, and the

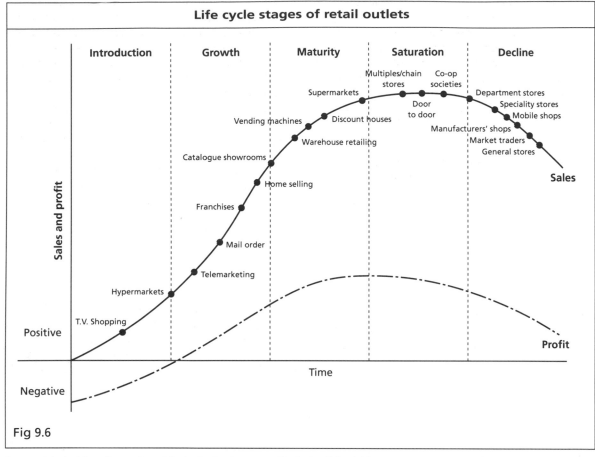

Life cycle stages of retail outlets

Fig 9.6

Source: Adapted from Boone, L. and Kurtz, D., *Contemporary Marketing* (6th edn) Transparency Acetate Teaching Notes, © 1989 Dryden Press (overhead transparency number 14.2). Reproduced by permission of the publisher

creation of large retail groups such as Burton, Kingfisher, Sears and W.H. Smith;

- the incorporation of new technology to improve service and economic efficiency, for example central warehousing and electronic point-of-sale (EPOS) systems monitoring transactions and orders for automatic stock replacement;
- corporate retail strategy employed to bring about economies of scale, although the industry has become capital intensive owing to the high costs of store development and necessary refurbishments;
- retailing focused on narrower market segments and more specific product lines, for example the emergence of Sock Shop and Tie Rack;
- less mass merchandising and more concentration on up-market images, in terms of presentation, store design and flow, and promotion;
- more emphasis on the creation of ambience and lifestyle retailing, as stressed by Laura Ashley,

Habitat, Next and even Tesco, DIY stores such as B&Q and some off-licences and video shops;

- improved ethical, environmental and quality standards of retailing, for example strict food dating and storing, and the emergence of natural, non-additive and 'green' products.

From the demand point of view, the 'consumer revolution' has affected retailing in several ways:

- An increase in real income has led to an increase in retail demand for all products.
- Changes in lifestyle have brought about a demand for good parking facilities, extended and weekend opening times, as time for shopping is more limited.
- Increased premium placed on price, value, image and environmental factors such as the 'green' movement.
- The need for ease and convenience has led to increased self-service facilities and an increase

in 'one-stop shopping' areas such as large stores and city centre precincts.

- Shopping increasingly being treated and marketed as a 'leisure' activity, leading to a move away from the high street and to the growth of out-of-town sites such as garden centres or shopping malls with entertainments and other attractions, e.g. the MetroCentre in Gateshead, Meadowhall in Sheffield or Brent Cross in North London.

Retailing is also considerably influenced by political legislation, such as government monetary policy, monopolies and mergers rules and local town planning laws, while shops and retail areas play a very important part in civic regeneration and urban planning policies.

PHYSICAL DISTRIBUTION

Having decided on the appropriate distribution channels for its products and selected wholesalers and retailers where necessary, an organisation must ensure that it oversees and manages the movement of the goods in order that the right quantity reaches the right destination at the right time and with the desired support services.

Rather than treating each of the physical distribution activities in isolation, the marketing orientated organisation will see the benefits of integrating them into a combined system, thus enabling economies to be made and allowing for an overall strategy to be pursued. The main components of an organisation's physical distribution system are illustrated in Figure 9.7.

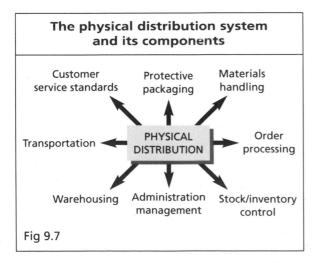

The physical distribution system and its components

Fig 9.7

Each of these components is increasingly taking advantage of computerisation and new technology, but each is potentially very costly. As we have seen, an organisation could pass on some of the problems and costs to a wholesaler, agent or factor, or deliver the product direct using their own or hired transport.

Another method is for warehouse depots to be established to provide ease of access to the main geographical concentrations of buyers which, together with bulk deliveries, could substantially reduce distribution costs in the long term. Warehouse storage must now be economic and purpose-built to take account of climate control, safety and security factors, space for handling movement and technological and legal requirements.

In addition, an organisation must consider questions of packaging and its suitability for transportation, materials handling arrangements, the processing of orders, monitoring of stock and inventory control, and associated management matters relating to administration and customer services. However, the most important and most costly aspect of physical distribution revolves around the question of the method or methods of transport to be selected.

The main factors to take into account when making such a choice of transportation are:

- cost;
- speed;
- dependability;
- frequency;
- availability in different locations, and convenience;
- flexibility in handling products;
- security;
- capability, and possession of appropriate equipment and conditions;
- traceability in case of loss;
- energy efficiency and environmental acceptability;
- the nature of the product, e.g. size and life span.

The five main modes of freight transport, together with their key advantages and disadvantages, are:

- *Road travel* – offers door-to-door access, frequency and speed, but subject to weight restrictions, weather conditions and traffic de-lays, and environmentally unfriendly. Examples: food, clothing.

- *Railways* – flexible, appropriate for heavy freight and a 'green' method, but unreliable and infrequent. Examples: coal, grain.
- *Airlines* – fast and useful for perishable goods and emergencies, but costly, limited in size, have also to rely on other modes and inefficient on energy. Examples: mail, health products.
- *Waterways* – cheap, flexible, large capacity and can be inland or offshore, but slow, subject to weather conditions, infrequent and have also to rely on other modes. Examples: petrol, vehicles.
- *Pipelines* – continuous, dependable and energy efficient, but slow, subject to shrinkage and leakage, inflexible and inaccessible. Examples: oil, gas, water.

Physical distribution management involves the efficient movement of goods and materials, both inwards to the point of manufacture and outwards from production line to customer. The two main considerations in the design of such a system concern the appreciation that it should begin with customers' needs and wants and should be constructed to provide the required level of customer service and utility at the minimum cost.

ARTICLES

A1

Squeeze on supermarkets

THE big three supermarket chains, Sainsbury's, Tesco, and Safeway, are poised to 'carve up' their smaller rivals, a report predicts today.

As the big three's share of the £50bn grocery trade expands, some middle-ranking supermarket chains – including Leeds-based Asda – face being squeezed out of the market altogether.

It could ultimately mean less choice for shoppers, according to the study by market analysts Mintel.

The total number of food stores has already shrunk by 25 per cent in the past five years and about a dozen major supermarket chains now take 80 per cent of all grocery spending.

But, as many other shops fold, the march of the superstores continues, with 730 giant outlets now in business compared with 238 a decade ago.

'The three leaders – Sainsbury's, Tesco, and Safeway – have between them £1.4bn of equity capital to assist in their development programmes,' said Mintel.

'Each expects to open between 15 and 20 new superstores a year over the next three years.

'The 'carve-up' of the grocery market by the big three is likely to hit the middle-ranking players hardest.

'Trade respondents identified the likely losers in the middle ground as being Asda, Gateway and Budgens,' said Mintel.

All three, however, are vigorously defending their share of the market and wooing shoppers with regular special offers.

Mintel's senior retail analyst, Caroline O'Neill, added: 'The development of discount shops is squeezing the bottom end of the market, while continued expansion of the superstore sector intensifies competition at the other end.

'Both approaches are to the detriment of smaller and medium-sized retailers.'

Source: By courtesy of *The Yorkshire Post*

1 The Mintel report referred to suggestions that the growth of the 'big three' could lead to less choice for consumers. Do you agree? What are the advantages and disadvantages of this trend?

2 Who are the 'smaller and medium-sized retailers' under threat from the march of the superstores? What might they do to counteract the threat?

3 How will the extension of shopping hours and Sunday trading affect these changes? Do you agree with these developments?

4 How long do you think the life cycle of the big superstores will be? What might eventually replace them and why?

A2

Discount store 'a boost for York'

TOMORROW'S opening of York's first American-style membership-only discount clothes warehouse will not hit city centre shops, said one of its directors.

Duncan Sutherland said the presence of Matalan on Clifton Moor will boost trade in and around York.

'The kind of customer we attract is very different. People tend to travel from a very wide catchment area to our store. And that has good knock-on effects for businesses near us.

'And also if people have travelled to see us they will probably stay and go and have a look in York. So it's good for the city centre.'

The new 20,000 sq ft store promises branded fashion goods at up to 50 per cent less than the price in many high street shops.

It cuts costs by buying in bulk from suppliers, cutting overheads, for example spending the minimum on store decor, and slashing mark-ups on goods.

'On average we have about a 30 per cent mark-up compared with some high street stores that have up to 100 per cent,' said Heather Glynn, development co-ordinator, whose job is to open new stores throughout the country.

Matalan are presently using data to compile a profile of their average customer.

But the stores prove very popular with men shopping by themselves, said Heather.

'I think it's largely because of the parking. Men can come here, buy what they want and then drive off. It's quick and simple. And if they come with their wives or family and get fed-up they can go and sit in the car.'

Tomorrow anybody can shop at the store. After that entry will be by membership card only, available through companies, organisations and clubs.

Already 2,200 businesses in York have applied for cards and Matalan expect to have between 60,000 and 80,000 members within the first year.

Around 30 local people are now working at the store, which estimates staff could double by the end of the first year's trading.

Matalan already operate 19 stores nationwide. The first opened in the company's base-town, Preston, in 1986. The York store is the first of 15 more the company plans to open this year.

Tomorrow the store's ten tills will be supplemented by four extra portable tills brought in to cope with expected demand.

Heather said: 'People love getting bargains. We expect people queueing at the doors, it usually happens.'

Source: The Yorkshire Evening Press

1 What do you believe will be the effect of Matalan on local consumers and retailing in the York area? What are the main advantages it offers and what are the disadvantages?

2 Describe the kind of customer most likely to shop at Matalan. In which circumstances would you shop there and why?

3 How does a discount warehouse such as Matalan manage to cut its costs? Describe the pricing strategy it will adopt to make a profit.

4 The hypermarkets and warehouse clubs are generally members-only retailers. Discuss the view that this breeds 'elitist, two-tier shopping' and is counter-productive in the long term.

A3

Centre attracts young and rich

THE AVERAGE shopper who visits the Gateshead MetroCentre is young, rich and upwardly mobile, according to a council report.

It also says the centre's supposed adverse affect on town centre shops has been offset by people generally spending more.

Researchers at the Oxford Institute of Retail Management were commissioned to produce a report on the impact of the MetroCentre and other retail developments on Tyneside shops.

The five-year study from 1986 to 1990 investigated if the out-of-town stores had changed shoppers' habits or taken away trade from Newcastle and Gateshead. A report to Gateshead Council's planning committee this week says the MetroCentre prompts less frequent but higher-spending trips than other centres, including Newcastle city centre.

When the MetroCentre opened local traders blamed it for a downturn in sales, says the report. But later, in 1990, most said the recession was the cause.

'The impact of the MetroCentre has been offset by the growth in retail expenditure in this period. Therefore the study concludes that the impact of such developments is heavily dependent on both local and national economic circumstances.'

The MetroCentre created 5,000 jobs by mid-1989 – almost half of them full-time – and at June 1988 prices it had an estimated annual turnover of £200-£240m, the report said.

'It now takes 7pc of the available retail expenditure within 30 minutes driving time of the centre.'

On the kind of shoppers it attracts, the report says: 'A social split is emerging in the patronage of such centres, in particular the MetroCentre, which is drawing the more affluent and younger members of society ... and higher spending trips.'

Source: The Northern Echo

1 What are the reasons for the growth of out-of-town shopping malls?

2 Do you believe retail developments such as MetroCentre have revolutionised shopping habits? If so, why?

3 What kinds of customers does MetroCentre attract? How might it segment its market? Who are its main competitors?

4 Shopping malls are often said to benefit from the 'magnet effect'. What do you think is meant by this?

A4

Prontaprint: Franchisor of the Year

DARLINGTON-based Prontaprint, 21 years old this year, has been named Franchisor of the Year.

The company, which has 285 print, copy and design centres, won the award for its franchise programme to fight recession.

It was judged on four main criteria: franchisee support, communications, marketing and assistance for franchisees in difficulty.

The award was presented at the British Franchise Association's convention. During the past two years of difficult trading conditions, franchisee failure at Prontaprint has been maintained at less than 3pc a year.

Derek Mottershead, managing director, said: 'The award is recognition of the success we have had in building a first-class support system for our franchisees.'

'We have constantly been improving and refining it to ensure maximum support for franchisees to enable them to develop their own business to the full even in recession. This they have done with remarkable success and the award recognises their achievements.'

The company, which has a turnover of £50m, is one of several franchise operators in Darlington which have established the town as a major centre for franchise business.

These include hairdressing company Saks and domestic services group Poppies.

Source: The Northern Echo

1 Describe how a franchise distribution operation works. Give examples.

2 List the advantages and disadvantages of a franchising arrangement such as Prontaprint.

3 From the article, what do you consider are the main features of a thriving franchise such as Prontaprint? What extra services, such as drive-in retailing facilities, could be important for its success?

4 Suggest the possible components of the 'first-class support system' referred to by Derek Mottershead.

A5

How hidden persuasion makes shoppers spend

Counter culture: In the second of a series on supermarkets, **James Erlichman** looks at the subtle psychology gearing soft sell to big profits

ENTERING a supermarket is like taking a seat in the psychiatrist's chair – the food shopper's deepest desires will be laid open and explored.

In-store cameras backed up by discreet human surveillance measure when and where we are tempted to pause and drop that unnecessary little luxury into the trolley.

The laser beam at the checkout records whether more mozzarella cheese is being sold after it was moved to an eye-catching display or featured in the supermarket's latest TV advertisement.

Everything is geared to increased sales and profits, which means getting consumers to buy things they don't really need, but cannot resist.

Supermarkets don't like talking openly about tactics. They wish to appear the friendly grocer who helps wash our salads, not our brains.

However, it is hard to disguise that virtually every new superstore has its primary doors on the left so the shopping is done clockwise, to the right. 'Nine out of 10 people are right handed and they prefer turning to the right.' said Wendy Godfrey, a spokeswoman for Sainsbury's.

She denies, however, that the smell of fresh bread from the in-store bakery is drawn by ventilation ducts to be wafted at customers as they enter the store. 'We used to do that, but now we don't need to because we bake throughout the day and the smell naturally pervades the store.'

Sainsbury's believes customers associate it with high quality fresh produce. That is why fruit and vegetables greet the shopper first at newer stores.

Profits from the store's own label products are normally higher than those from the big manufacturers. So own label baked beans are usually placed to the left of the Heinz display because the eye reads left to right and will spot the store's brand first.

The big manufacturers can rectify this by paying a premium for better display. How much they pay – especially when they may well be making the own brand version for the supermarket – is a closely guarded secret.

Of the 16,000 items of food which a superstore displays, only about 200 are KVIs – known value items – essentials such as tea, butter and coffee, the price of which will be known by most customers. Two rules apply here. Firstly, keep the cost competitive, which means halving gross profit margins to 15 per cent. Second, dot the KVIs around the store, so customers will have to hunt them out and walk past the frozen black forest gateau, or mange tout peas – items they do not really need.

Sainsbury's second largest susperstore, at Hampton in south-west London, covers 42,000 square feet, has 41 checkouts, a vast delicatessen, in-store bakery, coffee shop, a one-hour dry cleaning service and a bank of petrol pumps outside. Can a store be too big, threatening and confusing the customer? Current thinking is that abundance sells. A well-stocked 20-foot display of tomato ketchup sells more sauce than a depleted shelf 15 feet long.

'I don't think there is a maximum size unless it is how fast the average customer can get round without the frozen food defrosting,' said John Davidson, a lecturer in retail marketing at the University of Surrey.

'The jury is out on lighting,' he said. 'It is kept soft in the wine section to encourage browsing, but it is sharp and bright at the cosmetics counter to suggest cleanliness.'

Width of aisles is also a factor. 'If they move too fast they are missing buying opportunities,' said Andy Mitchell, research officer with the Institute of Grocery Distribution. 'They also try to bounce you back and forth across the aisle by putting the best-selling digestive biscuit on one side and most popular chocolate one on the other.'

Diversification into non-food products can also boost sales. Discount petrol often attracts people who end up filling a trolley as well as their fuel tank.

Convenience and cost are also behind Sunday trading. Round-the-clock running of freezer and chill cabinets means supermarkets cost a lot to operate after closing. Many perishables thrown away on Saturday afternoon could be sold on Sunday. Just as important, however, is the psychology of leisure shopping. Internal studies show that people buy more expensive, discretionary items when they are relaxed and browsing.

It is not only how much one buys, but what one buys. A supermarket makes more profit from its own brand, microwave cook-chill chicken kiev than it does from the ingredients needed to make it at home.

Many consumers appear willing to pay almost any price to avoid preparing food. Grated carrots wrapped in a nice plastic bag sell briskly for £1.18 a pound at Sainsbury's. Whole carrots, a few feet away, cost just 19p a pound.

Source: The Guardian, 11 August 1992

1 Describe technological advancements which have affected supermarket operations, including EPOS (electronic point-of-sale).

2 What is meant by the phrase 'abundance sells'? Give examples.

3 The article suggests that supermarkets aim to influence consumers 'to buy things they don't really need, but cannot resist'. Outline the psychology applied to achieve this.

4 What is merchandising? Describe the ways it is used to encourage consumers to make purchases in retail outlets.

ISSUES

CHANNELS OF DISTRIBUTION

Channel selection is a key component of the marketing mix.

1 Discuss the likely distribution channels for each of the following products: ice-cream, paperback books, 'fizzy' drinks, furniture, lawn-mowers, insulated cable.

2 Argue the case that cutting out the intermediary reduces costs and the case that it does not.

3 Consider whether one channel member can effectively perform all channel functions with reference to examples of vertical marketing.

4 What degree of channel exposure and market coverage – intensive, selective or exclusive – are the following products likely to adopt – Video games, 'designer' birthday cards, bathroom scales, Barbour wax jackets, Bic biros, BMW cars, ball-bearings, soap?

WHOLESALING

A vital channel member or a costly luxury?

1 Discuss the main roles and differences between agents and brokers and give examples of when each is used.

2 What could be the repercussions for (a) a consumer organisation and (b) an industrial company if wholesalers are not used?

3 How does an auction house act as a wholesaler? Give examples of successful auctioneers.

RETAILING

Changes in the purchasing environment have led to retail casualties.

1 It is said that superstore growth is leading to the 'death of the high street'. Discuss whether this is so and how the changes are affecting society at large. Do you believe the progressive historical developments illustrated by the 'wheel of retailing' are healthy for consumers in general and retailing in particular?

2 Is there room in the market-place for both the price-driven discount shops, such as Netto, and the traditional stores and supermarkets which offer ambience and quality?

3 Co-operative societies, department stores and marketing boards are all struggling to survive – why?

4 Outlets such as W.H.Smith are diversifying into e.g. travel and financial services. Is this movement (a) beneficial for the customer and (b) necessary for retail survival?

MAIL ORDER

Mail order has existed for 60 years and has now become a way of life for many consumers.

1 Mail order has been described as a 'painless way of shopping' – why? What are its limitations?

2 What products are most suited to mail-order methods? Discuss examples and try to account for their success.

3 What are the advantages and disadvantages of using catalogue warehouses for retail shopping?

HOME SHOPPING

By the next century ordering goods direct from home will be commonplace.

1 The name of the satellite television shopping channel QVC stands for 'quality, value and convenience'. To whom can television retailing offer these attributes?

2 What are the social and economic advantages and disadvantages of home shopping?

3 Have you ever made a purchase from a telephone or door-to-door sales person or party plan? Do you consider them to be an invasion of privacy or do you believe they have a role to play in future retailing?

PHYSICAL DISTRIBUTION

Choice of a suitable physical distribution system is *now affected greatly by considerations of technology and the environment.*

1 Warehouse storage and stock control methods are increasingly computerised. Discuss the implications of this for an organisation's finances.

2 What are the advantages and disadvantages of replacing people with robots in the various components of physical distribution?

3 A great deal of freight travels by road, which is neither environmentally friendly nor cheap. Argue the case for rail versus road and discuss how the use of transportation methods might change in the future.

QUESTIONS

1 What are the four main components of the distribution or place mix?

2 What is direct distribution?

3 Give two examples of direct distribution.

4 Give three reasons why organisations might not use direct distribution channels.

5 What are the three main intermediaries used by organisations?

6 Name four factors which will influence an organisation's choice of distribution channel.

7 What are the main differences between the distribution channels for consumer and industrial goods?

8 Name four of the main roles of the intermediary.

9 What is a vertical marketing system? Give an example.

10 What are the three levels of market exposure for a product? Give an example of each.

11 What is a wholesaler?

12 Define the two main types of wholesaler.

13 Give two examples of full-service wholesalers and describe their main features.

14 Give three examples of limited-service wholesalers and describe their main features.

15 What is the difference between an agent and a broker? Give an example of each.

16 List six functions of a wholesaler.

17 List three advantages a wholesaler offers to a manufacturer.

18 List three advantages a wholesaler offers to a retailer.

19 What is a retailer?

20 Give three examples of types of retail store which are not mass merchandisers and describe their main features.

21 Give three examples of kinds of mass merchandiser and describe their main features.

22 Give three examples of non-store retailing and describe their main features.

23 What is the 'wheel of retailing'?

24 List four aspects of the retail mix on which a retailer must make decisions.

25 Describe four features of the 'retail revolution'.

26 Describe three ways in which the 'consumer revolution' has affected retailing.

27 Name five components of a physical distribution system.

28 List three key aspects of effective warehouse storage.

29 Name five of the key factors to consider when selecting a method of transportation.

30 Name three modes of freight transport and give their main advantages and disadvantages.

PROJECTS

1 'The importance of place decisions is invariably underestimated and yet selecting the correct channels of distribution is probably the most important part of the marketing mix.' Do you agree with this statement?

2 What sort of distribution methods are used by an organisation or product with which you are familiar? Assess the costs, benefits and disadvantages of the system and compare it with channels used by services such as tourism.

3 In some industries many wholesalers have gone out of business, e.g. the food industry. Why do you think this has happened and what are likely to be the problems faced by wholesaling in the future?

4 Describe and account for the growth of the 'multiples' and the 'big three'.

5 What do you understand by the term 'the retail revolution'? Do you believe its effects have been driven by business or by the consumer?

6 Do you consider that the co-operative societies have a future in the retailing industry? Discuss the successes and failures of one such organisation in your answer.

7 'Home shopping will breed a society of robots in which the only winners will be the large retail organisations.' In your opinion, is this a realistic view of retailing trends?

8 'The three main strategies of retailing are location, location and location.' What is meant by this statement and how true do you believe it to be?

9 'Warehouse clubs offer items from just about every type of shop: power tools, computers, saunas, jewellery, plus the odd speedboat, grand piano and flatbed truck. The new American version is a vast tin shed with concrete floors, squinty lighting and industrial shelving. Sainsbury's it is not.' Consider this description of hypermarkets and discuss the role they could play in future retailing.

10 Describe the role played by physical distribution in ensuring that goods arrive at their destination in the right condition, place and time. Which do you consider to be the most important component of a physical distribution system and why?

GLOSSARY

Agent an intermediary who performs wholesaling functions for a buyer or seller but does not take title to the goods.

Auction house type of wholesale agent who brings buyers and sellers together in one location to enable examination of goods, then sells to the highest bidder and takes commission from the vendor.

Broker an agent wholesaling intermediary who brings buyers and sellers together on a temporary basis but does not take title to the goods.

Bulk buying purchasing of large amounts of goods by retailers or wholesalers for economic reasons.

Cash-and-carry wholesaler limited function merchant wholesaler selling to the retail market for cash.

Catalogue retailing selling products from a catalogue with some samples displayed in a showroom and customers placing orders which are usually met from a warehouse on the store premises.

Chain stores, multiples or variety stores group of retail outlets centrally owned and controlled, handling mass merchandise and similar product lines varied according to local needs.

Channel see 'Channel of distribution'.

Channel management the management of the system of distribution, including all the intermediaries used.

Channel member one of the channels of distribution used by an organisation in its distribution strategy for a particular product.

Channel of distribution organisation of a group of inter-related intermediaries designed to ensure goods move effectively from their point of origin to their point of sale or consumption, usually via wholesalers and retailers.

Commission merchant wholesale intermediary who acts as agent for the producer and controls the sale of the goods for a commission.

Consumer co-operatives see 'Co-operative society'.

Containerisation process of combining several items of goods into one centralised sealed load to facilitate safer and more economic transportation.

Convenience store small retail outlet offering a limited line of products and every service and convenience for local consumers.

Co-operative societies voluntary retail organisations run by producers, retailers or consumers, with profits distributed to owners or members.

Dealer loader an incentive or gift to a retailer in return for the purchase of a specified amount of merchandise.

Department store or 'shopping store' series of specialist shops under one roof forming a large store selling a wide range of commodities, usually located in urban centres.

Direct response marketing see 'Home selling'.

Discount houses mass merchandisers offering a wide range of standard goods and consumer durables at very low prices and with little service.

Distribution all those marketing activities which ensure that products can be purchased by consumers at the time, place and condition required.

Distribution channel see 'Channel of distribution'.

Distribution mix or place mix the mixture of all the place or distribution factors which an organisation decides best suits their objectives in selling products or services.

Door-to-door method of direct response non-store retailing involving the selling of goods by personal calls on householders or organisations.

Drop shipper limited-function merchant wholesaler who receives orders from customers and forwards them to producers, who ship directly to the customers.

Dumps large baskets or display units to be found in supermarkets, usually placed in the aisles or at the ends of gondolas, and often containing special offers.

Electronic point-of-sale (EPOS) retailing technology installed to monitor data, e.g. barcode scanning equipment.

Exclusive distribution market exposure decision where only one outlet is used for a particular product in a geographical area.

Facilitating agency organisation performing activities assisting in the movement of goods from producer to consumer, but not involved in buying or selling the product, e.g. a financial or transport company.

Factor agent wholesale intermediary acting for commodity sellers, arranging for the sale of products and involved in their processing.

Factory shop or manufacturer's shop retail selling by producers from an outlet, often on their premises, direct to consumers.

Franchisee small company operating a retail franchise for a larger organisation within certain guidelines.

Franchising or licensing method of retailing where a small operator is granted a licence to sell the products of the parent company under prescribed conditions.

Franchisor large organisation allowing smaller operations to sell its products independently but under specific conditions.

Full-service merchant wholesaler wholesaler who takes title to the goods and provides a complete range of functions.

General merchandiser full-service merchant wholesaler carrying a wide range of products.

General store small traditional independent retailer offering a convenient, local service to customers.

Gondolas main display units to be found in supermarkets which, put end to end, form the shelving either side of the aisles.

Home selling, home shopping or direct response marketing methods of buying and selling where demonstrations and purchaser interact in the buyer's home, e.g. party plans, home demonstration or TV shopping channels.

Horizontal marketing combining two or more channel members at the same level to exploit marketing opportunities.

Hypermarket or wholesale club very large self-service mass merchandising superstore away from the city centre, offering a very wide range of cheap products and service such as parking, but usually requiring consumers to take up membership of the club.

Independent stores small, traditional retail outlets, often privately owned and offering limited product lines and a convenient, local service.

Intensive distribution market exposure decision where the maximum number of outlets are used for a particular product in a geographic area.

Intermediary or middle person a distribution channel member performing various functions designed to facilitate the transfer of products from manufacturer to consumer – can be an agent or broker, wholesaler or retailer.

Inventory the amount of goods being stored.

Inventory management process of managing stock levels to ensure an efficient flow of goods at any stage from producer to consumer.

Jobber see 'Rack jobber'.

Just-in-time method (JIT) 'last minute' distribution system pioneered by Toyota in the 1950s and designed to minimise stock and reduce inventory control at warehouses and production plants.

Licensing see 'Franchising'.

Limited-line stores see 'Single-line stores'.

Limited-service merchant wholesaler wholesaler who takes title to the goods but provides only a limited range of functions.

Mail-order retailing non-store retailing method in which consumers purchase goods by mail after viewing catalogues, press advertisements or television product listings.

Mail-order wholesaling companies providing a limited-service wholesaling function, selling goods by distributing catalogues to other organisations.

Manufacturers' agent agent wholesaling intermediary selling similar products for several non-competing producers for a commission.

Manufacturer's shop see 'Factory shop'.

Marketing boards producers' organisations established to achieve an orderly supply and marketing of produce, often agricultural, and making provision for the protection of consumers, generally with assistance from public funds, e.g. Milk Marque.

Market traders small non-store retailers selling cheap products from market stalls.

Mass merchandisers large stores, generally self-service, selling to large markets with low prices and lower margins for fast turnover.

Materials handling physical handling of products – part of the physical distribution process.

Merchandising all activities aimed at selling goods at the point of sale, such as display, special offers or gifts, packaging and pricing, carried by the retailer with or without the help of the producer or wholesaler.

Merchants intermediaries performing wholesaling functions and taking title to the goods, buying and selling for a profit.

Middle person see 'Intermediary'.

Mobile shops selling a limited range of products from adapted vans, thereby offering convenience for customers.

Multi-level marketing, network marketing or pyramid selling form of continuous franchising operation where personnel are recruited to sell a product range and bring others into the scheme, thereby establishing an extended distribution network of agents and earning commissions on sales made by those participants. Its legality has frequently been challenged.

Multiples see 'Chain stores'.

Network marketing see 'Multi-level marketing'.

Non-store retailing method of retailing where consumers purchase products without visiting a store, not usually limited to a fixed site.

Off-price retailer retailer selling well-known designer label products at low prices.

One-stop shopping retail development allowing consumers to purchase all the goods they might need from a shopping unit or centre on one visit, sometimes associated with departments licensed to outside organisations.

Order processing part of the physical distribution process which receives and transmits sales order information.

Outlet retail or wholesale venue for selling or trading products.

Over-the-counter selling method whereby customers purchase products at a retail or wholesale location.

Party retailing or party plan non-store home selling method utilising product parties or demonstrations held in consumers' homes.

Place one of the Four Ps of the marketing mix, covering all aspects of distribution (see 'Distribution').

Place mix see 'Distribution mix'.

Producer co-operative co-operative society acting as a wholesaler to serve local co-operatives and retailers.

Protective packaging part of the physical distribution process which ensures safety and security of goods.

Pyramid selling see 'Multi-level marketing'.

Rack jobber or 'jobber' limited-service merchant wholesalers delivering direct without storing and specialising in non-food products sold in food outlets.

Retail audit study of retail outlets designed to provide information on sales, stocks, display, promotion, and so on.

Retailer co-operatives see 'Co-operative society'.

Retailing all activities involved in the sale or exchange of products or services to the ultimate consumer rather than for re-sale.

Retail outlet physical point or premises at which goods are sold by a retailer, often in the form of a shop or store.

Retail revolution all the changes which have taken place, for a variety of reasons, in the retailing industry during recent years.

Selling agent wholesaler intermediary representing an organisation and performing a range of marketing activities, including selling.

Selective distribution market exposure decision where a limited number of chosen outlets are used for a particular product in a geographic area.

Self-selection or self-service stores retail outlets where customers help themselves to merchandise from the shelves.

Shopping centre group of retail outlets, often developed and managed as a unit.

Shopping channel interactive television station, such as the QVC satellite shopping channel, dedicated to non-store home retailing.

Shopping store see 'Department store'.

Single-line or limited-line stores stores selling certain lines of related products rather than a wide assortment.

Single-line wholesalers full-service merchant wholesalers carrying a very narrow line of goods.

Speciality store retail outlet selling one product or a narrow product line and carrying a deep assortment in that line.

Speciality wholesalers full-service merchant wholesalers specialising in a limited variety of products.

Stock control counting and managing of trading stock by a wholesaler or retailer to ensure efficient physical distribution of products.

Supermarket large self-service mass merchandising retail outlet, specialising in low costs and prices and rapid turnover, and selling a wide variety of foods and other products.

Superstore large supermarket selling a wider range and larger number of products.

Telemarketing method of direct response non-store retailing involving the selling of goods by telephone calls to consumers' homes or places of work.

Trading stamps incentive vouchers issued by retailers according to the value of products purchased and later redeemed for cash or gifts. Used to encourage consumer loyalty.

Transportation part of the physical distribution process which concentrates on the method of transport to be used when moving goods.

Truck wholesaler limited-function merchant wholesaler marketing and delivering perishable items which normal wholesalers prefer not to carry.

Universal product code (UPC) special product identifying marks able to be read by electronic scanners in retail outlets.

Variety stores see 'Chain stores'.

Vending machines non-store retailing method involving selling a range of items via automatic coin or card machines in a variety of indoor and outdoor locations.

Vertical marketing or vertical integration distribution channel structure in which some or all channel activities are owned and managed by one channel member in a unified system.

Voluntary chain association of independent traders using collective power for purchasing, promotion and development and confining its membership to retail buyers.

Voluntary group similar to a voluntary chain but membership based on a wholesaler in association with a group of retailers.

Warehouse storage site for finished goods providing a local base prior to sale.

Warehouse showroom retail outlet based in or near a company's warehouse and selling goods selected by customers from a catalogue.

Warehousing part of the physical distribution process concentrating on the storage of goods after production and before transportation to the next channel member.

Wheel of retailing concept suggesting that retailers tend to begin as cheap, low-status operations then evolve into higher-priced, up-market organisations, eventually becoming vulnerable to the newer, cheaper retailers following them in the cyclical 'wheel'.

Wholesale club see 'Hypermarket'.

Wholesaler intermediary, usually an agent, broker or merchant, carrying out some or all of the functions of wholesaling.

Wholesaling channel of distribution involving organisations obtaining goods from manufacturers and distributing them to retailers, or acting as agents in that process. Sometimes involves selling of products direct to the end-user.

SUGGESTED REFERENCES

VIDEO MATERIAL

Business Economics 'One-stop Shopping', BBC, Open University, 1984.

What would you do? 'Gateshead MetroCentre', Tyne Tees Television, 1987.

Prontaprint! – a successful business formula, Prontaprint Ltd., 1988.

Retail Revolution, 'So we bought a computer', Open College, Channel 4, 1989.

Contemporary Marketing, Video Cases, No. 12 (Famous Amos); No. 13 (Northern Produce Co./Mushrooms Inc.); and No. 14 (West Ridge Mountaineering), Boone, L. and Kurtz, D., Dryden Press, 1989.

Business Studies, 'Marks and Spencer – Paris to Madrid', Thames Television, 1990.

Big Business, 'Meadowhall Shopping Centre', Yorkshire Television, 1990.

Critical Eye, 'Custom Eyes', Channel 4, 1991.

American Supermarket, Discovery Channel, 1991.

Walk the Talk, No. 1 (Body and Soul); and No. 2 (Magnificent Mouchoirs), BBC, 1991.

The Geography Programme, 'Retail Chain', BBC, 1992.

High Interest, 'Super! Markets', Channel 4, 1992.

France Means Business, 'Hypermarketing', BBC, 1993.

Me T.V.: the future of television, BBC, 1993.

High Interest, 'Terminal shopping syndrome', Channel 4, 1994.

Open Space, 'Dead centre', BBC, 1994.

MAGAZINE ARTICLES

Journal of Marketing Management, Vol. 1, No. 1, Winter 1985, p.139, 'Future trends in physical distribution'.

Journal of Marketing Management, Vol. 2, No. 1, Summer 1986, p.7, 'New technology in UK retailing: issues and responses'.

Journal of Marketing Management, Vol. 8, No. 3, July 1992, p.259, 'Motives for retailer internationalisation: their impact, structure and implications'.

Journal of Marketing Management, Vol. 8, No. 4, Oct. 1992, p.335, 'Motives for and the management of counter-trade in domestic markets'.

Journal of Marketing Management, Vol. 9, No. 4, Oct. 1993, p.393, 'Power and control in distribution channels: the case of automobile distribution in Turkey'.

Marketing Business, July 1988, p.8, 'New models of retailing'.

Marketing Business, Dec./Jan. 1991/92, p.32, 'Spread the word'.

Marketing Business, June 1992, p.30, 'Signed, sealed, delivered'.

Marketing Business, Sept. 1992, p.13, 'Joint effort'.

Marketing Business, Nov. 1992, p.24, 'A breed apart'.

Marketing Business, Mar. 1993, p.36, 'Marketing solutions'; 'Sweet dreams'.

Marketing Business, April 1994, p.11, 'Science of Marketing'; 'Killing off the competition'.

Quarterly Review of Marketing, Vol. 11, No. 4, Summer 1986, p.1, 'Direct Distribution systems in the marketing of Life Insurance'.

Quarterly Review of Marketing, Vol. 11, No. 2, Winter 1986, p.12, 'Retail classification: a theoretical note'.

Quarterly Review of Marketing, Vol. 13, No. 3, Spring 1988, p.1, 'Consumers' attitudes towards Tele-shopping'; and p.8, 'Retailing change: cycles and strategy'.

Quarterly Review of Marketing, Vol. 13, No. 4, Summer 1988, p.19, 'Franchising in the UK'.

FURTHER READING

Adcock, D., Bradfield, R., Halborg, A. and Ross, C., *Marketing Principles and Practice* (2nd edn), Pitman, 1995, ch. 12.

Baker, M. (Ed.), *The Marketing Book*, Heinemann/C.I.M., 1990, ch. 17.

Boone, L. and Kurtz, D., *Contemporary Marketing*, Dryden, 1989, chs 12–15.

Booth, Don, *Principles of Strategic Marketing*, Tudor Publishing, 1990, ch. 10.

Cannon, Tom, *Basic Marketing*, Holt Business Texts, 1980, chs 7, 14 and 15.

Dibb, S., Simkin, L., Pride, W. and Ferrell, O., *Marketing*, Houghton Mifflin, 1994, chs 10–13.

Foster, D., *Mastering Marketing*, Macmillan, 1982, ch. 8.

Giles, G., *Marketing*, MacDonald and Evans, 1985, ch. 9.

Kotler, P. and Armstrong, G., *Marketing*, Prentice Hall, 1993, chs 12 and 13.

McCarthy, J. and Perreault, W., *Basic Marketing*, Irwin, 1987, chs 11–14.

Mercer, D., *Marketing*, Blackwell, 1992, ch. 10.

Oliver, G., *Marketing Today*, Prentice Hall, 1990, chs 20 and 21.

Acknowledgements

The Guardian.
The Northern Echo.
The Yorkshire Evening Press.
The Yorkshire Post.

10

PROMOTION DECISIONS

DEFINITIONS

Communication is the process of establishing a commonness or one-ness of thought between a sender and a receiver . . . for communication to occur there must be a transfer of information from one party to another in which both receiver and sender play an active role.

WILBUR SCHRAMM, *THE PROCESS AND EFFECTS OF MASS COMMUNICATIONS*, UNIVERSITY OF ILLINOIS PRESS, 1955

The promotion mix consists of any combination of four major ingredients including advertising, personal selling, publicity and sales promotion.

DIBB, SIMKIN, PRIDE AND FERRELL

INTRODUCTION

As we saw in Chapter 1, a successful exchange of goods or services can only take place if an effective relationship has been established between buyer and seller. Communication is thus a vital component of marketing and it is important for an organisation to try to understand how it works.

Once it has opened up communication links with consumers, it is the company's task to decide how best to inform them of its products or services and persuade them to purchase these goods. The promotion function thus assumes significant importance within an organisation's marketing mix (see Figure 10.1).

Promotion involves decision making in several areas which will be covered in the next three chapters. The four key sectors of promotion, all important aspects of business in their own right, are personal selling and the three non-personal methods, i.e. advertising, sales promotion and public relations/publicity, all of which contain many variations and sub-divisions. The combination of methods selected by an organisation will constitute its promotional mix, to be monitored and adjusted as and when necessary.

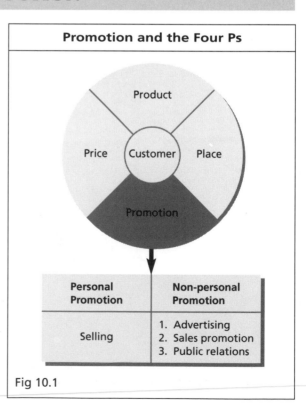

Promotion and the Four Ps

Personal Promotion	Non-personal Promotion
Selling	1. Advertising 2. Sales promotion 3. Public relations

Fig 10.1

KEY CONCEPTS

MARKETING COMMUNICATIONS

Communication takes place constantly, internally and externally, in every organisation, whether non-verbally, via the written or spoken word, or utilising the rapidly increasing range of electronic and machine-based methods which are developing into the so-called 'information superhighway'. Indeed, business could not function without communication and we are not far away from the day when any person is available and any fact can be relayed at the touch of a button.

Communication thus pervades every imaginable facet of an organisation's existence, from simple messages to employer–employee relationships and full-blown promotional campaigns. Although the all-encompassing nature of marketing, as discussed in Chapter 1, clearly embraces all

these areas, we will confine ourselves here to those aspects of communication directly related to the central role of marketing in the buyer–seller exchange process.

In this regard, the marketing communications system is a complex one. Its effectiveness depends on several inter-related factors, such as the target group, the medium used, the product or service involved and the nature of the message being relayed, all of which must be considered carefully by the organisation generating the communication. Essentially, however, effective communication is based around the simple process illustrated in Figure 10.2.

This views communication as a process of information exchange, with information about customers and the marketing environment flowing in to the organisation, which then decides what messages it

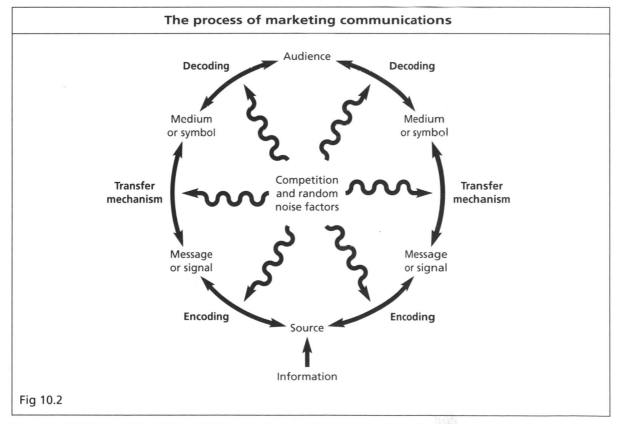

The process of marketing communications

Fig 10.2

Source: Engel, I., Warshaw, M. and Kinnear, T., *Promotional strategy* (6th edn), Richard D. Irwin, Inc. 1987.

wishes to transmit to which audiences through what media. So for marketing communication to take place four main elements are required:

1. An organisation or person wishing to relay a message.
2. A medium through which the message can be transmitted.
3. A piece of communication in verbal and/or visual form.
4. An audience capable of receiving the message.

As the piece of communication makes its passage from originator to receiver it is first put into an appropriate code, or *encoded*, to express effectively in understandable terms the message or signal to be delivered. The communication could thus be incorporated into an advertisement, a display, publicity release, sales presentation, and so on.

The next step is for the originator to determine what transfer mechanism best suits the encoded message and convert it into a symbolic medium. Here again there are many possible choices of channel, for example advertising media, sales people, exhibitions and public relations channels.

Upon arrival at its destination, the message will be interpreted, or *decoded*, by the receiver and, if all stages have been carefully researched and selected by the sender, the result will be the consumer understanding and acting on the information provided or making a positive purchase decision. The whole communication process can be summarised by posing five key questions:

1. Who (is generating the message)?
2. What (is the message)?
3. How (is the message being transmitted)?
4. To whom (is the message being directed)?
5. With what effect (is the message being transmitted)?

However, there are other complicating factors for an organisation to assess if it wishes to understand and capitalise fully on communication opportunities. For instance, at every stage of the process a message will face interference from many forms of distraction and competition, whether media generated or not. To withstand these random 'noise' factors a message must therefore be designed to stand out from the crowd by use of creativity, originality, media method and other marketing tools, in order to reach the desired audience successfully.

Again, the environment of marketing is always changing and an organisation must closely monitor these changes in order to ensure that its messages and media are effective and relevant to its target market and do not become obsolete. The main way of doing this involves close consideration of and appropriate action on all the information coming back to the organisation from its audiences in the form of feedback communication, either in response to the original message transmission or independently.

The choice of communication method open to an organisation is vast, as are the information sources used by consumers. Referring to the division between personal and non-personal communication mentioned in the introduction to this chapter, and the fact that we are all affected by general as well as marketing orientated messages, it is the task of the marketer to identify relevant communication channels, assess their comparative advantages and limitations, and select those deemed to be most suitable in the prevailing circumstances (see Table 10.1).

Another communication tool used by organisations is *networking*, a method of delivering a message, extending distribution channels and broadening a market by establishing links with individuals or firms, initially through informal contact such as social events and displays based on common needs and interests.

With an understanding of how marketing communications works, an organisation is then in a position to develop an effective promotional strategy as part of its overall marketing mix.

THE PROMOTION MIX

Any company wishing to market a product or service (or even itself) has to bring it to the attention of its potential market and possibly to the public at large, and try to ensure that consumers recognise, remember and want its particular offering in preference to any other. In order to achieve this aim, promotion focuses on the invention and transmission of appropriate messages using effective channels of communication, usually in one of the four mix categories mentioned in the introduction to this chapter.

Promotion in some form is always available to an organisation, however restricted it might be by resources. However, there are five general conditions which particularly favour the use of promotion as a marketing mix tool:

Table 10.1 Methods of communication and their benefits and drawbacks

Source	Personal communication	Non-personal 'mass' communication
1. General	Word-of-mouth influence	General media
2. Marketing dominated	Personal selling	Advertising Sales promotion Public relations and publicity
Assessment factors for marketing communication		
1. Reaching a large audience:		
Speed	Slow	Fast
Cost per individual reached	High	Low
2. Influence on the individual:		
Ability to attract attention	High	Low
Accuracy of message transmitted	Moderate	High
Clarity of content	High	Moderate
3. Feedback:		
Direction of message flow	Two way	One way
Speed of feedback	Fast	Slow
Accuracy of feedback	High	Low

Source: Adapted from Engel, I., Warshaw, M. and Kinnear, T., *Promotional Strategy* (6th edn), Richard D. Irwin, Inc., 1987.

- an upward trend in demand;
- strong product differentiation;
- hidden product qualities;
- existence of emotional buying motives;
- availability of adequate funds.

When making a decision to promote a product or service, an organisation will normally have one or more specific objectives in mind, the main ones of which are listed in Figure 10.3.

The main purpose of promotion is to smooth the path between consumer and product, so promotion will tend to be applied according to where such smoothing is most required and where the application of promotion is most likely to be effective. Of course, promotion should be consistent throughout the distribution chain, and it must be remembered that a channel member is often just as important a recipient of promotional messages and materials as the end-user and should therefore be targeted as such. Retailers, for example, have only limited shelf space for which producers must compete, whilst in their turn they will require evidence from producers of the likely success of the product. Promotion will help to clarify the position in both situations.

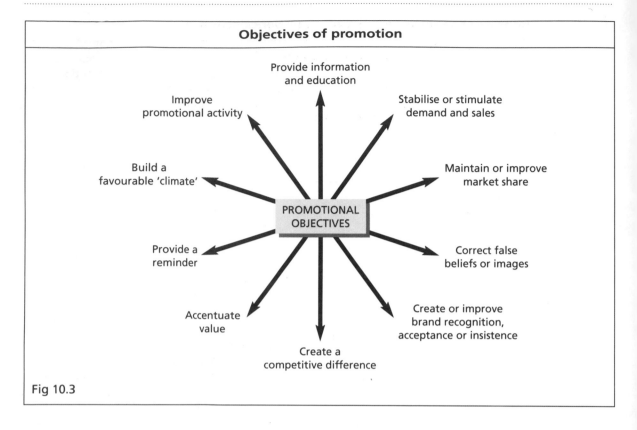

Objectives of promotion

PROMOTIONAL OBJECTIVES

Provide information and education

Stabilise or stimulate demand and sales

Improve promotional activity

Maintain or improve market share

Build a favourable 'climate'

Correct false beliefs or images

Provide a reminder

Create or improve brand recognition, acceptance or insistence

Accentuate value

Create a competitive difference

Fig 10.3

The necessity for a close relationship between promotion and place is an important ingredient in a balanced marketing mix. Depending on the nature of the product, the market and the desired objectives, an organisation has a choice between two main promotional strategies related to the channels of distribution it is using or intending to recruit.

It could choose to pursue a *pull strategy* which concentrates on promoting to the end-user direct, thereby 'pulling' them into the retail outlet and encouraging them to pull the product off the shelf, a method focusing on advertising and direct marketing to the consumer. Alternatively, an organisation could decide to use a *push strategy* which emphasises promotion to current or potential channel members, focusing on distribution penetration by 'pushing' the product hard into retail outlets and onto their shelves. This method utilises personal selling and trade promotions. Each strategy will support the other if they are used in conjunction, but an organisation should be conscious of the need to get the right balance between the two methods. The two companies in the detergent and washing-powder duopoly illustrate the use of these contrasting strategies: Procter and Gamble pulls while Lever Brothers prefers to push.

Whoever the target may be and whatever the promotional tool utilised, it is the main aim of promotion to reach customers at various stages of the product adoption process (see Chapter 5) and to move them along the continuum towards a purchase. The strong link between promotion and consumer behaviour is best remembered by use of the traditional marketing acronym, *AIDA*, referred to in Chapter 5.

Table 10.2 illustrates how consumers move through the four AIDA stages of product or service familiarity, which promotional tools generate most activity at each stage and what effects they produce. So advertising and public relations tend to draw customers in by arousing attention and interest, whilst sales promotion and selling methods tend to induce desire and prompt action. Advertising and public relations then re-establish themselves in the post-transactional period as the cycle is repeated. However, direct response marketing methods are starting to alter this traditional view of promotional methods.

Table 10.2 The AIDA concept applied to promotion

Stage	Promotional method	Effects
1. Attention	Mass media advertising	Consideration/awareness
2. Interest	Mass media advertising Public relations	Evaluation of evidence
3. Desire	Sales promotion Word of mouth	Trial and analysis
4. Action	Selling	Conviction and purchase

This kind of analysis helps an organisation to select its most effective promotional mix, along with a number of other key variables listed in Figure 10.4.

One of the most important of these factors is the nature of the product or service. Consumer products, and particularly fast-moving consumer goods, are more suited to advertising and sales promotion methods of communicating while in contrast, industrial goods emphasise personal selling and public relations very strongly in their promotional budgets.

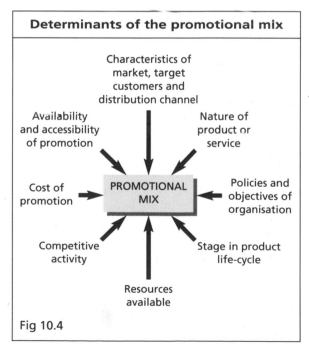

Determinants of the promotional mix

Characteristics of market, target customers and distribution channel

Availability and accessibility of promotion

Nature of product or service

Cost of promotion

PROMOTIONAL MIX

Policies and objectives of organisation

Competitive activity

Stage in product life-cycle

Resources available

Fig 10.4

The consultancy group PIMS (Profit Impact of Marketing Strategy) has produced considerable research on the allocation of promotional mix budgets, and some of its main conclusions are that:

- profitability depends on the mix of advertising and other promotional methods;
- companies which concentrate on advertising tend to be more profitable than those which rely on sales promotion;
- increased market share depends on the combination of advertising and other promotional expenditure;
- the larger the market share a product has, the greater the budget devoted to advertising rather than other methods, and the higher the return on capital employed.

As a result of these findings, PIMS suggests that it is wiser for organisations to use advertising in declining markets which require brand maintenance, and to use other promotional methods in growth markets; also that the amount invested in advertising should be reduced in markets containing fewer, larger buyers.

The management of promotion will also have to take account of the speed of consumer reaction required. Advertising tends to lead to an increase in sales which gradually slackens off to rest at a new, higher level, whereas sales promotion usually produces a sharp rise which can then be followed by a rapid sales decline if the right measures are not taken. In contrast, personal selling and public relations tend to generate a more steady, long-term improvement. As with most marketing tools, it is a case of 'horses for courses'.

Table 10.3 Promotional expenditure in the UK for 1991

Promotional method	Expenditure in £millions	%
Advertising	7, 575	55
Sales promotion	3, 300	24
Public relations	950	7
Direct mail	950	7
Exhibitions	600	4.5
Sponsorship	325	2.5
Total	13, 700	100

Source: Mintel Special Report, *Marketing Services Business*, 1992

As already discussed, there are many promotional tools available to an organisation and these can be categorised in four main areas along with other minor sectors. The amounts spent on each vary from company to company, for reasons described previously, and from country to country. Even without inclusion of the huge expenditure on personal selling, which is extremely difficult to quantify financially, the total amount spent annually on promotional activities is still over £13 billion in the UK alone. Table 10.3 summarises what percentage of this figure is allocated to the different marketing communication methods.

The rest of this chapter looks in more detail at the personal selling portion of the promotional mix, including sales management. The non-personal elements of communication are covered in Chapters 11 and 12. These are often divided into two segments known as 'above-the-line' and 'below the line', following traditional advertising agency practice of placing promotional activities which earned them a commission above an imaginary line for accounting purposes and those resulting in a fee below it.

Above-the-line promotion thus refers to situations where organisations pay various media for the space and/or time necessary to deliver a message, in other words advertising, whereas *below-the-line* promotion covers all other methods where this is not the case, such as sales promotion and public relations. However, some of the newer activities, such as direct marketing and sponsorship, tend to span both sectors; agencies are also starting to move away from the commission system, and a large component of the promotional mix fits neither of these categories, namely personal selling.

PERSONAL SELLING

Personal selling covers all the processes involved in informing consumers and persuading them to buy products or services by communicating with them orally or visually on a personal basis. It is an activity which has sometimes attracted a bad press and a down-market image because of 'cowboys' and foot-in-the-door sales people, yet personal selling still has a vital role to play in the promotional mix of many organisations.

The very nature of selling as a one-to-one communication method rather than a mass medium means that it is a promotional tool used more in circumstances when the conditions are particularly favourable, such as:

- when there are relatively few customers in the market;
- where customers are geographically concentrated;
- where the product or service is technically complex or custom-made;
- where the product or service has an associated trade-in or needs special handling;
- when the channels of distribution are short;
- where the price is relatively high.

Industrial marketing usually meets most of these criteria and thus tends to focus predominantly on personal selling, although consumer marketers will use this method, mainly with wholesalers and retailers and particularly when adopting a push strategy.

The locations in which selling takes place are innumerable, for instance on the organisation's own premises, at the customer's house or client's base, in neutral venues such as exhibitions, conferences and hotels, or at social events. The three main types of sales environment are:

- *field selling*, where sales people visit customers on their premises, usually having targeted them or made arrangements first. This category includes some of the direct selling and distribution methods mentioned in Chapter 9;

- *retail selling*, where customers visit shop or store outlets, often on a random basis;
- *telephone selling*, or telemarketing, in which sales people target customers and make direct contact with them by telephone.

The advantages and disadvantages associated with each of these methods are listed in Table 10.4.

In addition to these main categories, multi-level marketing is on the increase as a selling and distribution method, as discussed in Chapter 9, and direct marketing is a rapidly growing selling environment in which customers are individually targeted and contacted by mail. Although becoming increasingly personalised, direct marketing is not a face-to-face method linking buyer and seller orally or visually, and is thus bracketed with below-the-line promotion in Chapter 12.

The three methods of selling listed above all incorporate a variety of responsibilities for the sales person, of which the following are the most important:

- order taking, in which sales people play a relatively passive role to keep business 'ticking over' by ensuring the continuation of orders from established distributors and end-users;
- order getting or order processing, where the emphasis is on a strong sales force playing an

Table 10.4 Advantages and disadvantages of selling methods

Method	Advantages	Disadvantages
Field selling	Face-to-face contact Complexities explained Allows for looking around Organisation straightforward	Expensive Low control Can be hard to appraise or motivate Low coverage
Retail selling	Customer involvement Face-to-face contact Products can be discussed Cheap	Can be claustrophobic Unpredictable Difficult to evaluate Less time
Telemarketing	High control Organisation easy Accessible to customer Testable/measurable	Not face-to-face – easier to fob off/harder to build relationships Viewed as intrusive Can lead to confusion Relies on accurate telephone details

active role in demonstrating the product, attracting new customers and meeting quotas and targets;

- supporting the organisation's other promotional mix activities and ensuring that the sales function is fully integrated into the overall marketing effort;
- product delivery, and simultaneously encouraging greater volume;
- missionary selling, essentially a public relations role building goodwill, assisting in product use and display, educating customers and giving information;
- providing technical advice and support;
- keeping abreast of product and market knowledge and trends;
- making regular calls to customers and ensuring the maintenance of adequate stocks and promotional/merchandising materials;
- being competent with audio-visual and selling methods, such as lap-top computers, which help to reduce non-selling time;
- monitoring environmental factors and relaying customer comments and complaints;
- compiling records and writing reports on customers, products, markets and competitors, and attending sales meetings, courses and conferences;
- collecting payments, investigating/reporting account problems and dealing with other financial matters.

Every industrial sales call has been calculated to cost, on average, well over £100. So increasingly, organisations are insisting that sales people follow certain principles to achieve value for money. They should:

- be trained;
- make appointments;
- know the customer's business;
- know the products;
- not call too often or too rarely;
- ensure they have the authority to act.

Research has shown that over half of all sales people do not adhere to many of these basic principles.

Of course, the main role of sales people in any selling operation is to persuade customers to purchase the product or service by taking them through the AIDA stages referred to earlier in this chapter. To achieve this objective, a sequence of well-established, logical steps is generally followed, as illustrated in Table 10.5.

Each stage of this scientific approach contains a check-list of tasks for sales people to observe and complete in their search for and discussions with potential customers, tasks which are generally the subject of considerable thought and debate.

Before selling can take place, a great deal of research must be done into who and where the potential clients are. The list can then be narrowed down to the most likely names and tailor-made approaches designed. The sales person must in any given situation determine exactly whom to target; not always an easy task when several elements could contribute to the final decision, in either consumer, industrial or business-to-business markets.

An understanding of consumer and organisational behaviour and the composition of the decision-making unit (or DMU, referred to in Chapter 5) operating in different selling situations, is thus an important consideration for the sales person before meeting the potential customer. In order to maximise the chances of eventual success, the roles played by various individuals or groups must be distinguished so that they can be treated accordingly. These roles are identified by the acronym GUDBI:

- *Gatekeepers* – those potentially barring the way to the decision makers, e.g. secretaries.
- *Users* – those who will actually use the product and thus offer valuable opinions and advice.
- *Deciders* – personnel making the final decision, usually the most important category.
- *Buyers* – those physically responsible for completing the actual order or purchase.
- *Influencers* – individuals or groups who could affect the final purchase decision.

Much thought should also go into the method of communication itself. For example, organisation members acting in a selling capacity are always encouraged to ask 'open' rather than 'closed' questions – e.g. 'how many would you like?' (encouraging a figure in reply, thereby anticipating a sale) when closing a sale, instead of 'would you be interested in buying?' (which is far more likely to attract the answer 'no') – and qualitative 'why?' questions rather than quantitative 'which?' ones.

Again, sales people are recommended to anticipate possible objections, which usually focus on price, service, quality, image, timing, capacity, competition or personality, and devise a strategy for handling and countering them. The 'boomerang'

Table 10.5 Stages in the personal selling process

AIDA stages	Selling steps	Description of tasks
1. Attention	Prospecting Qualifying Pre-approach	Set guidelines, locate potential clients Evaluate/select suitable targets Research background and prepare/plan sales pitch
2. Interest	Approach Presentation Demonstration	Establish appropriate atmosphere and real needs, probe customers Highlight features/benefits/USPs Practical illustration/evidence/examination
3. Desire	Overcoming objections Negotiating Closing	Anticipate, listen to and counter negativity Offer incentives, discuss terms and differences, 'reduce the gap' Observe buying signals, finalise offer, exchange contact details
4. Action	Agreement Follow-up Feedback	Complete sale and administration, suggest other products, observe courtesies Deliver, communicate, remove dissonance Receive views, encourage further sales

method, which turns objections into benefits, is often used – for example, one response to the standard objection 'I'm too busy to see you' could be 'I know you are busy – that's the reason I've called. I have a service designed for busy executives.' Similarly, price objections can be answered by replies which emphasise value.

Considerable research has been done into how best to prospect for the right clients; putting potential customers at their ease and never giving them a reason to refuse or look elsewhere; developing graphic and computer-led presentations; negotiation skills designed to reduce the gap between buyer and seller; closing a deal; retaining clients through regular follow-up and feedback procedures, and so on. It has also been estimated that 70 per cent of interpersonal communication is non-verbal (body language), so this aspect of personal selling has attracted considerable attention as a result. The emphasis in selling has gradually shifted away from the traditional *hard sell* adopted by slick or aggressive operators and towards the *soft sell*, focusing on 'stroking' customers and establishing long-term relationships with them, known

as *relationship marketing*. Sales people are now less likely to indulge in *cold calling*, where a prospect is called on without being contacted beforehand, unless they are in possession of enough positive information or are involved in telemarketing.

In today's competitive business world, personal selling usually requires a creative imagination and the ability to find solutions for buyers' problems. This *creative selling* applies to all sectors, whether the products are tangible goods or intangible services.

In fact, effective selling requires many other qualities and characteristics on the part of the sales person. In addition to the ability to communicate precisely and persuasively using oral, written and technological means, possession of organisational skills such as time management and effective record keeping, enthusiasm, flexibility, receptiveness, tenacity and an appropriate personal appearance are also important attributes in the selling situation.

Sales people must also explain and observe the increasingly stringent ethical standards and legal requirements applying to selling – for example, there is now a 'cooling-off' period attatched to certain kinds of major sale, in case consumers change their minds or feel they have been pressurised. Above all, however, a sales person should be motivated and managed effectively.

SALES MANAGEMENT

Managing the selling function requires an organisation to consider, make decisions on and monitor certain activities which together form its *selling mix*, namely:

- selection of selling methods and sales technique to be used;
- management of customer accounts and financial matters;
- organisation of the sales force, including size, geography, duties, motivation and remuneration;
- establishing effective procedures for short- and long-term sales forecasting and the measurement of trends.

The various selling methods available have been covered in the last section. Sales techniques have always been the subject of considerable debate, the evangelistic and scientific approach of practitioners such as John Fenton contrasting with the more relaxed, soft-sell attitude adopted by other 'gurus'.

The management of customer accounts involves the location of relevant customer segments, their prioritisation according to importance, and associated monitoring of income and expenditure. Key accounts are the most significant contributors and often reflect the *Pareto 80/20 effect*, whereby 20 per cent of an organisation's customers account for 80 per cent of its business and thus a corresponding percentage of its effort. Other categories of customer are the new accounts, and those being developed, changed or phased out. The sales management of each will vary accordingly.

Initially, an organisation should consider whether it needs a sales force, a decision which will depend on the nature of the firm, its objectives, size, products, customers and outlets, as well as geographic factors. Having opted for a sales force, the size of that force will be set according to the following main factors:

- the number and location of current and prospective customers;
- the resources available to the company;
- the value of potential orders;

- the characteristics and buying habits of customers;
- the nature and range of the products or services involved;
- the marketing policy being adopted;
- the flexibility of the company's organisational structure;
- the availability of appropriate personnel.

Sales force operations can be organised in a number of ways. Where firms are selling a single or small range of homogeneous products through similar distribution channels or to similar types of customer, the system tends to be functional and straightforward in nature. When the organisation grows and its range of products, customers and distribution channels are more extended, more focused arrangements can be adopted, for example:

- *Geographic* – a sales person covers all the company's operations in a particular territory with sales managers in charge of different regions. This method saves on travel expenses, utilises knowledge of the locality and customers, and avoids unnecessary or annoying repeat calls.
- *Product or service based* – where homogeneous product groups can be easily identified and require separate treatment. Especially used in consumer durable and industrial selling to cope with the higher degree of differentiation between products in these sectors and the need for specialist sales people to deal with technical complexities and problems. Sometimes extended to incorporate the criterion of end-use.
- *Customer type* – allocating according to knowledge of organisations or individuals, company or customer attitudes and background, and market segments in general. Could thus include *systems selling*, i.e. supplying a range of items for one customer such as office carpets, curtains, filing cabinets and furniture. Sometimes large organisations or key accounts may be handled by the sales manager rather than a member of the sales force.
- *Compound or mixed system* – a combination of the above methods designed to sell diversified products to wide-ranging markets.

Whichever operation is used, sales management personnel will be needed to put it into effect. Figure 10.5 illustrates the roles of such people in the sales hierarchy and contrasts the likely scenarios for small and large organisations.

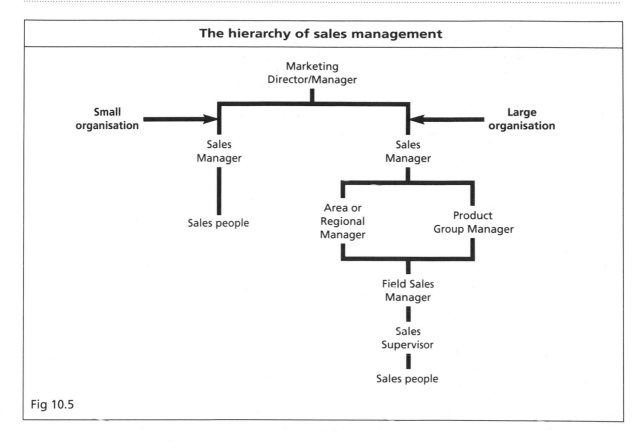

The hierarchy of sales management

Fig 10.5

Sales managers or their equivalents are responsible for assessing the comparative importance of the various sales force activities described previously and ensuring the appropriate selling mix is put into effect, as well as handling administrative matters such as keeping central records, arranging frequency of calls and managing economy of time and effort.

None of these management functions will be effective, however, if sales people are not sufficiently motivated, and this is therefore a prime consideration of personnel at sales manager level and above. The nature of the profession is somewhat uncertain and stressful owing to irregular hours, working alone and away from home, the lack of support, responsibility for company errors in delivery and so on, and the loss of confidence resulting from rejection or failure to achieve the required sales levels.

Performance can thus easily suffer and the sales person needs to be both self-motivating and motivated in order to sustain effort. Motivation should ideally have a lasting effect and this can be achieved

in many ways, the most important of which are listed in Figure 10.6.

Two key inter-related aspects of motivation are the ways in which sales people are evaluated and remunerated. Staff can be evaluated quantitatively, applying ratios, e.g. sales value per call, or by analysing performance measured against targets, past performance or business development in general. Alternatively, qualitative analysis could be applied by monitoring relative success in the sales process, judging initiative or assessing through an appraisal system.

Evaluation is invariably closely linked to targets and remuneration, and the methods by which sales people are paid depend on a company's circumstances, objectives, traditions and philosophies. Sales are usually encouraged by financial incentives so that additional payments accompany increased business and the beating of targets. There are three basic forms of remuneration and their advantages and disadvantages are described in Table 10.6.

The salary-only method is often used where situations other than order taking are involved or

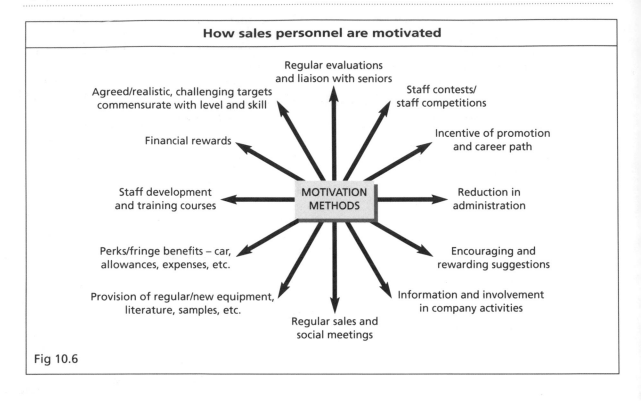

How sales personnel are motivated

Regular evaluations and liaison with seniors

Agreed/realistic, challenging targets commensurate with level and skill

Staff contests/ staff competitions

Financial rewards

Incentive of promotion and career path

Staff development and training courses

MOTIVATION METHODS

Reduction in administration

Perks/fringe benefits – car, allowances, expenses, etc.

Encouraging and rewarding suggestions

Provision of regular/new equipment, literature, samples, etc.

Information and involvement in company activities

Regular sales and social meetings

Fig 10.6

Table 10.6 Advantages and disadvantages of payment systems for sales people

Payment method	Advantages	Disadvantages
1. Salary only	Provides security Minimises tension Easy to administer Organisational and long-term goals encouraged Realistic long-term objectives	No financial incentive for extra effort Supervision and motivation required No achievement or reward base
2. Commission only	Maximises effort Strong achievement/reward relationship Full exploitation of major accounts Costs tied to returns Selling expenses reduced when revenue decreases Rates changed to suit organisation	Personal and short-term goals emphasised Jealousy and antagonism created Deterrent to many applicants Financial distress can occur Company has less control over sales force Independent sales people attracted No personnel stability – high turnover Costly to administer
3. Salary and commission or bonus	Management has some freedom of control Incentive/security balance Encourages new opportunities Favoured by sales personnel Reduces uncertainty/risk factor	Difficult to administer Incentives can be limited Can lead to confusion

when orders are infrequent. In contrast, salary plus commission or bonus tends to be used where orders are frequently taken, while commission only is usually preferred where speciality selling is concerned, such as the traditional door-to-door personal selling of encyclopaedias. The mixture of salary with a commission or bonus tends to be the most popular system as it offers an acceptable compromise between incentive and security.

In order to reduce the risk factor and plan ahead most organisations attempt to estimate future sales levels, in terms of numbers of products or total value/revenue over a short- or long-term period, and these figures will be used to set individual sales people's goals.

Sales forecasting is also necessary for preparing sales budgets and financial targets, co-ordinating and planning production schedules to cope with variable factors such as demand, labour and raw materials, formulating short- or long-term objectives and strategies, and serving as a decision-making tool for other elements of the marketing mix.

Forecasting methods are either quantitative or qualitative in nature. *Quantitative forecasting* applies statistical techniques and computer simulations to research data and makes numerical predictions, by using methods such as:

- *trend analysis and projections* from internal and external data – cheap but over-simplified and unreliable;
- *market testing and customer surveys* – usually reliable but costly and lengthy;
- based on *sales in the previous period* – cheap but naïve and inaccurate;
- *exponential smoothing* – a sophisticated trend analysis assigning a weight factor to historical sales data and giving greater weight to the most recent and more relevant statistics. Helps to reduce the risk factor.

Qualitative forecasting is more subjective in nature and includes techniques such as:

- *guesstimates* – educated guess-work;
- *composite opinion* of the sales force – 'grass roots'

information so should be accurate and valuable, but could be biased and informal;
- *intention-to-buy surveys* – can be unreliable and misleading;
- *jury of executive opinion* – consensus of senior personnel which is quick and easy but relies on opinion and not facts;
- *industrial surveys* – limited but accurate;
- *Delphi technique* – an extended jury of executive opinion, in which a series of anonymous viewpoints and forecasts are sought from practising and academic experts via a questionnaire, with the answers combined and averaged and other questionnaires sent until a consensus is reached. Accurate but expensive and time-consuming.

The usefulness and value of any sales forecasting method will depend on the economic climate, the organisation's market share and resources, the industrial outlook, product life cycle stage and factors such as accuracy, speed and cost, and it requires frequent review and modification to take account of environmental changes. Even then, errors, the unpredictability of demand and other variable factors make sales forecasting a very risky business.

An organisation can judge its performance by the volume of sales and the size of orders, breaking down this information for further evaluation and control by product sizes and styles, customer types, sales territories, channels of distribution, key outlets, terms of sale, and so on. This information should be compared to standards, forecasts, previous performance records and internal and external data.

The danger is that sales analysis information either arrives too late for corrective action to be taken or that other crucial data is not taken into account – for example, irregular discussions with sales force members can mean that vital information remains undisclosed and then disappears completely when a person moves, taking data, knowledge and possibly customers with them. An organisation proficient in the sales management function will take action to ensure these kinds of problems are not encountered.

ARTICLES

A1

Town bids to revive image with spa message in a bottle

BOTTLED spring water from Harrogate could join bestselling brands from all over the world on supermarket shelves this summer.

A deal utilising water from local springs is on the cards as the town seeks to revive its famous spa image.

Harrogate Borough Council is hoping to sign a deal with a company wishing to bottle up to 1m litres a year – and, if it meets with consumers' approval, this could be increased.

Sales would not only boost the district's profile but bring in thousands of pounds for the council through royalties.

It is the first stage of a campaign to recreate the spa fame associated with Harrogate in the Victorian and Edwardian eras.

The discovery of the town's first medicinal spring was made in 1571. The number of visitors peaked in the 19th century.

The last production of Harrogate spa waters for therapeutic purposes was in 1968, although there has been at least one unsuccessful bid to market bottled town water since.

The spa at Harrogate's twin town Luchon in the Pyrenees attracts more than 27,000 visitors a year generating an income of £6.5m.

Harrogate council leader Phil Willis said: 'I am anxious that what is an untapped resource should be tapped, and we hope this will accelerate the spa revival.'

The council is expected to authorise tests on the water next week which should eventually allow the bottled product to be labelled as 'mineral water'.

Source: The Northern Echo, 7 March 1994

1 Describe all the types of communication that Harrogate Borough Council might be involved in when preparing to market bottled spring water.

2 What do you think would be the most effective promotional mix and why? What factors would affect the decision? Which are likely to be more useful in this situation, above- or below-the-line methods?

3 Explain the role of the consumer in the communication process for the water product. Do you think the AIDA concept is relevant here? What noise factors might intervene?

4 Would you advocate a push or a pull strategy of promotion for the enterprise? Explain your reasons.

A2

The Second Oldest Profession

Hugh Herbert

PEOPLE who have money, said the Kleeneze man, 'the money they've got, they've got because they don't like to part with it.' This impeccable logic is one of the fruits (and there aren't many) of Mostyn Morgan's many years selling brushes door to door in Wales, the perfect nutshell explanation of the old truth that the rich get richer and the poor get poorer. The poor must obviously be suckers for door to door salesmen, while the well off say 'Not today, thank you,' slam the portals and loose the dogs.

Morgan has a hard row to till. He plods up muddy paths to remote houses where like as not the wife is hiding under the stairs till he goes away. When he does find a potential customer at home, he sells the odd pastry brush, price £1.29.

Still, it's an open air, serene life compared with those of some of the other salespeople shown in The Second Oldest Profession (BBC-1). Take the lady who used to give parties for plastic containers, or at least for those who might buy them. Now she gives boudoir parties where she shows off without actually wearing them, the products of a chain of sex shops.

See-through shifts, bras with peepholes, a nightie with a lift-up front. Buy one of these tonight, she says, and I'll throw in a pair of frilly panties free. These have a kind of ripcord at the side for speedy release: which brings a big laugh, whereas the vibrators in assorted shapes and sizes get only a titter. Tuppaware was never like this.

The necessary faith is that if you try hard enough you can sell anything anywhere, and to prove it we are selling pasta to Italy, tom toms to Nigeria, and brass bands to Pakistan. There are people like John Fenton who sell salesmanship, and outfits like Programmes Ltd which sells computers and conferences by phone while putting its employees through a course of mental body building.

Programmes Ltd is the commercial face of the Exegesis movement. Its sellers' day starts with aerobics, proceeds by way of bullying from instructors to group investigation, the claiming of brownie points and the confessions of failure. A collective mania sweeps the office, with sudden screams of 'order!'

These are not, it turns out, a desperate plea for calm, but the joy of landing a buyer. 'Good morning? *Good morning!*' shouts the instructor, to one seller unable to get enough enthusiasm into his telephone greeting. 'The first two words of the script, and you're lying!' And how.

Source: The Guardian

1 Why is selling viewed as a historically important profession?

2 Do you agree that 'if you try hard enough you can sell anything anywhere'?

3 What do you consider to be the main attributes of a good sales person?

4 List the selling situations mentioned in the article. Do you think they require different selling styles?

A3

Hard sell fails new approach to selling

LET it be said at the outset Mr Patrick Ellis – prophet of profit and author of what he hopes will become the business people's Bible, Who Dares Sells – is a charming, likeable man, and evangelistic in his zeal to promote his book.

It's just that, in pushing the near-800-page tome, he pushes, well ... just a little too hard. And for this buyer at least, that is not the way to sell.

Mind you, in a hurried nationwide whistlestop promotional tour he had to pack a lot of communication into a relatively short time.

Our first contact was not hopeful – he was arguing on a hotel foyer telephone, trying to persuade someone that his method would give the persons on the other end 'a better deal'.

But he was all smiles when we met.

He said: 'Demotivation is one of the major problems in the world today. And it is because man is not a logical being – he is an emotional being.

'The whole sales process is a battle – not physical, but persuasive.'

That is where he is convinced his book can transform people's approach to selling.

It ranges far and wide, from a potential customer's body-language to understanding the working's of the customer's mind; from planning ahead to sales techniques.

And it does pack in plenty of useful information and guidance.

'It is put in such a way that every word is designed to sell,' said Mr Ellis.

Source: By courtesy of *The Yorkshire Post*

1 Do you agree with Patrick Ellis's contention that 'the whole sales process is a battle – not physical, but persuasive'?

2 Why is 'demotivation' a problem in selling? How can it be prevented?

3 Why does selling have an 'evangelistic' image in the eyes of many people? Do you believe this to be a fair current reflection of the profession?

4 Patrick Ellis considers that selling 'ranges far and wide' and highlights four specific components. Discuss the role of each of these elements of selling, giving examples.

A4

Winners and losers in a big money game

A controversial sales system which once led to a series of spectacular crashes is having a revival. **MARTIN SHIPTON** spoke to converts who believe they can make their fortune – and he warns of the pitfalls.

A GROUP of people gathered in the Sundial Hotel at Northallerton last week, eager to hear how they could make big money selling a product whose marketing potential they were told is enormous.

All of them had responded to advertisements placed in local newspapers including *The Northern Echo*. If they agreed to be recruited, they joined a growing number of participants in schemes which describe themselves as examples of 'multi-level marketing'.

The system is better known as pyramid selling, and is so called because it trades at a number of tiers. People who join the pyramid buy goods or services from the person running the scheme or from other participants, and sell them to the general public in their homes.

Apart from the profit they make on selling, participants are offered other rewards which they can earn in various ways. These can include bonuses for recruiting new participants, commission on sales made by other participants and bonuses or higher commissions or extra discounts on goods when the participant is promoted to a higher level in the scheme.

In the Sixties and early Seventies, pyramid selling got itself a bad name after a series of spectacular crashes; many people who joined up with the dream of becoming rich ended up losing heavily.

But although the old name is rarely used because of its tarnished reputation, the same system is undergoing an upsurge of interest at the end of the Eighties.

Last week's meeting was organised by two agents of an American water filter company called National Safety Associates. Until two months ago, Debbie Cain and Vicky Harris ran a fruit and vegetable stall at York Market. They were recruited by Debbie's brother Colin, who decided to sell his removal business and organise an NSA network full-time.

Colin, 25, was impressed by an NSA exhibition he saw earlier this year. He reels off statistics about the vast market potential of his superior brand of water filter, and the phenomenal amounts of money he expects to earn (£150,000 by this time next year is a 'conservative' estimate, he reckons). Colin is anxious to build up as big a network as possible, because if he achieves a certain turnover he will earn commission on every sale made by those he recruits – and by everyone subsequently recruited at lower tiers of the pyramid. His immediate aim is to become a 'sales co-ordinator', which will entitle him to £96 commission on every £155 unit sold.

Isn't the high level of commission dependent on over-pricing the product? 'Not really,' says the former owner of racehorse transport business who has also been recruited.

'In a traditional company there are a lot of overheads, as well as high salaries for regional sales managers and so on. The mark-up on our water filters is a lot less than what you pay on a soft drink in a pub.'

Dos and Don'ts

THE Department of Trade and Industry issues the following advice to people thinking of joining a pyramid selling scheme:

DO choose a scheme which concentrates on selling rather than recruiting others.
DO make sure you have confidence and are interested in the goods or service you will have to sell.
DO make sure the company will give you proper training and back-up.
DON'T rush into joining because you feel under pressure.
DON'T commit yourself to spending large sums of money until you are confident that you really can sell.
DON'T get carried away by others' success stories. A few people right at the start might make extra money, but later entrants do not do so well.

Source: The Northern Echo, 23 October 1989

1 Why is multi-level marketing so called? Explain the NSA operation described in the article.

2 If you were asked to join the NSA network scheme, what information would you think it important to know before making a decision?

3 Why did pyramid selling get a bad name in the 1960s and 1970s?

4 How closely do you think multi-level marketing should be monitored and how far should its participants be legally protected?

A5

SOLD SHORT!

Sales teams must 'fight harder' to survive

SALES teams are not putting in enough effort to ensure the survival of their companies in the recession, according to research by a York firm.

'If you are going to survive in a recession, you have to get out there and fight for it,' said Frank Atkinson, senior partner at Haxby-based Sales and Marketing Solutions.

'When times are good you can, to a large extent, get away with trusting your sales people to bring home the orders. But when times are bad, companies cannot afford such a laissez-faire attitude.'

The firm's research found activity levels in the sales teams of one national firm had dropped by as much as 50 per cent.

In some cases it had ceased altogether.

Mr Atkinson said a drop in confidence, fuelled by increasing rejections, leads to lower expectations of making a sale.

Rather than face more rejection sales staff may stay at home, he said, or fill their days with non-productive work. Thus the recession can become self-perpetuating.

'I don't want to give the impression that sales teams are being lazy,' added Mr Atkinson, 'but in times of recession you start to believe your own bad publicity.'

Those sales people that do persevere may find their bargaining powers reduced. 'We have observed that prices are often driven downwards by sales people and not the buyers,' he said.

'The buyer asks if the price can be reduced, and the sales person responds by trimming the price rather than defending the company pricing structure.'

He said sales staff tend to relate more to the customer than to their own employer with the result that prices, and profits, are driven down.

Mr Atkinson has devised a range of solutions to these problems, centred around the idea of sales audits. The key, he says, is to give sales teams the motivation, skills and tools to do their job effectively.

Firms should adopt a more 'hands-on' approach to their sales teams and start looking in the longer term.

'Because sales people are set a target, they take a much shorter-term view – just trying to achieve their target,' he said. 'Instead of filling their day with ineffective activity, they should be thinking about longer-term calls.'

Source: The Yorkshire Evening Press, 26 October 1992

1 What does Frank Atkinson mean by a 'laissez-faire attitude' to selling? When is this philosophy not appropriate?

2 Does the setting of sales targets always lead to a 'shorter-term view'? What is meant by 'longer-term calls'?

3 Why might sales people drive prices down rather than buyers doing so? How important is confidence to a sales team?

4 What is meant by a 'hands-on' approach to sales management? How might such a policy improve the effectiveness of a sales force?

ISSUES

THE ROLE OF COMMUNICATION IN MARKETING

Communication happens automatically, it cannot be viewed as part of the marketing process.

1 In what ways, if any, do you think communication contributes to the marketing mix? Give examples of organisations which place a high value on a well thought-out communication process and those which do not.

2 Do you believe organisations should ensure their staff participate in communication training programmes, and if so, why? Is it necessary for all staff to take part?

3 How can organisations block out the 'noise' factor from competing messages? Discuss the main sources of such noise.

THE PROMOTION MIX

There are some broad guidelines to assist an organisation, but the selection of a promotional mix is really a lottery.

1 Do you agree with this statement? Suggest where the emphasis on the elements of the promotional mix might be for (a) a diesel engine manufacturer, (b) a company selling soft contact lenses, (c) an independent school and (d) a firm marketing breakfast cereals.

2 Are the above- and below-the-line divisions of non-personal promotion still relevant in contemporary business? Can you think of a better way to categorise the main components?

3 Explain push and pull strategies and when they are applied. How important is this distinction in an organisation's promotional mix decisions?

THE SELLING STIGMA

In some countries the sales function still has a down-market reputation.

1 Why do you think this might be so? What are your personal views of the selling function? Do you think there are differences in the image and operation of selling between consumer and industrial markets?

2 Discuss the contrast between hard and soft selling and give examples of both from your experience.

3 Do you think any modern methods help to improve the reputation and effectiveness of selling? If so, discuss which ones and why. Do you agree that 'a good marketing person can sell anything'?

THE AIDA CONCEPT

Applicable to practical promotional and selling situations or just another theoretical marketing acronym?

1 Do you think the four AIDA steps accurately reflect the stages consumers go through when considering the purchase of a product or service, and to what categories do they best apply?

2 Think of a purchase you have recently considered or actually made. Identify the roles played by promotional stimuli and sales people in moving you through the AIDA stages.

3 Split up into groups of three and appoint a buyer, a seller and an observer. The seller should try to sell to the buyer either this book or a product or service chosen by the group, observing the stages of the personal selling process where applicable. The buyer should raise appropriate objections and engage in relevant questioning before the seller closes the deal. Allow 20 minutes for this then spend 10 minutes listening to and discussing the observer's comments before reporting back to the main group and considering all the main issues which arose.

SALES FORCE MOTIVATIONS

Sales people are only motivated by financial incentives.

1 Do you agree with this statement? What other incentives are there?

2 What do you think an organisation can do to make sales people feel 'part of the team'?

3 Which method of remuneration do you think is most suitable and why?

4 What main sales activities are the following involved in: (a) a network seller, (b) a telemar-

keter, (c) a retail assistant, (d) a car dealer, (e) a merchant wholesaler, (f) a travelling computer sales person and (g) a door-to-door double glazing sales person?

SALES FORECASTING

Sales forecasting can only be arbitrary and is rarely accurate.

1 If sales forecasting is so unpredictable, why do organisations commit considerable amounts of time and money to this activity?

2 Which do you consider to be more reliable, quantitative or qualitative forecasting methods, and why?

3 Select the individual forecasting method you consider to be most suitable for (a) a consumer organisation, (b) an industrial firm and (c) a service company.

QUESTIONS

1 Name the four main components of the promotional mix.

2 What is the process of marketing communications?

3 Explain decoding and encoding.

4 What is 'noise' in relation to communications?

5 Name the four elements required for marketing communication to take place.

6 What is networking?

7 Give the main advantages and disadvantages of personal communication.

8 Give the main advantages and disadvantages of non-personal communication.

9 Name three conditions which favour the use of promotion.

10 List six main objectives of promotion.

11 What is a pull strategy?

12 What is a push strategy?

13 Explain the AIDA concept as applied to promotion.

14 List five key determinants of the promotional mix.

15 What is PIMS?

16 Give three findings of the PIMS research.

17 What is above-the-line promotion?

18 What is below-the-line promotion?

19 List four situations in which personal selling would probably be used.

20 What are the three main types of sales environment?

21 Give two advantages and two disadvantages of each of the three main types of selling.

22 List six of the main responsibilities of a sales person.

23 Name four of the principles sales people are usually encouraged to follow.

24 Name two of the main steps in each of the four AIDA stages of personal selling.

25 What are the hard sell and the soft sell?

26 List four qualities of an effective sales person.

27 Name three components of the selling mix.

28 What is the 'Pareto effect' related to the selling function?

29 List five factors determining the size of a sales force.

30 Name three organisational systems around which a sales force can be based.

31 List six motivating factors for sales force personnel.

32 What are the three main remuneration methods for sales people?

33 Give two advantages and two disadvantages of each of the three methods by which members of a sales force are paid.

34 What is quantitative forecasting? Give three examples.

35 What is qualitative forecasting? Give three examples.

36 Give two uses and two disadvantages of sales forecasting.

PROJECTS

1 'Marketing and communication are synonymous.' Discuss.

2 The Body Shop does not advertise but instead lays emphasis on good PR, merchandising, customer care and direct marketing. Describe and account for this promotional strategy and The Body Shop philosophy of 'instinctive marketing'.

3 'We believe that changes in media will increasingly blur the definitions between advertising and other communication disciplines . . . there are no advertising problems, only communications problems' (Andy Law, Managing Director, Chiat Day Advertising Agency). Discuss this view that all the promotional mix components are becoming increasingly similar.

4 Why do industrial marketers tend to favour personal selling and public relations while consumer organisations emphasise advertising and sales promotion? Give examples in your answer.

5 'Some companies are so entrenched in above-the-line, particularly in the use of television, that it is difficult for them to see the value of scaling down into a range of promotional activities' (*Marketing Business* magazine). What is the reason for this emphasis on above-the-line promotion and what are the advantages to an organisation of using other promotional methods?

6 'It is easier to sell to people with a friendly hand-shake than by hitting them over the head with a hammer. You should try to charm the consumer into buying your product' (David Ogilvy, *Confessions of an Advertising Man*). Is this a realistic view of the evolution of personal selling in the 1990s?

7 Discuss the contention that the sales person's interaction with the customer is the most important part of the selling mix.

8 'In times of recession, the first company activity to suffer is promotion' (*Marketing Business* magazine). Why is this so, and is the policy justified?

9 'The effectiveness of the sales force and the overall success of an organisation's marketing effort depend on sympathetic and thorough sales management.' How far would you go along with this statement?

10 How is the sales function organised in a company with which you are familiar? Describe the geographic breakdown of the sales force. Would you recommend any changes and if so, why?

11 'Nowadays, a job in sales is much more than just selling.' Explain this statement and discuss the relationship between selling and marketing.

12 You have identified a prospective customer for your product or service. Describe how you would approach the personal selling process and consider any background research necessary as well as presentation, closing and follow-up techniques.

GLOSSARY

Above-the-line refers to non-personal promotional methods where organisations pay various media for the space and/or time required to deliver a message, i.e. advertising in the mass media.

Action final stage of the AIDA promotion and selling process in which consumers are induced to purchase the product or service.

Agreement stage of the personal selling process in which both buyer and sales person arrive at a consensus of opinion.

Approach step in the personal selling process in which the sales person makes initial contact with a prospective customer to establish an appropriate link.

Attention first stage of the AIDA promotion and selling process in which consumers' awareness of the product or service is aroused.

Audience group of people exposed to, receiving and decoding a piece of promotional communication.

Below-the-line refers to non-personal promotional methods where organisations do not pay separate media to transmit a message, i.e. sales promotion, public relations, direct mail, exhibitions, and so on.

Bonus an incentive payment to sales people designed to increase motivation and productivity.

Buyers potential members of a consumer or organisational decision-making unit, one of the components of the GUDBI acronym.

Buying signal indication by a prospective customer that they are willing to make a purchase, thus inviting a sales person to use closing techniques.

Closed questions types of sales questions which are limited in nature and tend to attract a negative response from consumers.

Closing techniques various methods a sales person adopts as part of the selling process to end the communication and bring about consumer purchasing action.

Closing the sale the action of the sales person in securing an order from the customer.

Code system of symbols used to send a piece of communication or promotional message to an audience.

Cold calling sales people paying calls on prospective customers without warning in order to secure an interview and eventually an order.

Commission method of remunerating sales people where payment is based on an agreed share or percentage of the amount sold or business transacted, with no salary involved.

Communication the process by which an organisation or individual makes contact within and outside the organisation, through written, verbal, non-verbal or technological means.

Communication mix combination of different promotional methods designed to reach a target audience with a specific message.

Communications media the methods used to relay messages from their origin to the chosen target audience.

Compound sales system (or mixed system) combination of geographic and product-based methods of organising sales force operations which is appropriate when diversified products are being sold to wide-ranging markets.

Creative selling imaginative method of selling, which focuses on original material or ideas, their presentation to customers, finding solutions for buyers' problems and developing new sales territories. Can apply to any product or service.

Customer sales system organisation of a sales force according to knowledge of the customer's attitudes, behaviour, income, background, and so on.

Deciders potential members of a consumer or organisational decision-making unit, one of the components of the GUDBI acronym.

Decoding the process by which the recipient of a piece of marketing communication interprets and translates the message.

Delphi method qualitative method of sales forecasting in which experts and practitioners are anonymously surveyed several times until a consensus of opinion is reached.

Demonstration stage of the personal selling process in which the product or service is shown in action to the prospective customer.

Desire third stage of the AIDA promotion and selling process in which the consumer expresses a positive preference for the product or service.

Development account relatively new individual or corporate customer categorised by the sales person or selling organisation as suitable for expansion.

Encoding the process of translating a marketing communication message into an understandable form and transmitting it to a target audience through an appropriate medium.

Exponential smoothing sophisticated method of sales forecasting in which statistics are weighted to reflect their relative importance and produce a more accurate analysis of trends.

Feedback last stage in the communication and selling process whereby measurable response or reaction to a message is provoked, indicating to an organisation how that message is being interpreted.

Field sales manager person responsible for organising, motivating and training a sales force.

Field selling selling environment which involves visiting prospective customers on their premises on a face-to-face basis.

Follow-up stage in the personal selling process when a sales person contacts a prospective customer by telephone, letter or visit, after an initial approach has been made.

Gatekeepers potential members of a consumer or organisational decision-making unit, one of the components of the GUDBI acronym.

Geographic sales system organisation of a sales force according to particular geographic regions or territories.

GUDBI acronym used to help identify members of a consumer or organisational decision-making unit, who could be gatekeepers, users, deciders, buyers or influencers.

Guesstimate qualitative method of sales forecasting in which an estimation is made based purely on educated hunch or guesswork.

Hard selling technique of selling in which sales persons adopt determined and sometimes aggressive tactics to sell products or services to customers.

Influencers potential members of a consumer or organisational decision-making unit, one of the components of the GUDBI acronym.

Intensive selling selling a greater volume to existing customers through a concentrated campaign.

Intention-to-buy survey qualitative method of sales forecasting in which consumers are given questionnaires or asked orally whether they intend to buy a product or service.

Interest second stage of the AIDA promotion and selling process in which the consumer's curiosity in the product or service is aroused.

Joint promotion occurs when two organisations get together to market their products or services, thereby benefitting from each other's differential advantages and economies of scale.

Jury of executive opinion qualitative method of sales forecasting in which views of personnel in senior positions and departments are sought and combined to arrive at a consensus.

Key account individual or corporate customer identified by the sales person or selling organisation as important to keep and nurture because of its large or potentially large contribution to the firm's sales figures and profits.

Marketing communications all the ways in which an organisation contacts customers and transmits messages with a view to promoting and selling products and services.

Medium channel of communication through which a promotional message is relayed from an organisation to its target audience.

Message piece of promotional communication transmitted by an organisation to a target audience through a selected medium.

Missionary selling method of selling in which sales people concentrate on stimulating sales, often through third parties, by building up relationships and goodwill.

Mixed sales system see 'Compound sales systems'.

Motivation the combination of psychological, social and economic stimuli and incentives by which an organisation encourages its sales force to complete its tasks successfully and improve future performance.

Negotiation stage in the personal selling process in which the sales person makes offers, discusses differences and aims to reduce the gap between buyer and seller, with a view to seeking agreement on mutually acceptable terms.

Networking a method of marketing communication which involves establishing links through informal contact with individuals or organisations as a way of extending the market.

Noise any interference or distraction to a transmitted, promotional message that reduces the effectiveness of the communication process.

Non-personal promotion all the methods available to organisations to communicate messages about products and services which do not involve direct face-to-face contact with customers, i.e.

advertising, sales promotion, public relations, and so on.

Objections reasons given by customers for not purchasing a product or service, which the sales person must try to overcome.

Open questions types of questions which are discursive in nature and tend to encourage a customer to consider a purchase.

Order getting (or order processing) duties of the sales person emphasising a positive approach to the selling process leading to successful meeting of targets.

Order taking duties of the sales person emphasising the continuation of regular business, often with established customers.

Pareto effect situation affecting an organisation whereby a small percentage of customers often has a disproportionate effect on total sales. Often called the 80/20 rule, i.e. 20 per cent of customers might account for 80 per cent of sales.

Personal promotion methods available to organisations communicating messages about products and services which involve direct face-to-face contact with customers, i.e. personal selling.

Personal selling the process of personal promotion which involves a sales person informing and persuading customers about products or services by meeting them face to face.

PIMS Profit Impact on Marketing Strategy, a consultancy group which has researched into promotional mix budgets in order to assist organisations in formulating communications strategies, and has discovered a strong relationship between a firm's market share and its return on investment.

Pre-approach step in the personal selling process in which the sales person prepares all relevant material on products and customers before a selling approach is made.

Presentation step in the personal selling process in which the sales person meets prospective customers, usually formally, to present a product or service in its best light and encourage them to purchase.

Product sales system organisation of a sales force according to the nature and characteristics of the products or services involved.

Promotion communication with individuals or organisations by the use of various methods designed to inform them about products or services and persuade them to purchase.

Promotion mix the selection and blending of personal and non-personal promotional activities within a fixed budget, appropriate for the market and product concerned and designed to meet organisational objectives.

Prospecting step in the personal selling process in which the sales person sets guidelines for the project and identifies potential purchasers of a particular product or service.

Pull policy strategy which emphasises promoting direct to the end-user, using advertising and direct marketing to 'pull' customers into retail outlets where they are encouraged to 'pull' products off the shelf.

Push policy strategy which concentrates on promoting to current or potential channel members by 'pushing' products hard into and through distribution outlets using personal selling and trade promotions.

Qualifying step in the personal selling process in which the sales person evaluates and selects target customers for a product or service.

Qualitative forecasting methods of sales forecasting which are subjective in nature and involve using research surveys to gather data and opinions.

Quantitative forecasting methods of sales forecasting which use statistical techniques to analyse trends and make predictions.

Quota sales target set for sales people to achieve, either in terms of performance or as a basis for remuneration.

Relationship marketing marketing philosophy based on making sales by establishing long-term relationships with customers.

Remuneration the different ways in which a sales person may be paid, all of which can be strong motivational factors.

Retail selling selling environment which involves customers making purchases at shop or store outlets.

Salary and commission means by which a sales person is paid, involving a mixture of straight salary and commission based on performance

Salary only means by which a sales person is paid based purely on salary with no element of commission.

Sales analysis detailed investigation of an organisation's sales figures and patterns.

Sales folder portfolio of selling aids used by the sales person.

Sales force group of sales people within an organisation.

Sales forecasting a combination of qualitative and quantitative methods used by an organisation to project likely sales, in the future depending on certain criteria and assumptions.

Sales management all the activities involved in the management of the selling function in an organisation, including planning, training, motivation and forecasting.

Salesmanship skill of informing customers and persuading them to buy, practised by sales people in selling environments.

Selling process of informing and persuading customers to purchase products or services by directly communicating with them face to face.

Selling mix all the aspects of personal selling and sales management from which an organisation selects and which are combined in order to maximise its sales figures.

Signal message or symbol communicated by an organisation to a target audience via a medium of transmission.

Soft selling technique of selling in which sales people adopt calm tactics, focusing on getting to know customers and gently introducing products or services in order to encourage purchases.

Stroking technique of supporting and continually encouraging customers, used by sales people to generate purchases.

Suggestion selling a subtle method of presenting selling arguments by suggestion and encouraging customers to purchase associated products or services as a result.

Symbol representative signal used by an organisation or sales person to convey a message about a product or service to customers.

Systems selling sales operation involving selling a range of different products or services to the same customer.

Targets sales figure or other performance goal set by an organisation for a sales person to achieve and on which remuneration could be based.

Telephone selling (or telemarketing) selling environment which involves sales people using the telephone to contact potential customers and encourage them to make purchases.

Transfer mechanism means by which a message is relayed by an organisation via a medium of communication to a target audience of prospective customers.

Trend analysis (or trend projections) quantitative method of sales forecasting in which historical figures are compared and studied, and their significance evaluated.

Trial close a sales person's attempt to close a meeting or ascertain what progress has been made before the presentation has been completed.

Users potential members of a consumer or organisational decision-making unit, one of the components of the GUDBI acronym.

SUGGESTED REFERENCES

VIDEO MATERIAL

I could do that, 'Selling', ITV, 1984.

Marketing Today, 'Promotion', Marketing Today Publishing, Henley, 1985.

English File, 'Power of language – power to persuade', BBC 2, 1985.

It's a deal – Selling (series of five), Channel 4, Open College, 1987.

The second oldest profession – six faces of selling, BBC, 1987.

The Language of Persuasion, BBC, 1988.

The Big Company – the corporate ladder and the freedom net, 'Amway', Channel 4, 1989.

Contemporary Marketing, Video Cases, No. 16 (Apple Computer, Inc); and No. 18 (Lipton and Lawry's), Boone, L. and Kurtz, D., Dryden Press, 1989.

Watchdog, 'The hard sell', BBC, 1992.

Winning, 'Building a network', BBC, 1993.

RADIO MATERIAL

Sell, sell, sell, 'Sales', BBC Radio Leeds, 1984.

Selling to industry, InTech (Sales Training) Ltd, 1985.

Market forces, 'Selling', BBC Radio, 1985.

MAGAZINE ARTICLES

Journal of Marketing Management, Vol. 8, No. 4, Oct. 1992, p.365, 'The process of conflict in buyer–seller relationships at domestic and international levels: a comparative analysis'.

Journal of Marketing Management, Vol. 9, No. 2, Apr. 1993, p.105, 'How to create competitive advantage in project business'; and p.123 'Managing the industrial sales force of the 1990's'.

Marketing Business, Issue 11, June 1990, p.20, 'Motivation on the wing'.

Marketing Business, Issue 12, Aug. 1990, p.6, 'Sales professionals – the training gulf'.

Marketing Business, Issue 13, Oct. 1990, p.9, 'Marketing initiative'; 'Taking the lead in sales training'.

Marketing Business, July/Aug. 1991, p.40, 'Look who's talking'.

Marketing Business, Oct. 1991, p.32, 'Science of marketing'; 'Mix and match'.

Marketing Business, June 1992, p.28, 'Market Brief'; 'Multi-level marketing', and p.35, 'Ring my bell'.

Marketing Business, July/Aug. 1992, p.48, 'Briefly'.

Marketing Business, Nov. 1992, p.43, 'Doorstepping'.

Marketing Business, April 1994, p.6, 'Sales partnerships', p.45, 'Negotiation tactics'; and p.48, 'Briefly'.

Marketing Business, June 1994, p.35, 'Calling the shots'.

Quarterly Review of Marketing, Vol. 13, No. 2, Winter 1988, p.14, 'Key market-factor forecasting aids sales prediction'.

Quarterly Review of Marketing, Vol. 13, No. 3, Spring 1988, p.12, 'Using salesforce compensation as an effective management tool'.

FURTHER READING

Adams, Tony, *The Secrets of Successful Sales Management*, Heinemann, 1989.

Adcock, D., Bradfield, R., Halborg, A. and Ross, C., *Marketing Principles and Practice* (2nd edn), Pitman, 1995, chs 14, 15 & 18.

Allen, Peter, *Selling*, Pitman/Nat West, 1988.

Baker, M. (Ed.), *The Marketing Book*, Heinemann/ C.I.M., 1990, chs 15 and 16.

Boone, L. and Kurtz, D., *Contemporary Marketing*, Dryden, 1989, chs 16 and 18.

Booth, Don, *Principles of Strategic Marketing*, Tudor Publishing, 1990, chs 4, 5 and 6.

Cannon, Tom, *Basic Marketing*, Holt Business Texts, 1980, ch. 17.

Denny, Richard, *Selling to Win*, Kogan Page, 1988.

Dibb, S., Simkin, L., Pride, W. and Ferrell, O., *Marketing*, Houghton Mifflin, 1994, chs 14 and 16.

Elvy, B. Howard, *Salesmanship*, Heinemann Made Simple Books, 1978.

Engel, I., Warshaw, M., and Kinnear, T., *Promotional Strategy*, Irwin, 1987.

Foster, D, *Mastering Marketing*, Macmillan, 1982, ch. 7.

Giles, G., *Marketing*, MacDonald and Evans, 1985, ch. 10.

Kotler, P. and Armstrong, G., *Marketing*, Prentice Hall, 1993, chs 14 and 16.

McCarthy, J. and Perreault, W., *Basic Marketing*, Irwin, 1987, chs 15 and 16.

Mercer, D., *Marketing*, Blackwell, 1992, ch. 13.

Oliver, G., *Marketing Today*, Prentice Hall, 1990, chs 8, 15 and 18.

Smith, P.R., *Marketing Communications*, Kogan Page, 1993, chs 1, 2, 3, 8 and 10.

Acknowledgements

The Northern Echo.
The Yorkshire Evening Press.
The Yorkshire Post.

11

ADVERTISING

DEFINITIONS

Advertising is the use of non-personal paid mass communication media to inform, persuade or remind a target audience about an organisation or its products, and to influence their knowledge, attitudes and behaviour in such a way as to meet the objectives of the advertiser.

The aim of advertising is not to 'sell' but to induce people to try the product and to prepare them for satisfaction by presampling it verbally.   INSTITUTE OF PRACTIONERS IN ADVERTISING

INTRODUCTION

Advertising in one form or another has provided a ready means of communication for centuries. In the latter half of the twentieth century, however, it has experienced a huge growth to match that of marketing, of which it is an important part. This growth has been due to a whole range of social factors, in addition to the emergence of the fast-moving consumer brands and the expansion and accessibility of the mass media.

As a result, specialist organisations have developed to institutionalise and professionalise the advertising industry, which now embraces some key areas of strategic decision making, as illustrated in Figure 11.1.

In fact, the use of above-the-line promotion, or advertising as it is generally known, has grown to such an extent that it now accounts for over half the huge total of expenditure on non-personal communication, as observed in the last

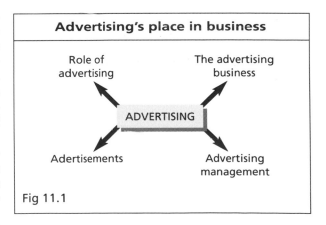

Fig 11.1

chapter. But advertising has always attracted controversy and there is much debate as to its actual value and general role within the marketing mix.

KEY CONCEPTS

THE ROLE OF ADVERTISING

Traditionally the most direct, noticeable and powerful method of promotion, advertising has invariably been the subject of criticism from many quarters. However, this can often be attributed to its role being misunderstood and, in fact, public attitude surveys have shown that only a minute proportion of people actually object to being exposed to advertising.

In most contemporary societies advertising fulfils a number of important economic and social functions which many individuals and organisations use to their benefit. Amongst the numerous purposes for which advertising can be employed the following are the most significant, and can be grouped into four main areas:

- *the product or service*
  - providing information about the availability of products and services and increasing awareness;
  - promoting them and stimulating demand or increasing use;
  - reinforcing previous messages and supporting other communication;
  - introducing product features, benefits or USPs;
  - describing new uses or modifications;
  - announcing special offers, price changes, packaging, and so on;
  - justifying performance or price.

- *customers and markets*
  - communicating with new areas or segments;
  - appealing to needs and triggering buying motivations;
  - building brand recognition and encouraging trial, preference and insistence;
  - inviting enquiries for direct selling, for example mail order;
  - developing international markets.

- *the advertiser*
  - manipulating product life cycles;
  - reducing fluctuations in sales;
  - increasing market share;
  - creating a reputation for service, quality, reliability, research and development, and so on;

  - enhancing company image and generating positive goodwill;
  - providing information on trading results, job recruitment, etc.

- *external organisations*
  - counteracting competitive activity;
  - satisfying and informing the trade;
  - supporting sales people;
  - increasing number of outlets and improving their quality;
  - increasing volume and visibility on the shelves and traffic in the store.

Whatever an organisation's objectives in using this form of communication, one of three main types of advertising will normally be employed which generally correspond to the product life cycle and AIDA stages, as illustrated in Table 11.1.

In addition, these three main forms of advertising can be product or service based, or corporate – in other words, advertising can be focused on promoting a particular item or the institution itself.

Julian Simon goes into more detail on types of advertising and suggests that there are seven key classifications of 'activation methods':

1. *Information* – straight facts with little explanation.
2. *Argument* – using logical facts or benefits to give a 'reason why'.
3. *Motivation with psychological appeals* – enhancing product appeal by attaching pleasant emotional connotations.
4. *Repeat-assertion* – the hard sell approach, based on constant re-iteration of the message.
5. *Command* – ordering consumers, particularly if they are susceptible.
6. *Symbolic-association* – subtle soft sell, linking the product positively and pleasantly to a person, piece of music or situation.
7. *Imitation* – presents celebrities and situations for the audience to identify with and imitate.

Advertising has always been controversial and contains many advantages and disadvantages which are the subject of constant debate. As well as all its positive uses described above, there are a number of other advantages often cited in the case for advertising. Advertising can:

Table 11.1 Types of advertising in relation to the product life cycle and AIDA concepts

Advertising type	Product life-cycle stage	AIDA stage	Organisational objectives	Relevant methods
1. Informative	Introduction	Attention and Interest	Short term – sales volume increase	Announcements Classified ads Jingles/ slogans Teaser, (Introductory) campaigns Descriptive ads
2. Persuasive	Growth and Maturity	Desire and Action	New market development or increased share of existing ones	Image ads – status/ glamour appeals/ celebrities Competitive ads, Testimonials/price deals 'Last chance'/direct action point-of-sale ads
3. Reminder	Saturation and Decline	All four stages	Long term – corporate image and favourable attitudes towards company	Reinforcement ads Informative 'why' ads, and as above

- help to provide a society of aware, up-to-date, informed and educated consumers;
- add value to goods and services beyond physical or functional properties;
- encourage competition and help to ensure freedom of choice;
- provide entertainment and brighten up the environment;
- publicise society's material and cultural advantages and disadvantages;
- help to maintain the provision of independent mass media and the 'freedom of speech';
- protect customers by giving details of products/services;
- act as a public servant by disseminating government communication and socially desirable information;
- generate mass demand to justify mass production, enabling costs to be lowered through economies of scale, thus reducing the price of the product to the consumer in the long term.

The economic argument, in particular, is one not always appreciated by advertising's detractors. In addition to suggesting that advertising is costly and wasteful, they would cite a number of other economic, social and environmental disadvantages, including:

- its effectiveness is very difficult to measure or evaluate;
- it demands a high commitment of resources in the short term;
- it promotes socially undesirable products and services;
- it is dominated by a few organisations in some markets, thus restricting competition by preventing new entrants;
- it interrupts the main media programmes and information services;
- it invades people's privacy and intrudes into their lives;
- it adds to noise and can be garish or cause environmental problems;
- it exerts unfair pressures on children and adults or the elderly;
- it encourages sexism;
- it can provide false trade descriptions or mislead;
- it exploits consumers through the use of psychological, subliminal methods;

- it unfairly denigrates competitors through the use of comparative advertising, or 'knocking copy', which Qualcast were accused of in their 'lot less bovver than a hover' lawn-mower campaign against Flymo.
- it portrays an unrealistically good life which we cannot attain, thus leading to frustration and dissatisfaction.

Of course, everyone has their own views as to the relative importance of these factors and undoubtedly advertising carries difficulties and dangers. However, in the current era it is indispensable as a means of communication, familiarising consumers and increasing the likelihood of a sale in the future rather than physically bringing together a buyer and seller immediately.

By investing in customers and building up goodwill, advertising provides greater control over changes in demand, helps to facilitate those changes and cushion their disruptive effects, and thus reduces the overall risk involved in marketing.

Although even the highest quality advertising cannot sustain the sales of poor or inferior products, the risk is limited considerably by the application of sound advertising principles within a professional business structure.

THE ADVERTISING BUSINESS

Three distinct elements make up the advertising business and can best be viewed as the corners of a triangle (see Figure 11.2).

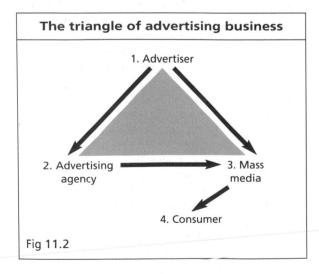

The triangle of advertising business

1. Advertiser
2. Advertising agency
3. Mass media
4. Consumer

Fig 11.2

When a person, group or organisation decides to advertise they have the choice of doing it themselves, either the individual concerned or a relevant in-house company department, or engaging a specialist advertising agency to do the work. Either way, the chosen mass media will then be approached to transmit the message which will eventually be relayed to the target audience of consumers. The three parts of the advertising business triangle will now be considered in turn.

Advertisers form the tail that wags the advertising dog in that it is they who control growth or shrinkage in the advertising industry. Every person or organisation is a potential or actual advertiser, and although advertising is predominantly used for consumer products, many other sectors now employ it as a tool of communication. Advertisers can be categorised as follows:

- individuals, using, for example, classified and small ads;
- companies, either sole traders, partnerships or limited liability organisations, using product/brand or corporate/institutional advertising, whether consumer, industrial or service orientated;
- political parties – all the major ones now advertise;
- pressure groups, such as Greenpeace, the Railway Development Society and Amnesty International;
- public service announcements, e.g. the Aids campaign and traffic safety;
- non-profit organisations, such as charities, the arts, religions and the forces;
- service organisations, e.g. education, tourism, health and transportation.

The use of advertising has now become more widespread in sectors of business which have not traditionally employed it as a central part of the promotional mix. An example is the industrial organisation which aims to sell to other producers, speed up sales and reduce the costs of personal selling by using the trade press and exhibitions to advertise technical goods and services.

Who exactly is responsible for advertising decisions within the organisation will depend on the characteristics of the company concerned. In smaller firms, all promotion decisions could rest with one individual, while larger organisations could place the responsibility with a product, brand or marketing manager, or even with an advertising manager backed up by a creative and media department, working on their own or liaising with a specialist agency.

Whether or not such an agency is used will depend upon the size, resources and expertise of the advertiser, together with the nature of the product or service involved, the perceived need for a specialist and the availability of an appropriate advertising agency to fill that role.

Advertising agencies exist ultimately to create and place advertisements which will sell products or services for companies, or *clients*, who wish to have this aspect of their marketing dealt with by a specialist offering services that even the largest companies cannot handle.

Having made the decision to use an agency, the client company will either let the fact be known, and await approaches from agencies, or, more commonly, it will invite a selection of such specialists to compete, or *pitch*, for the *account*. The agencies chosen are then required to prepare and present their ideas and suggestions to the client, based on a previously issued set of guidelines, or *brief*, in what is sometimes referred to as a 'business beauty contest'.

Choice of the short-list for presentation and decision on the final choice of agency will be based on a variety of factors relating to the client and its product or service. The Harris Research Centre identified certain key qualities that clients particularly look for when assessing agency image and performance and which agencies seek to develop:

- a record of creativity, style and flair and its effective utilisation to sell products successfully;
- evidence of the agency understanding the client's business and particular marketing problem;
- good personal chemistry and empathy between the two sets of staff, with the potential for a relationship built on respect in which information is exchanged freely, problems in both organisations are perceived to be mutual, and the agency can be regarded as an extension of the client company, making recommendations and discussing options;
- the ability to offer objectivity, experience, knowledge of relevant consumers, markets and products, and specialist skills and expertise.

An *account executive* will normally handle the work for a particular client on behalf of the agency, overseeing a variety of creative, administrative and production orientated tasks necessary for successful completion of the advertising *campaign*, in close liaison with the client. An agency's organisation structure reflects the wide range of advertising duties it is required to accomplish and Figure 11.3 illustrates the organisation chart of a full-service agency.

In addition, there are 'creative hotshops', agencies concentrating on design and ideas, media buying houses which buy media space and time for clients, and specialists, handling one type of client or advertising, such as financial, recruitment or the so-called 'detergent agencies'. Many have now diversified into other marketing services, such as marketing research, sales promotion, direct marketing, and PR. Some are in constant contact with their clients, while others specialise in one-off, *ad hoc* jobs.

Agencies have traditionally received their income in the form of a discount on rate card prices, usually 15 per cent, given by the media owners whenever advertising time or space is bought. Thus if the client pays the agency £1000, say, for advertising to be placed, on top of all the finance for preparation and production, the agency will pay £850 to the media owner concerned and retain £150 as its commission.

However, this method has proved to be rather inflexible in modern times and other systems have developed. Some agencies now use commission rebating, passing some of the discount back to the client and accepting a lower level of commission for themselves. Others work on a fee basis by negotiating an agreed payment for services rendered, and some combine the commission and fee methods. Recently payment by results has emerged, with income based on eventual sales or measures of shifts in awareness or image, and bonuses or penalties imposed for over- and underachievement.

Each method of remuneration contains advantages and disadvantages for both client and agency and will be evaluated according to the prevailing circumstances. The total worth of an advertising agency can be measured by calculating the cumulative value of all the accounts it possesses to give an overall *billings* figure. There are many large agencies in the thriving advertising industry,

Organisation chart for a full-service advertising agency

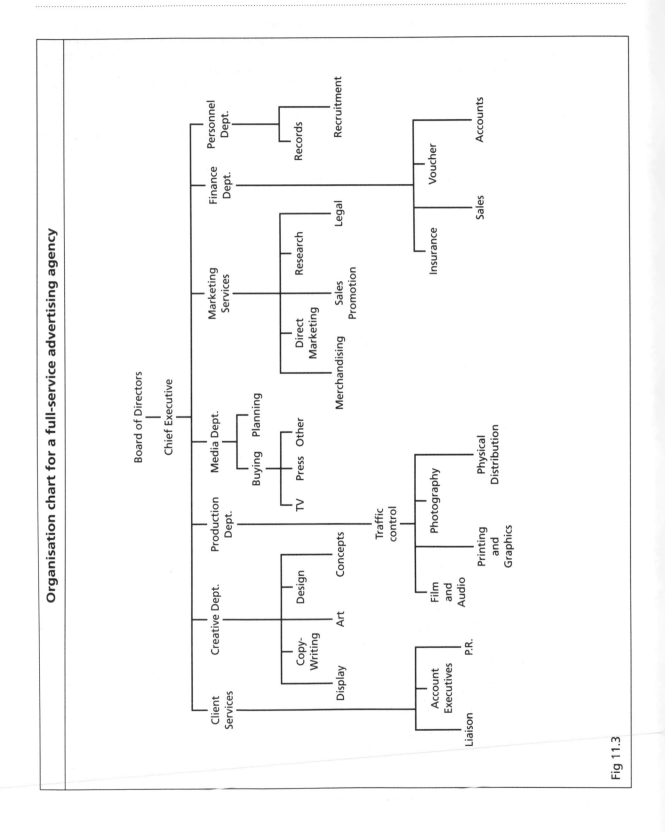

Fig 11.3

particularly in western Europe, the USA and Japan, but amongst the biggest are the WPP Group, incorporating J. Walter Thompson and Ogilvy & Mather, and Cordiant (formerly Saatchi & Saatchi) both handling the accounts of some of the world's largest advertisers.

Advertising is a volatile business and agencies can lose an account overnight as a result of many factors, such as:

- changes in personnel or the right chemistry with staff not developed;
- disagreements on either side over creative or ethical matters;
- senior client executives deciding their advertising is in a rut and the time is ripe for a change to introduce new ideas;
- problems not mutually understood;
- product launch or re-launch requiring a different approach;
- need to rationalise the agencies used (some large clients employ more than one agency for different accounts);
- economic reasons – results falling short of expectations or lack of value for money.

Table 11.2 Mass media advertising in the UK

Medium	Divisions	% of total in 1990	Projected % of total in 1995
Television	Terrestrial – independent television ITV – 15 regions + Channel 4 (over 43% of total TV audience) Satellite – BSkyB and others Cable (Overseen by the Independent Television Commission)	29.5	31.5
Press – papers	National dailies – popular/quality National Sundays – popular/quality Regional – daily/Sunday Local – evening/weekly/specialist/freesheets	40.0	35.9
Magazines	Colour supplements General interest Hobby/special interest Men's & women's interest Trade and technical	24.3	26.5
Outdoor	Poster sites – 4–96 sheet size Signs – basic/illuminated Transportation – railways/buses/stations/vans/lorries/planes Sports and music venues, etc. Aerial displays/balloons Sandwich-boards/town criers/other methods	3.7	3.5
Radio	Independent local radio (ILR) National radio – Classic/Virgin Other commercial stations (Overseen by the Radio Authority)	2.0	2.2
Cinema	1850 screens, inc. multiplexes £102.5 million admissions income in 1992	0.5	0.4
	Total	100	100

Source: Adapted from *The Book of European Forecasts*, Euromonitor plc 1992

Table 11.3 Characteristics of the TV and press media

Media	Advantages	Disadvantages	Developments
Television	Audio-visual, & colour Movement Creativity Attention Memorability Mass audience – network and regional spots 15 channels – test-marketing areas Associated with exciting programmes Different length of spot available	Temporary/fleeting Avoidable – breaks/video/ ad-zappers Expensive Clutter and 'noise' Non-selective Impersonal Limited in detail Franchise system makes programmes/audiences uncertain in long term	Cable Satellite Franchises De-regulation Research methods Segmentation Infommercials (look like programmes but are really long ads)
Press	Visual Sensory (magazines) Permanent and regular Mass audience – national, regional and local Possibility of particular editions/ positions/designs/gimmicks Flexible/selective Believable Involvement of readers Detail possible Colour and different insertion sizes available Can be passed around to others	Less memorable Unexciting Static Expensive nationally and for special features Only informational Clutter and 'noise' factors	Sophistication Colour Segmentation Research methods Technological processes

Agencies can be vulnerable if major clients withdraw their accounts, and the fickle 'musical chairs' nature of advertising is further evidenced by rapid staff turnover and creation of new agencies.

Some loyalties and ethics are observed in the advertising business, however. It is an unwritten law that agencies will not bid for or accept accounts which are competitive with ones they already hold. An agency working on the advertising of two similar or competing products or services would clearly have a clash of interests, which could prove embarrassing and eventually unacceptable to the clients concerned and would be counter-productive for agency business.

Advertising messages originating from company or agency are conveyed by the five *mass media*, as identified by the American sociologist, Marshall McLuhan – television, press, radio, cinema and outdoor. The use of each medium for advertising purposes varies from region to region and from country to country. For example, there is very little television advertising allowed in the Scandinavian countries, press is predominant in the UK, the cinema is a popular medium in Portugal as is radio in Spain and Austria, while outdoor is far more significant in Switzerland, Belgium and France. The sub-divisions of the mass media and the extent of their use for advertising in the UK are illustrated in Table 11.2.

Decisions on media planning involve scheduling, that is, consideration of the most appropriate sizes, timings and frequencies of advertisements, and, especially, media selection. These kinds of choices depend on a number of factors, of which the following are entirely the internal decision of the company or agency:

- the product or service to be advertised;
- the budget available;

Table 11.4 Characteristics of the outdoor, radio and cinema media

Media	Advantages	Disadvantages
Outdoor	Simple/brief message – can be memorable Flexible, and can be 3-dimensional Mobile audience Little competition High exposure in some areas Variety of methods, products and sizes Cheap locally Captive audience for venues and some transportation	Environmental problems Limited creativity Less interactive/depends on viewer mood Limited availability Expensive nationally Not selective Audience measurement difficult
Radio	Direct selling link – e.g. local food offers ILR and commercial stations and audiences increasing (4% market share in 1994 – Radio Advertising Bureau) Introduction of national commercial radio Opportunity to use catchy theme or jingle Flexible and selective Different lengths of spot available Cheap locally Low resistance factor Audiences well defined, particularly the young/commuters/house-persons	Very brief, temporary message Retention debatable Limited in scope and coverage Measurement difficult Audio only Much non-commercial competition
Cinema	Defined audiences particularly 16–25s Ads can be national, regional or local Audio-visual & colour Creativity and entertainment Captive audience and participation Cheap locally Growth of multi-screen centres Different lengths of film available	Audiences low Production expensive nationally Attractions elsewhere in intermission breaks nowadays Effectiveness research methods limited High cost per thousand reached

- convenience of communication between company/agency/media.

On the other hand, external factors are also important and can be to a great extent researched, such as:

- distribution support;
- the target market size, characteristics and media habits;
- production costs for the advertising;
- media availability;
- expense of media space and time, often based on guideline figures of cost per thousand consumers reached and measured by circulation, readership, viewing and listening statistics available in rate cards and publications such as *BRAD* (British Rate and Data). Outdoor and radio can be as low as £1 per thousand, whereas costs for press and TV are rather higher and cinema is usually the most expensive.
- effectiveness of media in presenting the product.

The choice usually boils down to an analysis of the relative advantages and disadvantages of the five mass media. It is often said about the 'front-line' media of TV and press that companies should use 'TV to sell and press to tell'. This is reflected in their main characteristics, summarised in Table 11.3.

By contrast, although they are trying to increase their share of the advertising market, outdoor, radio and cinema are generally regarded as reminder or re-inforcement media, supporting press and TV. Their key characteristics are identified in Table 11.4.

For their part the media owners concentrate on highlighting the virtues of their medium, attracting an audience and selling to the advertiser on the evidence of that audience. To do this, the media owner will employ sales people such as circulation and advertising managers to ensure that all their time or space slots are filled with advertisements from clients.

ADVERTISEMENTS

The key to successful advertising is the creation of stimulating and appropriate advertisements whose effectiveness can be measured. In order to fulfil the basic functions of providing information, persuading and moving consumers through the AIDA stages described previously, a press display advertisement, e.g. should contain all, or a relevant selection, of the following components:

- impact headline, either above or below illustrative material;
- sub-headings;
- brand name and/or company name;
- main body of copy/text;
- artwork;
- price;
- coupons or cut-aways;
- other inducements to act;
- trademark and/or identifying logo;
- contact address and/or telephone number;
- enough white space to make the ad clear and uncluttered.

In addition, an advertisement should be placed in a strategic and eye-catching position within the publication, if possible, such as 'facing matter', 'solus' (see Glossary), or on the problem, horoscope or TV pages.

Advertisements in the other mass media require different approaches because of their varied nature. However, all share common qualities in that they should be:

- focused on a major concept and aimed at prospects, not suspects, treating consumers as individuals even in a mass market;
- attention grabbing, utilising cartoons, humour, jingles, slogans, music, colour or black and white for effect, and so on;
- brief, using short, catchy words, phrases, sentences and paragraphs which answer questions, promise benefits and provoke curiosity;

- original – attractive, interesting, stylish and readable, with gimmicks where appropriate;
- logical and balanced in layout and content;
- designed to avoid pitfalls, such as being too clever, complex or unbelievable;
- geared to the marketing mix and other organisational objectives.

Some of these qualities can turn out to be surprisingly powerful tools of communication, one of the best examples being the use of old or modern music in TV advertisements. 'Jeans on', by David Dundas, was orginally for the Brutus jeans campaign and became a big hit in 1976 as a result, while Guinness successfully used Louis Armstrong's 'We have all the time in the world' and the soundtrack made it to number three in the UK popular music charts in 1994.

Another quality which advertisements should incorporate is appropriateness, in terms of suitability both for the product or service and the target audience, and for the media through which the advertisement will eventually be transmitted. For example, farms advertising 'fresh fruit available within' require a rustic approach normally associated with the product and to which the consumer would be quite happy to respond, whereas this style would be totally inappropriate for more technical products or services, such as the provision of driving lessons for which the expectations and therefore approach are far more professional.

Again, this appropriateness extends to the application of common-sense and inoffensive language which still accurately describes the merchandise being advertised. As a very simple example of this, Figure 11.4A is clearly far more appropriate than Figure 11.4B.

Advertisements vary widely in tone and style, even within the same medium. Press ads can be highly creative, utilising space, colour and so on,

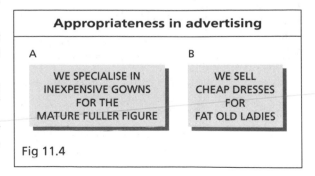

Fig 11.4

or purely functional, concentrating on delivering product or service information, whereas glossy magazine double-page spreads can be both lavish and very expensive.

The first ever UK commercial on ITV was for 'sparkling Gibbs SR' toothpaste in 1955. Television advertising has since evolved from these naïve black and whites to powerful colour ads, featuring subtle whimsicality (Carling Black Label and Hamlet Cigars), blunt exhortation (the detergent ads) and soap-style story-lines (Gold Blend coffee).

The support media offer variations on these styles of advertising. Due to limitations on space and viewing time the many outdoor methods have pioneered the memorable picture or short slogan, such as 'Guinness is good for you', 'Drinka Pinta Milka Day' and 'Skegness is so bracing'. Independent radio has specialised in informational public service ads and catchy musical jingles, while cinema advertising ranges from extravagant drinks commercials such as Martini, Gordon's Gin and Coca-Cola, to entertaining bank and building society ads, aimed at youthful audiences, and simple slides promoting local shops and services.

However much consideration is given to creativity or appropriateness, the abstract and subjective nature of advertising makes its effectiveness difficult to predict. Some renowned campaigns have scooped advertising awards but been unsuccessful commercially. One example of an advertisement which appealed to the connoisseur but not the consumer was the notorious campaign for Strand cigarettes by the S.H. Benson agency in 1960, which contained the slogan 'you're never alone with a Strand'. As the first advertisement to sell a mood it was considered highly innovative at the time, but its commercial failure was eventually put down by research to subconscious factors, i.e. consumers did not want to be associated with a product which implied they were lonely.

Another celebrated example of the hazards of advertising was the humorous 1980s' Cinzano commercial featuring Joan Collins and Leonard Rossiter, which focused heavily on the two stars and, despite its creativity and memorability, was generally considered to have done more for their careers than it did for the product, which many people believed in tests carried out afterwards to be Campari.

Lord Leverhulme of Unilever once said, 'I know that half my advertising works but I don't know

which half,' further illustrating the dilemma facing advertisers. In order to minimise wastage they search for scientific measurements, and various quantitative and qualitative research techniques are applied to evaluate responses to advertisements, audience size or media usage. Table 11.5 illustrates the different methods of measuring advertising effectiveness through consumer research, both in pre-testing the message before it is used commercially and post-testing it following its placement in the media.

All these methods can be run on a continuous or 'dip-stick' basis and all contain a variety of advantages or disadvantages. However, apart from direct measurement methods, such as response to advertising coupons and so on, the measurement of advertising effectiveness is by its very nature generally qualitative rather than quantitative. This is emphasised by the DAGMAR study (Defining Advertising Goals, Measuring Advertising Results), which contends that the communication aspects of advertising usually provide the only measurable results, that sales and profit figures are very difficult to relate directly to advertising, and that in order to assess the success of advertising an organisation must first clearly understand and outline the particular objectives it seeks.

So it is impossible to say with any certainty exactly what part the choice of media plays in the sale of a product or service. It is also difficult to be accurate in the measurement of audience size and media effectiveness, although the organisations responsible for such research are continually updating and improving their technical methods and sampling procedures. These industry bodies thus provide best estimates on advertising opportunities rather than guaranteeing audiences for advertisers, and on their figures media rate costs are generally calculated. There is at least one such organisation for each of the main mass media, namely:

- BARB (British Audience Research Bureau), which measures television audiences using a 'people meter' attached to the set to record the station being watched and hand-held units to monitor who is watching, in a sample of 4500 homes throughout the ITV areas.
- NRS (National Readership Surveys), covering the national press and main regional dailies by carrying out 28,000 annual interviews, supplemented by ABC (Audit Bureau of Circulation)

Table 11.5 Methods of evaluating advertising effectiveness

Nature of test / Consumer involvement	Advertisement-related test (reception or response to the message itself and its contents)	Product-related test (impact of message on product awareness, liking, intention to buy or use)
Laboratory measures (respondents) aware of testing and measurement process)	**Pre-testing:** 1. Consumer jury – 50 to 100 interviewed from target audience to ascertain order of merit or rating scale. 2. Portfolio tests – exposure to a portfolio of test and control ads seeking recall of content. 3. Readability tests – assessing appeal, length, familiarity and difficulty of advertising copy. 4. Physiological measures – e.g. eye camera (tracking eye movements), tachistoscope (measuring physical perception at varying speeds/illuminations) and GSR (galvanic skin response – measures arousal) or PDR (pupil dilation response – measures information processed).	**Pre-testing:** 1. Theatre tests – respondents offered a choice of gifts, in a central location, before and after exposure to ads, to measure changes in consumer product or brand preferences. 2. Trailer tests – respondents shown ads for the same product with different copy themes and asked to select preferences. 3. Laboratory stores – respondents exposed to ads then given coupons to purchase merchandise in a nearby store, enabling measurement of preferences.
Real-world measures (respondents unaware of testing and measurement process)	**Pre-testing:** 1. Dummy advertising vehicles – magazine read by respondents ostensibly to measure reaction to editorial content, but ad recall is measured in follow-up. 2. Inquiry tests – measure return of ad coupons. 3. On-the-air tests – measure response to ads in TV or radio programme test markets.	**Pre-testing and post-testing:** 1. Pre–post tests – measurements of respondents' awareness, attitudes or preferences before and after exposure to advertising to ascertain changes. 2. Sales tests – direct questioning of buyers, or formulation of experimental test designs to isolate the role of advertising in the final purchase decision, as against other marketing mix elements. 3. Mini-market tests – measurement of advertising effects with small panels in narrow, tightly controlled markets. Can include retail audits or EPOS (electronic point-of-sale) measures.

Nature of test ⟍ Consumer involvement	Advertisement-related test (reception or response to the message itself and its contents)	Product-related test (impact of message on product awareness, liking, intention to buy or use)
	Post-testing: 1. Recognition tests – measure readership of printed ads by interview in respondent's home. 2. Recall tests – measure impression ads make on the memory, either spontaneous (unaided) or prompted (aided). Often timed, e.g. DAR (day after recall). 3. Association measures – tests supplying brand or theme clues and requiring completion by respondent. 4. Combination measures – a mixture of recognition (over-stimulation) and recall (under-stimulation) tests.	

Source: Adapted from Engel, I., Warshaw, M. and Kinnear, T., *Promotional Strategy* (6th edn), Richard D. Irwin, Inc., 1987, p.407

which surveys the sale of 2000 different publications and measures circulation (purchase total) and readership (numbers actually reading).

- JICREG (Joint Industry Council for Regional Papers), supplying a variety of data on the readership of regional publications by field interviews, and VFD (Verified Free Distribution system), monitoring the readership of freesheets or local newspapers.
- OSCAR (Outside Site Classification and Audience Research) and PAB (Poster Audit Bureau), which measure 'opportunities to see' or 'view' (OTSs or OTVs) for billboards and other outdoor media, based on position, size, site and local population/traffic.
- RAJAR (Radio Joint Audience Research), measuring radio audiences using self-completion diaries issued to a sample of 14,500 adults and 2400 children per quarter.
- CAVIAR (Cinema and Video Industry Audience Research), monitoring cinema and video audiences and profiles.

All these statistics and related media costs are listed in *BRAD* (British Rate and Data), along with detailed information on many other aspects of advertising in all the available mass media.

Additionally, media owners research into the effectiveness of their own media. For example, More O'Ferrall (outdoor poster contractors) proved the power of billboards by placing the face of a small girl on bus shelter sites with a meaningless message (the 'Amy' campaign), bringing an enormous response from the public who wanted to know what was being advertised and thought it was a build-up (or 'teaser campaign') to a major launch. It was estimated from this independent research that two-thirds of the population of the UK had seen the poster within three months, thus stressing the effectiveness of the medium for potential users. The same company repeated this research some years later with its 'Sheila' poster and the caption 'the first Australian perfume (also kills flies)', another spoof advertisement which produced the same positive results.

ADVERTISING MANAGEMENT

The process of advertising can be said to involve consideration of and decision making in the 'Six Ms':

1. *Mission* – the objectives that advertising should accomplish.
2. *Message* – the nature of the advertising transmitted.
3. *Medium* – through which channel the message is relayed.
4. *Money* – the budget committed to advertising.
5. *Monitoring* – measuring the advertising's effectiveness.
6. *Management* – co-ordination of all the above activities.

The message, the medium and monitoring have been covered in the three previous sections. In the final section the mission, money and management will be considered.

Advertising can be used to achieve a wide range of quantitative and qualitative objectives, ranging from awareness raising and brand introduction to specific sales levels or profit targets. It is important that these objectives and the advertising mission are specified for the following reasons:

- advertising is integrated with other marketing mix elements leading to a consistent marketing plan;
- the agency can prepare and evaluate plans and recommend appropriate media;
- advertising budgets can be determined accurately;
- management can appraise advertising plans and control advertising activities;
- it permits the measurement of advertising performance.

Before planning and commencing advertising, objectives need therefore to be clearly defined and the following key stages then observed in chronological order:

- deciding who will do the work;
- assessing consumers' attitudes and needs;
- understanding the competition and their strategy;
- defining the target market;
- establishing the benefits and getting the product and packaging right;
- getting the price right for both the consumer and the retailer;
- ensuring adequate distribution to justify advertising;

- establishing the advertising budget;
- deciding on creative and media strategies.

The campaign can then be executed and its effectiveness evaluated. Various approaches can be used to fix the sum to be devoted to advertising, or the *appropriation*, the commonest being:

- *arbitrary allocation* – no real system, advertising regarded as 'the done thing' and available funds used with no consideration for promotional objectives other than for building goodwill;
- *percentage of sales or profits* – a fixed, inflexible method based on figures applied in previous years;
- *unit assessment* – a fixed amount or percentage set aside for each unit sold;
- *return on investment* – budget depends on a calculation of returns compared to other investment areas;
- *competitive parity* – spending roughly the same as competitors based on market share and total advertising spend in the industry;
- *'all you can afford' approach* – spending as much as can be afforded;
- *marginal analysis* – continuing advertising expenditure until costs of new business exceed sales revenue;
- *objective and task* – setting the budget by defining objectives and calculating costs necessary to accomplish them.

In addition to the problem of where to advertise, organisations must also carefully manage the timing of expenditure, the 'when' factor. Advertising campaigns could be planned on an annual, seasonal, weekly, hourly or other system and could be intermittent, continuous or concentrated on a level, rising, falling or alternating basis, related to sales patterns or other marketing strategies. Advertisers must also decide whether to schedule a few large or long advertisements, or several smaller or shorter ones.

All these decisions should be the result of both financial and research considerations as well as media availability, but whatever strategy is adopted, advertising continuity is vital because populations, markets, habits and fashions are constantly changing. Research has shown that advertising companies will gain sales over rival, non-advertising ones, and consumers forget, particularly where products are purchased only occasionally.

The sequence of activities involved in the management of advertising and the relationship between advertiser, advertising agency, media owner and consumer is summarised in Figure 11.5.

Advertising has always been controversial, as observed earlier, and open to abuse. It is thus one of the most highly regulated areas of marketing and subject to various controls in all countries. These range from restrictions on the advertising of certain products or services, such as alcohol, tobacco, politics or medicine, to limitations on poster sizes and the banning of commercials exerting unfair pressure on people, such as Rowntree's famous 'don't forget the Fruit-Gums, Mum' advertisement catch-line in the 1980s, believed to be aimed at parents via their children. Again, there are limitations imposed on the amount of television advertising allowed per hour - in the UK, this is seven minutes on average and $7\frac{1}{2}$ minutes at peak time for ITV and Channel 4, and nine minutes on average with a maximum of 12 minutes for satellite TV.

Controls affecting advertising can be legal, such as the laws preventing blatant misleading or misrepresentation (see Chapter 16) or non-statutory voluntary codes, which offer guidance to enable organisations to avoid problems before they arise and are thus cheaper and quicker to implement.

Many branches of marketing have their own codes of practice, and to maintain the credibility of their professions they will ensure that advertisements conform to three main measures of quality, i.e. they should:

- be legal, decent, honest and truthful;
- follow the basic business principles of fair competition;
- show responsibility to the customer and society.

Different voluntary bodies administer these standards, depending on the media involved. For the press and all non-broadcast media, the non-statutory *Advertising Standards Authority* fulfils this role. Consumers' complaints are directed to the ASA, which compiles reports and can ask companies to withdraw advertisements or blacklist them. The ASA also publishes the *Code of Advertising Practice* which deals with the trade and advertisers directly and is overseen by the *Committee of Advertising Practice*, which is made up of representatives of advertisers and media agencies.

The advertising codes were originally drawn up in 1961 and in the 1995 review (the first for seven years) covering all bar TV and cinema commercials, advertisements are required to be 'truthful and socially responsible' and reflect the recent changes in attitude by adhering to new standards in the areas of decency, alcohol, children, motoring, environmental claims, health and beauty, slimming, sales promotions and distance selling.

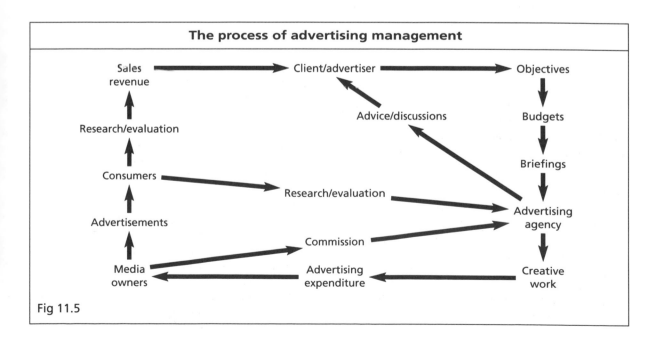

The process of advertising management

Fig 11.5

The broadcast media, television and radio, come under the non-statutory ITC, the *Independent Television Commission*, and the *Radio Authority*, which also publish guidelines on good practice in the form of codes. They both monitor advertisements and scripts before they are broadcast and give their approval, or alternatively they can ask for an advertisement to be taken off air following consumer complaints. It is thus important for organisations to abide by the rulings of these voluntary bodies.

ARTICLES

A1

Stop annoying the viewers

RESOLUTION for advertisers: stop spending millions on TV adverts which succeed only in annoying the viewers.

Banks, building societies and public utilities are the worst offenders, with the Oscar for patronising obnoxiousness going to the Anneka Rice excursions on behalf of British Gas.

In fact the gas people seemed to go beserk in 1991. Whatever possessed them to pay a fortune to Larry Hagman, Burt Reynolds and Joan Collins? Was it some kind of social security for ageing film stars?

Then there was National Power, with its sinister walking pylons. British Rail, swathing a train in 2,000 yards of black silk. Tesco, spending a million pounds on traipsing Dudley Moore around on a chicken hunt.

It was all part of the 1980s spending brainstorm. Bank and building society chiefs in particular thought they were Sam Goldwyn, hiring top directors at astronomical fees. Natwest had a gripping drama about the chap who loads the cashpoint machine. Lloyds nearly turned me off the incomparable Rumpole by putting him into a series of allegedly comic sketches. Nationwide had an impenetrable ad about a father writing a letter to his drone of a son.

Probably the rot started with the splurge of privatisations. I pity anyone called Sid at that time. But even the brilliant Maureen Lipman should accept that it is possible to overstay your welcome with viewers.

I sometime wonder how effective these TV ads are anyway. Advertising a specific product such as Gold Blend is one thing: corporate advertising on TV is something else. Doubtless the ads are noticed but often they just annoy. And a survey showed that a quarter of all commercials play to an empty room while viewers make a cup of tea or chat. Many flick over to other channels during the breaks. One man spent the time practising his golf swing.

Indeed when the TV advert for one brand of margarine was banned for some reason and was switched to newspapers, the makers found to their delight that sales immediately soared. There must be a moral there somewhere.

Source: By courtesy of *The Yorkshire Post*

1 Describe and discuss the advertisements which annoy you and those which you enjoy. Select three of each from any of the mass media.

2 What do you consider to be the aspects of financial advertising which the writer of this article most dislikes? Do you feel the same way about it?

3 What are the main differences between product and corporate advertising and what is each trying to achieve? Give an example of each.

4 If 'a quarter of all commercials play to an empty room' and if the selection of media is as arbitrary as implied in the final paragraph, why do companies still advertise?

A2

Agency doubles billings to £12m

Ian Green
Business Editor

BRAHM, the Leeds-based advertising agency, has doubled its billings in the first six weeks of 1994.

According to the agency, billings at the group have risen by £6m to £12m.

The rise in turnover follows three major national account gains and a clutch of new regional appointments.

Brahm claims the rush of business to Leeds will further aid the city's push to become a major creative centre in the advertising industry. A spokesman said: "We are trying to do for advertising in Leeds what the financial services sector has done."

The company made it clear that it wants to take away business from Manchester, the North's major advertising centre.

Brahm, which lost the Yugo Cars account with the outbreak of war in former Yugoslavia, has picked up a £3.5m account from Russian car maker Lada. Brahm won the account after a six-way pitch.

The Lada win comes just five weeks after Brahm won the account for Nuffield Hospitals, Britain's largest private hospital group.

Other account wins include: Silentnight, Rakusen, Leeds Leisure Services, Yorkshire Post Training, Brewers Heritage and Coda, the recently floated software group based at Harrogate.

Source: By courtesy of *The Yorkshire Post,* 21 February 1994

1 What is meant by the term 'doubled its billings'? What effects might this have on Brahm's organisational structure?

2 How might the agency have approached the task of gaining the Lada business? What is meant by 'won the account after a six-way pitch'?

3 The range of Brahm's accounts is very wide. What are the benefits and disadvantages of such a broad portfolio?

4 Brahm is both a local and national advertising agency. Could this geographic spread give rise to problems for the company? If so, what sort of problems?

A3

Radio gains over falling TV audiences

Natasha Narayan

Radio is gaining ground over television, with more people tuning in, says a report published today.

Nine out of 10 people spend about three hours a day listening to the radio, a survey by the Policy Studies Institute has shown.

In the last quarter of 1992, 89 per cent of the population listened to radio, closing the gap with TV's 98 per cent. TV viewing, which rose in the early 1990s with the launch of satellite channels, has since dropped. On average viewers spent 25 hours a week watching last year – three hours less than in 1991.

Classic FM, the national commercial radio station launched in September 1992, is already the fourth or fifth most popular station – well ahead of Radio 3.

The report, Cultural Trends, says Classic FM's "popularising" style has done much to bridge the gap between classical and popular music. The station has bypassed the worst effects of the advertising recession and has also drawn some listeners from Radios 2 and 4, although the BBC maintained a 58.4 per cent share of listeners.

However, the recession has knocked the cable and satellite industry off course. They account for no more than 5 per cent of TV viewing, with only 2.7 million homes receiving satellite. It is predicted that by the year 2000 9.5 million homes are likely to have a dish or cable TV – 800,000 fewer than was expected.

"The economic situation over the past few years has inevitably caused problems with regard to the massive funding necessary for a major project like cabling the UK," the report said.

Despite the Oscars won for Howard's End and The Crying Game, Britain's film industry has had another bad year, with 40 per cent less spent on production in 1991 than in 1984.

Cinema-going enjoyed a revival, with 101 million tickets – the most since 1980 – sold last year. But the report says people spend as much time each week watching films on TV as they do at cinemas in a year. The films people go out to see are likely to be Hollywood blockbusters.

The new ITV franchises also proved a mixed blessing to their shareholders, with audiences for the breakfast station, GMTV, 15 per cent below forecasts.

Source: The Guardian

1 Estimate how much time you spend per day and per week, on average, listening to the radio. Which independent stations do you listen to and which advertisements have the most effect on you?

2 How often do you watch television? Do you consider TV adverts to be more memorable than those on the radio, and if so, why? Give examples.

3 Describe two cinema commercials you have enjoyed. Do you believe the advertising industry has capitalised on the cinema revival, and if so, how?

4 Contrast the advertising styles used in the press and outdoor media. What features contribute most to the effectiveness of each, in your opinion? Give examples.

A4

No, no, Nanette is not going anywhere

SOAP giant Procter & Gamble has played down market rumours that it is to ditch Nanette Newman from its Fairy Excel washing-up liquid TV adverts.

The actress has been the star of the ads, firstly for Fairy Liquid then Fairy Excel, for the past 13 years.

She has regularly promised that by using Fairy, the consumer will save cash, "because Fairy goes further." But P&G's advertising agency, Grey London, has unveiled a new ad featuring two men washing up. Nanette is not in sight.

Account manager Adam Collins would only offer a terse "no comment" but a P&G spokeswoman in Newcastle, where Fairy Excel was devised by its soap boffins, said rumours of Ms Newman's demise were premature.

"We have a new commercial being aired at the moment that doesn't feature Nanette. But that doesn't mean she won't be used again," she said.

However, one marketing expert said it is unlikely that Nanette will be seen. "Fairy's angle about it doing twice as many dishes as other washing-up liquid has been wiped out by supermarket policies."

Source: The Northern Echo, 19 February 1994

1 Describe the possible reasons for the shift in emphasis of the advertising for Fairy Excel.

2 What is the style of advertising adopted by the detergent industry? Why is it often criticised?

3 Why should both Procter & Gamble and its advertising agency be evasive about the strategy being adopted for Fairy?

4 What other creative ideas might be used by Procter & Gamble and Grey London for this product in the future? Is television the only appropriate mass medium for detergent advertising?

A5

Reg bows out but still upsets MP

A NEW poster advertising campaign for Embassy Regal cigarettes has been launched in direct contravention of the Government's voluntary agreement on tobacco advertisements, it was claimed yesterday.

Rother Valley MP Kevin Barron claims the new poster – which says "Farewell address" and shows a suitcase with a tag saying: "Dunadvertisin, Bognor Regis. BYE 2U" – is part of a campaign criticised by the Advertising Standards Authority.

The ASA demanded last year that the "Reg" campaign be withdrawn after complaints from the Health Education Authority about its direct appeal to children. Imperial Tobacco, manufacturers of Regal, has launched the new advert in the North where Regal is the most popular brand among young people.

It emerged yesterday that Spencer Hagard, HEA chief executive, is writing to the ASA in protest.

Mr Barron, who is sponsoring a Bill to ban tobacco advertising, said: "This is a flagrant breach of the Government voluntary agreement with the tobacco industry and demonstrates just how toothless these so-called agreements are.

"This revelation, on the eve of the Health Secretary's announcement of fresh talks with the industry on a new voluntary agreement, shows how pointless such an approach is if the intention is to keep tobacco ads in check."

Source: The Northern Echo, 7 February 1994

1 Despite criticism from the Advertising Standards Authority, Embassy has gone ahead with its poster campaign. What do you feel about this? Describe the relationship between the ASA and the advertiser.

2 Argue the case for the banning of tobacco advertising, referring to relevant ethical factors.

3 Argue the case against the banning of tobacco advertising, referring to factors such as the importance of brand switching.

4 Do you believe advertising should be more tightly controlled, and if so, why? Discuss examples.

ISSUES

THE ROLE OF ADVERTISING

Advertising is wasteful and only adds to the cost of the product.

1 Do you agree with the above statement? Give your reasons.

2 Give the economic arguments for and against advertising.

3 Discuss all the non-economic reasons for using advertising, giving examples.

4 Describe the main disadvantages of using advertising, giving examples.

ADVERTISERS

The use of advertising is now open to everyone and is no longer purely the domain of the large multi-nationals.

1 What are the main categories of advertiser? Are there any circumstances in which companies do not need to advertise?

2 Discuss how the use of advertising has widened in recent years, giving examples.

3 What options does an advertiser have when considering how and when to prepare an advertising campaign?

4 Describe the different occasions in which you have advertised and why. Was it cost effective?

ADVERTISING AGENCIES

Advertising agencies are one of the most volatile areas of business.

1 Compile the 'top ten' of world-wide or UK advertising agencies currently, in terms of billings. Discuss why these listings are so changeable.

2 Choose two agencies. List the accounts they possess and compare their advertising philosophies, histories and organisational frameworks.

3 Describe the ways in which an agency can win and lose an account. Do you think quality is always the crucial factor?

4 List the ways in which agencies are remunerated. Which do you think are the most effective and why?

THE MASS MEDIA

Use of the media for advertising is arbitrary and its success difficult to measure.

1 Do you agree with the above statement? Discuss your reasons.

2 What is meant by 'TV to sell, press to tell'? Do you agree with this view of the main media, and if so, why?

3 What are the 'support media' and when might each be used? How useful do you believe them to be?

4 For which types of product or service do you think the following media are most appropriate and why? Cinema, local freesheets, trade and technical journals, independent local radio, general interest magazines, transport panel cards.

ADVERTISEMENTS

There is no magic formula for the success of an advertisement.

1 Record the advertisements you see in any one day and classify them in terms of product type and media. Which had the most effect on you and why?

2 Why do you consider that the 'story-line' ads, such as Gold Blend, have become popular? Does this necessarily make them a commercial success?

3 List adverts which are or were based on catchy slogans or musical jingles, such as Club chocolate biscuits, and discuss why they have been successful.

4 Describe the main methods used for measuring the effectiveness of advertisements. Discuss which you believe are the most useful and accurate.

ADVERTISING MANAGEMENT

Advertising can only work if the whole process is carefully planned and co-ordinated.

1 Discuss the Six Ms of advertising management. Do you believe each must be followed rigorously for a campaign to be successful?

2 What is the nature of the relationship between the advertiser, the agency and the media? How important do you believe it to be in terms of advertising industry effectiveness?

3 Discuss the main methods of establishing advertising budgets. How rigid do you feel organisations should be when fixing appropriations?

4 Describe the voluntary controls which serve advertising. How effective and important do you think they are? Give examples.

QUESTIONS

1 Provide a definition of advertising.

2 List three purposes of advertising related to the product or service.

3 Name three purposes of advertising related to customers and markets.

4 List three purposes of advertising related to the advertiser.

5 Name three purposes of advertising related to external organisations.

6 List three of Simon's major advertising types.

7 Name six of the main advantages of advertising.

8 List six of the main disadvantages of advertising.

9 What is the triangle of advertising business?

10 Name four categories of advertiser.

11 What are accounts, billings, clients, campaigns and pitches?

12 Name two qualities of an agency looked for by advertisers.

13 List the four main methods of agency remuneration.

14 What are the main ways in which an agency wins an account?

15 Name four reasons for an agency losing an account.

16 List five of the main departments in an advertising agency.

17 What are the mass media?

18 Name five criteria on which media selection is based.

19 List four advantages and four disadvantages of television as an advertising medium.

20 Name four advantages and four disadvantages of the press as an advertising medium.

21 List three advantages and three disadvantages of outdoor as an advertising medium.

22 Name three advantages and three disadvantages of radio as an advertising medium.

23 List three advantages and three disadvantages of the cinema as an advertising medium.

24 Name five of the components of a press advertisement.

25 List three qualities of a successful advertisement.

26 Name two laboratory methods of evaluating advertising effectiveness related to the advertisement itself.

27 List two real-world methods of evaluating advertising effectiveness related to the advertisement itself.

28 Name two laboratory methods of evaluating advertising effectiveness related to the product.

29 List two real-life methods of evaluating advertising effectiveness related to the product.

30 Name the organisations responsible for measuring audiences in each of the mass media.

31 What are the Six Ms of advertising management?

32 List three reasons for the importance of advertising objectives.

33 Name the main chronological stages of advertising management.

34 List five methods of establishing advertising budgets.

35 Name the main non-statutory voluntary controls for advertising.

36 What are the three main measures of quality to which advertisements are expected to conform?

PROJECTS

1 'Advertising offers an unattainable eldorado and is thus bound to disappoint.' Discuss this view of advertising.

2 'For most consumer orientated companies, advertising is the main marketing cost, yet, to a great extent, it is an act of faith.' Do you agree that advertising is so uncertain?

3 It has been said that a client doesn't need an agency but an agency needs its clients. Discuss the importance of the advertising agency in contemporary business.

4 'The client gets the standard of advertising it deserves from an agency which is as good as the client allows it to be.' How much control should the advertiser exercise over its agency and its advertising?

5 Edward Stern has stated that advertisers are bombarded by 'a great mass of media statistics that relate, at best, only to superficial media vehicle exposure and really tell us nothing about the ability of the medium to help communicate what we are trying to say.' How true do you believe this statement to be in the light of increasingly sophisticated media research?

6 Discuss the contention that advertising in the mass media must be effective otherwise organisations would not advertise.

7 What are the main methods employed to try to ensure that advertisements are different and make consumers sit up and take notice? Give examples of such advertisements.

8 In what ways is the advertising industry open to ethical abuse and how are these abuses controlled? Give examples.

9 'Estée Lauder cosmetic products are designed to appeal to the subliminal romantic in us all.' What is meant by this statement and do you think it leads to the exploitation of customers?

10 You are a tourism marketing manager with a large budget for a new package holiday in the Caribbean. Describe your creative and media campaign strategies, with reference to intended dealings with your advertising agency and projected costs.

11 Describe the advertising management structure and specific policies adopted by a firm with which you are familiar.

GLOSSARY

A.B.C. Audit Bureau of Circulation, which measures the sale, circulation and readership of a large number of publications, for advertising purposes.

Account piece of advertising work offered by the client, for which an agency has to compete.

Account executive person in an advertising agency responsible for supervising all the advertising for a client's product.

Advertisement a specific, individual piece of advertising transmitted through the mass media.

Advertisement-related test advertising-effectiveness test measuring reception or response to the message itself or its contents.

Advertiser any individual or organisation designing and/or placing an advertisement through the mass media.

Advertising informing, persuading or reminding consumers to purchase products or services by transmitting a message through the non-personal, paid, mass communication media.

Advertising agency specialist marketing organisation used to assist advertisers in planning and implementing advertising policies.

Advertising manager member of organisational staff responsible for the company's advertising programme.

Advertising Standards Authority (ASA) non-statutory, voluntary body which handles advertising complaints, monitors organisations and issues guidelines on advertising.

Advertorial extended promotions for a product or service in the press media, a combination of advertisement and editorial in style.

Aided recall see 'Prompted recall'.

'All you can afford' approach method of establishing advertising budgets based on spending as much as can be afforded.

Appropriateness ability of an advertisement to suit its product or market, through use of design or copy.

Appropriation amount spent on advertising, i.e. the advertising budget based on no specific timings, amounts or layouts.

Arbitrary allocation method of establishing advertising budgets, based on no specific timings, amounts or layouts.

Artwork finished layout of type, drawing and photographs ready for reproduction by the printer.

Association measures method of evaluating advertising effectiveness.

Billings total value of an advertising agency, calculated by the addition of all the financial values of its accounts.

Bleed where a press advertisement runs to the edge of the page to improve visibility.

Body copy type matter filling the areas below the headline.

Brief set of guidelines used by a client to advertising agencies competing for its account.

BARB British Audience Research Bureau, organisation measuring television audiences for advertising purposes.

BRAD British Rate and Data, publication which lists all the available mass media, the costs of advertising with them and other relevant information.

Broadsheets see 'Qualities'.

Cable new media development involving the transmission of television programmes and advertising, by means of underground wiring methods.

Campaign structured course of advertising action, based on advertising types, timings, media, and so on.

Campaign planning the strategic planning of an advertising campaign to take in all the relevant advertising and marketing variables.

Celebrity advertising using celebrities to advertise products or services.

Centre spread see 'spread'.

Cinema one of the main mass media used for advertising purposes.

CAVIAR Cinema and Video Industry Audience Research, organisation measuring cinema and video audiences for advertising purposes.

Circulation the actual number of newspapers or magazines distributed.

Classified advertising or 'small ads' press adverts, usually grouped together, e.g. situations vacant, properties, and so on.

Client advertisers who place their advertising with advertising agencies.

Client services department section of an advertising agency concentrating on client accounts and public relations.

Code of advertising practice (CAP) a non-statutory guideline on good advertising published by the ASA.

Colour supplements magazine sections of newspapers, used extensively for advertising.

Combination measures methods of evaluating advertising effectiveness.

Commission the traditional system of agency remuneration whereby the company receives a discount, usually 15 per cent, from media owners when advertisements are booked.

Commission rebate method of agency remuneration involving a lower level of commission.

Committee of Advertising Practice a group of people who oversee the application of the CAP.

Comparative advertising or 'knocking copy' advertising (legal in the USA) which unfairly denigrates the competition by directly referring to their weaknesses.

Competitive parity method of establishing advertising budgets based on spending a similar amount to the competition.

Consumer jury method of evaluating advertising effectiveness.

Copy the verbal and written sections of advertisements, including headlines.

Copy-writers advertising personnel specialising in the creation and writing of copy.

Corporate advertising advertising an organisation rather than its products or brands.

Creative department section of an advertising agency concentrating on writing, design and ideas for new advertisements.

Creative hot-shops advertising agencies specialising in design and ideas for the client.

Dealer listing an advertisement promoting a product and identifying the names of participating retailers selling it.

DAGMAR defining advertising goals, measuring advertising results, a study concluding that advertising effectiveness is only measurable in communication terms and depends on stated objectives.

Direct response measurement method of evaluating advertising effectiveness.

Display advertising larger non-lineage advertising usually involving an element of design.

Double page spread (DPS) see 'spread'.

Dummy advertising vehicle method of evaluating advertising effectiveness.

Facing matter preferential position for press advertisement opposite an editorial page.

Fee basis system of agency remuneration whereby the firm receives a straight fee for advertising services performed.

Franchise system method whereby independent television channels must regularly bid to retain the licence to run their network.

Full-service agency advertising agency performing the complete range of advertising services.

General interest category of magazine relating to a wide range of themes.

Generic advertising the use of brand and product advertising, rather than corporate advertising.

Independent local radio (ILR) commercial radio stations used for advertising purposes.

Independent Television Commission (ITC) organisation issuing guidelines on good practice in television advertising.

Infommercial form of promotion for a product or service on the television media, an idea originating in the USA and involving an organisation sponsoring part, or all, of a programme, in order to produce an extended information commercial.

Informative advertising advertisements concentrating on providing facts and awareness.

Inquiry test method of evaluating advertising effectiveness.

Island position press advertisement surrounded entirely by margins or editorial.

JICREG Joint Industry Council for Regional Papers, organisation measuring readership of regional publications for advertising purposes.

Knocking copy see 'Comparative advertising'.

Laboratory stores method of evaluating advertising effectiveness.

Laboratory tests methods of evaluating advertising effectiveness where respondents are aware of the testing and measurement process.

Lineage small advertisements measured and priced by the line.

Marginal analysis method of establishing advertising budgets based on continuing expenditure until costs exceed sales.

Marketing services department section of an advertising agency concentrating on promotional mix methods other than advertising.

Mass media the 'above-the-line' media used for advertising purposes and identified by Marshall McLuhan as television, the press, outdoor, radio and the cinema.

Media buying house advertising agency specialising in the analysis and purchase of media for the client.

Media department section of an advertising agency concentrating on the planning and purchasing of media advertising.

Media mix the combination of media advertising considered appropriate for a particular product or service campaign.

Mini-market test method of evaluating advertising effectiveness.

Multiplex multi-screen cinema complex.

NRS National Readership Survey, organisation measuring readership of the national press and main regional dailies, for advertising purposes.

Objective and task method of establishing advertising budgets based on defining goals and calculating their costs.

On-the-air test method of evaluating advertising effectiveness.

Opportunities to see or view (OTSs or OTVs) the measurement of poster and other outdoor advertising audiences, based on position, size, site and population.

Outdoor advertising one of the main mass media used for advertising purposes and consisting of many different methods.

OSCAR Outside Site Classification and Audience Research, organisation measuring OTSs for advertising purposes.

PAB Poster Audit Bureau, which measures billboard audiences for advertising purposes.

Payment by results system of agency remuneration whereby the firm is paid according to specific sales, awareness or public relations results achieved.

People meter device attached to television set in sample homes by BARB to measure audiences for advertising purposes.

Percentage of sales or profits method of establishing advertising budgets based on figures applied in previous years.

Persuasion a process aiming to change or influence a person's attitude or behaviour, with respect to the purchase of products or services.

Persuasive advertising advertisements concentrating on provoking desire through the use of status, image, gimmicks, and so on.

Physiological measures methods of evaluating advertising effectiveness, including eye camera, tachistoscope, GSR (galvanic skin response) and PDR (pupil dilation response).

Pitch an advertising agency's actions and efforts when competing for an account.

Populars or 'tabloids' group of national newspapers reaching mainly the C1, C2, D and E social class groups.

Portfolio test method of evaluating advertising effectiveness.

Post-testing tests on the consumer's knowledge/opinion of an advertisement after the main campaign has taken place.

Pre–post test method of evaluating advertising effectiveness.

Press one of the main mass media used for advertising purposes and divided into types of newspaper and magazine.

Pre-testing tests on the consumer's knowledge/opinion of an advertisement before the main campaign has started.

Product-related test advertising effectiveness test measuring the impact of the message on product awareness, liking, intention to buy or use.

Production department section of an advertising agency concentrating on the actual production of the finished advertisement.

Prompted recall or 'aided recall' test in which respondents are asked questions about adverts, after being prompted, to assess the effectiveness of advertising.

Qualities or 'broadsheets' group of national newspapers reaching mainly the A, B and C1 social class groups.

Radio one of the main mass media used for advertising purposes.

Radio authority organisation issuing guidelines on good practice in radio advertising.

RAJAR Radio Joint Audience Research, organisation measuring radio audiences for advertising purposes.

Rate cards listings issued by the mass media identifying available advertising and its costs for potential buyers.

Readability test method of evaluating advertising effectiveness.

Readership the number of people who actually read a newspaper or magazine (usually more than the circulation).

Real-world tests methods of evaluating advertising effectiveness where respondents are unaware of the testing and measurement process.

Recognition test method of evaluating advertising effectiveness.

Recruitment advertising advertising designed to recruit staff for jobs.

Reminder advertising advertisements concentrating on reinforcing messages about products or services and jogging consumers' memories.

Return on investment (ROI) method of establishing advertising budgets based on a calculation of returns compared to other investment areas.

Run of paper (ROP) indicating no special position sought for advertisement in the press.

Sales test method of evaluating advertising effectiveness.

Satellite recent media development involving the transmission of television programmes and advertising, utilising space satellite dish methods.

Sheet basic measurement of poster advertisement size, from 4–96 sheet.

Single column centimetre (SCC) method of measuring advertising in the press.

Six Ms the process of advertising, covering the Mission, Message, Medium, Money, Monitoring and Management.

Small ads see 'Classified advertising'.

Solus preferential position for press or poster advertisement, separated from other competing messages.

Space amount of advertising available in a publication for purchase by 'space buyers'.

Special interest category of magazine relating to specific hobbies or interests.

Specialist agency an advertising agency concentrating mainly on one of the advertising functions, e.g. media or creativity.

Spontaneous recall test in which respondents are asked questions about adverts without guidance or assistance, to assess the effectiveness of advertising.

Spot single radio or television advertisement, of various lengths.

Spread two press advertisement pages facing each other – can be centre-spread or double-page spread.

Subliminal advertising psychological audio or visual advertising method, illegal in some countries, in which the message is not immediately obvious but registers in the consumer's sub-conscious.

Super-sites very large poster advertisements.

Tabloids see 'Populars'.

Teaser campaign advertisements deliberately designed to withhold information about the product or organisation in order to arouse consumers' attention and curiosity and thus boost eventual sales – the poster medium is often used for this purpose.

Television one of the main mass media used for advertising purposes.

Theatre test method of evaluating advertising effectiveness.

Trade and technical category of magazine relating to specific trades.

Trailer test method of evaluating advertising effectiveness.

Triangle of advertising the three corner-stones of the advertising business, namely the advertiser, the advertising agency and the mass media.

Unit assessment method of establishing advertising budgets based on a fixed amount or percentage set aside for each unit sold.

VFD Verified Free Distribution system, organisation measuring the readership of freesheets or local newspapers for advertising purposes.

Voucher section part of advertising agency involved in checking that advertisements have appeared and logging the financial details.

Zapper device used in some video recorders to eliminate advertisement breaks.

SUGGESTED REFERENCES

VIDEO MATERIAL

Art of Persuasion, Series, Channel 4, 1985.

Two too many and *So you think you know the code*, Advertising Standards Authority, 1985.

The Marketing Mix, No. 5, 'Using the Media', Yorkshire Television, 1986.

Advertising Agencies, Marketing Week, Centaur Communications, 1986.

Economics, 'A question of choice – to buy or not to buy', BBC, 1986.

A sense of the past, 'And now . . . a short intermission' (Cinema Advertising), Yorkshire Television, 1986.

Communication and Education, 'Talking to the tea folk – the making of a T.V. ad', BBC, 1986.

QED on Advertising, 'It's not easy being a dolphin', BBC, 1988.

T.V. Advertising Clinic, Institute of Marketing Travel Industry Group/YTV, 1988.

Contemporary Marketing, Video Cases, No. 17 (Chiat/Day), Boone, L. and Kurtz, D., Dryden Press, 1989.

Advertising – the Image-makers, Thames Television, 1990.

Omnibus, 'But the client loved it', BBC, 1990.

Walk the Talk, No. 9, 'Race for the pitch', BBC, 1991.

Commercial Mania, Polygram Video Ltd., 1991.

Advertising Education Foundation, 'Behind the scenes – the advertising process at work', Marketing Videotape, Dibb, S., Simkin, L., Pride, W., and Ferrell, O., Houghton Mifflin, 1991.

The Robinson Report . . . on Advertising, Yorkshire Television, 1991.

Whipped into Action, Open University, Open Business School, 1991.

Public Eye, 'Tobacco – smoke without fire', BBC, 1991.

Answering back, Maurice Saatchi on advertising, 1991.

Without Walls, 'Ducking the issue' (United Colours of Benetton), Channel 4, 1993.

High Interest, 'Leader of the Pack', Channel 4, 1994.

Plus Agency (Feature film, with Robert Mitchum and Lee Majors, on subliminal advertising), 1989; Jasper Carrott's *Commercial Breakdowns*, *Tarrant on Advertising*, Peter York on Advertising, and the annual TV and Advertising Awards (all regularly featured).

RADIO MATERIAL

The Manipulators, series, BBC Radio, 1980.

Twenty-five years of ITV advertising, BBC Radio, 1984.

Sell, sell, sell, 'Advertising', BBC Radio Leeds, 1984.

Oldies and Advertising, BBC Radio, 1989.

The Ad Break, series, BBC Radio, 1994.

MAGAZINE ARTICLES

Campaign, Admap and *Advertiser's* magazines.

Euro-Marketing magazine.

Institute of Practitioners in Advertising literature.

British Rate and Data (BRAD).

Marketing Business, Oct. 1991, p.14, 'Sex sells'; and p.29, 'Consumer Speak' (Radio advertising).

Marketing Business, Nov. 1991, p.29, 'Consumer Speak' (Benetton).

Marketing Business, April 1992, p.15, 'End of an empire'.

Marketing Business, June 1992, p.16, 'Headline news', p.24, 'Battle of the airwaves', and p.41, 'Going solo'.

Marketing Business, Sept. 1992, p. 22, 'Advertising credit'.

Marketing Business, Oct. 1992, p.48, 'Briefly'.

Marketing Business, Nov. 1992, p.23, 'Consumer speak' (Electricity Board).

Marketing Business, Dec./Jan. 1992/93, p.9, 'What Auntie did next'; and p.14, 'Big time boy'.

Marketing Business, Feb. 1993, p.6, 'Survival of the fittest'.

Marketing Business, April 1993, p.31, 'Consumer speak' (Gold Blend).

Marketing Business, June 1993, p.18, 'Protection Racket' (Tampax).

Marketing Business, July/Aug. 1993, p.24, 'Action Jackson'; and p.29, 'Called to account'.

Marketing Business, Oct. 1993, p.13, 'Guardian angel'.

Quarterly Review of Marketing, Vol. 15, No. 4, July 1990, p.12, 'A structured approach to planning creative strategy'.

FURTHER READING

Adcock, D., Bradfield R., Halborg, A. and Ross, C., *Marketing Principles and Practice* (2nd edn), Pitman, 1995, ch. 16.

Baker, M. (Ed.), The Marketing Book, Heinemann/C.I.M., 1990, ch. 16.

Boone, L. and Kurtz, D., *Contemporary Marketing*, Dryden, 1989, ch. 17.

Booth, Don, *Principles of Strategic Marketing*, Tudor Publishing, 1990, ch. 6.

Cannon, Tom, *Basic Marketing*, Holt Business Texts, 1980, ch. 16.

Dibb, S., Simkin, L., Pride , W. and Ferrell, O., *Marketing*, Houghton Mifflin, 1994, ch. 15.

Douglas, Torin, 'The Complete Guide to Advertising', Macmillan, 1984.

Dyer, Gillian, *Advertising as Communication*, Methuen, 1982.

Engel, I., Warshaw M. and Kinnear, T., *Promotional Strategy*, Irwin, 1987.

Foster, D., *Mastering Marketing*, Macmillan, 1982, ch. 7.

Giles, G., *Marketing*, MacDonald and Evans, 1985, chs 6 and 7.

Jefkins, Frank, *Advertising*, MacDonald and Evans, 1985.

Kotler, P. and Armstrong, G., *Marketing*, Prentice Hall, 1993, ch. 15.

McCarthy, J. and Perreault, W., *Basic Marketing*, Irwin, 1987, ch. 17.

Mercer, D., *Marketing*, Blackwell, 1992, ch. 11.

Ogilvy, David, *Confessions of an Advertising Man*, Longman, 1964.

Oliver, G., *Marketing Today*, Prentice Hall, 1990, chs 16 and 17.

O'Sullivan, Tim, et al., *Key Concepts in Communication*, Methuen, 1983.

Packard, Vance, *The Hidden Persuaders*, Penguin, 1960.

Simon, Julian L., *The Management of Advertising*, Prentice Hall, 1971.

Smith, P.R., *Marketing Communications*, Kogan Page, 1993.

Williamson, Judith, *Decoding advertisements*, Marion Boyars, 1978.

Acknowledgements

The Guardian.
The Northern Echo.
The Yorkshire Post.

12

BELOW-THE-LINE

DEFINITIONS

Sales Promotion is an activity and/or material that acts as a direct inducement, offering added value or incentive for the product, to resellers, salespersons, or consumers.

DIBB, SIMKIN, PRIDE AND FERRELL

Public Relations practice is the planned and sustained effort to establish and maintain goodwill and mutual understanding between an organisation and its publics.

INSTITUTE OF PUBLIC RELATIONS

Direct Marketing is the planned recording, analysis and tracking of customers' direct response behaviour over time . . . in order to develop future marketing strategies for long-term customer loyalty and to ensure continued business growth.

INSTITUTE OF DIRECT MARKETING

INTRODUCTION

As described in Chapter 10, below-the-line promotion involves the use of techniques which do not normally pay a commission or fee to an advertising agency, and where there is no media owner to pay for transmitting the message through a specific medium – in other words, all promotional methods other than mass media advertising. Below-the-line thus involves a vast array of promotional tools, the most important of which are listed the Figure 12.1, and each of which contain a number of different methods and sub-divisions.

These methods are usually harder than advertising to quantify but the boundary between the two is sometimes difficult to define, particularly regarding direct marketing and sponsorship, for example. However, below-the-line methods of promotion are generally more within the control of the organisation, and are often operated or owned by it. This chapter will deal with the main instruments of pro-

motion available to a company under this heading, their uses and characteristics and how they function within the context of the promotional mix.

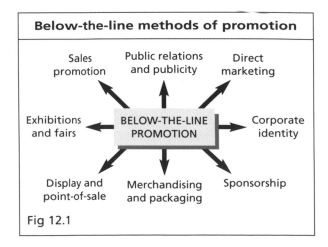

Below-the-line methods of promotion

Sales promotion — Public relations and publicity — Direct marketing

Exhibitions and fairs ← BELOW-THE-LINE PROMOTION → Corporate identity

Display and point-of-sale — Merchandising and packaging — Sponsorship

Fig 12.1

KEY CONCEPTS

SALES PROMOTION

Traditionally a promotional method used to support above-the-line mass media advertising, sales promotion has become one of the fastest growing areas of activity in marketing. Much of this growth has been stimulated by the direct purchase link which often occurs with a sales promotion, i.e. the product has to be bought, sometimes repeatedly, if the promotion is taken up. This is important in building up short-term sales volume and provides an effective means of directly measuring the pay-offs and effectiveness from any promotional activity.

Sales promotion comes in many forms, and different types are used according to whether the campaign is directed at consumer or industrial markets or aimed at the trade. The most common in each category are listed in Figure 12.2, although some techniques can clearly be used in all three classifications.

Every type of sales promotion is linked by a number of common characteristics, i.e. they are normally:

- specific and clearly identifiable;
- short term or limited period;
- out of the ordinary and non-recurrent;
- featuring an offer and/or suggesting a tangible advantage;
- designed to achieve promotional and marketing objectives.

Although it still tends to have a lower profile than advertising, sales promotion is rapidly losing its down-market image as more money is spent on it, as it is subject to more legal and non-statutory controls and as the number of specialist sales promotional or below-the-line organisations increases.

In addition to the advantages of direct measurement and short-term market building mentioned previously, there are a number of other important reasons for firms using sales promotion to achieve their promotional mix objectives. Sales promotion:

- helps to obtain trial and acceptance of a new product/new use, increase the purchase of an established product, or revive demand for an ailing/slow-selling one near the end of its life cycle;
- complements mass media advertising and other below-the-line methods;

- is generally cheaper than advertising and quicker to implement;
- can often be targeted at a specific market segment or in a particular geographic area;
- combination promotions can encourage the use of other products in addition to the original one;
- can be used to attract the marginal, uncertain buyer;
- encourages off-season and off-peak sales;
- creates trade and dealer interest and acceptance, and helps to stock the product and secure shelf space;
- moves excess stock;
- assists sales force presentations and develops sales leads;
- helps to off-set price competition;
- builds customer goodwill and loyalty;
- develops product positioning and image;
- matches the competition;
- helps to formulate a database of respondents;
- can lead to a higher level of sales in the longer term, e.g. the *Daily Telegraph's* Fantasy Football League has led to large increases in sales of the newspaper on Wednesdays, when the tables are issued, and a general sales improvement overall.

Naturally, these varying advantages or objectives will require the use of different sales promotional tools, but all such methods should result in an increase in sales, at least in the short term, and all should be able to be evaluated to exploit the close relationship between the piece of sales promotion and the respondent. For example, specific offers will result in specific, measurable responses over and above the normal enquiries or business, and their relative effectiveness can thus be compared with other methods, unlike advertising.

However, the use of sales promotion can also lead to certain difficulties and dangers for an organisation, for example:

- measurement and evaluation can still be difficult or inaccurate;
- consumers could reject the campaign outright or regard it as a worthless gimmick;
- the product could suffer from an image of being 'cheap and nasty' or always on offer;
- short-term sales increases do not always compensate for the costs of the promotion;

Methods of sales promotion

SALES PROMOTION

Consumer products/services

Industrial products/services

Trade – sales force/distributors

Competitions or sweepstakes	Industrial literature	Trade literature
Free gifts	Money-off deals	– catalogues
On-pack offers (product attached to another)	Trade-in allowances	– brochures
Free samples	Systems and installation support	Trade shows
Tokens	Service offerings	Price deals
Coupon and premium inducements	Special guarantees	Allowances
In-store demonstrations	Industrial offers	Discounts/rebates
Price offers	Executive desk-top gifts	Display and packaging
– reductions	– pens	Merchandising
– special discounts	– key-rings	Point-of-sale material
– buy now, pay later	– calendars	Sales and retail contests
– beat price rise	– ash-trays	Incentives
Money refunds	– beer-mats	– cash
Special offers	– bookmarks	– materials
– free draw	– matchboxes	– travel
– self-liquidators	– diaries	Bonuses
– 2 for the price of 1	Industrial fairs	Meetings/conferences
– next one free		Training materials
– mail-in offers		Trade gifts
Time offers, e.g. laundry back in 2 hours		Sales aids
Time limits		
Personality appearances		
Restricted to privileged few		
Seasonal gimmicks, e.g. Santa's grotto		
Free trials or previews		
Leaflets etc.		
Scratch cards		
Give-away material		
– mugs		
– stickers/badges		
– carrier-bags		
– T-shirts		
– hats and caps		
Trading stamps, e.g. Green Shield		
Air Miles		

Fig 12.2

- when the campaign comes to an end and product sales fall, it can take a long time for the previous figures to be regained;
- bad organisation or environmental influences could lead to unfavourable publicity, poor responses or consumer anger if an offer is not properly fulfilled (for example, the Hoover 'free air tickets' offer of 1992/93);
- market penetration is generally low – it has been estimated that maximum total awareness of a sales promotion campaign is rarely higher than 20 per cent, and an organisation would consider it had been successful if 2 per cent actually took part;
- the code of Sales Promotion Practice insists on a high standard of ethics in this area.

For these reasons, organisations tend to use sales promotion techniques as a part of their long-term communications mix. An effective balance of above-the-line media advertising and below-the-line non-media promotions should sustain brand image while building long-term volume. Before settling on the final mix components, however, the value of other below-the-line methods needs to be assessed.

PUBLIC RELATIONS

The growth of and need for public relations as a central component of the promotional mix has been mainly due to the emergence of several important factors, notably:

- more effective pressure groups;
- new customer values and ethics;
- the desire for more corporate information;
- new investor criteria;
- increasing media interest in business;
- environmental forces – economic, legal, political, social, technological, competitive;
- constant search for cost-effectiveness.

The Institute of Public Relations considers that PR is all about 'reputation – the result of what you do, what you say and what others say about you.' It believes that the practice of public relations is therefore 'the discipline which looks after reputation with the aim of earning understanding and support, and influencing opinion and behaviour.'

So it is important for an organisation to establish credibility and a good reputation and to generate goodwill, before it launches into the kind of high-profile visibility generated by more expensive advertising. Public relations should certainly build awareness, but it is also concerned with gradually obtaining mutually beneficial and favourable publicity and establishing or improving good relationships between an organisation and all the different groups of people with which it deals, through successful inter-communication and constructive feedback.

As well as responding to external developments and building confidence in the organisation and its products or services, PR is necessary for:

- illustrating that the company is public-spirited and aware of its social responsibilities;
- maintaining close contact with the public, enabling easier and prompt attention to grievances and gaining public support and feedback;
- increasing public understanding, particularly regarding sensitive issues such as expansion or environmental factors, and putting people at their ease by providing explanations;
- facilitating information flows into and out of an organisation;
- keeping employees interested, motivated and performing well with high morale by focusing attention on policies (e.g. on quality, profitability or marketing issues), objectives, programmes or clients (their opinions, expectations, brand image, and so on);
- giving a good impression, correcting false ones and creating a favourable climate of opinion in which a firm can pursue its objectives;
- being seen to have an effective and valuable influence on the well-being of the trade and general environment in which it operates;
- supporting and complementing the other promotional activities of the organisation and its overall business philosophy;
- providing research information (e.g. changes in public opinion about it or its products) and thus indicating policy implications and actions;
- building up brand awareness and knowledge for new and established products;
- showing the organisation to be worthwhile, vigorous and a leader or innovator in its industry;
- satisfying the demand for follow-up contact, relationship building and general customer care, as referred to in Chapter 1.

Almost everyone is potentially a recipient of PR messages but, in addition to the general public, an

Target publics for PR messages

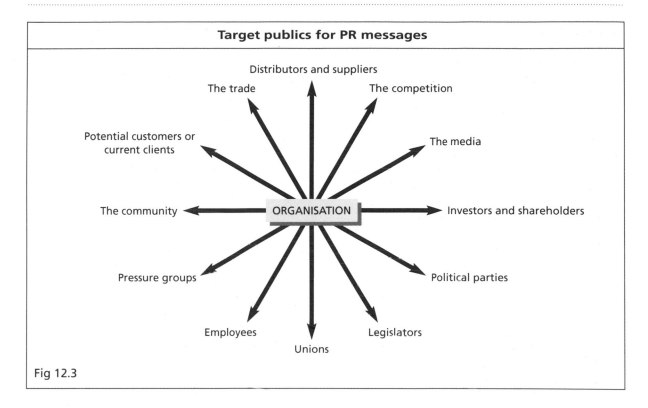

Fig 12.3

organisation will often have specific internal and external groups or 'publics' it particularly wishes to address, as listed in Figure 12.3.

As with sales promotion, there are a number of general types of public relations message, again both internal and external, which can be communicated to the target group by a multitude of specific methods, depending on the prevailing circumstances, as indicated in Figure 12.4.

Organisations tend to concentrate on certain general types of PR and specific techniques to deal with them, but an ability to use as many methods as possible is clearly desirable in case of unforeseen circumstances. This is particularly so regarding *complaints management*, the art of handling or heading off unfavourable rumours, stories or events; and *crisis management*, which requires rapid, positive action to deal with drastic situations. For example, Exxon did not handle the 1989 Alaskan oil spill well and lost considerable business as a result; but Perrier dealt quickly and successfully with contamination difficulties in 1990.

Another crucial area of public relations is *publicity*, defined as non-personal, below-the-line promotion in news story form concerning an organisation or its products and transmitted through a mass medium at no charge. Publicity often involves the use of press releases or editorial on company policies, marketing or economic/trade developments, personalities and events, slogans/symbols, endorsements, or news of general interest.

To be effective, and to be considered for use in the first place, press releases should be short, simple, clear, accurate, interesting and relevant, and should provide answers to the key questions, the Five Ws and One H – who, what, when, where, why and how. They should also include illustrations and photographs where possible, observe appropriate language/style and feature attractive layout, be dated and timed sensibly and focus on a news angle. A good working relationship with the media could also ensure that the press release is used.

One particular aspect of PR, *word-of-mouth recommendation*, is believed by many to be the most effective form of promotion. However, it can work both ways and research has shown that whereas four out of every ten satisfied customers tell someone else, seven out of every ten who are dissatisfied pass on their negative message.

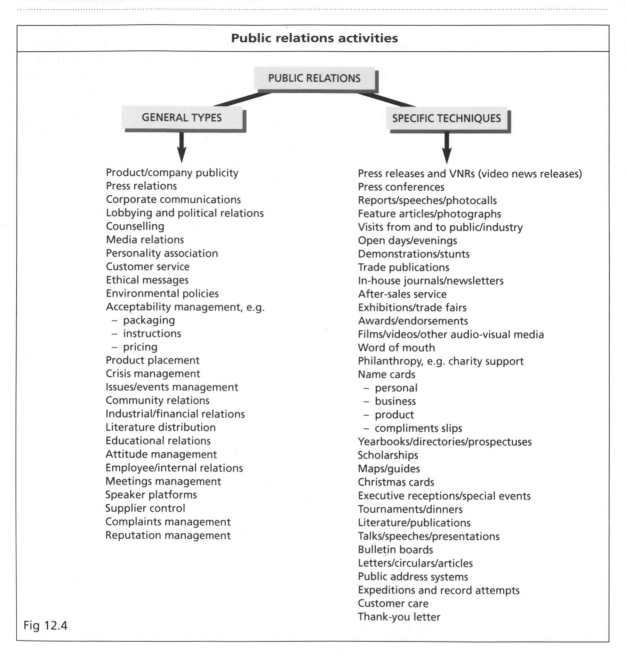

Fig 12.4

The main advantages shared by all these tools of public relations is that they are generally cheaper and more objective, factual and believable than advertising and sales promotion; rely less on methods of persuasion and can remove misunderstanding or ignorance and create goodwill. But there are also problems associated with PR, such as the following:

- the use of celebrities can backfire if their image is dented for any reason, e.g. Michael Jackson and Pepsi-Cola;
- lobbying can arouse fierce opposition;
- extensive campaigns can be very costly;
- media publicity depends on availability of space or time, whilst important points could be edited out or unfortunate choices of words/expressions could provoke an unfavourable reaction, if not monitored by the organisation;
- many day-to-day factors can create bad publicity or morale and lose business if not corrected, e.g. unfriendly receptionists or unhelpful staff, rude telephonists, poor parking facilities, lack of drinks

machines or refreshments, incomprehensible or confusing literature/instructions, unsatisfactory work conditions, misleading advertising, and lack of safety, cleanliness or internal support.

In order to avoid these pitfalls and create effective public relations, organisations should thus observe certain rules:

- PR must be founded on correct information and honest self-analysis;
- it should form part of a concerted marketing strategy, rather than being a casual or *ad hoc* activity;
- it should be used positively to disseminate good news or deal with criticisms rather than as a means of attempting to excuse company failings;
- staff should be trained in 'best practice';
- it should involve research, planning, objectives and appropriate action;
- effectiveness should be evaluated through measurement of quantity v. quality in media coverage, changes in attitude and behaviour, research, direct response levels and performance results against plans.

The management of all these PR functions is usually handled internally by an in-house department or within a marketing section, together with employees through all their personal contacts. Alternatively, an organisation can choose to use an advertising agency or specialist PR consultant.

Public relations is often used in conjunction with advertising. The spectacular successes of the Sellafield nuclear power station and Bradford city tourism campaigns, and the Moscow McDonald's media exposure coup, all illustrate how successful this can be.

According to Peter Gummer, chairman of Shandwick plc, the largest PR group in the world, the art of modern public relations lies in controlling the whole process and 'ensuring that whatever route the message ends up taking, it addresses the overall objectives, is constant, and thus credible.' PR has often been described as a steady 'drip-drip' process of attitude forming and, although not appreciated by all, the 'have a nice day' slogan at McDonald's has long been a good example of this.

One of the underpinning elements of PR is the establishment of a favourable reputation. In her article 'The best and the worst corporate reputations', Tricia Welsh describes how reputation can be created through various criteria, or attributes, such as

quality of management and of products and services, financial soundness, value as a long-term asset, use of corporate assets, innovativeness, community and environmental responsibility, and the ability to attract, develop and keep talented people.

So PR is not an activity which 'just happens', and although it is easier to build a good image from scratch than change a bad one, public relations should be practised by everyone. As an agent for change, it is often a slow method of promotion. However, with the current vogue for information exposure, employee communications, community and green movements, crisis management and globalisation, the use of PR will undoubtedly undergo an even more rapid increase in the future than it has already experienced.

DIRECT MARKETING

Another fast-growing below-the-line communications tool is direct marketing, which now accounts for nearly 10 per cent of all promotional expenditure. It includes any technique which provides the opportunity for a potential customer to respond to an offer direct to the supplier, without involving a third party, and can be described as 'the cost-effective delivery of pre-tested, customised propositions to identified and targeted prospects.'

Many factors have given rise to the rapid growth of this type of communication process, in particular:

- more accurate research methods resulting in more detailed and identifiable target segments;
- changing demographics and lifestyles, e.g. the traditional family unit now only accounts for 27 per cent of all households;
- alternative channels of distribution emerging;
- fragmentation of the media;
- increasing costs of sales force and the media;
- falling costs of data processing;
- a changing focus of business.

Direct marketing methods exhibit certain common denominators in that they:

- are based on accurate targeting and segmentation (dealt with in Chapter 4);
- involve direct responses from customers;
- can be measured for effectiveness;
- feature the use of databases, the 'bridge' between marketing and sales;
- emphasise long-term customer development;
- are strategic in nature.

Table 12.1 Advantages and disadvantages of direct marketing

Advantages	Disadvantages
Increased product/service visibility aids launches and improves sales	Intrusion into people's privacy
Personal contact builds loyalty	Can be pressurising and alienate people
Targeted to individual niche market needs (rifle, not scatter-gun)	Little time to examine propositions
	Proliferation of 'junk mail' – the 'binning factor'
Acts as a 'door-opener' for sales force	Boredom can reduce response
Confidential and selective	Some methods can be costly
Precise measurement and testing possible	Still produces 'cowboy' operators
Generally cost-effective	Large wastage factor
Responses build up database and better market information	Consumer lists quickly obsolete
	High cost of database access/maintenance
Databases profile and analyse	Low response rates – 2% is average for most methods
Creativity arouses interest	Feedback can be limited
Consumer laws improving, e.g. Data Protection Act	Relationships formed might not be deep
Life-time values cemented	Difficult to monitor encoding
Timing controllable	Creative and postage costs can be high
Supports existing channels	
Allows multi-media planning	
Can replace sales force	
Integrates with other promotional techniques or stands alone	
Few restrictions on format	
Flexible – easily adapted to special events etc.	

Several methods of promotion fall within these guidelines and the most important is *direct mail*, which will be concentrated upon here. The others are closely related to either distribution, selling, sales promotion or advertising, and have been covered in the last three chapters. They include:

- network database methods;
- mail order;
- door-to-door selling;
- multi-level marketing;
- business directories;
- home shopping by TV or computer/household deliveries;
- party plan marketing;
- telemarketing/telesales;
- direct response advertising, e.g. coupons or 0800 numbers.

All these methods seek to establish details about individual customers and communicate with them directly. From this and the other common features listed above, several benefits and problems accrue to an organisation from the use of direct marketing, as indicated in Table 12.1.

Whether dealing with consumers or in the 'business-to-business' market, organisations aim to avoid the problems and exploit the benefits by developing a staged approach to direct marketing known as the *'spiral of prosperity'*, illustrated in Figure 12.5.

From this programme of response invitation, information gathering and customer care, an organisation hopes to pull people through the AIDA stages (more quickly than might be achieved by other promotional methods) and retain them, thus establishing a chronological 'ladder of loyalty' up which customers can be lifted:

1. *Suspects* – reached through broadscale media.
2. *Prospects* – reached through selective media.
3. *Converts* – including previously unconverted enquiries.
4. *Customers* – including following up former customers.
5. *Clients* – including present satisfied ones.
6. *Advocates* – endorsing through personal testimony.

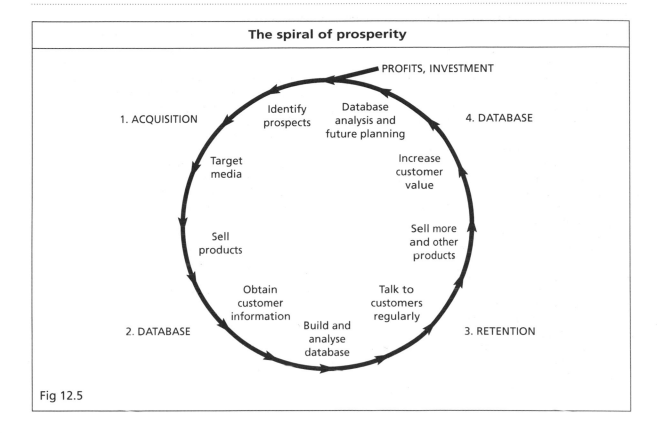

The spiral of prosperity

PROFITS, INVESTMENT

1. ACQUISITION

Identify prospects

Database analysis and future planning

4. DATABASE

Target media

Increase customer value

Sell products

Sell more and other products

Obtain customer information

Build and analyse database

Talk to customers regularly

2. DATABASE

3. RETENTION

Fig 12.5

Direct marketing is founded on three fundamental principles, known as the *Three Rs*, which underpin any campaign:

- *Response* – eliciting customer reaction through the specific method used, the accuracy of the database and targeting techniques, creative appeal and imagination employed (how direct mail goes about this will be covered later), the reliable generation of leads, and so on, then measuring the response to ascertain the effectiveness of the methods used
- *Relationships* – establishing positive and lasting contact with clients, based on understanding/meeting needs and aimed at retaining/increasing custom and expanding the client base, as every satisfied customer tells three others (but every dissatisfied customer tells 11 others). Interactive *'relationship marketing'* is preferable because if people participate, the barriers tend to come down. Relationships can be forged by welcoming, thanking, informing, explaining, rewarding, producing incentives or time limits,

adding value, introducing surprises or other propositions, emphasising cost or quality, acknowledging or personalising, all of which can be reassuring and add credibility. Relationships can be further built or retained by regular, supportive communication and service, the so-called 'massaging' or 'smoothing' factor.

- *Revolution* – utilising the increasing sophistication of testing, targeting, segmentation, database systems, mailing lists, effectiveness measurement methods, accountability and cost procedures, and legal protection. Although only 20 years old, direct marketing is no longer about 'junk mail' and is growing rapidly. The 'direct marketing culture' is also growing, with many people enjoying being on lists and having another dimension in their lives. There are now many agencies and companies specialising in the area and a number of large mailing houses and mailing list organisations. Direct marketing now has the capability to define, identify, locate, target, pre-test, deliver, measure and evaluate.

Many organisations now use direct marketing techniques, either as the only form of promotion in their mix, such as Reader's Digest; integrated with other methods, such as the RAC or Barclays Bank; or for peripheral support, such as Marks and Spencer and the Mirror Group.

The method of direct marketing used by most companies is *direct mail*, which involves the sending of unsolicited sales promotional and advertising matter to known targeted recipients through the post at specific named addresses. This incorporates most of the advantages and disadvantages of direct marketing previously listed.

Direct mail is used particularly for informing, accompanying a launch, maintaining awareness and loyalty, generating leads, and often for selling products or services to large markets, in contrast to some of the other direct marketing methods. It is relatively quick, cheap and confidential, offers high coverage and the literature can be retained for future reference. However, it is easy to ignore, can be primarily one-way communication with little feedback, and does not always lead to the forming of deep relationships which are the general aim and characteristic of direct marketing.

The success or failure of direct mail depends to a great extent on four main factors, namely content, creativity, mailing lists and management.

1. Content of the mail shot

The literature mailed could come in a variety of colours, shapes and sizes, depending on the nature of the product or service being advertised, the market targeted, the message being communicated, the budget allotted and the objectives envisaged. The direct mail package generally consists of:

- outer envelope, clearly addressed and labelled;
- letter, leaflet, brochure or invitation, including a worthwhile offer, such as discussed earlier in the chapter under 'sales promotion', a list of features and benefits or USPs, a PS to encourage action, and an order form;
- reply device to elicit a quick response, via a pre-paid business reply card or a freepost or stamped pre-printed envelope, and to aid measurement of effectiveness.

2. Creativity

It is said that 'the more you tell, the more you sell', but direct mail isn't only about volume. Design and wording are also crucial in maximising effectiveness and encouraging consumers to progress through the AIDA stages:

- *Attention* – touching off a sympathetic nerve in the reader.
- *Interest* – describing the proposition.
- *Desire* – explaining what the product should mean to the reader.
- *Action* – urging the reader to respond positively.

Various ways of achieving this are practised, but there are a number of basic ground-rules which need to be followed. Direct mail should:

- focus on the customer as a friend, using a familiar style and a name;
- emphasise importance, enthusiasm and individual needs;
- try to sell happiness and paint 'word pictures';
- be imaginative – use colour, three-dimensional designs, vouchers, or other unusual inclusions – and eye-catching, attractive layout and presentation;
- employ copy which is in the present tense, uses arresting headlines and short words/sentences/paragraphs, avoids unnecessary humour and includes power selling words such as 'you', 'free' and 'now';
- be appropriate, brief and get to the point quickly;
- illustrate where possible – 'a picture is worth a thousand words';
- encourage the reader to do something, e.g. answer a quiz, test or compare something, or tick a box;
- reward early response by setting a time limit or closing date;
- be easy to understand and handle, and simple to respond to.

3. Mailing lists

The possession of an adequate and accurate list of names and addresses of prospective customers is required for sending out the direct mail shot and building up the database. To be effective the list should:

- contain as much useful information as possible;
- be up to date and reliable;
- conform to the target group profile;
- be regularly revised and expanded.

Thousands of mailing lists are available covering the entire range of professions, interests and industries. Such lists can be gathered or compiled from many sources, including:

- in-house details of past and present customers and related products;
- sales records and sales force information;
- correspondence and telephone enquiries;
- trade shows and trade directories;
- direct response advertising and sales promotion replies;
- friends and recommendations;
- magazine subscribers and mail order and book club members;
- geodemographic and lifestyle information – ACORN, MOSAIC, etc;
- telephone directories, *Yellow Pages* and *Thomson's;*
- national directories, e.g. *Kompass, Kelly's, Dunn and Bradstreet*, etc;
- professional and shareholders' registers;
- register of electors;
- other sources, such as football pools promoters, publishing houses, charities, holiday operators, and so on.

In reality, most organisations will use rented lists, which are usually easily obtained in commercial, industrial and professional businesses with their own well-defined boundaries. Consumer lists are now more segmented and sophisticated, but still many sectors are untapped. It has been said that lists can supply '90 per cent coverage and 80 per cent accuracy', but they do have their drawbacks:

- they can be costly to compile and maintain;
- they are often reckoned to be out of date in six weeks and obsolete inside six months, due to people moving house or job, and so on;
- addresses can be inaccurate or wrongly entered;
- multiple entries can be misleading;
- there may be changes in the buying attitudes of the target group.

4. Management

Direct mail strategy involves consideration of the proposition, objectives, targets, timing, list compilation or selection, creative solution and production, budgeting, operational implications, testing, handling replies and evaluation. The responsibility for all these functions can be taken on by specialist direct mail houses or consultancies, or conducted in-house, using computerised methods. Either way, there should be provision of suitable facilities for the preparation and despatch of regular, professional mailings, often using special Post Office services and discounts.

Evaluation of the cost-effectiveness of direct mail can be tailored to specific groups and defined audiences and involves measurement of numbers of replies, orders, unopened returns or degree of interest. Although 81 per cent of mailings to business and 63 per cent to homes are read, a 5 per cent response is still considered a successful operation in most markets. However, direct mail has the ability to process large amounts of data quickly and cost-effectively and reach a specific target rather than offer blanket coverage. As such it opens up many opportunities for organisations and is a burgeoning area of business rapidly changing its 'junk mail' image.

OTHER METHODS

There are many other below-the-line promotional methods, as indicated at the start of this chapter. Packaging has been dealt with previously, so the techniques considered here will be corporate identity, sponsorship, exhibitions and fairs, and merchandising/display/point-of-sale.

Corporate identity is one of the fastest growing sub-sections of promotion. It involves an organisation developing a distinct image which is reflected in all aspects of its business, rather than being product specific, and is thus closely allied to public relations. Corporate identity is reality or what a company actually is, whereas *corporate image* is perception, or what people think the company is.

In recent years there has been growing pressure for a company to be seen as a brand and to pay the same attention to making its image and personality harmonious as it does to its individual products or services. The reason for this is that a well thought-out and implemented corporate identity has the following benefits:

- it encourages consumers to look more favourably upon the company and its products as opposed to the competition, by raising profile and credibility, reinforcing or sharpening positioning, and ensuring the organisation is up to date;
- it can improve internal morale by creating a sense of common purpose;
- it enables better products of more consistent quality to be produced;
- it allows an organisation to attract a higher calibre of employee than its more anonymous competitors;
- it heightens the company's profile in financial circles;
- it enables companies to establish themselves more effectively in new markets and adds value to the product range generally;
- it provides a constant reminder to both employers and the market-place about the organisation's achievements and aspirations, and thus helps during a crisis;
- it reassures customers and instils confidence, trust, reliability, quality and security, as opposed to uncertainty and negativity.

There are many means by which a corporate identity or image is fostered, enabling the organisation to benefit from these advantages. The most important work in combination and are listed in Figure 12.6.

Thus in the three main areas of products/services, environments and communications, a corporate image can be generated from observation or experience of sight, sound, smell, touch, taste and feeling. Corporate identity is thus projected through all the points of public contact, reflecting the personalities, core values and direction of the company, and has been fittingly described as 'corporate strategy made visible'.

Corporate identity is complex and needs constant monitoring and adjustment. It is a long-term strategy and cannot be altered overnight, but should move with the organisation or be supported by real organisational changes. It should

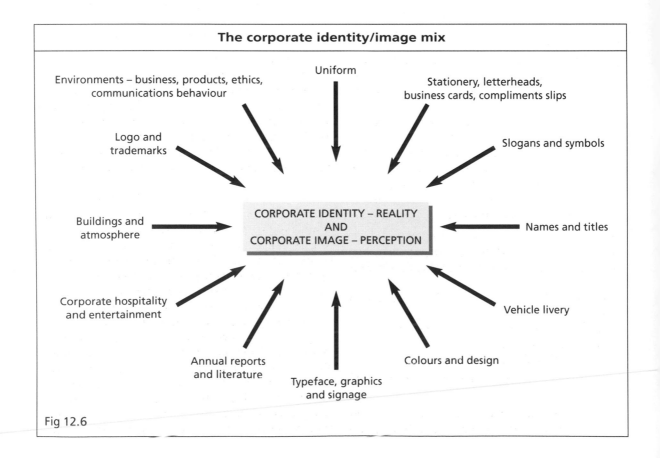

The corporate identity/image mix

Environments – business, products, ethics, communications behaviour

Uniform

Stationery, letterheads, business cards, compliments slips

Logo and trademarks

Slogans and symbols

Buildings and atmosphere

CORPORATE IDENTITY – REALITY AND CORPORATE IMAGE – PERCEPTION

Names and titles

Corporate hospitality and entertainment

Vehicle livery

Annual reports and literature

Colours and design

Typeface, graphics and signage

Fig 12.6

take account of fickle human behaviour and pay great attention to detail, for example the creation of a distinctive and memorable logo, easily identified and understood. Management of corporate identity thus involves considerable research, concept development and selection, refinement, implementation, launch, maintenance and evaluation procedures.

Many organisations place the establishment of a favourable corporate identity high on their list of promotional priorities, aiming either for instant recognition or a more fundamental reassurance. Examples are:

- Coca-Cola, Shell and McDonald's, with their familiar logos;
- companies centring on slogans, such as Midland – 'the listening bank', and British Rail with 'the age of the train' and 'we're getting there';
- the AA, with its distinctive yellow vans and livery;
- campaigns run by IBM, British Airways, Benetton, and so on.

Of course, problems also have to be faced with corporate strategy, in that identities can take a long time to build, some products within a range can require different treatment, and discarding a cultivated, long-term image can be an abuse of loyalty and lead to customer rejection, as Coca-Cola and Levi's have both found.

Exhibitions and Fairs are also closely related to public relations and widely used as a promotional tool. They are held at venues such as Kensington Olympia in London, the National Exhibition Centre in Birmingham, and many indoor and outdoor national or international locations, and can be mobile or involve seminars and demonstrations. They include:

- consumer goods exhibitions for the general public, such as the Ideal Home Exhibition and the Motor Show;
- national trade exhibitions for wholesalers and retailers, e.g. the Toy Fair;
- technical exhibitions for manufacturers, such as the Machine Tools Exhibition;
- international trade fairs;
- local trade fairs, often sponsored by a trade association.

Exhibitions provide a market-place where national and international sellers and potential buyers can

meet, customers can discuss the goods on offer and competitors can keep tabs on each other. They incorporate a number of advantages for the organisation:

- goods can be displayed, explained, discussed, examined and tested, and orders taken, agreements negotiated informally or follow-up planned;
- research information can be obtained from first-hand reaction to new or established products, their distribution and promotion, and from customer details;
- media coverage is often provided;
- product and competitive trends can be analysed;
- customer goodwill and corporate identity can be generated;
- a high profile can be established from 'showing the flag';
- a range of information can be disseminated to customers, who potentially include everyone attending;
- every minute is selling time with no travelling or waiting;
- they are often the only way to communicate with the total market;
- they can open up international markets.

For attendance at an exhibition to be effective, a great deal of thought has to go into designing appropriate stands, literature and displays, selecting the right location and staff to convey the desired atmosphere, and utilising available publicity. But exhibitions are complicated to stage, expensive to participate in (particularly site and equipment costs) and difficult to measure in terms of cost-effectiveness.

Like direct marketing, *sponsorship* straddles the borders of above- and below-the-line promotion. It is an under-rated medium that is often used in conjunction with other media such as advertising. In this relationship, advertising provides the message while sponsorship provides the vehicle and reinforces it. Of course, sponsorship is also used by organisations, such as the tobacco companies, to whom mass media advertising is prohibited.

Sponsorship takes many forms but generally involves an organisation paying to be associated with an appropriate event, usually in sport or the arts. In return the company may well receive advertising rights at the event, which is particularly worthwhile if this is to be televised, and should benefit from people buying more of its products. In practise, sponsorship can be local or national and is usually either:

- indirect promotion, where the sponsor's name is added but incidental to the main activity taking place; or
- direct advertising, where advertising space at the event is given to the sponsoring organisation.

Examples of sponsorship deals include TV programmes, NatWest Bank in cricket, Embassy Snooker, Beazer Homes in soccer, Marlboro' in motor-racing and Johnson's Wax for the New Shakespeare Company. By the use of logos, slogans, and so on, these organisations hope to attain extra sales, brand awareness, goodwill, perceived values and identity, and qualities such as globalism or sophistication, through close public contact and exposure.

In addition, firms see other advantages of sponsorship, such as:

- the value of the event having a favourable effect in the long term on their company or product;
- sponsorship being used as a basis for an eventual media advertising campaign or backing up other promotional activities;
- high cost-effectiveness, particularly if names are mentioned by commentators or advertisements strategically placed for TV cameras;
- greater intrusion into events, such as Formula One motor racing, where cars are practically mobile bill-boards.

However, sponsorship suffers from certain problems, namely:

- it can be very expensive;
- its intangibility makes effectiveness difficult to measure;
- rapid changes of sponsor weaken the event and its image;
- it takes time to build up public awareness and goodwill;
- companies can become better known for their sponsorship than their products, as was the situation with Gillette and cricket 20 years ago.

Merchandising, including *display* and *point-of-sale* promotions, is generally associated with retail outlets and as such has been mentioned briefly in Chapter 9. Merchandising is the total effort to encourage consumers and sell goods at the point of sale by maximising product, packaging, pricing and promotional offerings by the use of planned displays, store layout, point-of-sale advertising material and other buying incentives. The function has grown in importance as a result of the advent of self-service and associated impulse purchases, and it can be carried out by the retailer, the producer or both, sometimes aided by specialist merchandisers. Merchandising involves:

- assembling and locating distinctive and recognisable display material in visible, busy parts of the outlet and keeping them well stocked, clean and up to date;
- encouraging the buying process by ensuring a steady traffic flow, introducing diversions such as dump bins or aisle displays, changing product locations regularly, placing slow-moving lines in more prominent positions and awkward, bulky items near the exits, grouping related products together to eliminate confusion, using space sensibly, arranging attractive but functional displays which invite handling and examination, and siting goods at appropriate prime selling spots (such as counter ends and eye-level shelves, e.g. for children);
- employing creativity to win shelf and advertising space by providing consumer point-of-sale material, such as showcards and headboards, 'mobiles' and end-of-counter displays, signs and banners, 'crowners' to fit over containers, window displays, free gifts, and the sales promotional methods covered previously. Such material should inform, remind and attract the consumer, be short term and suggest value, secure retailer support and increase sales, whilst supplementing and integrating with other above- and below-the-line promotional activities, avoiding clutter and keeping within legal and ethical guidelines;
- providing appropriate and attractive industrial merchandising material, such as technical displays and literature;
- reflecting house style and corporate identity across all materials used, to maintain a consistent image, produce a collective impact, reinforce previous messages, encourage the development and purchase of own-label brands, and reassure consumers.

Wastage in merchandising, display and point-of-sale has been reduced over the years as quality has improved but, like all promotional activities, its effectiveness is difficult to evaluate.

ARTICLES

A1

ROMANCE GROWS AMONG THOSE SOAP COUPONS

By VIVIAN BROOKS

A FEW months ago, you had to be cautious when you set about doing any hand or machine washing. The packet of powder which was going to do all the work for you almost certainly had no top to it.

The top was swiped by the fastest member of the family, as soon as the packet was pulled from the shopping basket, to go towards taking someone else on a free train trip.

That sales campaign probably did not only the soap people, but the railways as well, a power of good. Most people I know sped around on more long-distance trips with those coupons than they would go in three years in normal circumstances.

The soap manufacturers must have been bubbling over with praise for the sales promoter who worked out that idea.

You'd need to be an average adjuster to work out how much the railways benefited. They run so many 'bargain offers' simultaneously – day returns, weekend returns, special rates to London, etc. – that it's hard to guess who would be making the journey anyway and ready to meet a higher price and who would be staying at home, leaving BR with empty seats and no income.

But, by and large, my guess is that the free-with-a-packet-of-soap offer promoted nearly as good business for the railway as it did for the soap manufacturers.

Now, the soap people have come up with their next idea. You can start collecting their coupons to get a sizeable amount knocked off your restaurant bill.

There's been some sound psychology applied in working out that one. You get a reduction on the total bill when you buy three adult meals, or two for adults and two half-portion meals for children. The reduction is calculated to meet the cost of the third meal free.

The railway tickets weren't worked out on threesomes. They gave you a free ticket for every one paid-for ticket.

But that's a scheme which wouldn't go down so well when it comes to eating out.

When a husband takes his wife for an "evening out," or it's incorporated into the courting routine of a lad and a lass, the female of the species wouldn't find it half as romantic if the whole bill weren't paid with a flourish.

Somehow, romance and soap coupons don't seem to flourish in the same atmosphere.

It's a different matter when it's dad giving mum a break from slaving over a hot stove by taking the family out for a nosh; or when it's three individuals who occasionally enjoy a 'Dutch treat' dinner together.

Then the food will have extra relish because one bite out of every three is coming free.

And, who knows, romance may break in after all. How many hungry threesome dinner dates may be formed just because everyone has enough coupons, which gradually develop into a twosome and a benevolent matchmaker under the mellow influence of good wine and tasty cooking?

Source: The Yorkshire Evening Press

1 Describe recent sales promotion campaigns which have had the same effect as the one in the article. Were they ultimately successful?

2 Why should BR use this method of below-the-line promotion rather than advertising?

3 What are the main advantages of this promotional strategy for the soap manufacturers?

4 What other sales promotion methods might be applicable in future for both BR and the soap companies?

A2

Sellafield wins PR award for 'regaining' public confidence

Susan Tirbutt

THE public relations department of British Nuclear Fuels yesterday won an award from the Institute of Public Relations for its work in 'regaining public confidence in Sellafield'.

The citation for the institute's sword of excellence award praised BNFL for being open and honest in inviting the public to visit and judge the Cumbrian plant for themselves.

The company launched its PR campaign in 1986, after widespread publicity in 1983 had linked radioactive discharges affecting nearby beaches with a high incidence of cancer in children in the area.

Visits to the centre rose from 29,000 in 1985, to 156,000 in 1988. The visitor centre has recently won English Tourist Board awards for its growth as a tourist attraction.

A BNFL spokesman said the campaign was delayed because the Independent Broadcasting Authority at first refused to take advertising for the centre. He added that it aimed to show the company was not secretive.

The award was last night criticised by environmental groups.

Mr Simon Roberts, a Friends of the Earth energy campaigner, said: 'No amount of well-packaged and multi-million pound advertising will hide the rot of the nuclear industry.'

Source: The Guardian

1 Why do you think BNFL originally decided on a public relations campaign as its main promotional weapon?

2 Which PR methods do you consider most effective for Sellafield and why?

3 As PR director for Sellafield, how would you deal with the environmental pressure groups?

4 How do you think BNFL should go about the future expansion of Sellafield as a tourist attraction?

A3

How to duck a shot in the post

Clare Sambrook

The average UK household gets six items of direct selling mail a week.

Most – 80% – is opened. And believe it or not, 63% of it is actually read.

Business by post is currently worth £945 million a year: 74% of it deals direct with the consumer, 26% deals business to business. Financial services account for £255 million, 27% of the total.

So junk mail, as the recipients tend to call it, and the senders *never* do, is a growth industry. Financial services companies account for one third of the mail shots. They sent nearly 30% more campaigns by post in 1992 than in 1991, according to research by Royston-based Market Movements. Sun Life alone sent ten million items to five million people. Companies like it because it is a cheap way to reach the customer. Why advertise on TV to millions when you can mail 20,000 carefully targeted potential customers? The best campaigns can achieve 15 sales for every 100 letters sent, a conversion rate some sales people would kill for.

But what's in it for the consumer, apart from the odd incentive like a discount or bonus allocation, or surprise, surprise, a clock radio? Isn't it just a nuisance?

Not according to Direct Line, the Royal Bank of Scotland's fast-growing insurance company, which claims to offer cut-price deals because it is cutting out the middle men.

Buying direct doesn't always work out cheaper. Some companies don't want to be seen undercutting their brokers.

But there can be other advantages.

Jeff Painter, managing director of Sun Life's direct marketing subsidiary, claims the life insurance, pensions and investments he sells at the lower end of the market are easier to buy through the mail. 'Brokers often aren't interested in spending time with people who have less than £50 per month to save.'

But the big argument in favour of direct mail is that its close targeting gives people a message they want to hear.

Source: The Mail on Sunday, 21 March 1993

1 If 80 per cent of direct mail is opened and 63 per cent is read, why do you think the term 'junk mail' has come into common parlance?

2 Why should financial services companies account for one-third of all mail shots?

3 What tactics might be adopted by these organisations to build a relationship between them and the customer?

4 Have you responded to any direct marketing for financial services? If so, describe it and whether the outcome was satisfactory. If not, why not?

A4

New image for council

RYEDALE is to project a new corporate image.

District councillors last night voted to spend £10,000 on developing an image and logo in a bid to promote the area.

Chief marketing officer Harold Mosley told the council's policy committee a corporate identity had to be created through the actions of staff, customer care and promotion, featuring a visual identity.

He said: 'The aim is to project who you are, what you stand for and most importantly what you do and how you do it.

'We can all decide on pretty pictures of Ryedale to promote the district but if we don't maintain the performance that goes with that there is a problem.'

Mr Mosley said a corporate image was needed to help five important factors:

- The establishment of a complaints procedure.
- The local government review.
- To enable members to get closer to the people.
- The work of the marketing office.
- Relations with the media.

The project will be allocated £10,000 through the council's budget.

Committee members debated whether this was the right time for the council to form a new identity.

Councillor Bob Eccles said: "We are going to meet parish councils in November about the local government review, discussing Ryedale as it is, Ryedale as they know it and Ryedale as the people know it.

'If we are going along this road, we ought to be going along it with the confidence of managing a new Ryedale. We should do it on the day we get to know we are a unitary authority.'

Councillor Gary Hobbs said: 'With a project like this we are better not to do it at all rather than do it badly.'

Councillor Eurig Thomas countered: 'If you don't do it, you are open to the charge that you have done nothing to address your image.'

Source: The Yorkshire Evening Press

1 Do you feel that spending £10,000 on a corporate identity programme is an appropriate action for a Local District Council?

2 Describe all the activities in which Ryedale might be involved to achieve the desired image.

3 If the 'person in the street' complains that they want to know when the dustbins will be emptied and not how the council is perceived, how might you try to convince them that a corporate identity will be of benefit?

4 Design a logo, slogan and business card to reflect Ryedale's new image, and explain the importance of each.

A5

Courage is taken by British team

BY MARTIN HAMER

COURAGE are the new sponsors of Great Britain international rugby league in a record-breaking £1.3 million deal spread over the next three years.

The agreement, announced yesterday, means all home internationals involving Britain, England and Wales will be under the John Smith's bitter banner.

New-style Great Britain jerseys, featuring the John Smith's logo, will be worn for the first time in the Wembley Test against New Zealand on Saturday October 16th.

The package includes this autumn's visit from the Kiwis, next year's tour by champions Australia, all annual clashes with France, and the 1995 centenary World Cup, being held in this country.

RFL, chief executive Maurice Lindsay said: 'The record sponsorship fee is two-and-a-half times the previous annual figure, reflecting the stature of the three-year calendar.

'Courage's expensive support also mirrors Great Britain's ever-improving record, highlighted by two recent victories over Australia, and being runners-up in the 1992 World Cup.'

He added that the popularity of modern-day international rugby league was confirmed by the British Test record gate being broken twice in recent times.

A new world record attendance for an international of 73,631 was also set in last October's World Cup final at Wembley, with the famous stadium now becoming a regular home for Great Britain fixtures.

Courage have previously been associated with rugby league through the Foster's World Club Challenge and the John Smith's Yorkshire Cup.

They succeed British Coal, who ended their four-year sponsorship of the British team last season.

Source: The Northern Echo/Martin Hamer

1 Why should Courage pay so much for sponsoring the Great Britain rugby league team?

2 What are the benefits of the Courage sponsorship accruing to (*a*) the rugby league team, (*b*) the supporters and (*c*) the media?

3 Do you think the sponsorship of sport is more effective than the sponsorship of other leisure or business activities? If so, why?

4 Describe another example of sponsorship of sport, the arts or business, and account for its success or failure. What are the disadvantages of sponsorship, if any?

ISSUES

SALES PROMOTION

Just a cheap and tacky attempt to sell more products?

1 List all the sales promotion schemes you have taken advantage of recently. What attracted you to them?

2 Do you consider that coupons, special offers and price reductions make consumers more 'brand loyal'?

3 The Hoover free air tickets offer was mismanaged and caused much controversy. Discuss the implications for the company and what lessons they may have learned in retrospect

PUBLIC RELATIONS

Does PR really help to sell products or is it an expensive luxury?

1 Debate the methods of PR which might be used in the short term and those more suitable to long-term strategies.

2 Select and discuss an example of (a) a consumer and (b) an industrial organisation which in your opinion need a PR campaign. What activities ought they to pursue?

3 Research and discuss an example of a company which has used PR (a) effectively, e.g. Perrier, and (b) to negative effect, e.g. Exxon. What has been the outcome in each instance?

DIRECT MARKETING

Promotion is steadily moving towards contact and relationship building.

1 Which direct methods do you think work best in establishing a rapport between organisation and consumer? Give examples from your experience.

2 Do you feel direct marketing (a) is an irritant, (b) violates privacy, (c) exerts pressure, or (d) encourages wastage? Give your reasons.

3 Do you object to being included on mailing lists? Argue the case for and against.

4 If direct mail costs so much to produce and send, why don't organisations just bring down the price of the product or service instead?

CORPORATE IMAGE

An unnecessary irrelevance which diverts an organisation away from the business of making money?

1 Argue the case for and against organisations spending large sums of money on comparatively minor alterations in logos, symbols or slogans, rather than on their products or services. Give examples.

2 Select an organisation which has adjusted its corporate identity recently. Debate whether it has been a successful change and explain why.

3 Corporate image essentially involves intangible aspects of promotion. Suggest ways in which its effectiveness can be evaluated, giving examples.

EXHIBITIONS AND FAIRS

A key part of the promotional mix or just an executive 'jolly'?

1 Which of the above descriptions do you think best applies to exhibitions, and why?

2 Do you consider exhibitions and fairs to be more relevant to industrial rather than consumer goods? Give examples of each.

3 Describe an exhibition you have visited personally or viewed on television, and list all the other promotional methods you noticed in evidence there.

MERCHANDISING, DISPLAY AND POINT-OF-SALE

Costly clutter which does nothing to influence the customer?

1 To what extent would you calculate you are affected by the layout of retail stores? Which features do you like and which do you dislike, and why?

2 List the key aspects of display or point-of-sale materials which you consider any organisation selling consumer or industrial products must use, and give reasons.

3 In your opinion, does merchandising 'get in the way' or is it an acceptable side of modern retailing?

QUESTIONS

1 Give four examples of below-the-line promotion.

2 Give a definition of sales promotion.

3 List six examples of consumer sales promotion.

4 Give four types of industrial sales promotion.

5 List four examples of trade sales promotion.

6 Give three characteristics of sales promotion.

7 List six advantages of using sales promotion.

8 Give three disadvantages of using sales promotion.

9 Provide a definition of public relations.

10 Give three reasons for the emergence of PR.

11 List five reasons for using PR.

12 Name six potential target 'publics' for PR.

13 List six general types of public relations.

14 Name six specific techniques of public relations.

15 What is the difference between PR and publicity?

16 Give three advantages of using PR.

17 List three disadvantages of using PR.

18 Name three rules companies should observe when using PR.

19 Give a definition of direct marketing.

20 List three factors which have led to the growth of direct marketing.

21 Name three common characteristics of direct marketing methods.

22 List four methods of direct marketing.

23 Give six advantages of direct marketing.

24 Name five disadvantages of direct marketing.

25 What is the 'spiral of prosperity'?

26 What is the 'ladder of loyalty'?

27 What are 'the Three Rs' of direct marketing?

28 Provide a definition of direct mail.

29 What are the three main contents of a mail shot?

30 List five aspects of creativity which organisations should observe when designing direct mail.

31 Name three characteristics of an effective mailing list.

32 Give five sources of mailing lists.

33 Name three disadvantages of mailing lists.

34 Provide definitions of corporate identity and corporate image.

35 List four benefits of corporate identity.

36 Give six examples of corporate identity techniques.

37 Name three examples of types of exhibition or fair.

38 List five advantages of using exhibitions.

39 Provide a definition of sponsorship.

40 Give two advantages of using sponsorship.

41 List two disadvantages of using sponsorship.

42 Provide a definition of merchandising.

43 Name three features of merchandising.

44 List two features of display.

45 Give four types of point-of-sale material.

46 Name two advantages and two disadvantages of merchandising.

PROJECTS

1 'Sales promotion appeals to the consumer's gambling instincts.' How much of sales promotion do you consider to be a gamble, for both the organisation and the consumer, and how much the result of careful analysis?

2 Describe all the sales promotion methods used by an organisation with which you are familiar. Which do you consider to be effective, which ineffective, and why?

3 How does public relations help to build a 'bank of confidence'?

4 'Advertising is the art of paying someone to say nice things about you or your product, while PR is the art of getting other people to say how good they think you or your products are.' Do you agree with this comparative view of advertising and PR?

5 Which types of product or business are most suitable for public relations activities, and why?

6 'If people participate, the barriers come down.' Discuss this view of the importance of establishing relationships in direct marketing.

7 It is said that direct mail should never miss the opportunity to give customers something they were not expecting. How important is the surprise factor in a mail shot and does it contribute to value?

8 Plan and design a direct mail campaign for one of the following:

   (a) a charity trying to raise funds for its activities;

   (b) a bank wishing to promote a new bank account;

   (c) a retailer stimulating demand for its in-house charge card;

   (d) an up-market clothing manufacturer promoting its new mail-order catalogue.
   Identify the objectives, targets, creative and distribution methods.

9 'One name is a name, two names is a list and three names is a database.' Discuss the importance of the mailing list to the effective operation of direct marketing.

10 'Direct selling is a one-way street – a database, junk mail, and hopes that it will be encoded, but no useful direct feedback.' Do you consider this criticism is justified or do you agree that 'there's no such thing as junk mail provided it's well produced and directed at the right person'?

11 Corporate identity is 'the essential glue that holds a company together'. Discuss this statement.

12 Choose an organisation and list all the 'faces' that it presents to its publics. How are those images projected, what other methods could be utilised and what are the potential pitfalls?

13 Some organisations are known more for the events they sponsor than the products they are trying to sell. Giving examples, in what situations would you regard sponsorship as an effective promotional tool?

14 'Everyone's a winner in sponsorship.' Is this a realistic viewpoint and if so, why?

15 It has been said that organisations cannot afford not to be represented at trade exhibitions and fairs. To what extent do you believe this to be true?

16 Describe the layout of a local store you are familiar with, and the merchandising, display and point-of-sale materials it employs. Analyse its good and bad points, giving your reasons.

GLOSSARY

Acceptability management type of public relations involving monitoring of customers' acceptance of product features and benefits.

Advocates stage of the 'ladder of loyalty' at which people become regular customers and tell others about the product or service.

Air Miles method of sales promotion whereby miles are credited on purchase of certain goods and accumulate until they can be redeemed for free flights.

Ambush marketing occurs when an organisation heavily sponsors an element of a sporting or other attraction in order to achieve saturation promotion levels and hijack consumer attention away from the event or override the main event sponsors.

Attitude management type of public relations involving monitoring of customers' attitudes towards the organisation.

Business to business marketing and promotional activities taking place between commercial or industrial organisations rather than involving end-user consumers.

Code of Sales Promotion Practice non-statutory guidelines concerning the production and mailing of sales promotion material.

Community relations type of public relations involving an organisation establishing good relations with the local community.

Competition method of sales promotion.

Compiled lists mailing list of names and addresses derived from directories, newspapers, public records, retail sales records, trade show registrations, and so on.

Complaints management type of public relations involving an organisation monitoring and dealing with customer complaints.

Converts stage of the 'ladder of loyalty' at which people are positively convinced about the product or service and become customers.

Corporate communications creating internal and external communication to promote understanding.

Corporate hospitality the provision of organisational favours and special treatment to current or potential clients.

Corporate identity the real image or impression an organisation wishes to create of itself in the public mind by means of various techniques.

Corporate image the perception of an organisation which is held by the public as a result of exposure to various oral and visual stimuli.

Counselling advising management about public issues, and company positions and image, used in public relations.

Coupon redeemable voucher used as a sales promotion incentive, either mailed or forming part of a direct response advertisement.

Crisis management type of public relations involving monitoring and handling difficult situations and problems associated with negative publicity as sensitively and appropriately as possible.

Cross selling encouraging the consumer to purchase different but related products or services.

Crowners point-of-sale advertisements fitting over bottles, cans, jars or other containers, at a retail outlet.

Database a computerised record of customer or prospect details used to compile mailing lists for direct marketing activities.

Demonstration sales promotion or public relations technique of showing the product or service in action, often in a retail store or exhibition.

Direct mail brochures, advertisements, letters and other personalised literature sent to potential customers through the post.

Direct marketing method of marketing whereby the producer supplies direct to the consumer – by post, through the media or other methods – without the use of retail outlets.

Direct response advertising method of selling using press or television advertisements which invite a direct reply from the consumer without going through intermediary channels of distribution.

Display the showing of merchandise within a retail outlet, store window, industrial exhibition, and so on.

Editorial publicity non-advertising space in a newspaper or other publication in which an organisation or product aims to gain a favourable mention free of charge.

Embargo limit put on a press or news release in terms of a time or date before which the particular item must not be published.

Enclosure or 'insert' material included within a direct mail shot envelope or package, usually in addition to the main content.

Endorsement sponsorship support given by an organisation or individual agreeing to lend its name to a product or service for promotional purposes.

Events management type of public relations involving planning and overseeing special promotional occasions.

Exhibitions or fairs method of public relations involving the promotional display of commercial or industrial trade products to gain eventual sales.

Fairs see 'Exhibitions'.

Financial relations type of public relations involving the development and monitoring of favourable relationships between an organisation and the financial sector.

Flyers a single mail shot or an additional insert in a direct mail package.

Free gift method of sales promotion.

Gift voucher sales promotion incentive, involving an opportunity for a special purchase or money off the next purchase.

Gimmick novel or unusual idea used for sales promotion.

Give-away material free literature or merchandise used to encourage purchase.

Goodwill intangible asset of customer satisfaction and feeling of benevolence towards an organisation generated by effective public relations.

Incentive or inducement a promotional offer such as a free gift or competition aimed at encouraging potential customers to purchase.

Inducement see 'Incentive'.

Industrial relations type of public relations involving the development and monitoring of favourable relationships between an organisation and the industrial sector.

In-house literature method of public relations involving the production of magazines, journals, newsletters and so on, within the organisation, and aimed both at internal and external publics.

Insert see 'Enclosure'.

Internal relations type of public relations focusing on the establishment of favourable relationships between an organisation and its employees.

Interviews method of publicising an organisation, usually conducted on the television or radio, or through the press.

Issues management type of public relations involving the monitoring and handling of situations central to the organisation.

Junk mail derogatory term often given to direct mail because of the large wastage in the industry.

Ladder of loyalty method used in direct marketing whereby relationships are established between organisations and people, who are moved up through six chronological stages – suspects, prospects, converts, customers, clients and advocates.

Lead generation activity designed to generate enquiries for follow-up.

List broker specialist concentrating on all the activities necessary to enable organisations to make use of each other's mailing lists.

Lobbying public relations activity dealing with building relationships with and influencing legislators, political figures and government officials.

Logo or logotype badge, name style, design or other representative symbol of an organisation's corporate identity.

Mail-in invitation for prospective customers to send by post for a free gift, used in sales promotion.

Mailing list list of names and addresses in a certain segment or category suitable for distributing a mail shot.

Mail shot single mailing operation within a direct mail campaign.

Massaging, stroking or smoothing direct marketing method of ensuring customers are satisfied by regularly meeting them, putting their minds at rest and cementing positive public relations to generate goodwill and sales.

Media relations type of public relations concentrating on the establishment and maintenance of a good relationship between an organisation and the media.

Meetings management type of public relations involving the effective planning and management of all meetings involving the organisation.

Merchandising see Chapter 9.

Mobiles moveable advertisements used in retail outlets, usually at ground level.

News release see 'Press release'.

Offer sales promotion incentive, including free gifts, refunds, and so on.

On-pack gift, price reduction or information attached to product, usually at the point of sale, for promotional purposes.

On-pack offer inviting purchasers to send for a gift or respond to a competition, usually with evidence of product purchase, for promotional purposes.

Open days or evenings invitations to press or other targets to visit an organisation for public relations purposes, sometimes for a special event, opening or launch.

Personality promotion or association type of public relations or sales promotion involving the use of celebrities to endorse a product or organisation and create interest and goodwill.

Philanthropy public relations technique involving an organisation supporting good causes, charities, and so on, and gaining goodwill as a result.

Photocall public relations technique whereby the media is offered an opportunity to photograph or film people or events, relevant to the product or organisation, in newsworthy situations.

Point-of-sale (POS) sales promotion, advertising or publicity material visible at the retail outlet or wherever the sale is made.

Political relations type of public relations involving the establishment of good relationships between an organisation and its political environment.

Premium gift used as an incentive for purchase or trial and for sales promotional purposes in general.

Press conference or press reception public relations activity involving meetings to which press representatives are invited, in order to be informed of an event and have the opportunity to question or comment.

Press pack promotional package on the organisation issued to relevant people, including a press release, photograph, background information, and so on.

Press relations technique of public relations used to foster favourable relationships between an organisation and the press and make it easier for newsworthy information to be given publicity.

Press release or news release a carefully written short article describing an interesting event or situation and designed to gain publicity for an organisation in the press or other media.

Prospect stage of the 'ladder of loyalty' at which certain people are identified as more likely to purchase a product or service.

Publicity public relations material in news story form concerning a product or organisation, designed to secure public attention via a mass medium at no charge.

Public relations (PR) the management and promotional function responsible for effectively communicating a controlled message to an agreed audience to achieve a planned response.

Publics groups of people identified as target recipients of public relations campaigns.

Redemption centre shop or warehouse operated by a trading stamp company where customers may exchange their books of stamps for cash or gifts.

Rented lists mailing lists rented from a specialist or other organisation in order to mount a direct mail campaign.

Reply card self-addressed card to facilitate an easy, quick response from the recipient.

Reputation management type of public relations involving the establishment and safeguarding of a positive reputation for the organisation and/or its employees, thus increasing its chances of business expansion.

Response rate level at which enquiries or orders are received from a sales promotion campaign.

Sales promotion indirect, below-the-line promotional activity offering customers, sales people or re-sellers incentives or offers, designed to add value to the product and boost sales.

Sample sales promotion method whereby customers are offered or given a free product or lower-priced trial pack as an incentive to buy.

Scratch card sales promotion competition method whereby special cards are issued on purchase of products and scratched to reveal numbers, etc., the winners receiving gifts or prizes.

Secondary marketing term often used for sales promotion activities.

Self-liquidator sales promotion offer or gift designed to raise sufficient revenue to pay for itself.

Slogan catchword, jingle, phrase or sentence associated with a product or organisation for the purpose of establishing corporate identity.

Smoothing see 'Massaging'.

Spiral of prosperity chronological sequence of activities in direct marketing, involving the acquisition and retention of customers and the use of databases.

Sponsor person or organisation financing an event or activity in order to gain promotional publicity or prestige from their association.

Sponsorship the act of a sponsor in paying money to be associated with a product or organisation in order to receive favourable publicity in return.

Stroking see 'Massaging'.

Stuffer piece of sales promotional literature or publicity material included within general mail distribution inside an envelope or package.

Stunt unusual trick or demonstration used in sales promotion or public relations to attract customers.

Suspects stage of the 'ladder of loyalty' at which

most people are perceived as potential pur-chasers of a product or service.

Symbol distinctive sign, logo, pictorial presenta-tion or graphic design denoting a product or organisation, as part of its corporate identity.

Three Rs of direct marketing three fundamental principles of direct marketing – response, rela-tionships and revolution.

Time offer sales promotion offer requiring response within a specified time period.

Trade-ins sales promotion incentive involving the selling of products or gifts to off-set the cost of a major purchase, e.g. cars.

Trading stamps method of sales promotion whereby stamps or vouchers are issued on pur-chase of goods, then collected and redeemed for cash or products, thereby acting as an incentive to buy (e.g. Green Shield stamps).

Trials sales promotion technique involving the free trial (and sometimes return) of a product before purchase, to give an incentive to buy.

Typeface particular distinctive print design or let-tering style used by an organisation as part of its corporate identity.

Vehicle livery identifiable design, logo, etc., on a car, lorry or other means of transportation, for the purpose of corporate identity.

Video news release short, broadcast-quality, news-worthy video designed to gain TV coverage for publicity purposes.

Window dressing arranging and displaying goods attractively in a retail outlet window in order to impress and attract potential customers.

Word of mouth method of public relations which involves seeking to generate and spread favourable comment about an organisation or its products/services, thereby expanding its markets.

SUGGESTED REFERENCES

VIDEO MATERIAL

Design Matters, 'Can you see what we do?' Channel 4, Malachite Ltd., 1983.

The Marketing Mix, No. 6, 'Corporate Image'; and No. 7, 'Display and Exhibition', Yorkshire Television, 1986.

The Business of Excellence, 'Corporate Culture', Open College, Channel 4, 1986.

Equinox, 'Junk Mail', Channel 4, 1990.

Work in Progress, 'It's a winner', Yorkshire Television, 1991.

Creative Management, 'Rover's return', BBC, 1991.

Business Matters, 'Taking care', BBC, 1991.

Actions speak louder than words, P.R.T.V., 1991.

Corporate image: high profile, P.R.T.V., 1991.

The John Bull business, 'The Big Game', BBC, 1992.

The Look, 'Scenting money'; and 'The Power of the Press'; BBC, 1992.

More than a game, 'Sold on Sport'; and 'Who's in the control room?', BBC, 1992.

The Training Hour, 'Into Print – the Persuasion Game', BBC, 1992.

Food File, 'Off your trolley', Channel 4, 1992.

The absolute essentials of direct marketing, series, the Institute of Direct Marketing, 1993.

MAGAZINE ARTICLES

Journal of Marketing Management, Vol. 9, No. 1, Jan. 1993, p.55, 'Dimensions of trade show exhibiting management'.

Journal of Marketing Management, Vol. 9, No. 3, Jul. 1993, p.255, 'Sales promotion – playing to win?'; and p.271, 'Sales promotion competitions – a survey'.

Marketing Business, Aug. 1989, p.12, 'Direct Marketing – vying for pole position'; p.14 – 'The power of the post'; and p.16, 'The only mailing-list in town'.

Marketing Business, Oct. 1989, p.10, 'Kingfisher – the logic of change'.

Marketing Business, June 1990, p.14, 'Sales promotion – will the boom come to an end?'.

Marketing Business, Aug. 1990, p.3, 'Judith Donovan – straight-talking success'.

Marketing Business, Oct. 1990, p.20, 'Cinderella grows up'.

Marketing Business, Dec. 1990, p.3, 'Leica – the market comes into focus'; and p.4, 'Corporate identity – value for money?'.

Marketing Business, June 1991, p.30, 'Get noticed' (sponsorship).

Marketing Business, July/Aug. 1991, p. 30, 'Consumer speak' (sponsorship).

Marketing Business, Sept. 1991, p.12, 'Meet the press'.

Marketing Business, Oct. 1991, p.40, 'Balancing act' (sponsorship).

Marketing Business, Feb. 1992, p.32, 'Public image'; and p.37, 'Waste not want not'.

Marketing Business, Mar. 1992, p.36, 'Free . . . and easy!'.

Marketing Business, April 1992, p.36, 'Pin-point accuracy'.

Marketing Business, May 1992, p.48, 'Briefly' (word of mouth).

Marketing Business, Sept. 1992, p.37, 'Sales promotion 1 – Perfect partners'; and p.41, 'Sales promotion 2 – Supplementary benefits'.

Marketing Business, Oct. 1992, p.12, 'Distinguishing marks'; and p.33, 'Conferences and Exhibitions special'.

Marketing Business, Nov. 1992, p.13, 'Taking issue'; and p.35, 'Presentation techniques'.

Marketing Business, Dec./Jan. 1992/93, p.39, 'Gifts and incentives 1 – power promotion'; and p.43, 'Gifts and incentives 2 – handle with care'.

Marketing Business, Feb. 1993, p.30, 'The cost of giving it away'; p.37, 'Stage show'; and p.42, 'Travelling light'.

Marketing Business, Mar. 1993, p.39, 'Direct marketing – hot data'; and p.45, 'Direct marketing – on target'.

Marketing Business, Apr. 1993, p.28, 'Price promises'; and p.40, 'Meeti ng needs'.

Marketing Business, May 1993, p.41, 'Sourcing – which widget?'.

Marketing Business, June 1993, p.22, 'A bit of a lottery!', p.39, 'Consumer speak'; p.40, 'Getting the message across'; and p.45, 'Pressed for space'.

Marketing Business, Jul./Aug. 1993, p.34, 'Post impressions'; and p.39, 'Direct competition'.

Marketing Business, Sept. 1993, p.43, 'Added incentives'.

Marketing Business, Oct. 1993, p.21, 'Sales promotion'; p.24, 'Conferences and Exhibitions'; p.25, 'Public Relations'; p.28, 'Direct Marketing'; p.30, 'Sponsorship'; and p.43, 'Corporate values'.

Marketing Business, Nov. 1993, p.28, 'Dell Boy', p.33, 'Venue menu'; p.45, 'Logo-land'; and p.48, 'Briefly'.

Marketing Business, Dec./Jan. 1993/94, p.36, 'Childish things'; p.41, 'The profitable power of the response'; and p.44, 'Winning combination'.

Marketing Business, Feb. 1994, p.8, 'Double exposure'; p.24, 'Can the EC deliver postal harmony?'; p.39, 'Incentive travel'; p.41, 'Videoconferencing'; and p.45, 'Interactive exhibitions'.

Marketing Business, Mar. 1994, p.39, 'The names game'.

Marketing Business, May. 1994, p.35, 'Hi-tech promotions'; and p.40, 'Longer shelf-life for design'.

Marketing Business, June 1994, p.29, 'Game of chance'; p.35, 'Calling the shots'; p.38, 'Continental contacts'; p.43, 'Stand and deliver'; and p.48, 'Briefly'.

Fortune Magazine, Feb 7th 1994, p.32–36, 'The best and the worst corporate reputations', including the 12th annual Corporate Reputations Survey.

FURTHER READING

Adcock, D., Bradfield, R., Halborg, A. and Ross, C., *Marketing Principles and Practice*, (2nd edn) Pitman, 1995, ch. 17.

Boone, L. and Kurtz D., *Contemporary Marketing*, Dryden, 1989, ch. 17.

Booth, Don, *Principles of Strategic Marketing*, Tudor Publishing, 1990, ch. 6.

Booth, Simon, *Crisis Management Strategy – competition and change in modern enterprises*, Routledge, 1993.

Cannon, Tom, *Basic Marketing*, Holt Business Texts, 1980, ch. 16.

Cram, Tony, *Relationship Marketing*, Pitman, 1994.

Cutting, S., Center, A., and Broom, G., *Effective Public Relations*, Prentice Hall, 1994.

Dibb, S., Simkin, L., Pride, W. and Ferrell, O., 'Marketing', Houghton Mifflin, 1994, chs 15 and 16.

Engel, I., Warshaw M. and Kinnear, T., *Promotional Strategy*, Irwin, 1987.

Foster, D., *Mastering Marketing*, Macmillan, 1982, ch. 7.

Giles, G., *Marketing*, MacDonald and Evans, 1985, ch. 7.

Gillies, Caroline, *Business Sponsorship*, Butterworth-Heinemann, 1991.

Jefkins, F., *Public Relations*, MacDonald and Evans, 1980.

Jefkins, F., *The Secrets of Successful Direct Response Marketing*, Heinemann, 1990.

Kotler, P. and Armstrong, G., *Marketing*, Prentice Hall, 1993, ch. 15.

McCarthy, J. and Perreault, W., *Basic Marketing*, Irwin, 1987, ch. 15.

Mercer, D., *Marketing*, Blackwell, 1992, ch. 12.

Royal Mail International, *Marketing Without Frontiers – the R.M.I. guide to international direct marketing* (annual).

Smith, P.R., *Marketing Communications*, Kogan Page, 1993.

Acknowledgements

The Guardian.
Martin Hamer, freelance journalist for *The Northern Echo.*
The Mail on Sunday.
The Northern Echo.
The Yorkshire Evening Press.

13

PRICE DECISIONS

DEFINITIONS

Price is the value placed on that which is exchanged.   ANON

Sum or consideration or sacrifice for which a thing may be bought
or attained.   *OXFORD ENGLISH DICTIONARY*

INTRODUCTION

Few decisions that a firm makes stimulate as much interest as those concerning price. Customers, intermediaries and company personnel are all directly involved. Politicians, economists and consumers study, comment on and try to take action over price because of the vital role it plays in the exchange process between buyers and sellers. However, establishing an appropriate pricing strat-

egy is a difficult procedure which depends on many internal and external variable factors.

The theory of pricing has its roots in classical economics, with the concepts of demand and supply curves elasticity and marginal costs and revenues. By contrast, the accounting approach to pricing tends to emphasise fixed and variable costs and financial considerations such as shareholders' divi-

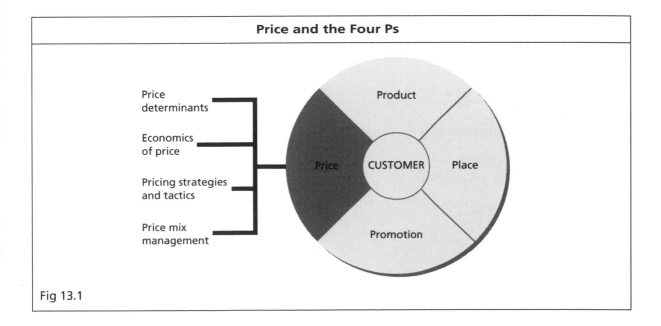

Price and the Four Ps

Price determinants

Economics of price

Pricing strategies and tactics

Price mix management

Price

Product

CUSTOMER

Place

Promotion

Fig 13.1

dends. For marketing purposes the key issues are practical ones, i.e. the pricing methods used in business and how they are best determined in order to satisfy the needs and wants of target customers.

Product, place and promotion have all been referred to previously. Pricing, the last of the Four Ps, is a vital element of the marketing mix (see Figure 13.1). It is not a mechanical process determined in isolation, but should be compatible with and lend support to the other three key elements.

It is useful to differentiate prices from costs. Costs are important and must be recovered through prices, but costs are a matter of fact, whereas prices are a matter of policy and therefore a marketing consideration. A marketing orientated business treats pricing as a key creative decision area and not an accounting or costing responsibility.

KEY CONCEPTS

DETERMINANTS OF PRICE

There are many inter-related, variable factors which a firm should take into account when making pricing decisions, any one or a combination of which could be the crucial determinants. For clarity, these can be broadly grouped into four categories, related to:

1. *The customer*
   - ability of customer to pay, i.e. the demand;
   - value of the product perceived by the customer;
   - willingness of customer to buy, or 'elasticity'
   - seasonal spending patterns, and sales;
   - nature of the product, and whether it is fashionable;
   - introducing new products or special promotions to the consumer;
   - susceptibility to psychological factors.

2. *The competition*
   - what other companies are charging for similar products;
   - the market segment in which the product is placed;
   - responses by competitors to changes in price;
   - trade agreements or cartels operating in the industry;
   - market share enjoyed by the competition;
   - reputation of the competition;
   - price flexibility in the market.

3. *The environment*
   - local, national and international (e.g. EU) policies;
   - country's general economic situation;
   - societal factors, e.g. social class;
   - political decisions, e.g. tax, VAT;
   - legal limitations imposed;
   - geographical characteristics;
   - expectations/needs of channel members and resellers.

4. *The company*
   - long- and short-term obligations;
   - volume of sales required;
   - production costs involved;
   - type and cost of promotional material;
   - brand image and quality of product and company;
   - ability of manufacturer to produce – the supply;
   - strategies adopted, e.g. market share and profit level;
   - policy on discounts/allowances;
   - product life cycle policy.

One key factor, of course, is the nature of the organisation. The key concepts illustrated in this chapter are relevant for all markets, but the focus generally tends to be on the consumer market.

Industrial organisations tend to be fewer and larger than their consumer counterparts, and operating in markets where there is more direct contact with customers and an emphasis on bulk quantities, product and service performance and technical specifications. Determinants of price in these situations will thus often include factors such as relationships with the customer, quality standards and traditional arrangements, such as

Table 13.1 Main determinants of price adjustments

Factor	Price increases (%)	Factor	Price decreases (%)
An increase in costs	97	A reduction in costs	48
Objective to increase profits	48	A reduction in rivals' price	47
A rise in competitors' price	47	Objective to increase market share	39
Improvement in own non-price competitiveness	25	A decrease in demand	30
		New rivals attempt to enter the market	26
An increase in demand	22	Objective to increase sales revenue	22
Objective to increase sales revenue	21	Decline in own non-price competitiveness	15
Decline in rivals' non-price competitiveness	11	Improvements in rivals' non-price competitiveness	10
Rivals exit the market	10		

discounts and allowances. Price discounting is generally operated in these markets within specific trades, for quantity or cash purchases and for seasonal variations. Geographic and internal transfer pricing are the most common methods used, and discrimination on pricing often results from factors such as income, tradition, location, status, product use and quality, size and volume, brand labelling, seasonal demand, and so on.

For all types of market, research has shown that some factors tend to be more important determinants of price adjustments than others, as indicated in Table 13.1.

Price is a central ingredient in the marketing strategy of many organisations, but competition is not always purely on price. Depending on the product or service involved, competitive strategies could be based on many factors in addition to or other than price, such as:

- distinctive product features;
- product quality;
- packaging;
- service aspects;
- promotional methods;
- other brand characteristics.

Non-price competition will tend to emphasise the role of customer and brand loyalty rather than financial considerations. In reality, organisations will often compete on a combination of price and non-price factors.

ECONOMICS OF PRICE

Decisions on price usually follow analysis of a combination of those factors perceived to be the most crucial in any given market. Most are related in some way to the market forces of supply and demand, in which the consumer plays a vital role. Figure 13.2 illustrates a simple model of how the average consumer would behave when faced with differing prices for the same product over a period of time.

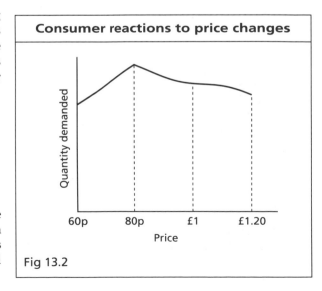

Fig 13.2

Of course, consumer demand depends largely on the nature of the product, but if £1 is the standard price, then the following are probable reactions to price variations which explain the shape of the graph:

- 60p – The product is considered 'cheap and nasty' and demand falls. The consumer is suspicious of such a low price and questions the product's quality and reliability.
- 80p – demand increases as existing consumers take advantage of an apparent bargain and some new buyers enter the market.
- £1 – the standard price, which most customers would expect and most would be prepared to pay.
- £1.20 – demand falls as consumers question whether the product is worth the higher price and possibly turn to cheaper alternatives (n.b. demand could rise for prestige products with perceived 'added value').

Underlying this principle is the notion of a 'fair' price which everyone is agreed upon, on the basis of social consideration and prior discussion. But when buyer and seller enter into an exchange of goods and money, both are seeking some degree of profit as a result:

- *the seller* wants some excess of income over costs; and
- *the buyer* wants an excess of satisfaction from the goods over the satisfaction gained from holding on to his/her money or purchasing something else. This element of alternative choice, or 'opportunity cost', is to a certain extent measurable.

So in determining pricing policies, companies need to understand the costs involved, alternatives available and the responses of the different customer groups and the values they place on the product. The relationship between a customer's costs and values is illustrated in Table 13.2.

But consumers rarely act with total rationality and cannot always judge quality from product attributes, often using price as the main indicator.

Table 13.2 Relationship between customer costs and values

Customer costs	Customer values
'Affordability'	Acceptability
Alternatives	Aesthetics – look, feel, sound, taste, smell
Costs of use	Conformance to standards
Installation	Credit and terms
Life span of product	Dependability
Monetary price	Durability
Service costs	Economy in purchase
Time needed for search and purchase	Image perception
Transportation	Performance and features
	Quality
	Safety/security
	Serviceability
	Variety

Table 13.3 Economic markets and price

Type of market	Characteristics	Role of price
Perfect	Many producers and buyers Unrestricted entry to the market Cartels/oligopolies may form Products are homogeneous Buyer/seller indifferent about with whom they trade	Price uniformity – only one price prevails in the market at any given time, subject to minor local variations One firm or customer cannot affect price
Imperfect	Many producers/buyers Restricted entry to the market Products are differentiated Back-up promotion and product innovation utilised	Prices not uniform Firms may change prices, thereby affecting other firms Price wars may occur, often destructive
Oligopoly	Small number of large producers controlling the total market	Firms control the price, but compete against each other
Duopoly	Only two suppliers in a market, e.g. Unilever and Procter & Gamble have 87% share of the detergents business	Two companies regulate price, depending on market share
Monopoly	Only one manufacturer of a product, who can control supply, e.g. British Gas (a monopolist in gas but not energy)	Company can stipulate price (but is subject to Monopoly Commission investigation if this is against public interest and the company has at least a 25% share of the market)

Although there are many exceptions, price can generally be said to offer a reasonable guide to quality, and vice versa, because:

- better quality products are likely to attract higher prices and cost more to buy because they usually cost more to make;
- price is usually determined by the forces of supply and demand, which tend to indicate quality;
- consumers often feel that prices are the outcome of collective experience and previous customer behaviour, and therefore are an acceptable measure of quality, perhaps reflected by an established brand name, e.g. Rolls-Royce cars.

Economic factors are also important in understanding the role of price, and pricing decisions are considerably influenced by the nature of the market in which the company and product is operating, as indicated in Table 13.3.

Imperfect markets are the most common, but firms have to remember price is also related to value and products must have utility (i.e. be capable of satisfying a want) and transferability. Also, both price and products are subject to the economic laws of supply and demand, cost factors and economies of scale, and the less predictable consumer reactions measured by elasticity.

Price tends towards an equilibrium figure where supply and demand are equated, as illustrated in Figure 13.3.

At point A, there is excess demand, insufficient stocks and prices rise.

At point B, a price equilibrium figure is achieved where supply and demand are equated.

At point C, there is excess supply, stocks accumulate and prices fall.

The main economic variable here is the elasticity of the product, i.e. the reaction of demand to a marginal change in price:

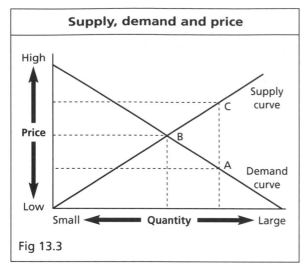

Fig 13.3

2. *Economic*   – cash flow;
                – ensure corporate survival;
                – return on investment;
                – analysis of break-even point.

3. *Sales*   – unit growth;
                – geographical areas;
                – growth in market share;
                – sales maximisation.

4. *Profit*   – target returns;
                – profit maximisation;
                – geographical areas.

5. *Stability* – retention of status quo;
                – meeting the competition;
                – using non-price competition.

Naturally, companies have different priorities and will organise their pricing objectives in a hierarchical form. Whilst the emphasis may well be focused on one key aspect, many firms have complex multiple pricing objectives.

Recent research, however, has shown that certain objectives are more usually pursued than others, as indicated in Table 13.4.

From the multitude of variable factors influencing price, an organisation must select those which are of most relevance and set about constructing a pricing strategy. Many companies have no clear pricing policy and final prices are still often market inspired, i.e. set at the market level which has already been established by competitors and which management knows, from experience, will be accepted by the consumer. The four main basic strategies available to a company are illustrated in Figure 13.4.

- *Competitive* – prices at the average or 'going rate', around which most firms are bunched. Used in large, stable, competitive markets where

- if a change in price leads to a measurable change in consumer demand, the product is said to be elastic, e.g. luxury products such as fur coats.
- if a change in price does not lead to a significant change in demand, the product is said to be inelastic, e.g. necessities such as bread.

Elasticity is also affected significantly by the availability of acceptable substitute products. All companies should be aware of which general economic category applies to their products, in order that an appropriate price can be fixed which reflects the importance placed on the commodity by the consumer.

PRICING STRATEGIES AND TACTICS

One of the most important determinants of price is based around a company's objectives, briefly referred to previously. Pricing objectives are general goals which identify what the company wishes to achieve from the pricing element of the marketing mix, and are consistent with the organisation's overall mission statement.

Firms usually set pricing objectives which fall into certain categories, orientated towards one or a combination of the following aspects of their businesses:

1. *Image* – setting a 'fair price';
            – emphasising product quality;
            – concentration on market retention;
            – prestige objectives.

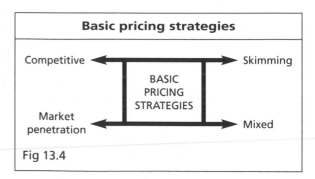

Fig 13.4

Table 13.4 Main pricing objectives

Main pricing objectives	Included among set of objectives (%)	Principal objectives (%)	Rank
Target profit or return on capital employed	88	67	1
Prices fair to firm and customers	49	13	2
Price similarity with competitors	48	8	3
Target sales revenue	47	7	4
Stable sales volume	25	5	5
Target market share of sales	18	2	6
Stable prices	17	2	7
Others (as specified)	5	1	8

it is possible to make accurate sales estimates. Requires product homogeneity, knowledge of the competition and analysis of costs.

- *Market penetration* – setting a price below that of the competition (even if that means making an initial loss) in order to get a foothold in the market, and then raising prices later when the product has become established. Used with 'elastic' products and responsive customers, but dangerous in times of inflation and price constraint, no clear segments identifiable, competitors will enter the market quickly and products will be undifferentiated.
- *Skimming* – pricing on the high side for short-term maximisation of profits before leaving the market or reducing price when faced by competition or resistance from consumers. Often used for specific segments or when launching a unique prestige product with a short life span (e.g. books, fashion) which cannot be protected from competitors. Such products are usually 'inelastic' and the market can be segmented on the basis of price. Also used where there is strong patent protection for a new product and in situations where demand could outstrip production capacity. Allows early recovery of costs (e.g. for research and development), but quality is vital and competitive costs are unknown.

- *Mixed* – a combination of the above. A company will begin with skim-pricing and, as competition builds up, lower the price to a competitive level (sometimes even below cost to eliminate competitors) before settling on a penetration price. Figure 13.5 illustrates a mixed pricing approach.

In addition to the main long-term strategies there are a number of short-term tactical variations which can be utilised if circumstances are appropriate. These are listed in Table 13.5.

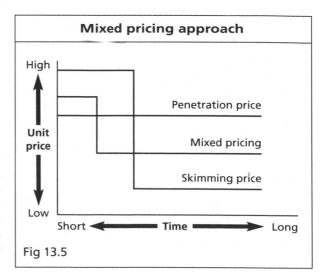

Fig 13.5

Table 13.5 Tactical pricing methods

Method	Characteristics
Bid pricing	A competitive price calculated by companies to win contracts by tender, e.g. government jobs or large-scale construction.
Cost-plus price	All costs calculated, a profit margin added and the result is the price. Traditional method, which ignores current/future demand and market potential. Also 'mark-up' pricing where a predetermined percentage of the cost is added.
Customary pricing	Fixing a product's price within a band to which the customer has become accustomed (companies might alter other elements of the marketing mix rather than exceed a perceived maximum and risk a major demand reduction), e.g. 10p telephone calls, 30p chocolate bars.
Differential pricing	Charging different prices for the same product according to location or type of customer, and value or size of order. Often considered unethical.
Diversionary pricing	Concealing the 'real' price by incorporating additional charges for necessary extra services, e.g. domestic wall-to-wall carpeting.
Dumping	Products offered in bulk at prices below cost, allowing additional profits to be made. Used where one large customer exists and includes own-label products and overseas trading.
Experience-curve pricing	Cumulative production experience enables an organisation to reduce prices and gain an advantage over competitors.
Loss leaders	Pricing at less than cost to attract customers in the hope that they will then buy other normally priced and profitable items. Can infringe legal guidelines (misleading prices can also be illegal if explanations are not offered whenever price comparisons or reductions are made).
Market pricing	Where the seller has no control over daily or hourly fluctuations, caused by supply/demand, e.g. commodities such as minerals and grain.
Predatory pricing	Pricing designed to accept short-term losses in exchange for long-term gains.
Prestige pricing	Prices set at an artificially high level to provide a prestige or quality image, e.g. cars, jewellery. High prices are often associated with high quality.
Price discrimination	Different prices are charged to give a group of buyers a competitive advantage. Used to satisfy segments, modify demand, support other lines, move stock and respond to competition. Bases can be customer's age/location/income, product use/size/quality, etc. But this is illegal in some countries, requires distinct segments, needs careful costing and can lose customer goodwill.
Price or product-lining	Based on relationships between a firm's products, rather than viewing each in isolation, to reflect quality, profit yield and use. Difficult to adjust and can be confusing. Often used in industrial markets.

Table 13.5 Tactical pricing methods (continued)

Professional pricing	Used in situations where great skill is associated with a particular activity, e.g. medical services. Ethical responsibility not to overcharge is assumed by customers.
Promotional pricing	Prices below normal to reflect special promotions, often on a product's launch, or boost ailing lines.
Psychological pricing	Pricing based on emotional responses, such as just below a round figure, to give the impression of a bargain, e.g. £4.99. Research has shown that as many customers round a figure down as up, often as a subconscious self-persuasion to buy.
Single price for all	One price charged to everyone, e.g. units of energy, standard transport fares.
Special event pricing	Price raised or lowered to attract customers, lower costs or increase revenue for a one-off occasion.
Target pricing, or rate of return	Prices fixed on a basis of rate of return over a given time, related to risk or investment. Requires accurate costing/forecasting, but ignores demand factor and influence of price on volume.
Variable pricing	Can be seasonal (varied according to annual trends, e.g. hotels, holidays) or diurnal (daily variations, e.g. transport fares, telephone charges).

The Price – Value Cycle

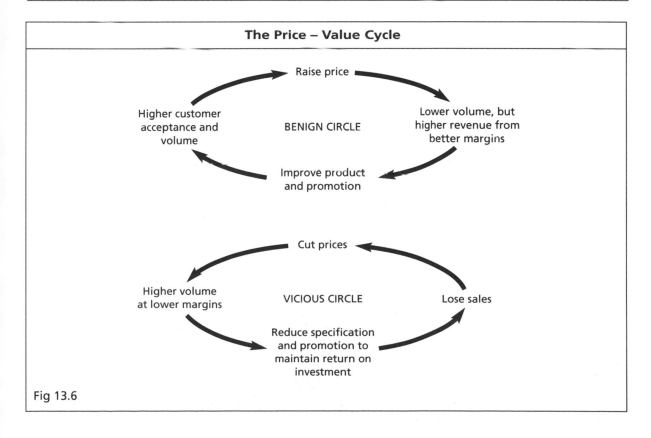

Fig 13.6

The results of such strategies and tactics are manifold, and companies need to keep a wary eye on variations in reactions and conditions. Sometimes firms can find themselves caught in a 'strategy circle' from which it is difficult to escape – this could have adverse or beneficial effects. The 'Price–Value Cycle' is a model which illustrates this (see Figure 13.6).

PRICE MIX MANAGEMENT

Clearly, price is a crucial part of the marketing mix and getting the price right requires analysis of many practical and theoretical considerations. Decisions made by a firm will constitute its price mix, which can involve some or all of the aspects we have referred to previously, as indicated in Figure 13.7.

Firms of all sizes are given advice on pricing. For instance, the doyen of pricing, John Winkler, suggests six practical points for organisations to remember when making price increases:

- Put prices up when everyone else does (don't hold back for the sake of competitive edge – you will have to increase eventually and the action will be more noticeable then).
- Not too much at any one time (incremental increases – around the level of inflation – are less noticeable).
- Not too often (buyers react against too frequent change).
- Move something down when you move something up (try to lower a price even if it is only that of a minor product).
- Look after your key accounts (the 80–20 rule says that it is the reactions of your key accounts which are most important).

- Provide sound – and true – explanations (customers understand that prices sometimes have to go up when costs increase).

Despite such advice and the wealth of research on price now available, the difficulty of establishing the most effective pricing policy is highlighted by many organisations which take the attitude that there is no uniform formula by which a price can be judged, and that it will be a good price or a bad price according to how well it serves the aims of the firm.

So in order to limit the risk factor and maximise the potential for successful pricing, organisations co-ordinate the key functions into a logical progression of tasks which ultimately lead to the determination of a price. Figure 13.8 depicts such a chronological process.

Such a methodical approach to the pricing problem will certainly ensure that decisions made are based on a thorough investigation of the many variable factors related to price, and are therefore far more likely to achieve the desired objectives.

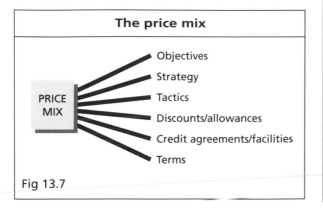

The price mix

PRICE MIX
- Objectives
- Strategy
- Tactics
- Discounts/allowances
- Credit agreements/facilities
- Terms

Fig 13.7

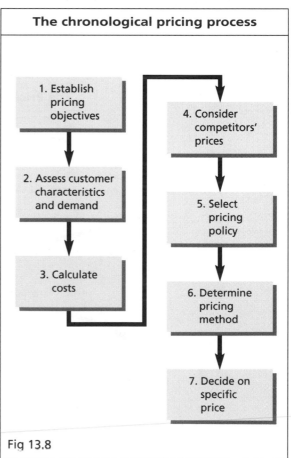

The chronological pricing process

1. Establish pricing objectives
2. Assess customer characteristics and demand
3. Calculate costs
4. Consider competitors' prices
5. Select pricing policy
6. Determine pricing method
7. Decide on specific price

Fig 13.8

ARTICLES

A1

BT unveils pricing package

DISCOUNTS for frequent phone users, up to 20 per cent off international calls and a freeze on many other call charges were announced by British Telecom today.

Average private phone bills will rise 4.87 per cent and go up by about £2 a quarter from September, under a new BT charging structure.

But more than one million customers who make few calls but regard the phone as a lifeline, can expect cheaper bills from a new BT scheme, Supportline, involving half-price quarterly rentals.

And people who use the phone a lot, including residential and business customers whose quarterly bill is more than £100, will also get automatic savings, said BT, which makes more than £3 billion a year.

The price package was hailed as a 'radical new approach' by BT vice-chairman Mike Bett. 'There is good news here for most of our customers,' he said.

Local calls will cost up to 4.7 per cent more when assessed on the number of seconds allowed for the basic charge unit fee of 4.2p, which itself stays unchanged.

But the cost of a three-minute, cheap-rate local phone call will still be 4.2p – less than the cost in 1981 despite inflation of 79 per cent over the past decade, said BT.

The typical residential bill would rise from its present £41.55 a quarter to £43.57 under the new tariffs.

BT insisted customers' bills would be cheaper in real terms as rises overall were not keeping pace with the annual 5.8 per cent inflation figure.

The quarterly rental will cost 7.8 per cent more – £1.57 extra for residential customers after adding VAT.

And installing a line will cost residential customers £11.86 more after VAT.

The biggest cuts will be in dialling abroad with international calls falling by an average of 10 per cent and some charges slashed by up to 20 per cent.

Source: The Northern Echo

1 What type of pricing policy is operated by British Telecom?

2 What are the implications, both positive and negative, of this policy?

3 How is BT likely to respond in future to the threat of competition?

4 Does BT operate any form of price discrimination?

A2

Dangers of the discount strategy

by Daniel Robins

THE supermarkets may have started a price war to fight their way out of the recession – but small firms are being warned about dangers in this strategy.

Marketing expert John Winkler says there are rules which must be adhered to following the 'cut prices, increase business' advice recently given by Chancellor Norman Lamont.

Brighton-based Winkler Marketing took a look at liquidations in the south of England and found that seven in 10 were businesses using a low-price strategy to attract customers.

The consultancy found that the companies most likely to succeed were those supplying goods and services at the upper end of the market and at firm prices.

The company's booklet – Pricing: Action Points – guides small firms through this tricky area which Winkler says can create conflicts.

'Of all the things likely to cause an internal row, pricing comes out on top.

'Marketers with their sights firmly fixed on the marketplace think they know just what the price should be.

'Finance people with an eye on costs often think differently.'

The Winkler discounting strategy starts by urging firms to keep their business aim in mind.

Be creative with discounting and don't copy everyone else. 'Ten per cent off' if you buy 10 is dull but 'one product free if you buy nine' is exciting.

Use discounts to clear stock and don't cut prices when there is no need. Apply time limits on discounts as this produces the opportunity to change the discount or to renew it.

Mix the discounts with payment terms. Do not give discounts if they do not pay on time, do not order in adequate quantities or require rush deliveries.

You discount for extra business, says Winkler, and must make sure they are passed on by the trade. Don't let them stick in the trader's pocket.

Stay flexible and keep reviewing the strategy. 'Copying everyone else in the market gives you no edge. Try to avoid giving money away, and a price reduction to buyers who settle their bills promptly can nearly always be avoided.'

With an eye to the future, and the eventual economic upturn, Pricing: Action Points also gives advice on how to make price increases.

Do it when everyone else does and not too much at any one time because consumers relate to competitors' prices and 'norms' such as inflation.

But the consultancy warns: 'Don't make increases too seldom either. Some people and trades only move prices once a year which plays into buyers' hands.'

Save up product improvements to explain away price increases which causes less irritation for buyers. Look after key accounts and give them advance warning, possibly also a moratorium.

Source: The Northern Echo/Daniel Robins

1 What role should pricing play in the marketing mix of a small business?

2 Why should 'low-price strategies' be unsuccessful, as mentioned in the article?

3 Describe the advantages and disadvantages of discounting.

4 How relevant for different types of business are Winkler's action points on pricing?

A3

Wraps come off car prices

Julie Wolf in Brussels

CAR MAKERS have agreed to demands by Sir Leon Brittan, the EC's competition commissioner, to publish cross-border price lists to make it easier for British consumers to compare domestic and Continental prices.

The commission said yesterday that lists of main models and options will be published by European car makers every six months, beginning next May, including the price of buying a car with right-hand drive.

The car makers have agreed also to inform their official dealers in writing that they are free to sell cars for export. Many dealers previously feared they would be penalised by the car makers for selling to customers from another EC country.

The move is the latest in a campaign by the commissioner to get car makers to reduce the big differential in car prices between one EC country and another.

Although Sir Leon maintains one reason for the differences is the car makers' exclusive distribution system, other commissioners do not agree.

This has stopped the commissioner from threatening outright to end the EC exemption, which allows car makers to maintain exclusive distribution, when it expires in mid-1995.

The Association of European Car Makers, which in the past had threatened not to co-operate with the demand for price lists, yesterday expressed confidence that the lists would back its belief that price difference had not been due to exclusive distribution.

However, consumer groups argue that price gaps will only be narrowed if full competition is established in the car trade through the ending of the selective distribution system.

Source: The Guardian

1 What can UK car dealers do to reduce the effects of the large price differential between their cars and those of other countries?

2 Discuss the variations in price strategy between one car manufacturer and another. Give examples.

3 Examine the legal obligations of car makers to publish their full list of different prices.

4 Where does price come in the hierarchy of factors which customers take into account when considering the purchase of a car?

A4

Why they're disc-gusted with the price of a CD

CHRIS LLOYD looks at the latest moves in the battle between record companies and music lovers

THE managers of Dire Straits and Simply Red – two of the world's biggest rock groups – yesterday accused record companies of creaming off "massive hidden profits" from the sale of compact discs.

They told a parliamentary committee that CDs should be up to £2 cheaper.

Yesterday's hearing was the latest round in a long and acrimonious fight between record companies and music-lovers that centres around why a chart CD in the U.S. can sell for as little as £7 whereas a UK customer has to fork out as much as £14.

Over the next few weeks, the national heritage select committee will hear much contradictory evidence and, under the chairmanship of Gerald Kaufmann, will decide whether the great British public is being ripped off.

Record companies sell shops CDs for £7–£9 and make just a pound profit. Or so they say. To manufacture the five-inch bits of plastic costs them £1.05, but mass production could cut this to just 58p. The companies reckon £1.50 goes to the artists, but royalties were said yesterday to be "diabolically low".

Ed Bicknell, Dire Straits' manager, says there are just ten artists in Britain who earn more than £1 for each CD sold.

The shops add about £4 to the price of a CD, of which about £1.40 is profit once VAT and overheads are taken into account.

And yet WH Smith, whose chain sells 25pc of all CDs, broke industry ranks in January and called for a £2 price cut.

Ironically, WHS supports the Net Book Agreement which keeps book prices artificially high to protect small publishers. Books are educational, says WHS; CDs are entertainment. But why, as one commentator asked, does Jackie Collins deserve more support than Phil Collins?

WHS wants cheaper CDs to encourage more people to buy music, but there is no evidence that this would work. Over the last two years, sales of recorded music as a whole have fallen by ten per cent; sales of "expensive" CDs actually rose 12pc last year and are now worth £380.5m.

The record industry thinks it is being picked upon. It makes profits of ten per cent whereas pharmaceutical companies rake in 45pc, and yet it was investigated last year by the Office of Fair Trading. The OFT concluded that as seven major companies control less than 80pc of the market they could not be price fixing, but it is currently looking into copyright issues.

It will not be until the end of the month before MPs have heard all the evidence. In the meantime it will still be cheaper to have CDs posted to your home from America than to pop down to your local record shop.

Source: The Northern Echo

1 What part is played by the concept of value in the sale of compact discs?

2 Is it justifiable for a CD company to charge above the odds on the grounds of better quality?

3 Describe the role of the retailer in the 'fixing' of prices.

4 What short-term tactical pricing manoeuvres could companies indulge in to offset consumer discontent?

A5

Bookshop chains in discount battle

**Nicholas de Jongh
Arts Correspondent**

A DISCOUNT war between Britain's two largest bookshop chains, the Pentos Group and Waterstone's, was joined yesterday amid claims that the rivalry would threaten the quality and variety of the publishing industry and the books it produces.

Tim Waterstone, chairman and chief executive of his chain of 85 stores, announced cuts of between 20 and 30 per cent on 40 titles. He said his move was in response to 25 per cent cuts last week by the Pentos chain of more than 100 stores which trade under the names of Dillons, Claude Gill, Hatchards and Athena.

His action was greeted with jubilation by the chief executive of Dillons, Frank Brazier.

Mr Brazier said that the developments meant that the net book agreement, which fixes the price of 90 per cent of Britain's books, was 'a dead duck'.

But Mr Waterstone accused the Pentos Group of behaving like a 'playground bully'.

He predicted the change might lead to fewer books of quality, threaten the maintenance of Britain's list of 450,000 books in print, and cause difficulties for Britain's smaller bookshops and independent publishers.

'I did not want this discount war,' he said. 'I think it will be very bad for the trade, which is a fragile enough industry.' Discount wars in America and France had had adverse repercussions.

In a statement yesterday, Dillons predicted that there would be 'a Gadarene rush for price freedom'.

Several leading publishers have stuck within the constraints of the Net Book Agreement 'only because of intense pressure from W H Smith, who have now deserted the cause'.

Mr Brazier said that Mr Waterstone was talking 'nonsense'. The cuts in prices of books meant that more people visited bookshops and 50 per cent of those buying a discounted book bought another which was not discounted.

'People who believe in the status quo believe that the number of books sold is fixed.' This was not so. 'We sell five to seven times as many books when we discount.'

His view was not shared by the Publishers' Association, whose director of public affairs, Ian Taylor, said the Net Book Agreement was 'beneficial to readers, the public and the book trade'. Every country in Europe, apart from Belgium and Luxembourg, had some form of agreement and recognised its worth.

If it was abandoned, it was unlikely that more than 1 per cent of books would be discounted. But the Pentos Group would gain a larger share of the total market.

'People not near the main urban centres with a Dillons or Waterstone's will lose out, and so will independent booksellers,' he added.

Source: The Guardian

1 In what circumstances could the sale of books justify a prestige pricing strategy?

2 How could a discount war be to the detriment of all publishers and bookshops?

3 What price strategies could small booksellers adopt to ensure survival?

4 In what ways could analysis of the elasticity of demand for books help publishers to set prices and fix the numbers sold ?

ISSUES

PRICE PHILOSOPHIES

Different viewpoints on price: (a) the economics approach, (b) the accountancy approach, (c) the marketing approach.

1 Research and describe the three approaches to pricing.

2 Discuss the relative merits and de-merits of each philosophy.

3 Give examples of small or large companies which have adopted each of these approaches and comment on their apparent success or otherwise.

THE ROLE OF 'ABSTRACT' MARKETING FACTORS

Two concepts inseparable (in marketing terms) from price: (a) volume, (b) quality.

1 Describe the price/volume relationship.

2 Describe the price/quality relationship.

3 Discuss the importance of each concept within the parameters of a company's price mix, including examples of organisations utilising each (to good or bad effect).

UNFAIR TRADE PRACTICES

The legal environment has an important bearing on a firm's pricing policies.

1 Research current regulations affecting how companies may price their products.

2 Are such restrictions 'unfair' and if so, to whom?

3 Describe methods which firms may employ to avoid infringing such legislation whilst retaining consumer confidence, and give examples.

FIXED PRICES

It is sometimes argued that manufacturers should be required to set fixed prices on all products, which retailers are obliged to adopt.

1 How would such an obligation alter an organisation's marketing philosophy generally and its marketing mix in particular?

2 What would be the repercussions of such a change for the retailer?

3 Discuss the likely reactions of the consumer to this scenario.

PRICE COMPETITION

Many firms still compete on price, despite the availability of several other marketing options.

1 In what situations is price competition more effective than non-price competition?

2 In which markets are consumers most price sensitive?

3 How effective is price in building brand loyalty?

PRICE DISCRIMINATION AND DIFFERENTIATION

Companies often put different prices on the same product in response to different market situations.

1 Debate the ethics of charging different prices for identical products.

2 Discuss the legality and effectiveness of 'loss leaders'.

3 In what situations might the consumer response to price discrimination/differentiation be positive?

QUESTIONS

1 Name three factors connected with the customer which influence price.

2 List three factors related to the competition which affect price.

3 Name three factors connected with the environment which influence price.

4 List three factors related to the company itself which affect price.

5 List three ways in which organisations can compete on factors other than price.

6 If the usual price of a product is £1, what would be the probable consumer reaction if it were priced at 80p?

7 Name five costs for the customer in buying a product.

8 Name five values a customer might take into account when considering the purchase of a product.

9 List three reasons for price being a measure of quality.

10 Name three of the economic markets in which a company could operate.

11 Give two examples of elastic goods.

12 Give two examples of inelastic products.

13 Name two examples of the main pricing strategies which could be adopted by a company.

14 Name seven examples of pricing tactics which a firm could consider.

15 Identify the seven stages which make up the process of establishing prices.

16 Describe briefly why pricing decisions are so important to an organisation.

17 Define price differentiation.

18 Describe briefly how pricing decisions are affected by the legal environment.

19 Name five of the objectives that firms could adopt when establishing a price strategy.

20 Define prestige pricing, and give a current example.

21 Give two examples of variable pricing.

22 Describe a practical example of psychological pricing.

23 Name two benefits of using a skimming price strategy.

24 Describe a situation in which penetration pricing might be used.

25 Name five of the business decision areas which make up an organisation's price mix.

26 Name three of Winkler's points which a firm should remember when considering a price increase.

PROJECTS

1 Select a local or regional retailer and describe the strategic and tactical decisions which such an organisation must consider within the area of price.

2 How important are ethical considerations to a company involved in establishing a pricing policy? Discuss a recent example of a firm whose pricing appears to breach ethical standards.

3 Price is only one part of the marketing mix. Discuss how the other elements of the mix affect the pricing activity. Select and describe a situation where price plays the main role within the mix variables.

4 Choose a consumer or industrial product or service and conduct a marketing research survey to examine its price sensitivity. Suggest an appropriate pricing strategy for the product.

5 What pricing strategy operates in a company with which you are familiar? Who decides the strategy, what are their objectives and what are the main influences on such decisions? Do the prices operating indicate product quality, ser-

vice, image and value and how might investing in design, packaging or promotion affect price?

6 'You get what you pay for'. Discuss whether this is always so.

7 How important is price as a competitive tool in

industrial markets? Use examples to illustrate your answer.

8 Describe the circumstances in which an organisation might use competitive, penetration, skimming and mixed pricing strategies, giving examples.

GLOSSARY

Administered prices consciously set prices aimed at reaching objectives.

Allowances price reductions given to consumers, customers or channel members in exchange for a return benefit.

Average cost pricing adding a 'reasonable' mark-up to the average cost of a product.

Barter price expressed in the form of an exchange of products or services.

Basic list prices prices that final customers or users are normally asked to pay for products.

Bid pricing offering a specific price for each job rather than setting one price for all customers.

Break-even analysis accountancy technique studying costs and revenue to determine at what price a firm can break even, i.e. cover all its costs.

Cartel informal organisation of firms in one market in order to control prices and/or minimise competition.

Competitive pricing pricing a product or service at a price comparable with that charged by the competition, i.e. the average or 'going rate'.

Complementary product pricing setting prices on several related products as a group, e.g. fish and chips.

Cost-plus pricing price set as a result of adding a fixed profit margin to the calculated costs.

Cost-related pricing prices set mainly on the basis of cost (fixed and variable overheads).

Customary pricing setting a price to which the customer has become accustomed.

Demand want for a commodity accompanied by an ability and willingness to pay for it.

Demand-backward pricing setting an acceptable final consumer price and working backwards to what a producer can charge.

Differentiated pricing setting specific prices to the advantage of different market segments.

Discounts reductions from list price that are given by a seller to a buyer for a return benefit.

Diversionary pricing concealing the 'real' price by incorporating additional charges.

Dumping getting rid of products by offering them in bulk at prices below cost.

Duopoly economic situation where only two producers control a market.

Economies of scale as a company produces larger numbers of a particular product, the cost for each unit goes down. This reduction can be passed on to the consumer in the form of lower prices.

Elasticity sensitivity of customer demand to changes in price (affected significantly by the availability of acceptable substitutes). Products can thus be elastic or inelastic.

Equilibrium price the point at which the level of demand exactly matches the level of supply. The going market price acceptable to both buyers and sellers.

Experience-curve pricing price reductions possible due to accurate estimations of costs from cumulative production experience.

Fixed costs costs remaining the same in the short term, e.g. salaries and rates/rent.

Flexible-price policy offering the same product and quantities to different customers at different prices.

Freight-absorption pricing absorbing freight costs so that a firm's delivered price meets the price of the nearest competitor.

Full-line pricing setting prices for a whole line of products.

Gross profit margin difference between direct cost and selling price.

Imperfect market economic market situation in which the products for sale are not homogeneous, where there are few buyers and sellers and barriers to entry.

Long-run target return pricing pricing to cover all costs and over the 'long run' achieve an average target return.

Loss leaders products offered to consumers very cheaply to attract them to retail stores in the hope that they will buy other merchandise at normal or inflated prices.

Marginal cost the change in total costs which arises as a result of producing one more unit.

Marginal revenue the change in total revenue which occurs as a result of producing one more unit.

Mark-down a retail price reduction that is required because customers will not buy at the original price.

Market pricing the seller has no control over demand/supply fluctuations, e.g. in the commodities market.

Mark-up a fixed amount or percentage added to the cost of products to arrive at the selling price.

Monopoly economic situation where one supplier has total control of a product (although a supplier can be a monopolist by definition with only a 25 per cent share of the market).

Non-price competition competing on elements of the marketing mix other than price.

Odd–even pricing setting prices ending in certain numbers.

Oligopoly economic situation where a market is controlled by relatively few suppliers who are usually large and concentrated. Products are homogeneous and demand curves fairly inelastic.

One-price policy offering the same price to all customers who purchase products under the same conditions and in the same quantities (also called 'single price for all').

Opportunity cost costs associated with choosing an alternative strategy (and which should be taken into account when pricing).

Penetration pricing selling to the market at a low price to stimulate growth and capture a larger share of a price sensitive market.

Perfect market an economic situation with large numbers of buyers and sellers, homogeneous products and perfect information and freedom of entry (such a market cannot, in practice, exist).

Predatory pricing setting a price designed to accept short-term losses in exchange for long-term gains.

Prestige pricing setting a high price to suggest high quality or status and to appeal to image-conscious consumers.

Price what is charged in exchange for a product.

Price competition competition based purely on price.

Price discrimination selling the same products to different buyers at different prices.

Price fixing sellers illegally combining to raise, lower or stabilise prices, possibly to the detriment of consumers.

Price leader seller who sets a price followed by all others in the market.

Price lining setting a few price levels for a product line and then marking all items at these prices.

Price mix the combination of pricing elements which an organisation applies to a product or service.

Product-line pricing see 'Price lining'.

Professional pricing pricing to reflect great skill associated with a particular activity, e.g. medical services.

Profit/volume ratio relationship between the volume of sales and the level of profit which results when the total of fixed and variable costs has been met.

Promotional elasticity change in level of demand for a product occurring as a result of a change in promotional effort and/or expenditure.

Psychological pricing setting prices which have special appeal to target customers, and/or can suggest a bargain, e.g. £9.99.

Quality a product's distinctive characteristics of excellence for which customers are often prepared to pay extra.

Quantity discounts discounts offered to encourage customers to buy in larger amounts.

Rebate refund to consumers after a purchase has been made.

Return on investment ratio of net profit (after taxes) to the investment used to make the net profit.

Revenue amount of money which an organisation receives in return for provision of a product or service at a set price.

Satisficing situation occuring when a company is satisfied with a price because it is considered conventional within a given level of risk and offers the possibility of an increased return.

Semi-variable costs those costs which do change but are not directly proportional to the level of output (includes elements of fixed and variable costs, such as telephone charges).

Single price for all see 'One-price policy'.

Skimming price policy pricing at a high level initially to maximise short-term profits.

Special event pricing setting a price to suit a particular occasion or situation.

Stable prices situation where prices are steady and inflation and depreciation in the value of money are minimal.

Strategic pricing price decisions/objectives affecting the whole organisation, usually over the long term.

Substitute product different product purchased as a result of a price rise in a product which performs a similar function.

Tactical pricing price decisions made which affect the firm in the short term and are usually easier to change than strategic price decisions.

Target return pricing setting a price to cover all costs and achieve a satisfactory target rate of return.

Turnover the total revenue which a company obtains from its volume of sales.

Uniform delivered pricing making an average freight charge to all buyers.

Unit pricing placing the price per gram or some other standard measure of the product.

Utility the usefulness, in terms of satisfaction or fulfilment, derived from consuming a product. Measured in terms of the value (or price) which a consumer is prepared to put on it and its power to satisfy human needs.

Value advantages of a product perceived by customers and for which they are prepared to pay a price.

Value-in-use pricing setting prices that will capture some of what customers will save by substituting the firm's product for the one currently being used.

Variable costs costs which change proportionately with the level of output, e.g. raw materials and energy.

Variable pricing setting prices according to likely changes in demand at different times and in different situations, e.g. diurnal telephone charges or seasonal holidays.

Zone pricing making an average freight charge to all buyers within specific geographic areas.

SUGGESTED REFERENCES

VIDEO MATERIAL

The Marketing Mix, No. 8, 'The Price is Right', Yorkshire Television, 1986.

Economics – a question of choice, 'The right price', BBC, 1986.

Contemporary Marketing, Video cases, No. 10 (Yamaha Motorcycles); and No. 11 (Looking Good Calendar Co.), Boone, L. and Kurtz, D., Dryden Press, 1989.

MAGAZINE ARTICLES

Marketing Business, Nov. 1991, p.36, 'Science of Marketing – Price Wars'.

Marketing Business, Apr. 1993, p.28, 'Market Brief – Price Promises'.

Marketing Business, June 1993, p.28, 'How to profit from premium-priced brands'.

Quarterly Review of Marketing, Autumn 1986, Vol. 12 No. 1, 'The Contribution Method of Price Determination'.

FURTHER READING

Adcock, D., Bradfield, R., Halborg, A. and Ross C., *Marketing Principles and Practice* (2nd edn), Pitman, 1995, ch. 13.

Baker, M.,(Ed.), *The Marketing Book*, Heinemann/ C.I.M., 1990, ch. 14.

Boone, L. and Kurtz, D., *Contemporary Marketing*, Dryden, 1989, chs 10 and 11.

Booth, Don, *Principles of Strategic Marketing*, Tudor Publishing, 1990, ch. 7.

Cannon, Tom, *Basic Marketing*, Holt Business Texts, 1980, ch. 13.

Dibb, S., Simkin, L., Pride, W. and Ferrell, O., *Marketing*, Houghton Mifflin, 1994, chs 17 and 18.

Foster, D., *Mastering Marketing*, Macmillan, 1982, ch. 5.

Giles, G., *Marketing*, MacDonald and Evans, 1985, ch. 5.

Kotler, P. and Armstrong, G., *Marketing*, Prentice Hall, 1993, chs 10 and 11.

McCarthy, J. and Perreault, W., *Basic Marketing*, Irwin, 1987, chs 18 and 19.

Mercer, David, *Marketing*, Blackwell, 1992, ch. 9.

Acknowledgements

The Guardian.
The Northern Echo.
Daniel Robins, freelance journalist for *The Northern Echo.*
John Winkler, 'Pricing – Action Points', from M. Baker (Ed.), *The Marketing Book,* Heinemann/C.I.M., 1990.

14
MARKETING MANAGEMENT

DEFINITIONS

Marketing management is 'a process of planning, organising, implementing and controlling marketing activities to facilitate and expedite exchanges effectively and efficiently. '

DIBB, SIMKIN, PRIDE AND FERRELL

There is no such thing as marketing skill by itself. For a company to be good at marketing it must be good at everything else, from R. and D. to manufacturing, from quality controls to financial controls.

HOWARD MORGENS, FORMER CHAIRMAN OF PROCTER & GAMBLE

INTRODUCTION

Marketing is an approach to business, to re-iterate the point made in the first chapter. Its role is to relate the strengths and performance of the organisation to the needs of the customer and the opportunities in the market-place, in such a way as to maximise company profits and consumer value. But it cannot thrive in isolation and must be integrated with all aspects of organisational activity to be truly effective.

Successful management of the marketing function thus requires a broad understanding of all the many aspects of business in which firms are involved and the application of the marketing concept to them in both the short and the long term, within a co-ordinated overall programme. The core areas of marketing management at the heart of such a policy are outlined in Figure 14.1.

In formulating policies to deal with these considerations, marketing management cannot ignore all the constraints placed upon it by the internal and external environments, discussed in Chapter 2, and the 'Three Ms':

- *Movement* – the management of human resources, the 'who does what?' aspect;

Key aspects of marketing management

Implemention of the marketing concept

The marketing audit

MARKETING MANAGEMENT

Marketing planning

Strategies and controls

Fig 14.1

- *Money* – budgetary limitations;
- *Minutes* – demands made by time horizons.

However, as previously mentioned, the most influential factor is communication. As Hugh Davidson puts it in *Offensive Marketing*:

'The effective operation of the integrated marketing approach really depends on the spirit of the organisation . . . the best results are achieved in an atmosphere of co-operation, where the quality of an idea matters more than the seniority or background of its originator. To this end, a marketing department . . . is in a very strong position to persuade others since it possesses all the facts about the market-place which underlie action plans, and has a clear picture of the total corporate operation.'

It is thus the function of marketing management to emphasise its central role by combining all the theoretical and practical information described in the previous 13 chapters, selecting and utilising what is relevant in a particular situation and designing programmes aimed at successfully achieving the desired objectives, whilst taking into account all the variable factors and other organisational dimensions.

KEY CONCEPTS

IMPLEMENTING THE MARKETING PHILOSOPHY

In order to convert marketing theory into effective practice, organisations should undertake a series of logical steps which serve to complete an individual task efficiently whilst applying and reinforcing overall company policy. These broad stages form the backbone of this chapter and can be identified by the SOSTE mnemonic (see Table 14.1).

If followed closely, this staged process will ensure that the building bricks are in place sufficiently firmly for the marketing philosophy to be implemented throughout the organisation. It should provide the framework for effective communication within the marketing department and the company as a whole and for proper understanding and co-ordination of all marketing activities, enabling all personnel to be motivated to work towards the common goal of putting the customer at the centre of everything they do.

For this to happen, however, certain conditions must be present, one of the most important being the establishment of an appropriate corporate or organisational culture in which business activities can flourish, as mentioned in Chapter 2. Furthermore, marketing's key role as an 'influencer' of all types of business activity necessitates that senior management must adopt it whole-heartedly as a basis for all goal setting and decision making. Only then can the philosophy permeate downwards and convince all organisation members to change their policies, operations and attitudes accordingly.

Again, all levels of management must adapt to the customer-centred approach by such procedures

as establishing comprehensive information systems and restructuring the organisation (for instance, elevating marketing units, appointing product or brand managers and abolishing or creating departments) to reflect the new emphasis, as indicated in Chapter 2.

Even then, many problems can be experienced by firms implementing the marketing philosophy within their existing frameworks, at managerial and other levels. The most common are:

- the difficulty of tailoring products or services to fit the exact needs of each customer or target group;
- the uncertainty surrounding what customers actually want – research is often unreliable despite the fact that considerable time and money may be expended on it;
- satisfying one segment of the market could alienate others;
- resistance of employees to what is seen as a change in philosophy and thus becomes suspicious or threatening;
- the inability of employees to interpret the marketing philosophy and/or incorporate it into their routines and behaviour;
- the difficulty of maintaining employee morale during the re-structuring of the organisation;
- the reluctance of managers to communicate effectively the reasons for the changes and their enthusiasm for them;
- rigid and inflexible adherence to adopted marketing management procedures, which can sometimes be counter-productive and lead to the organisation being unable to respond appropriately and speedily to changing customer and market situations.

Table 14.1 Stages of marketing management

Stage	Questions posed	Description/solution
S–Situation	Where are we now? Where are we going?	Market audit analysis: appraisal of company, market, competition, products, productivity, internal and external environments
O–Objectives	Where do we want to get to?	Hierarchical destination analysis: 1. Corporate goals – long term, e.g. development of corporate culture. 2. Business objectives, e.g. production, financial, human and marketing resources. 3. Marketing objectives – markets, market share, marketing mixes. 4. Specific objectives – e.g. promotion (personal selling, advertising, etc).
S–Strategies	How do we get there in the long term?	Selection by senior management of best long-term routes for achieving objectives – choice and organisation of resources/broad product areas/marketing mixes/target markets, and so on
T–Tactics	What must be done in the short term?	Selection by middle management of the best short-term routes to chosen destinations and detailed execution of strategies, e.g. product USPs/packaging, promotional methods, research/sales plans etc
E–Evaluation	How well are we doing?	Controlling strategies/tactics/budgets, monitoring plans, measuring success

Customer-centred organisations will seek to overcome these potential problem areas by positively espousing the virtues of the marketing concept and ensuring that everyone has a part to play in its implementation and success.

THE MARKETING AUDIT

Before a company can start planning future operations a complete situation analysis is required, covering every aspect of its past, current or potential activities, organisation, strategies and tactics, systems, profitability and philosophies. These management considerations are all touched upon elsewhere, but the main part of the *marketing audit* concerns a thorough and exhaustive review of the internal and external environments in which the firm is operating, regularly undertaken to ensure its findings remain current.

One particularly useful method of achieving this is to conduct a *SWOT analysis* which outlines specific details under various headings, rather than

Table 14.2 SWOT analysis

Component	Description	Environmental position
Strengths	Capabilities and assets	Internal
Weaknesses	Limitations	Internal
Opportunities	Chances	External
Threats	Dangers	External

generalising, in order to enable the organisation to cope with change, deal with influences and prepare for the future. The component parts of a SWOT analysis are described in Table 14.2.

An *internal audit* is necessary to examine *strengths* and *weaknesses*, in order to:

- identify shortcomings in the company's present skills and resources;
- pinpoint areas in which the firm can build or expand;
- provide a 'capability profile', a statement of organisational resources and assets in quantitative and qualitative terms.

Some of the main factors included in an internal audit are listed in Table 14.3.

Significant strengths and weaknesses will warrant further attention and will indicate the company's capacity to deal with the *opportunities* and *threats*, which comprise the *external audit*. Opportunities need to be engineered and exploited while threats should be anticipated and resisted.

However, the external business environment is wide in scope and can operate at local, regional, national or international levels and involve many factors. As described in Chapter 2, these are usually grouped into areas covered by the PEST acronym (Political/governmental, Economic/commercial, Social/sociological and Technical) and also include the competitive environment.

Many organisations use this SWOT information to develop simple, objective techniques to appraise their respective situations, such as *matrix* frameworks and analysis. There are many variants of this approach but the most common are:

- the Ansoff matrix, referred to in Chapter 7, which presents four basic types of market and product situations and opportunities;
- Hofer and Schendel's product/market evolution matrix;
- the General Electric business screen, which presents a ranking grid based on business strengths and industry attractiveness factors;

Table 14.3 The internal audit

Strengths and Weaknesses	
Research capabilities	Market share
R and D/innovation	Access to markets
Evaluation of products and services	Financial resources
Product range	Human resources/skills profile
Known brands/brand leaders	Labour relations
Traditional/modern profile	Equipment/IT systems
Creativity and design	Physical facilities
Quality reputation	Organisational abilities
Distribution network	Managerial skills
Promotion performance	Productivity
Price control and strategies	Technical competence
Established market segments	Corporate image/identity
	and so on

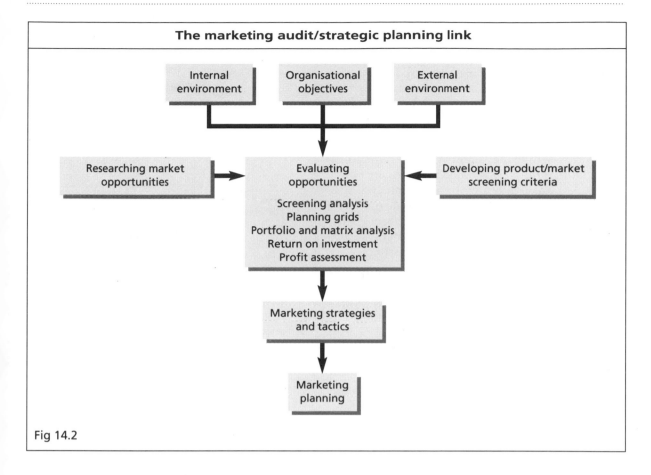

The marketing audit/strategic planning link

Fig 14.2

- the Boston Consulting Group's product portfolio analysis, known as the 'Boston box', again described in Chapter 7, which places companies in categories based on market share and market growth, but ignores market size, threats of entry and the risks associated with different markets.

These methods of evaluating the situations and opportunities open to organisations are a natural extension of the marketing audit, as illustrated in Figure 14.2.

This kind of analysis, based on all the information derived from internal and external audits, helps to provide the background necessary to enable marketing strategies and tactics to be devised, controlled and evaluated.

STRATEGIES AND CONTROLS

There are three broad levels of strategy:

1. *Corporate strategy*, which answers the question 'what business are we in?' by determining the overall use of resources in all operational areas, in order to achieve organisational objectives.
2. *Business strategy*, which answers the question 'how do we compete?' by considering distinct business areas or units within the organisation, such as production, finance, personnel and marketing, and satisfying their resource requirements within the overall framework.
3. *Functional strategy*, which answers the question 'how do we support the business-level strategy?' by determining how each individual function, e.g. marketing, is organised and resourced in detail.

Strategies are derived from a combination of the following factors at the theoretical research stages of marketing management:

- the need to implement a marketing orientated philosophy;
- the gathering of all relevant marketing information from the environment;
- the application of target market analysis;

- the blending of marketing mix components to suit the target market;
- the incorporation of short- and long-term marketing objectives, including budgetary considerations.

They are typically broad in scope and long range in nature, and focus on overall organisational objectives, thus requiring fundamental decision making by senior management, underpinned by financial planning. This could involve concentration on key areas indicated by SWOT analysis and selection of a particular long-term route designed to establish competitive advantage. Michael Porter, for example, has suggested three 'generic strategies' which help companies to be successful:

1. *Cost leadership* – achieving market penetration through low cost structures.
2. *Differentiation* – developing a product or service which is unique or superior in some way.
3. *Focus* – concentrating efforts and resources on particular market segments and gearing marketing mixes to them.

However, Porter also warns that organisations can become 'stuck in the middle' of these three strategies, leaving customers confused and without a clear reason for buying their products or services.

Marketing strategies serve as a basis for decision making on *marketing tactics* which, in contrast, are typically narrow and short range in nature and focus on the ways to implement the activities specified by marketing strategies. Thus they are generally conducted by middle or supervisory management levels and involve such considerations as departmental policies and procedures, short-term budgets for individual units and selection of specific research methods, media mixes, and so on.

Strategies and tactics should always be under review and flexible enough to permit easy adaptation to all the possible changes in circumstances. The most effective way to achieve this is to build in control and evaluation procedures which monitor decision making and results on a systematic basis throughout the company's marketing operations, as indicated in Figure 14.3.

Control and evaluation systems vary from organisation to organisation. Some are highly formalised and rigorously cover all aspects of the firm's marketing programme, while others are conducted on an informal basis and applied only to certain activities. The most common areas covered

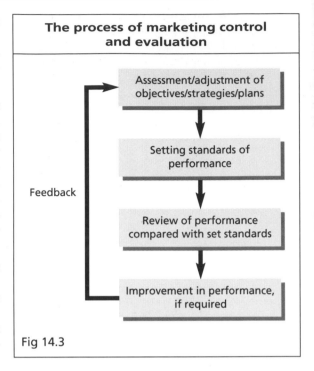

The process of marketing control and evaluation

Assessment/adjustment of objectives/strategies/plans

Setting standards of performance

Review of performance compared with set standards

Improvement in performance, if required

Feedback

Fig 14.3

by such procedures can be grouped into four main categories:

- *tactical*, including effectiveness of marketing information systems, product, distribution, promotion and pricing procedures;
- *strategic*, such as market share/growth/changes /inforrmation, the competition, internal management structures and organisation;
- *quantitative*, including sales analysis and forecasting, research and general statistical information, cost/profit/overhead and other financial areas;
- *qualitative*, such as control and measurement of internal consistency, development plans, reaction to external needs and requirements, and so on.

On a wider scale, control and evaluation mechanisms can also be used to measure and appraise annual marketing cycles and long-term marketing plans, either in terms of general progress or specific results. For whatever purpose they are used, such methods should be accurate, flexible, rapid, easy to administer and cheap, for maximum effectiveness.

MARKETING PLANNING

All the elements of marketing management referred to previously can be incorporated into an organisation's *marketing plan* for a specific product or campaign, along with the crucial, ever-present financial projections and budgetary considerations. These provide a formal, quantitative and authoritative statement of the firm's plans, expressed in monetary terms.

There are several reasons for the importance of *budgets* in marketing plans, not the least being that budgeting forces management to stand back from their regular activities and consider the organisation's goals and detailed ways of achieving them, i.e. it forces them to plan. Budgeting also reveals new data about the firm's future and thus reduces operating risks, it encourages communication and

the co-ordination of activities, provides a guide to action, helps to synthesise a company's various objectives, and acts as a basis for controlling, measuring and evaluating marketing performance.

Marketing budgets can cover marketing expenditure as a whole, focus on individual mix elements such as sales, advertising or research, or concentrate on general profitability or contribution in comparison with other areas of organisational activity.

Various models are used to try to describe accurately how marketing planning works, but the fact is that all organisations interpret the process differently and there is no one blueprint. Most examples incorporate some, if not all, of the SOSTE stages of

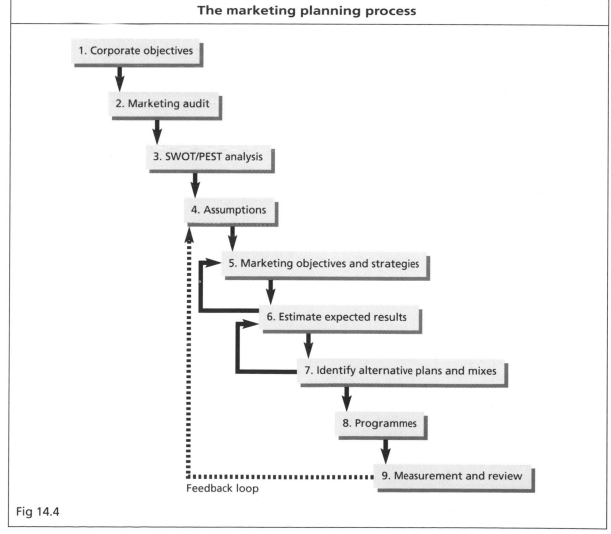

The marketing planning process

1. Corporate objectives
2. Marketing audit
3. SWOT/PEST analysis
4. Assumptions
5. Marketing objectives and strategies
6. Estimate expected results
7. Identify alternative plans and mixes
8. Programmes
9. Measurement and review

Feedback loop

Fig 14.4

Source: McDonald, Malcolm, *Marketing Plans,* Butterworth-Heinemann, 1984

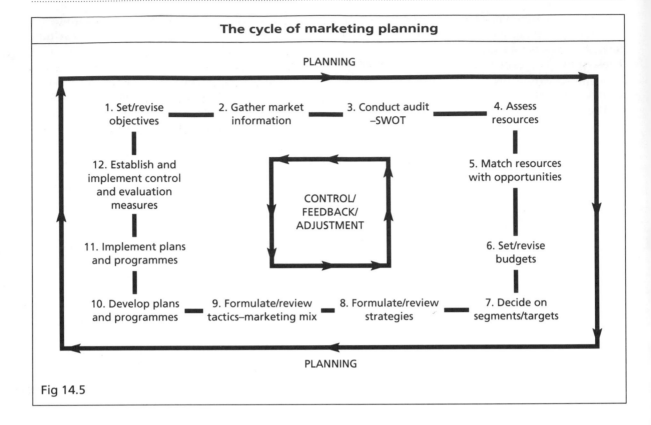

The cycle of marketing planning

PLANNING

1. Set/revise objectives — 2. Gather market information — 3. Conduct audit –SWOT — 4. Assess resources

12. Establish and implement control and evaluation measures

CONTROL/ FEEDBACK/ ADJUSTMENT

5. Match resources with opportunities

11. Implement plans and programmes

6. Set/revise budgets

10. Develop plans and programmes — 9. Formulate/review tactics–marketing mix — 8. Formulate/review strategies — 7. Decide on segments/targets

PLANNING

Fig 14.5

marketing management referred to previously, such as the version favoured by Malcolm McDonald and illustrated in Figure 14.4.

These tend to reflect the need for organisations to produce different plans aimed at specific time-scales, whether relatively short term in nature, annual or over a longer period. Alternatively, other firms view marketing planning as a never-ending cycle of activity, as depicted in Figure 14.5.

Either way, marketing planning produces considerable benefits for an organisation, amongst the most important of which are that it:

● encourages systematic thinking ahead by management;
● leads to better co-ordination of company efforts and activities;
● makes the organisation sharpen its policies and objectives;
● results in more flexibility and better preparation for change;
● makes staff more aware of their responsibilities and roles in communication and interaction;
● leads to better use of a firm's resources;

● results in an improvement in environmental awareness;
● provides a better base for a customer-centred philosophy and culture;
● produces a significant impact on profitability through the creation of competitive advantage.

However, there are also a number of potential problems which can be experienced by any organisation, and McDonald lists the ten most common pitfalls of marketing planning as:

1. Confusion between marketing tactics and strategy.
2. Isolating the marketing function from operations, i.e. lack of integration.
3. Confusion between the marketing function and the marketing concept – marketing viewed purely as sales, advertising, product management or customer service, for example.
4. Organisational barriers such as bureaucracy.
5. Lack of in-depth analysis.
6. Confusion between process and output, e.g.

between audit data and the planning activities themselves.

7. Lack of knowledge and skills.
8. Lack of a systematic approach to marketing planning.
9. Failure to prioritise objectives.
10. Hostile corporate cultures, e.g. amongst senior management.

In addition to these fundamental problems of organisation, attitude, process and understanding, which can occur before or during planning development, companies can also make a number of mistakes in their practical interpretation of marketing plans. The most common mistakes are:

- lack of knowledge about markets, based on the false assumption that the information is not available;
- competing on price rather than developing a unique selling proposition;
- pitching prices too low, leaving inadequate margins for the costs of advertising or sales promotion;
- expanding sales of the least profitable products or services;
- expanding sales with insufficient working capital;
- launching new products or services with inadequate prior research of the market;
- using sales people who may have good technical knowledge but who have not been trained to sell;
- allowing excessive credit to customers and continuing to supply slow payers;
- staying too long in declining and unprofitable markets;
- becoming complacent when all seems to be going well;
- not involving middle and operational management in strategic issues or senior personnel in tactical decisions.

If the organisation can overcome all these obstacles, it will be involved in meaningful and successful marketing planning. The total sum of all the firm's marketing plans viewed together produces its overall *marketing programme*, which completes the picture as the final layer in the hierarchy of marketing management. In its crucial, pivotal role, marketing can then feed its analyses, plans and programmes into all aspects of the policy and operation of a customer orientated company.

ARTICLES

A1

Marketing seizes a wider role

In a more sophisticated competitive world, companies have to develop new attitudes in all departments, and train men and women to acquire strategic vision, MICHEL SYRETT writes

THE DRIVE by British companies to compete effectively in the more sophisticated international markets of today has elevated the role of the marketing function from pure promotional support. It is now of central strategic importance. The demands made on marketing managers have undergone dramatic changes.

"Most organisations have solved the problems of poor industrial relations, manufacturing inefficiency and overmanning which dogged their profitability prior to 1979," says Tony McBurnie, director-general of the Institute of Marketing.

"Now they realise that the only route left for profit improvement and growth is through an increased share of existing markets or the exploration of new ones. They are therefore looking to marketing people to take the lead in achieving this."

Senior marketing personnel, he says, require a far greater knowledge of the competitive world in which their organisation operates. "They need to bring an accurate analysis of market changes to boardroom meetings, and specific strategies enabling the company not only to meet the challenges of competitors but to outflank and overtake them."

Marketing managers therefore base their activities on detailed market research, either done internally or commissioned outside. This enables them to identify unexploited market niches and to conduct analyses known by the acronym SWOT – examining their company's strengths, weaknesses, opportunities and threats.

The process goes much further than knowledge of external developments. To understand a company's strengths and weaknesses, marketing managers need a proper grasp of how it creates its products or services. This requires close liaison with the heads of other departments.

Marketing managers need to brief design departments and research and development departments to keep creative output in line with market needs; they need to provide manufacturing managers with information about pricing policy if prototypes are to achieve cost-effective mass production; and they need to work closely with financial directors to ensure that overheads are built into the price of products.

Above all, the marketing ethos of the company needs to be reflected in the attitude of the workforce, and the way they are recruited, trained and supervised. Recent corporate philosophy is based on the principle that marketing is part of everyone's job and dictates the way in which all employees perform their day-to-day work.

One illustration is the growth of "corporate image" in recruitment campaigns, which are increasingly seen as marketing exercises that require an input from key marketing staff.

Another example is a successful motivational exercise recently conducted by Luncheon Vouchers. Lacking a major British competitor, the company ran a two-week competition during which all staff were invited to compare their performance against employees in a fictitious competing organisation.

The competition was the brainchild of LV's managing director, Olivier de Bosredon, and its sales and marketing director, Sue Harvey. "Although the exercise was purely internal, a major motivation was the improvement of customer service," she says. "Customer inquiries and complaints were slashed to just over a fifth of their normal level during the two weeks of the competition."

The gradual transformation of the marketing role has led to a demand for people who are better communicators and have a far greater strategic vision. This is reflected in the training provided by the Institute of Marketing (at Cookham, Berkshire), which places great emphasis on the skills needed to develop and implement marketing policies.

The institute's courses are increasingly attended by senior as well as junior managers, many lacking a traditional marketing background. The typical marketing director in the 1980s could easily be an engineer who crossed into the sales function; or a young partner of a professional firm that needs to compete more effectively in the more sophisticated market for financial services.

Marketing is being transformed from a profession to a discipline required by managers from all parts of the organisation. Tony McBurnie goes further and calls it "an attitude of mind".

"Many marketing managers in the past made the mistake of concentrating on the tools of the profession – advertising, public relations, promotions," he says, "rather than how these contributed to their company's marketing position. Given the straight choice, I would rather have a board and chief executive that are really market-driven than a small marketing department struggling and getting nowhere."

Source: The Sunday Times, 26 July 1987/Michel Syrett

1 Outline the main changes in the demands made on marketing managers as described in the article. Explain the reasons for these changes.

2 The article was written in the late 1980s, before a recession. Do you think that the role of marketing management has changed at all since then, and if so, in what direction has it moved?

3 How was Luncheon Vouchers successful in implementing marketing management? Would you recommend its methods to all companies?

4 Why would Tony McBurnie 'rather have a board and chief executive that are really market-driven than a small marketing department struggling and getting nowhere'?

A2

Lennox Lewis: the package waiting for delivery

Keith Wheatley on the marketing of a potential world heavyweight champion

BOXING has always produced strange bedfellows. It's a thought that occurs to Mark Thomas as he moves from a grave, grey-suited meeting with the Law Society to a brain-storming session with the Lennox Lewis camp.

Thomas is an executive with RTG Ltd, a Chelsea-based marketing consultancy hired to promote Lewis into the British public's hearts and minds. The agency has never handled a boxer before. It tends to see itself as more blue-chip than blue-corner.

"The first problem boxing has is an image of an ugly street sport, with brutal men in the ring and crooks outside it manipulating them," Thomas said. But he admits his own preconceptions have taken a battering in the past two weeks. "Somebody like Lewis could start to change that. He's an intelligent athlete. He could be boxing's answer to Gary Lineker."

At a press conference last week, Lewis was impressive as he handled the issue of personally donating 200 tickets – paid for from his $600,000 purse – to redundant miners. It could have looked a tacky stunt. Lewis explained the gesture with simple dignity.

Not the least of Thomas's strategies is to develop the appeal of Lewis to women. Pre-fight interviews and photograph sessions have been arranged for women's magazines as well as newspapers. Television and radio advertising for the fight will often be timed to address a largely female audience.

"Compared with Frank Bruno, Lennox Lewis has started from a low awareness base. He's known to the cognoscenti but when you have 17,000 tickets at Earls Court to sell you have to go outside that audience," Thomas said.

But the crucial economic component of Lewis's future success is in the USA. Lewis will fight at 1am London time on Sunday in order that the American cable station Home Box Office can show the fight at prime-time in the eastern United States.

"Among boxing people, this is regarded as a very, very important fight," said John Hornewer, the Chicago attorney who has been Lewis's lawyer and guided many of his career moves since he won the Olympic gold medal in 1988. "They believe it's a better and more significant match than Holyfield versus Bowe on November 13. It will set out the heavyweight pecking order for some time to come.

"As far as America's concerned, Ruddock's got the biggest name and the biggest punch right now. Although Lennox has got the British and European titles, he is still seen as the young contender over there."

Already the salesmen, Thomas included, have got their eyes on the big target beyond this fight. "Patch deals", similar to those found in motor racing and tennis, are being talked about should Lewis become the world champion. It may become a source of regret that boxers fight in shorts rather than voluminous flame-proof overalls.

"From Lennox Lewis's point of view, it's a lot easier earning money through having labels stuck on you than going into the ring and being beaten up," Thomas said. "There's no reason why, given his image and appeal, brands as diverse as Rolex and Nike shouldn't want to be on a world champion boxer's kit."

Most knowledgeable observers say that on the evidence of every past fight Lennox Lewis is what his handlers and promoters claim. The one misgiving is that none of those fights have been against anyone as tough, experienced or skilful as "Razor" Ruddock.

Frank Maloney, promoter of Saturday's fight and a kingpin in the Lewis management team, admits his boxer's early bouts were designed to shield him from defeat but claims his recent fights have been against "reasonable opponents".

"We did what was necessary to bring him to this point. People in the fight game love looking at the past. I'm only interested in the future," said Maloney, who has been told by a Tarot card reader – who knew nothing of his boxing involvement – that he will manage a world champion athlete.

Lewis's handlers have spent over $40,000 on sparring partners in the past month, including former heavyweight champions such as Tony Tubbs and Mike Weaver. "Various people have invested a fortune in Lennox since 1989," said John Hornewer. "But when you're just one step away from the title there's no expense that can be spared."

Source: The Sunday Times, Keith Wheatley, freelance sports journalist

1 In what ways is the marketing concept applicable to personalities and celebrities from all walks of life?

2 Undertake a SWOT analysis for Lennox Lewis and suggest how it might be used.

3 What do you consider would be the main emphases in a marketing mix for the sport of boxing?

4 Acting as the boxer's marketing manager, suggest (a) the key short-term tactics, and (b) a long-term strategy for marketing Lennox Lewis.

A3

Euro Disney in debt but on the mend

EURO Disney, the theme park operator rescued from the brink of collapse by a huge financial survival package, has reported halved operating losses for the three months to June 30.

Trading at the park near Paris in the third quarter of its financial year lost 194 million francs (£23.5m), compared with 381 million francs a year earlier.

However, further one-off charges of 352 million francs linked to the financial restructuring were also incurred.

The improvement at the operating level came despite a fall in revenue at the park and its associated hotels to 1,162 million francs from 1,466 million francs.

"The company believes this drop is due to lower attendance largely resulting from the uncertainty which surrounded the company's future impeding the company's marketing efforts, and to the new aggressive pricing strategy," it said.

Source: *The Northern Echo*, 28 July 1994

1 What might be Euro Disney's (now known as Disneyland Paris) main corporate, business and marketing objectives after being rescued from collapse in 1994?

2 In the light of its past troubles, what do you think would be the main features of a revised marketing audit for the company?

3 How might the uncertainty surrounding Euro Disney's future have impeded its marketing efforts? Propose ways in which the company can remove this uncertainty.

4 Euro Disney blames lower attendances on 'the new aggressive pricing strategy'. Suggest why the company may have chosen such a strategy and what they could do to reverse the negative trend.

A4

Full benchmarks for a 'best in class' business

David Harvey

BRITISH business is notoriously introverted. A study by management consultant KPMG showed that fewer than half the UK's largest organisations combined market and external information in their strategic planning.

It is therefore not surprising that benchmarking – the comparison of a company's performance and processes with its best-performing peers – has yet to take root as standard business practice – even though it is well entrenched as a management buzzword.

According to Rank Xerox consultant Paul Leonard, a CBI study in which 67 per cent of companies claimed to benchmark paints a flattering picture. 'My follow-up showed only 10 per cent were using benchmarking,' he says. Robert Luchs, managing director of PIMS, which has been comparing business performance in the UK since the 1970s, is also sceptical of company benchmarking claims. 'Out of every 100, maybe five are doing it right,' he says.

Benchmarking proper is much more rigorous than unfocused 'industrial tourism', says Leonard. Its purpose is to help companies create market-beating strategies by evaluating performance standards set by 'best-in-class' businesses.

The underlying logic is compelling: unless you know what the competition is doing, and how customers rate your efforts on a comparative basis, how can you establish meaningful goals for improvement? Without those benchmarks, the impact of improvement programmes is a lottery: raising standards to an industry average, for example, is not the same as leap-frogging rivals.

Whether companies are planning to re-engineer their processes or launch quality or other performance improvement programmes, benchmarking helps to set targets which give these initiatives their competitive thrust.

Take the example of Cigna UK, the British arm of the American insurance giant. Cigna knew that it faced an uphill struggle when it started selling employee insurance schemes in a UK market dominated by large, established players such as Bupa and Private Patients Plan.

Its strategy was to carry out a comparative assessment of a variety of key aspects of its operations. Its market survey showed where, and how far, the company needed to improve its performance to achieve superior service.

The findings set the framework for Cigna's plans to re-engineer its customer-service processes. Fourteen months on, the company saw a 40 per cent rise in revenue. Benchmarking has been instrumental for bottom-line gains in other companies. 'There is an irrefutable link where benchmarking is part of total quality programmes,' says Leonard.

For Xerox, the company largely responsible for defining benchmarking in the 1980s, the practice has become a way of life, applied as a discipline with its own well-established rules. Initially, the practice was the company's reaction to the Japanese onslaught on its markets. Xerox set out to find out exactly where it was losing out in the price-performance battle and how it could close the gap. The findings underpin its drive for quality and, more recently, the reorganisation and re-engineering of its global business.

Since Xerox won the Baldrige Award in the US in 1989 and Rank Xerox the European Quality Award three years later, a steady stream of companies have clamoured for a glimpse of the prize-winning processes in exchange for revealing their own. The majority do not pass the first test.

'We always ask their objective for benchmarking and 80 per cent never reply,' says Leonard. 'To carry out benchmarking, a company must have a clear vision and a five-year plan,' he advises. 'It must understand the connection between the factors which are critical for its success and its processes. Then benchmarking is relatively easy.'

Luchs agrees that posing benchmarking question in a strategic vacuum is a pointless exercise. 'Many people just want to compare practices,' notes Luchs, 'but there's no strategic linkage. Benchmarking is most valuable for those who have thought about their strategy.

'Otherwise it's rather like someone who hasn't learnt their alphabet trying to write a novel.'

Source: The Observer, 13 February 1994

1 Describe the process of 'benchmarking'. In which functions of marketing might its application prove to be most useful?

2 Do you believe control procedures such as those illustrated in the article can accurately measure the success of marketing management? What are their drawbacks?

3 Describe how Rank Xerox and Cigna UK have used benchmarking. What other methods of evaluating performance could they use?

4 Explain why benchmarking without a strategy is 'rather like someone who hasn't learnt their alphabet trying to write a novel'.

Grand Met's drive in the burger war

BURGER KING is planning a new offensive to knock McDonald's off the top slot as the UK's biggest hamburger chain.

The fast food group owned by Grand Metropolitan is to launch three new types of outlet this year.

The sites, which will include kiosks and drive-through restaurants, will each cost £500,000 less to develop than their current restaurants and will open up new markets for the chain. The first kiosks will open in July in sports stadiums, airports and railway stations.

Sites earmarked for future developments include hospitals, universities and cinemas.

Burger King's vice-president of marketing, Joyce Myers, said: 'The new formats will provide added impetus to our aggressive expansion plans in the UK.'

Susan Gilchrist

Source: The Mail on Sunday

1 Draw up a marketing plan for Burger King in its long-term offensive against McDonald's.

2 Describe the company's distribution strategy. How effective do you feel it will be and why?

3 How useful is portfolio and matrix analysis in aiding Burger King's growth? Discuss its likely position in the Ansoff matrix and Boston box, and which of Porter's generic strategies it could be using.

4 What are the marketing pitfalls of which the company should be aware in mounting its 'aggressive expansion plans'?

ISSUES

IMPLEMENTING THE MARKETING PHILOSOPHY

In many organisations there is confusion about the actual role of marketing management.

1 Discuss the difference between the marketing 'function' and the marketing 'concept'.

2 How might corporate culture be changed to improve the implementation of marketing management?

3 Do you agree that marketing decisions should always be implemented before, for example, production, financial or personnel decisions?

THE MARKETING AUDIT

Situation analysis can only provide a general overview and is not a significant factor in marketing management.

1 How true do you think this statement is? How much time and effort do you think a firm should expend on establishing its current position, and why?

2 Devise a SWOT analysis for a company of your choice. Which are more significant, the internal or external environmental factors, and for what reasons?

3 Select an organisation and discuss its objectives at different levels. Do you believe them to be realistic?

STRATEGIES AND CONTROLS

Marketing strategies are only effective if they are closely controlled.

1 Explain the difference between strategies and tactics. Why are the two often confused? Is either more important than the other?

2 Discuss the relative merits and de-merits of matrix and portfolio analysis as a tool of strategic marketing, giving examples.

3 How much progress can an organisation make without control and evaluation measures? How rigidly should they be enforced, and why?

MARKETING PLANNING

Despite the general acceptance of marketing, few organisations indulge in thorough, long-term marketing planning.

1 What benefits do marketing managers gain from planning? Is planning necessary for long-term survival – why or why not?

2 How strictly do you think companies should stick to their marketing plans to be effective?

3 Outline the marketing plan or plans adopted by the institution in which you are studying or any other organisation with which you are familiar.

MANAGING THE MARKETING OF IDEAS, EVENTS, CAUSES, PLACES AND PEOPLE

Marketing is the same, no matter what it is applied to.

1 In what ways do you agree with the above statement? How does the marketing of ideas, events, causes, places and people differ from that of goods and services?

2 Design a marketing plan for (*a*) a bid by the City of Leeds to stage the Olympics, or (*b*) an attempt by the city of Hull to become a major tourism centre.

3 Suggest a marketing mix for Madonna (or another performer of your choice) and consider how it could be controlled and evaluated.

CONSUMER V. INDUSTRIAL MARKETING MANAGEMENT

Consumer marketing is very different in nature to industrial marketing.

1 How do industrial marketing mixes differ from those of consumer products and what are the main similarities? Give examples.

2 Why might entry into a particular market segment entail greater commitment by an industrial firm than by a consumer products company?

3 Are industrial marketing plans likely to be more or less detailed than consumer ones, and why?

QUESTIONS

1 What are the 'Three Ms'?

2 What are the SOSTE stages of marketing management?

3 Name four problems experienced by firms when implementing the marketing philosphy.

4 What is situation analysis?

5 List three levels of objectives in hierarchical destination analysis.

6 What is the marketing audit?

7 What is SWOT analysis?

8 Give four examples of each stage of SWOT analysis.

9 What is the difference between an internal and an external audit?

10 What is a 'capability profile'?

11 Why do organisations use matrix and portfolio analyses?

12 Give three examples of matrix or portfolio analysis.

13 Provide a definition of marketing strategy.

14 Name three of the factors giving rise to marketing strategies.

15 What are Porter's 'generic strategies'?

16 Describe the three broad levels of strategy.

17 Give a definition of marketing tactics.

18 List three examples of tactics.

19 Provide a definition of marketing control and

evaluation systems.

20 Name three examples of types of control and evaluation mechanisms.

21 Give a definition of a marketing plan.

22 Give three reasons for the importance of financial budgets in marketing planning.

23 What is the Malcolm McDonald marketing plan?

24 What is the cycle of marketing planning?

25 List five benefits of marketing planning.

26 Name five common pitfalls of marketing planning.

27 List five common mistakes in the practical interpretation of marketing plans.

28 What is a marketing programme?

PROJECTS

1 'Marketing is the art of gentle seduction.' Do you agree? Describe how this philosophy might be implemented within an organisation's marketing management procedures and the problems it could cause.

2 If marketing is the business of trying to satisfy unpredictable human beings, can it really be 'managed' reliably?

3 On what criteria should the determination of objectives be based and how far in advance of strategy implementation should they be set? Refer to examples in your answer.

4 How important is it for a marketing audit to be undertaken on a regular basis and why might the time interval vary between different types of organisation?

5 'Tactical and strategic marketing are complementary rather than contradictory policies.' Discuss what is meant by this statement and give examples of where each might be used alone and where they might be used together.

6 Which do you think are the most effective control and evaluation methods for (a) consumer and (b) industrial organisations, and why?

7 The pitfalls of marketing planning have been well documented. Which do you think are the most dangerous and why? Discuss examples of companies which have felt their effects.

8 Compare Malcolm McDonald's marketing plan with the marketing planning cycle models. What differences are there and how significant are these differences for marketing management?

9 Devise a marketing plan for an idea, place or person of your choice and describe the reasons behind it.

10 How useful to practical organisations is a marketing management policy based on theoretical models?

11 Select and research an organisation and describe and criticise its strategies, tactics and overall marketing programme. Do these adequately reflect its background philosophy and objectives, in your opinion?

12 It is often said that 'a business has to speculate to accumulate'. How can marketing contribute to this process?

GLOSSARY

Audit see 'Marketing audit.'

Business strategy the level of strategy which involves decision making on resources to be committed to the individual areas of business in an organisation.

Capability profile part of the marketing audit which examines organisational resource strengths.

Control all the methods used by organisations to monitor the effectiveness of and retain a firm hold over all the aspects and stages of their marketing plans.

Corporate culture a combination of philosophies adhered to by an organisation within the framework of which its business activities are performed.

Corporate strategy the level of strategy which involves decision making on resources to be committed to all operational areas of the organisation in total.

Cost leadership one of the three generic strategies suggested in Porter's model.

Destination analysis survey of corporate, business, marketing and specific objectives which indicates the direction in which an organisation wishes to go.

Evaluation all the methods used by organisations to measure performance standards in all aspects and stages of their marketing plans, part of the process of marketing management.

External audit examination of the opportunities and threats (the O and T of SWOT analysis) facing an organisation, the PEST environmental component of the overall situation analysis.

Feasibility study a process of assessing the likelihood of success of a product or service, generally expressed in financial or economic terms.

Feedback measured response or reaction to all or part of a marketing plan, enabling adjustments to be made where appropriate.

Focus one of the three generic strategies suggested in Porter's model.

Functional strategy the level of strategy which involves decision making on resources to be committed within individual business areas, such as marketing.

General Electric business screen a matrix analysis used by organisations for strategic planning purposes.

Goals corporate or departmental objectives or aims which an organisation wishes to achieve as part of its marketing plans.

Hofer and Schendel's model a product/market evolution matrix used by organisations for strategic planning purposes.

Internal audit examination of an organisation's strengths and weaknesses (the S and W of SWOT analysis), part of the overall situation analysis.

Marketing audit close examination of an organisation's internal and external environments, often by means of a SWOT situational analysis, in order to provide background information for marketing decision making.

Marketing concept philosophy of customer orientation implemented within an organisation by marketing management.

Marketing functions every aspect of the marketing process planned and implemented within an organisation by marketing management team.

Marketing management the co-ordination and processing of all marketing functions within an organisation.

Marketing plan all the stages of marketing decision making incorporated into a chronological cycle of activities and applied to a specific product, service or organisation.

Marketing planning the process of formulating marketing plans undertaken by an organisation's marketing management team.

Marketing programme an organisation's total marketing activity, the sum of all its marketing plans.

Market share a company's percentage of sales of a particular product or service, expressed in relation to the total sales in the market.

Marketing strategies all the methods used by an organisation, as part of the marketing management process, to achieve its long-term objectives.

Marketing tactics all the methods used by an organisation, as part of the marketing management process, to achieve its short-term objectives.

Marketing tools all the activities, processes and techniques which an organisation uses to implement its marketing plans.

Matrix analysis method used by marketing management to assess an organisation's current position and indicate possible areas of strategic action in the future.

Minutes time, one of the 'Three Ms' constraining marketing management.

Money finance, one of the 'Three Ms' constraining marketing management.

Movement human resources, one of the 'Three Ms' constraining marketing management.

Objectives corporate or departmental goals or aims which an organisation wishes to achieve, part of the process of marketing management.

Opportunities organisational chances, an external component of SWOT analysis.

Planning implementation putting into effect marketing plans previously devised by the organisation.

Porter's 'generic strategies' a model for strategic planning which suggests that there are three basic strategies for business success (cost leadership, differentiation and focus) and one for failure (the 'stuck in the middle' situation).

Portfolio framework method used by marketing management to assess an organisation's current position and indicate possible areas of strategic action in the future.

Screening analysis method used by marketing management to assess an organisation's current position and indicate possible areas of strategic action in the future.

Situation analysis examination of the organisation's current position, including internal and external marketing audits, as the initial stage in the process of marketing management.

SOSTE a mnemonic used to represent situation, objectives, strategies, tactics and evaluation, the five main stages of marketing management.

Strategic business unit (SBU) the different businesses into which a firm's activities can be broken down, either on a regional, national or international basis.

Strategic planning outline of an organisation's long-term solutions designed to achieve its

more extended objectives.

Strengths organisational capabilities, an internal component of SWOT analysis.

Stuck in the middle business failure situation, described in Porter's 'generic strategies' model, in which organisations fall in between three successful strategies without fitting into any of them.

SWOT analysis acronym used to represent the four internal and external environmental areas (strengths, weaknesses, opportunities and threats) examined by organisations, in order to find background information to support future marketing plans.

Tactical planning details of an organisation's short-term solutions designed to achieve its immediate objectives.

Threats organisational dangers, an external component of SWOT analysis.

Three Ms minutes, money and movement, three of the main constraints placed on marketing management which limit the implementation of marketing plans.

Weaknesses organisational limitations, an internal component of SWOT analysis.

SUGGESTED REFERENCES

VIDEO MATERIAL

Marketing in Action, 'Corporate Fitness', BBC, Open University, 1985.

The Marketing Mix, No. 10, 'Marketing in Action', Yorkshire Television, 1986.

Marketing for Managers – the bottom line, Henley Distance Learning, 1987.

Managing in the Competitive Environment, 'Survival in the competitive environment' (Premier Drums), BBC, Open University, 1988.

Contemporary Marketing, Video Cases, No. 3 (Pizza Hop; and No. 6, (SkyFox Corp.), Boone, L. and Kurtz, D., Dryden Press, 1989.

The Big Company, Coca-Cola and Federal Express, Channel 4, 1989.

Business Studies, 'Menu for a multinational' (McDonald's), Thames TV, 1989.

Business Studies, 'Business Structure and Organisation' (Sock Shop); 'Business Behaviour' (British Airways); and 'Discs and games and planes' (the Virgin Group), Thames TV, 1990.

Business Matters, 'Front-line Managers', BBC, 1990.

Strategy in Action, No. 1, 'Strategic Intent' (Cable and Wireless); No. 2, 'Competitive advantage' (Ratners Jewellers); and No. 3, 'Strategic Implementation' (Bank of Ireland), Open College, Channel 4, 1990.

The Manager, 'Effective Marketing', Open College, Channel 4, 1990.

Walk the Talk, No. 4, 'B. Elliott expects'; and No. 5, 'Managing Change', BBC, 1991.

Business Matters, 'The one dollar bargain', BBC, 1991.

The Trainer Wars, (Nike, Dunlop, Reebok, etc), Channel 4, 1991.

Ideas in Hand, and *Our World Tomorrow* (3M Company); *Challenge of the 90s* (Royal Crown Cola); *The Momentum is Building* (Pier One Imports); and *Energy Return System* (Reebok International Ltd.), Marketing Videotape, Dibb, S., Simkin, L., Pride, W. and Ferrell, O., Houghton Mifflin, 1991.

Marketing in the Real World, (Rose Toys), TV Choice, 1992.

Troubleshooter, series (Sir John Harvey-Jones), BBC, 1992.

Business Matters, 'The dream in jeans' (Levi Strauss), BBC, 1992.

Business Matters, 'Making the most of things', BBC, 1993.

MAGAZINE ARTICLES

Journal of Marketing Management, Vol. 1, No. 1, Summer 1985, p.21, 'Marketing planning and Britain's disoriented Directors'; p.35, 'The anatomy of strategic marketing planning'; and p.65, 'Marketing lessons from UK's high-flying companies'.

Journal of Marketing Management, Vol. 1, No. 2, Winter 1985, p.157, 'Strategic marketing concepts and models'.

Journal of Marketing Management, Vol. 1, No. 3, Spring 1986, p.227, 'Formulating objectives – what can really happen'; and p.259, 'Planning: an effective management tool or a corporate pastime?'.

Journal of Marketing Management, Vol. 2, No. 1, Summer 1986, p.39, 'The contribution of marketing to competitive success: a literature review'.

Journal of Marketing Management, Vol. 3, No. 2, Winter 1987, p.121, 'Marketing and the British Chief Executive'; and p.205, 'Successful implementation of new market strategies – a corporate culture perspective'.

Journal of Marketing Management, Vol. 4, No. 1, Summer 1988, p.1, 'Marketing: in search of a competitive role model'.

Journal of Marketing Management, Vol. 8, No. 2, April 1992, p.177, 'Corporate culture: is it really a barrier to marketing planning?'.

Journal of Marketing Management, Vol. 8, No. 3, July 1992, p.199, 'Talking straight about competitive stragegy'; p.219, 'Historical perspective in marketing management, explicating experience'; and p.239, 'An empirical study of firms' co-ordination of functional and market entry timing strategies'.

Journal of Marketing Management, Vol. 9, No. 2, April 1993, p.155, 'Marketing planning decision-making in UK and US companies: an empirical comparative study'.

Marketing Business, July 1988, p.6, 'The marketing of ICI'; p.10, 'How Rolls-Royce regained its shine'; and p.12, 'Removing the blinkers – the importance of strategic marketing'.

Marketing Business, Oct. 1988, p.12, 'Seizing advantage – strategic marketing in practice'.

Marketing Business, June 1989, p.6, 'How marketing sharpened Allied Dunbar's edge'; and p.12, 'F1 Group – the future of work'.

Marketing Business, Dec. 1989, p.6, 'Sir Simon Hornby: setting the tone for W.H. Smith'; and p.14, 'Macallan finds its niche'.

Marketing Business, Feb. 1990, p.20, 'Making strategies happen in the real world'.

Marketing Business, June 1990, p.12, 'Porsche – the myth and the marketing'.

Marketing Business, Dec. 1990, p.20, 'Putting strategy to work'; and p.22, 'Tools of the trade'.

Marketing Business, April 1993, p.11, 'Marketing industry'; and p.24, 'The price of peace'.

Marketing Business, Feb. 1994, p.13, 'The transformation of marketing – new generation marketing'.

Marketing Business, March 1994, p.21, 'From tiny acorns'.

Marketing Business, June 1994, p.18, 'Getting the processes right'.

Quarterly Review of Marketing, Vol. 11, No. 2, Winter 1986, p.1, 'The domain of marketing – marketing and non-marketing exchanges'.

Quarterly Review of Marketing, Vol. 12, No. 1, Autumn 1986, p.10, 'POSIT-ive marketing: towards an integration of core concepts'.

Quarterly Review of Marketing, Vol. 13, No. 1, Autumn 1987, p.1, 'A re-appraisal of the role of marketing planning'.

Quarterly Review of Marketing, Vol. 15, No. 4, Summer 1990, p.1, 'Technique inter-relationships and the pursuit of relevance in marketing theory'; and p.16, 'Marketing planning in style'.

FURTHER READING

Adcock, D., Bradfield, R., Halborg, A. and Ross, C., *Marketing Principles and Practice* (2nd edn), Pitman, 1995, ch. 19.

Baker, M. (Ed.), *The Marketing Book*, Heinemann/C.I.M., 1990, chs 3, 18 and 19.

Boone, L. and Kurtz, D., *Contemporary Marketing*, Dryden, 1989, ch. 3.

Booth, Don, *Principles of Strategic Marketing*, Tudor Publishing, 1990, ch. 11.

Cannon, Tom, *Basic Marketing*, Holt Business Texts, 1980, chs 8 and 18.

Davidson, Hugh, *Offensive Marketing*, Penguin, 1987.

Dibb, S., Simkin, L., Pride, W. and Ferrell, O., *Marketing*, Houghton Mifflin, 1994, chs 19–21 and 23.

Foster, D., *Mastering Marketing*, Macmillan, 1982, ch. 6.

Giles, G., *Marketing*, MacDonald and Evans, 1985, ch. 11.

Kotler, P. and Armstrong, G., *Marketing*, Prentice Hall, 1993, ch. 2.

McCarthy, J. and Perreault, W., *Basic Marketing*, Irwin, 1987, chs 20 and 21.

McDonald, Malcolm, *Marketing Plans: how to prepare them and how to use them*, Heinemann, 1984.

Mercer, D., *Marketing*, Blackwell, 1992, ch. 15.

Mroz, Ralph, *The Formula for Successful Marketing*, Avant Books, 1990.

Oliver, G., *Marketing Today*, Prentice Hall, 1990, chs 9–11 and 24.

Porter, Michael E., *Competitive Strategy: techniques for analysing industries and competitors*, Macmillan, 1980.

Acknowledgements

The Mail on Sunday.
The Northern Echo.
The Observer.
The Sunday Times.
Michel Syrett and Keith Wheatley, freelance journalists for *The Sunday Times* newspaper.

15

INTERNATIONAL MARKETING

DEFINITIONS

The marketing of goods and services across national boundaries; the development of overseas subsidiaries or associates which market products developed and controlled by the parent company.

ALAN WEST, MARKETING OVERSEAS, MACDONALD AND EVANS, 1987

The globalisation of markets is at hand. With that, the multinational commercial world nears its end, and so does the multinational corporation. The global corporation operates as if the entire world (or major regions of it) were a single entity; it sells the same things in the same way everywhere.

PROFESSOR THEODORE LEVITT, HARVARD UNIVERSITY

INTRODUCTION

The 1980s and 1990s have seen the pace of geographical and political change quicken world-wide. The collapse of communism has resulted in international boundaries being re-drawn in eastern Europe and the old USSR, with new countries emerging to take their place on the global stage, while South Africa and a united Germany have re-entered the world scene and the countries of eastern Asia and the Pacific Rim grow ever more quickly both in population and influence. In addition, the world has shrunk in size as technological advances have given rise to huge improvements in communications and transportation.

All these effects have run parallel with an increasingly volatile economic world as many nations undergo rapid changes in their relative stages of market development. The so-called 'third world' and subsistence economies have made great strides, backed by the main global powers, while the growth of the raw material exporting countries has continued and the industrialising economies, such as India and China, are expanding massively to challenge the traditional economic strongholds of western Europe, the USA and Japan. This combination of geographical, political and economic factors, alongside social changes such as the convergence of ideas and tastes, has resulted in a considerable upsurge in global business activity as the world's nations and companies jockey for favourable positions in the international trade scene of the twenty-first century. On a national level, tariff distribution and institutional barriers have been eliminated and powerful trading blocks created, such as the European Union, while internal mechanisms have been set up to take advantage of these developments and produce initiatives for encouraging exporting.

At the company level, organisations of all sizes have started to exploit new international opportunities as domestic markets become too limited or saturated and global markets open up, and as governments provide incentives for such expansion. The application of marketing has thus become increasingly international in nature and

Main elements of international marketing

The international environment

Market entry methods

INTERNATIONAL MARKETING

Globalisation

International marketing strategies

Fig 15.1

any country or company involved in or contemplating such a move must cover the essential elements outlined in Figure 15.1.

International marketing has become highly sophisticated, and success in the global marketplace at any level demands a thorough understanding of the theoretical principles and a strong commitment to the practical issues involved, whether an organisation is importing or exporting.

KEY CONCEPTS

THE INTERNATIONAL ENVIRONMENT

In addition to the broad background already covered, many specific factors can push a company towards internationalisation, including:

- the requirement for increased sales volume and/or profits;
- the benefits arising from economies of scale in all aspects of the operation;
- recovery of research and development and other costs;
- acquisition of resources unavailable domestically;
- the need to utilise human and financial resources better;
- following up leads from current markets and other contacts;
- policy of diversification into new products and/or markets;
- the importance of meeting and beating the competition;
- incentives and encouragement offered by governments and membership of regional agreements and institutions.

When the decision to explore the feasibility of international trade has been made, an organisation must consider how best to implement and manage the marketing concept outside national boundaries.

The marketing philosophy and its attendant principles described throughout this book remain the same in essence whether applied locally, regionally, nationally or internationally, to products or services in consumer, industrial or non-profit markets. However, each situation involves different emphases on different aspects or components, and the management of international marketing activities can for this reason be far removed from the situation pertaining in domestic markets.

An understanding of the trading environment is therefore vital before a company can decide whether and how to proceed and which international markets to enter. Such an environmental survey would include not only standard SWOT and PEST analyses referred to previously, but also some of the many factors relating to the country, region and market to be targeted. Amongst the most important of these are:

- *Economic* — costs, taxation levels and import controls;
  - relative prosperity and growth;
  - foreign currency exchange and financial policies;
  - membership of economic organisations and trading groups, such as the EU, EFTA, GATT, OECD, OPEC and the WTO.

- *Political* – relationships between the countries involved;
  – ideological attitudes and level of stability;
  – degree of state or private ownership operating;
  – legal systems, regulations and controls;
  – membership of political unions.

- *Geographic* – location of country or region;
  – size and population of country or region;
  – demographic spread and ethnic groupings;
  – climate and physical topography.

- *Social* – educational structure and literacy levels;
  – cultural background, including religions and philosophies;
  – income, wealth and living standards;
  – language and linguistic considerations;
  – social class structures and family patterns;
  – environmental attitudes.

- *Technological* – transportation network;
  – communication systems and administrative procedures;
  – incorporation and growth of information technology;
  – scientific and commercial advances.

In conjunction with this research, specific marketing information must also be sought, including the current situation and likely future developments in such areas as:

- the nature of the product or service, whether visible goods or invisible services (such as banking, shipping, insurance or tourism), and their acceptance in each trading country;
- the structure and accessibility of the chosen markets and distribution channels;
- the availability of marketing services, e.g. advertising and research services, and the nature and availability of the media;
- consumption trends in the markets and products concerned;
- analysis of industry market potential and company sales potential;
- levels of sophistication and understanding exhibited towards the marketing concept in general;
- perceptions of and attitudes prevailing towards specific elements of the marketing mix, such as pricing and promotion;
- the nature and extent of the competition.

Surveys have revealed that the four aspects of the overseas environment of most concern to businesses are political stability, the foreign investment climate, profit remittances and exchange controls, and taxation. However, there are clearly many potential areas where different international viewpoints and practices could result in mistakes being made if accurate, comprehensive research has not been undertaken beforehand.

The following are some of the main problems commonly experienced by exporting companies and countries:

- The product or service might be too expensive, basic or sophisticated, or wrong in specification, colour, flavour, appearance, and so on.
- Customs, traditions, religions, beliefs or other ethnic and cultural factors might not be understood or allowed for and could cause offence.
- Product or market potential might be inadequately assessed and insufficiently researched.
- Political and economic guidelines could be misunderstood or ignored.
- Legal requirements and/or promotional regulations might be incorrectly assessed and not properly complied with.
- Words, symbols or other aspects of language and oral, written or visual communication could be wrongly translated or interpreted, e.g. in advertising.
- Inability to comply with administrative procedures.
- Distribution channels and transportation networks used inappropriately.
- Failure to develop a local as opposed to 'foreign' image or lack of identification with national aims and economic aspirations.
- Operations attempted too far in advance of the stage of development reached by the 'host' nation.
- Failure to develop local nationals to take decision-making positions within the exporting organisation.
- Mistakes made in estimating long-term investment requirements and risks, budgets, information flows and controls, and so on.
- Organisation too limited in size, resources or ambitions.

To avoid these potential pitfalls, there are many sources of international marketing information available to exporting organisations, both within and outside the country of origin, and much of this is provided free. In addition to those listed in Chapter 3, these information sources include:

- internal information already possessed;
- home government – overseas Trade Boards, the British Council and its equivalent in other countries, embassies abroad, Customs and Excise and other information offices, and export reports;
- international – embassies in the home country, the United Nations, overseas branches of banks, trade organisations;
- regional trade associations and organisations – Business Venture centres, Training and Enterprise Councils, libraries, Chambers of Commerce;
- professional bodies – e.g. Chartered Institute of Marketing, specialist marketing organisations, and so on;
- international publishers, journals, and newspapers such as *The European*, etc;
- the competition – catalogues, prospectuses, observational research;

- national and international trading institutions, such as OECD.

If such sources do not prove adequate an organisation will have to resort to primary field survey methods, also outlined in detail in Chapter 3. However, these can be very expensive and subject to problems of bias and mis-interpretation when conducted in another country.

Armed with the appropriate research information, a marketing philosophy and the corporate will to expand overseas, an organisation must then choose the scale of its international commitment. The four basic stages of overseas trading involvement are illustrated in Figure 15.2.

An organisation can move successfully through these four stages if it possesses a sufficient understanding of the international marketing environment coupled with the appropriate method of entering the market and effective strategies and tactics.

MARKET ENTRY METHODS

There are many options which firms can choose between when attempting to break into overseas markets. The method selected will depend upon

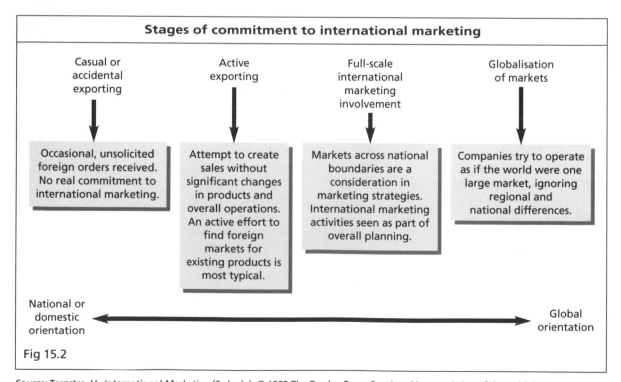

Stages of commitment to international marketing

Casual or accidental exporting

Active exporting

Full-scale international marketing involvement

Globalisation of markets

Occasional, unsolicited foreign orders received. No real commitment to international marketing.

Attempt to create sales without significant changes in products and overall operations. An active effort to find foreign markets for existing products is most typical.

Markets across national boundaries are a consideration in marketing strategies. International marketing activities seen as part of overall planning.

Companies try to operate as if the world were one large market, ignoring regional and national differences.

National or domestic orientation ⟷ Global orientation

Fig 15.2

Source: Terpstra, V., *International Marketing* (3rd edn), © 1983 The Dryden Press. Reprinted by permission of the publisher

the organisation's objectives and range of activities, together with all the environmental factors listed above. However, in practice a company is generally also limited, by the resources it can commit, to a series of gradual steps into the international trade arena, phased over a period of time. These stages, and the organisational implications they contain, are described in Table 15.1.

Mirroring these key stages, an organisation has the following market entry methods available to it, either individually or in combination, when ascending the ladder of international trade involvement:

1 Indirect Exporting

The informal use of intermediaries to handle the purchase and distribution of goods from domestic based firms to overseas markets. Various methods including:

- *buying offices* – represent retail stores in consumer markets;
- *buying houses* – deal in a wide range of goods;
- *buying representatives* – individuals trading for foreign firms;
- *confirming houses* – buy on principals' instructions, arrange transport and finance, and receive commission;
- *export houses* – agencies acting as a company export department, undertaking all activities. Often specialists in specific or inaccessible markets;

- *export merchants or wholesalers* – act independently, buying in one country and selling overseas, sometimes using export houses, for a profit;
- *co-operative groups* – enable small firms to combine to develop export opportunities by carrying other lines overseas;
- *international trading companies* – set up to purchase in the home market and distribute abroad.

2 Agent Exporting

The use of intermediaries or distribution channels in specific overseas markets where a formal contractual relationship exists between the two parties, such as:

- *overseas sales agents* – individuals or organisations bringing companies into contact with markets but not owning the goods, and providing local knowledge and specialisms. Include commission houses (obtain orders and pass back to company, working on a fixed percentage basis), stocking agents (acting as wholesalers with warehouses), and spares and servicing agents (particularly useful in industrial markets);
- *distribution agents* – maintain product stocks in the market with sole right to purchase and sell on for a profit. Provide a full-service local sales effort.

Table 15.1 Stages of international market development

Stage	Nature of company	Form of involvement	Organisational implications
1	Essentially domestic	Limited exports	Small export department
2	Semi-international	Exports & foreign sales/service offices	Export division
3	International company	As above & manufacturing facilities	International division
4	Multi-national enterprise	Ownership of local company & related business functions	International divisions abroad
5	Global corporation	Worldwide business ownership and manufacturing	Various headquarters worldwide

3 Direct Exporting

The use of a company's own personnel and methods within the overseas market, including:

- organisational field representatives, sales force and supervisors (sometimes acting as employees), either working alongside agents or on their own. Especially useful for technical products and services;
- *direct selling* – occurring where end-users are limited in number and easily segmented and located, and where products or services are technical and costly;
- *direct mail order houses* – overseas or domestic operations distributing catalogues and goods direct to the consumer from mailing lists, e.g. in fashion-wear;
- *representation* at exhibitions and trade fairs, and on trade missions.

4 Licensing and Franchising

The establishment of rights and agreements to enable international market entry/production through:

- *licensing* – involving one organisation paying another for legal contracts and limited rights to hold patents or use trade-marks/brand names/specific expertise for overseas operations;
- *franchising* – one organisation granting another the right to operate a particular business for a price in a specific overseas country or outlet, with the franchiser usually retaining links with the franchisee and providing them with expertise.

5 Joint Ventures

Two or more organisations joining together to invest in an overseas project, create a new company or otherwise combine to exploit a market where the need is for speed, human resources, expertise or the overcoming of legal/technical/financial entry barriers. This can include:

- *mixed ventures*, involving different firms or products from different countries;
- *group selling agreements* and 'piggy-back' schemes;
- *manufacturing consortia* and partnerships;
- *strategic alliances*, with specific marketing objectives;

- *industrial co-operation ventures*, where long-term technological expertise or production are shared;
- *management contracting*, involving one organisation being contracted to run some or all of the activities of another, in order to utilise and be paid for its expertise.

6 Overseas Operations

Establishing a local trading company, branch office or sales outlet, as an overseas subsidiary of the domestic organisation, in order to buy, sell, manage or support existing operations. Can be achieved by:

- creating a new set-up from scratch; or
- acquiring a local organisation for the purpose.

7 Foreign Production

Establishing a local manufacturing facility, as an overseas subsidiary of the domestic organisation, in order to produce goods and services in or near the target market, either by independent development or by local acquisition. Variations of this method are:

- *contract manufacturing*, where the facilities of overseas organisations are used for short production runs to reduce costs and adapt to local conditions;
- *local assembly*, which utilises overseas plant facilities to assemble finished goods from exported components, again for reasons of cost.

8 Direct Ownership

The acquisition of an overseas firm and its expertise, facilities and brands, through a merger, take-over or purchase, for full local production and marketing purposes. Creates a *wholly-owned subsidiary* of the parent company which can operate independently, but requires a high level of overseas commitment and investment. As the organisation expands, it will acquire companies and bases in other countries and develop into a full multi-national corporation and ultimately a global operation.

All these progressive market entry methods incorporate their own advantages and disadvantages (as they are closely linked with distribution, some have already been covered in Chapter 9) and organisations will seek the regular advice of international marketing consultants as to their next step. However, the main factors influencing their choice, in addition to the natural historical growth stage they have reached, concern the issues of cost, risk and control. The value assessment of each method in relation to these key variables is illustrated in Figure 15.3.

Clearly, the more an organisation becomes involved in international marketing the greater the risks and costs it incurs, but the greater the degree of control and influence it exerts. Whether the overall equation is successfully calculated will depend on the strategies which accompany each stage of overseas market entry.

INTERNATIONAL MARKETING STRATEGIES

When considering the relative merits and demerits of entering overseas markets and the methods available, organisations must establish a framework on which to base future policy. The three main approaches to initial strategic decision making are:

- *do nothing* – the 'wait-and-see' approach, the intention being to maintain the present position until further evidence is available;
- *defensive* – improving awareness and conducting preliminary research into environmental and marketing factors, with a view to future involvement overseas;
- *active* – conduct serious research and planning in order to set up international operations immediately.

Having established the degree of intended involvement and the necessary organisational arrangements, the firm can embark upon its marketing programme for the international arena by developing marketing plans for each overseas market it intends to pursue. As the main principles of marketing management apply in most situations, the planning model outlined in Chapter 14 can be followed, with adjustments where required to reflect the differences and demands of overseas trade.

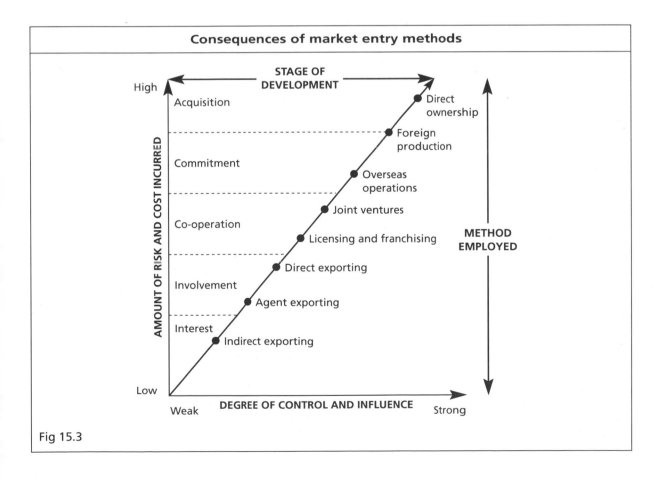

Fig 15.3

The international marketing environment has been referred to previously and, as indicated, this is the area where most differences occur and thus where most care has to be exercised. With objectives re-affirmed, the audit completed and budgets tentatively set, specific marketing mix strategies and tactics can be considered, the most important of which will concern the markets to be targeted and the products or services to be sold.

Detailed research will be required in both these areas, as attitudes to products and their associated features, benefits and unique selling points vary greatly from country to country and even region to region. Segmentation methods tend to be standard throughout, but additional criteria, such as the degree of political involvement, could also be used to establish segments and decide on targeting strategy. It is important for an organisation to balance its product and target market strategies. Figure 15.4 provides a three-dimensional view of how this could be done over a range of product types.

Similarly, companies must consider international variations in the other mix elements (whilst remembering that research methods and reliability could themselves also be affected). For example, promotion varies considerably in the theatre of international trade, with different emphases on the mass media, as mentioned in Chapter 11, sales promotion, direct marketing, personal selling, and control and legislation issues. For this reason international advertising and public relations agencies have developed specialist skills to deal with this potential minefield, for clients who can afford them.

Again, physical distribution and transportation methods vary from country to country and have to be taken into account, as do marketing channels, and all the factors which contribute towards the determination of pricing strategies. With a broad knowledge of all these effects in the chosen international market, an organisation can use portfolio or matrix analysis to help it assess potential strategies and indicate how to pitch, alter or adapt product, place, promotion and price tactics to suit the overseas market.

When contemplating further expansion plans, international marketing strategies require even more detailed knowledge and sophistication. Figure 15.5 is adapted from General Electric's screen for evaluating strategic business units, and provides an illustration of the criteria that might be

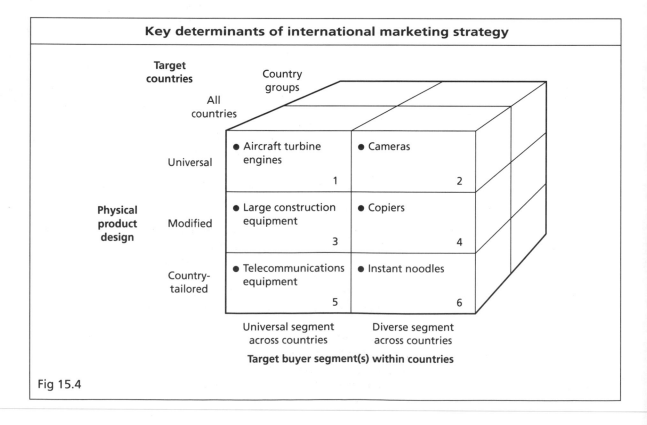

Fig 15.4

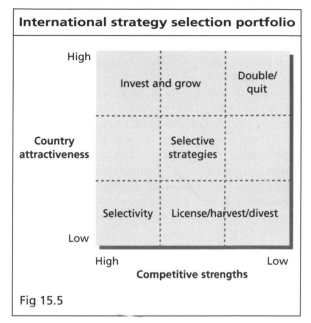

International strategy selection portfolio

Fig 15.5

Source: Adapted from Albaum, G., Strandskov, J., Duerr, E. and Dowd, L., *International Marketing and Export Management*, Addison-Wesley Publishers, 1989. Reproduced with permission

used in such a situation and some of the strategies which could be considered as a result, in relation to the relative stability, prosperity and trading potential of the countries concerned.

Depending on market opportunities, financial and organisational considerations and a host of variable factors already referred to, the firm will decide upon certain broad strategies, such as whether to target geographically dispersed or concentrated country-centred markets, before deciding on the best ways of implementing them. Together with the selected methods of control and evaluation, which again will have to be adjusted according to overseas variations, this will complete the international marketing plan. But in the eyes of most organisations the ultimate objective of overseas involvement in this era of free trade, opportunity and market expansion, is *globalisation*.

GLOBALISATION

For the big multi-nationals to become truly global demands a commitment to identical strategies, on behalf of both the organisation and its products or services, in different markets and countries around the world, rather than applying country-specific adjustments to the same basic marketing policies.

Achieving successful global growth thus requires an organisation to undertake a plan of expansion by introducing its common strategies to different countries at a realistic pace, thereby benefiting from the resulting economies of scale and gradually building up consumer confidence and acceptance.

Different companies have chosen different ways of going about this, but for most the development of distinctive *global branding* is central to marketing strategy. Whereas local brands are tailored to specific national or regional tastes, global brands will exhibit an identical formula, packaging and positioning in every country, whether directed to niche markets (e.g. Porsche and American Express) or mass markets (Castrol GTX).

When deciding whether or not to expand a brand internationally, the organisation must consider its relative transferability value in addition to the standard brand strength audit. This will involve many questions being posed, the most important of which will be to determine if the brand is:

- universal;
- modern;
- portable;
- cross-cultural;
- suited to overseas tastes;
- appropriate for international lifestyles;
- economically transferable;
- consistent with corporate objectives;
- adaptable to marketing environment and mix considerations.

An assessment can then be made of the relative difficulty of converting and managing a global as opposed to local brand and the benefits and economies of scale to be derived.

In *Marketing Strategies for Global Growth and Competitiveness*, the Business International Corporation suggests that a global brand is 'a product that bears the same name and logo and presents the same or a similar message all over the world. Usually, the product is aimed at the same target market and is promoted and positioned in much the same way.'

In 1990, the Lander Image Power Survey conducted a global assessment of the relative strengths of major corporate, service and consumer brand names across international markets and industry categories, by asking 10,000 people in the USA, Japan and Europe to evaluate more than 6000 brands for such qualities as 'share of mind' and 'esteem'. The following emerged as the 'Top Ten' global brand names according to this survey:

1. Coca-Cola
2. Sony
3. Mercedes-Benz
4. Kodak
5. Disney
6. Nestlé
7. Toyota
8. McDonald's
9. IBM
10. Pepsi-Cola

The growth in global branding has been brought about mainly as a result of the explosion of media consumption amongst the young, and in particular the interaction with television, music, sports and video sources. Donald Casey, President of Lauder Associates, has said that 'in every country, the data shows that the younger consumers are significantly more aware of international brands than their parents and have a higher opinion of international brands.'

World branding can be accompanied by other global strategies related to international market entry and expansion. For example, the Coca-Cola Company has concentrated on worldwide licensing agreements, while other companies, such as Kentucky Fried Chicken, Benetton and Budget Rent-a-Car, have focused on the development of global consumer and retail franchising arrangements.

Table 15.2 Globalisation strategies

Strategic area \ Type of organisation	Multi-domestic or multi-national e.g. retailing, insurance, motels, banking	Global industries e.g. automobiles, tyres, TV sets, cameras
Strategic arena	Collection of essentially domestic industries with overseas outlets in selected target countries	World industry, including most countries with critical markets for the product
Business strategy	Highly autonomous units, products tailored to fit circumstances of each country	Some basic unified strategy worldwide, with interdependent units and few product adjustments unless unavoidable
Strategy co-ordination	Little co-ordination	Highly co-ordinated and integrated worldwide
Production strategy	Plants scattered across host countries	Plants located on basis of maximum competitive advantage
Product strategy	Adapted to local needs	Mostly standardised and sold worldwide
Supply sources strategy	Host country sources	Sources anywhere in the world
Marketing and distribution strategy	Adapted to host country practices	Standardised worldwide approach, with minor local adaptions if unavoidable
Organisation structure strategy	Subsidiaries generally autonomous	Global structure to unify operations, major strategic decisions closely co-ordinated at global headquarters

Whichever method is used, an organisation will seek to support and enhance its universal brands and complete the process of moving along the continuum of international trade, from being primarily multi-domestic or multi-national in nature to assuming full global status. The main features of each situation are described in Table 15.2.

Worldwide, organisations are taking advantage of the speed with which the old order is disappearing and markets are opening up, in order to move towards globalisation. In the European Union, for example, new economic legislation has already resulted in:

- prices harmonising towards the lowest levels across Europe;
- purchasers buying on a pan-European basis to gain maximum financial advantage;
- distribution channels growing in number and efficiency, along with methods of transportation;
- major distributors and importers operating transnationally to exploit price differentials and low-cost suppliers;
- variety and availability of products and services increasing;
- methods of research, segmentation and promotion commonly applied across national boundaries.

The overall effect has been to increase competition between companies and countries, thus providing more choice and value for the customer, while business has grown rapidly in both the new and traditional geographic, product/service and trading sectors, despite a recession. This is a trend which will undoubtedly continue as the world moves towards the creation of one global market in the 21st century.

At the centre of these contemporary changes is the role of international marketing, and no company or country can afford to ignore the inexorable march of progress. As Theodore Levitt says, 'corporations geared to this new reality can decimate competitors that still live in the disabling grip of old assumptions about how the world works.'

ARTICLES

A1

Chippy to take bite of the Big Apple

Exclusive by Catherine Kelly

THE world's most famous chippy looks set to batter the American fast food market.

While McDonald's has swept through Britain in the last 20 years, bosses at Harry Ramsden's are hoping to strike a blow in return by moving into New York.

The idea sprung up following a visit to the Big Apple by Leeds Lord Mayor, Councillor Keith Loudon.

Served

Touring the World Trade Centre, the economic heart of America's East Coast, Coun Loudon suggested that the only food not served daily to the 25,000 diners in the building's Great Food Hall was good old British fish and chips.

"There's definitely a gap in the food spectrum in New York and this seemed ideal for Harry Ramsden's," he said.

Since the Lord Mayor's return, phone lines on both sides of the Atlantic have been as hot as the food served at the Guiseley-based emporium.

Ramsden's director Richard Richardson is now hoping World Trade centre officials will travel to Yorkshire to discuss the project and sample the goods which are already due for tasting at new restaurants planned for Hong Kong and Singapore.

"We're very flattered by the interest and I have to say we're not surprised it was a canny Yorkshireman like Keith Loudon who spotted the opportunity," he added.

With the World Trade Centre being a powerhouse of trade with tentacles stretching into Europe, the Far East, and Eastern Europe, such a move could be another lucrative string to the bow of the Ramsden empire.

The immense complex is home to 400 companies and 50,000 employees, with 350,000 people passing through every day. In the Great Food Hall, executives and workers dine daily on a choice of world cuisine, Thai to Italian, French to Yiddish.

Brendan J Dugan, from the London office of The Port Authority of New York and New Jersey, said he had no hesitation in furthering discussions.

"New York has expanded far in excess of its English namesake over the last 300 years. Having lived in London for the last eight I have discovered one thing that they still need to learn about back home – fish and chips.

"I will be returning to New York very soon and all my family would like to discover a good fish and chip shop in Manhattan."

Source: Yorkshire on Sunday, 24 April 1994

1 Where do you consider Harry Ramsden's main competition might come from in its bid to enter the American market?

2 Which are likely to be the most important environmental factors the company should be aware of in this international venture?

3 How could Ramsden's obtain the information it needs before entering the market?

4 Do you think the characteristics and potential problems of the North American market for fish and chips are any different to those in Hong Kong and Singapore, and if so, where might the differences lie?

A2

Elddis kits out in Far East

by COLIN TAPPING

A LUCRATIVE market in the Far East has opened up for Elddis Caravans.

The Consett-based manufacturer is sending out containerised kits to transform standard vans into motor caravans.

Under a new agreement, kits are being sent out to a firm in South Korea which will put together the motorhomes.

As well as the South Korean market, it is hoped sales will soon expand into the growing markets of Japan, China and Taiwan.

The kits manufactured by Elddis and shipped out include kitchens, sleeping accommodation, furniture and fittings, right down to bolts and screws.

The kits have been specially designed to convert Hyundai vans.

Development work is also taking place at Elddis to provide kits for mobile snack units used in South Korea for factory and office meal breaks.

A vehicle which can be adapted for use as a mobile stage is also being developed in time for next year's regional and national elections in South Korea, which will be contested by around 50,000 candidates.

Elddis sales director Paddy Doherty said: "The South Korean market is developing quickly for us.

"There is also potential for motor caravans to be exported via Hyundai's Far Eastern trading network to Japan, China and Taiwan."

Elddis inherited the South Korean contact on its takeover of rival Autohomes, in Dorset, bought out of receivership two years ago.

In the UK Elddis is market leader in caravans with a 17 per cent share of total sales. It is in second place for motorhomes with 20 per cent of the market.

In the 12 months to August 1993, Elddis turned in pre-tax profits of £2.8m, out of sales totalling £31m.

Increased attention to overseas sales was forecast earlier this year when property and transport group Constantine bought a majority stake in Elddis, which employs more than 350 workers.

Source: The Northern Echo, 17 May 1994

1 Which market entry method is Elddis concentrating upon? Describe how it will operate.

2 What are the pitfalls of this operation for the manufacturer?

3 What are the main benefits of dealing with Elddis for the Far Eastern countries involved?

4 Recommend further ways in which Elddis might devote 'increased attention to overseas sales'.

A3

CU lines up mega-bid for French firm

INSURANCE giant Commerical Union last night unveiled a £1.46 bn French takeover plan.

It said it was in exclusive negotiations to acquire the majority of the insurance operations of Groupe Victoire, part of the Compagnie de Suez conglomerate.

The businesses include France's sixth largest life insurer and its 11th largest general insurer. They will be paid for by a mixture of shares, debt and CU's internal resources.

Chief executive John Carter said he believed the French insurance market offers good growth opportunities, especially in life insurance and pensions products.

"The acquisition would improve the quality of Commercial Union's earnings by increasing our life profits and by improving the quality of our general insurance earnings," he said.

"It would further develop our position as a major European insurer with an important spread of international business."

Mr Carter added that the deal is consistent with the group's strategy of expanding its life insurance operations.

Source: The Northern Echo, 11 June 1994

Outline the main advantages for Commercial Union in taking over Groupe Victoire.

2 How else might CU consider pursuing its expansionist strategy?

3 How do you think the creation of the new European trading community has helped the company to expand?

4 In what ways might Commercial Union's international marketing mix change following this acquisition?

A4

Competitors click in for a better profile

BY ROGER TRAPP

KODAK and Canon are both household names in photography. By adapting their know-how, both have also entered the photocopier business. It seems odd, then, that they should have launched a strategic alliance.

But not as odd as all that. In the automobile industry such relationships are rife. For instance, the leading US companies have joined forces to develop an electric car, while some firms – like Rover and Honda in the UK – have started to co-operate with the Japanese "enemy".

Similarly, Apple has linked with Sony to take on Microsoft in the market for integrating business equipment with computer systems.

The justification is that nobody has all the answers when technology is developing all the time. It is becoming increasingly hard for one company to bear the costs of research and development and marketing and sales, and then deliver an ever-more sophisticated product at the right price. As a result, businesses are identifying their own core strengths and those of their competitors and seeking alliances.

Although the partnership route is not without its difficulties, more and more companies seem to prefer it to going alone. As Mike Mansell, Kodak's manager for the UK office-imaging business, says: "There is little sense in investing huge amounts of capital in areas outside your core expertise if a good complementary fit with a business partner can be identified."

Mr Mansell feels such a fit should allow the partners to achieve both a stronger business position and a maximum return on capital investment. But he cautions against putting all your eggs in one basket, pointing out that Kodak has a number of arrangements with such companies as IBM, Lotus, Olivetti and Unisys.

Nevertheless, at a time when the parent company, Eastman Kodak, has announced another round of job cuts, the link with Canon is seen as an important potential boost to profitability.

In the UK, the company's office-imaging arm has consistently produced double-figure growth. But for this to continue in a sector still dominated by Rank Xerox, it needs to transform a strong market position into "an extremely powerful" one. Hence the tie-up with Canon.

Although this may appear to be a case of two direct competitors getting into bed with each other, the companies have identified a number of distinguishing characteristics that they feel make them a well-suited couple.

For instance, Kodak believes its basic strengths are design and development allied to customer service and support, while Canon's are manufacturing and distribution. And although both are strong on marketing, they have different sales channels, with Kodak selling direct and Canon via dealers. Finally, the products are complementary in that Canon deals with the low to medium-volume end while Kodak serves the upper reaches.

Moreover, the two companies have had an informal relationship since the late 1980s, under which they market each other's products in their own territories. This suggests, says Mr Mansell, that they recognised the benefits of alliances earlier than most.

Doubters might feel that such cosy arrangements would make the companies softer than if they were conducting all-out war with each other. But Mr Mansell is adamant that they are still rivals in many ways.

"We don't want to compete on project development. But if you've got two salesmen going for the same customer, keen competition helps there. You lose a lot of the energy of an alliance if you don't compete."

Perhaps the strongest fear is that a friendly alliance

Source: *The Independent on Sunday*

1 What are the main advantages of strategic alliances for the organisations mentioned in the article?

2 Do you consider that such partnerships will aid or impede the creation of global brands and corporate identities for the individual companies involved?

3 Produce an international SWOT analysis for both Kodak and Canon to show how their respective situations appear to dove-tail.

4 With the partnerships highlighted, what are the relative chances of a 'friendly alliance' becoming 'an unfriendly take-over', and why?

GM company forms S American venture

PONTIAC, Michigan – General Motors Corp's Automotive Components Group Worldwide (ACG) has formed an organisation to oversee its operations and coordinate marketing and customer programmes in South America.

ACG South America, to be headquartered in Sao Paulo, Brazil, will operate along the lines of ACG Europe and ACG Asia Pacific, said J T Battenberg, a GM senior vice-president and president of ACG.

ACG has component manufacturing plants in Brazil, plus joint ventures and licensing agreements in Argentina, Colombia and Venezuela.

Jabes da Costa Cabral becomes executive director of ACG South America, effective immediately. Mr Cabral, 51, will retain the responsibilities he held in his previous job as managing director for GM's Packard Electric do Brasil.

"South America is a high potential market for our original equipment manufacturer customers, and our presence will help meet their needs for local content and delivery of components and systems," Mr Battenberg said.

Mr Cabral joined GM do Brasil in 1959. His assignments there included statistician, tool and die engineer, superintendent of tool and die, manufacturing manager and plant manager. He joined Packard Electric do Brasil in March 1988 at its operations in Paraisopolis.

ACG has 169,000 employees and 190 operations in 23 countries. Its six divisions – AC Delco Systems, Delco Chassis, Inland Fisher Guide, Harrison, Packard Electric and Saginaw – make components, modules and systems for nearly every car maker in the world. – Bloomberg Business News.

Source: Singapore Business Times, 10 August 1994 and *Bloomberg Business News*

1 Do you consider General Motors to be a multinational or a global corporation? Explain why.

2 Why is it necessary for the company to install a subsidiary organisation to oversee its continental operations?

3 Describe all the market entry methods and international strategies employed by GM and

referred to in the article, and explain how they might operate.

4 Do you think that industrial organisation GM's international marketing co-ordination is any more complex than that of a consumer corporation such as Coca-Cola? Why or why not?

ISSUES

THE INTERNATIONAL SOCIO-LEGAL-TECHNOLOGICAL ENVIRONMENT

National cultures, laws and technological standards are so diverse that the risk of overseas marketing is too great.

1 Research and describe examples of organisations committing mistakes in international marketing by misunderstanding cultural attitudes or language, in the areas of (*a*) advertising, (*b*) brand names, (*c*) colour or other product features.

2 Which legal and technological areas do you think cause most difficulty for (*a*) consumer, (*b*) service and (*c*) industrial organisations, and why?

3 Discuss what you believe to be the main reasons for Euro-Disney's poor performance in the international market, and what you think it should do to survive.

THE INTERNATIONAL POLITICAL AND ECONOMIC ENVIRONMENT

Political and economic instability renders reliable international marketing planning almost impossible.

1 Describe how changes in political and economic structures in eastern Europe and Russia have changed international marketing in those regions.

2 Choosing a relevant example of each, explain how companies marketing abroad can be affected by changes in (*a*) political organisation, and (*b*) economic decision making.

3 Discuss all the ways in which firms can go about trying to offset these difficulties.

INTERNATIONAL MARKET ENTRY METHODS

An organisation has to 'think big' if it is to retain control of its overseas interests.

1 Discuss the relative merits and de-merits of exporting via agents abroad, giving examples.

2 Research an established international licensing or franchising operation. Explain how it works and how successful it has been.

3 ICI's International Polyester business has numerous manufacturing plant facilities in countries such as Taiwan and Pakistan. List all the benefits and any difficulties of using this method of market entry.

INTERNATIONAL MARKETING STRATEGIES

International targeting and marketing mix strategies are no different to domestic ones.

1 How accurate do you believe the above statement to be? Describe where the main differences might be, using examples.

2 Explain the possible international strategies behind British Airways' investment in the American airline US Air.

3 Choose a university or organisation with which you are familiar and discuss its international marketing strategy.

GLOBAL BRANDING

A brand is not global if it is not instantly recognisable anywhere in the world.

1 Consider the 'Top Ten' global brands. What common denominators make them so memorable and successful?

2 Select examples of 'globalisation' and 'customisation' of brands and explain the reasons behind the different strategies.

3 Discuss the advantages and the disadvantages of the Mars confectionery company changing the brand name 'Marathon' to 'Snickers' in the UK market.

INTERNATIONAL MARKETING IN THE FUTURE

The world is heading towards one global market.

1 Describe and discuss the trading agreements between countries and companies which have led to this trend.

2 Debate whether one global market is (*a*) feasible and (*b*) desirable.

3 Which countries and trading blocks do you think will be most successful at the turn of the century, and why? Discuss the factors that are likely to have most affect on these trends.

4 Is the rapid emergence and strength of the Far Eastern economies an opportunity or a threat to the traditional trading powers? Why?

QUESTIONS

1 List four factors which can move a firm towards internationalisation.

2 Name two factors relating to the economic environment which an organisation should understand before trading overseas.

3 Describe two aspects of the political environment which a company should appreciate before contemplating international trade.

4 List two factors relating to the geographic environment which an organisation should research before entering international markets.

5 Name three aspects of the social environment which a company should understand before moving into international marketing.

6 Describe two factors relating to the technological environment which a firm should appreciate before trading overseas.

7 Give five areas of general marketing information invaluable to an organisation considering entering international markets.

8 List seven problems commonly experienced by organisations trading overseas.

9 Name four of the main sources of specific information available to a firm marketing abroad.

10 What are the four general stages of commitment to international marketing?

11 What are the five general stages of international market development?

12 What is indirect exporting?

13 Name three examples of types of indirect exporting.

14 What is agent exporting?

15 What are the two types of agent exporting?

16 What is direct exporting?

17 List two types of direct exporting.

18 Provide a definition of licensing.

19 What is franchising?

20 What is a joint venture?

21 Name three examples of types of joint venture.

22 Describe what is meant by 'overseas operations'.

23 What is the foreign production market entry method?

24 Name two types of foreign production.

25 Describe the direct ownership method of market entry and list its main features.

26 Explain the relationship between market entry methods and the key variables of risk, cost, control and influence.

27 What are the three main approaches to international strategic decision making?

28 List the main areas of strategic differences between a domestic and an international marketing mix.

29 Describe the main differences between domestic and international marketing research.

30 List the main differences between domestic and international market selection.

31 Name two methods of international marketing strategy selection.

32 Provide a definition of globalisation.

33 List five of the features of a global brand.

34 Name five of the world's top global brands.

35 List the policies and characteristics of (a) a multi-national company and (b) a global industry, in three selected strategic areas.

36 Describe three of the effects of European economic legislation.

37 Name three of the main trends affecting international trade.

PROJECTS

1 'There are so many pitfalls to beware of when entering the international trading arena that the expenditure is not worth the effort.' Do you agree with this viewpoint? Explain your reasons.

2 The most difficult thing about overseas trade is often said to be understanding the customs and systems of other countries. Discuss the importance of the international marketing environment, citing specific examples.

3 If few companies have either the financial or the human resources to move in a single step from trading nationally to marketing internationally, describe the most likely stages of market entry which they will go through.

4 'If you want to compete in a particular market segment in a particular country, the chances are that local companies are responding very precisely to local needs.' What organisational structures and strategies might companies adopt to meet the local competition? Give examples.

5 Joint venture agreements are opening up new markets around the world. Discuss their advantages and disadvantages and refer to specific cases.

6 Choose an example of an organisation adopting an offensive strategy for its international marketing and compare it with a company preferring to use a defensive strategy. What are the main differences and implications of the two approaches?

7 Michael Porter believes that standardisation is the key to international expansion. He cites brand name, product positioning, service quality and warranties as examples of relatively straightforward standardisation, and distribution, personal selling, sales training, pricing and media selection as areas of greater difficulty. Explain the thinking behind this viewpoint and say if you agree or disagree, and why.

8 If the concentration of international trading power increasingly lies with a limited number of global corporations, how might the small exporter hope to survive?

9 International trading restrictions have caused legal and political problems on both a company level (the pressure exerted on Laker and Virgin Airlines by British Airways) and a country level (Japanese import limitations and worldwide breaches of copyright). Using these or other examples, discuss the reasons behind these problems and whether they are likely to continue to figure prominently in the future.

10 Choose your own or any organisation and outline the international trade it undertakes, how it does so and what market opportunities exist for it in the future.

GLOSSARY

Agent exporting market entry method involving the use of intermediaries or distribution channels in overseas markets where a formal relationship exists between the exporter and the agent.

Balance of payments the total of credit and debit transactions of one country with all its international trading partners, including visible trade and invisible services.

Balance of trade a country's balance of payments for visible import and export trade.

Buying house helps indirect exporters by dealing in a wide range of goods.

Buying office aids indirect exporters by representing retail stores in consumer markets.

Buying representative an individual conducting trade for indirect exporters.

Commission agent or house intermediary working for an exporter by obtaining orders and passing them back for a fixed percentage.

Confirming house organisation buying on the

indirect exporter's instructions, arranging transport and finance, and receiving a commission.

Contract manufacturing method of foreign production market entry whereby facilities of overseas firms are used for short production runs.

Co-operative exporting method of indirect exporting where several products are taken overseas by one or a few companies to benefit smaller organisations and reduce costs.

Direct exporting market entry method involving an organisation using its own personnel and systems in the overseas market.

Direct mail order house method of direct exporting involving international catalogue and product distribution.

Direct ownership market entry method whereby an organisation acquires an overseas company by means of a merger or take-over, thus creating a wholly-owned subsidiary.

Direct selling method of direct exporting whereby organisations deal with the end-user direct.

Distribution agent acts on behalf of the exporting company with rights to purchase and maintain product stocks in the market, provide a full sales service and make a profit.

Dumping the sale of products in foreign markets at lower prices than those charged in domestic markets. Often considered unfair, and subject to legal controls.

Embargo restriction on the import of specified goods into a country, imposed either by the importing or the exporting country.

EFTA the European Free Trade Association, a group of European countries with reduced customs and tariff barriers.

EU the European Union trading block, including most of the countries in western Europe, established by the Treaty of Rome in 1962.

Exchange controls limitations on financial and trade dealings imposed by countries in the international market.

Exchange rate fixed price at which one country's currency may be exchanged for another's or for an agreed commodity of value, such as gold.

Export product or service sold directly or indirectly into international markets.

Export houses organisation specialising in selling into foreign markets, acting on behalf of indirect exporters.

Exporting activity entered into by organisations when selling products or services directly or

indirectly into international markets.

Export merchants or wholesalers organisations acting independently for indirect exporters, buying from them and selling overseas for a profit.

Floating exchange rate where an exchange rate is not fixed but allowed to find its own market level in trading negotiations.

Foreign investment the allocation and use of financial resources for particular projects, by one company or country in another country.

Foreign manufacturing or production method of market entry whereby an organisation establishes a local production facility in another country, either independently or as a subsidiary to the parent company.

Franchising method of international market entry whereby one organisation grants another the right to operate a particular business in a specific overseas country or outlet.

GATT the General Agreement on Tariffs and Trade, a treaty covering many countries world-wide which provides guide-line rules on the level and structure of import and export duties, subsidies, non-tariff barriers, and so on.

Global branding the development by international organisations of brands with identical characteristics for instant world-wide recognition.

Globalisation the development by organisations of strategies involving firms, products or services being marketed identically everywhere, thus treating the whole world as one market and enabling the company to trade globally.

IMF the International Monetary Fund, an organisation which acts as a central bank collecting money from countries and providing them with loans, so as to expand world trade and maintain economic growth.

Import product or service bought directly or indirectly from the international market.

Importing activity entered into by organisations when buying products or services directly or indirectly from the international market.

Indirect exporting market entry method involving an organisation using intermediaries informally to handle the purchase and distribution of goods to overseas markets on their behalf.

Industrial co-operation venture type of joint venture market entry method in which organisations share long-term technological expertise or production.

ational environment all the political, economic, legal, social, technological and competitive variable factors which affect organisations involved in overseas marketing.

International market entry overseas marketing strategy involving an organisation using any of several methods to sell its products or services abroad.

International marketing the act of employing the marketing concept and performing marketing functions carried out by organisations across national boundaries.

International marketing strategy all the ways in which an organisation develops and implements methods of entering foreign markets.

International trade the importing and exporting of goods carried out by companies and countries across national borders.

International trading company an organisation set up to purchase in the home market and distribute abroad on behalf of indirect exporters.

Joint venture type of market entry method involving two or more organisations forming a partnership to break into an overseas market by combining resources.

Licensing type of market entry method involving one organisation agreeing legally to transfer rights to another for the use of patents, trade-marks, brand names or expertise in overseas marketing.

Local assembly method of foreign production market entry whereby overseas plant facilities are used to assemble finished goods from exported components.

Management contracting type of joint venture market entry method involving one organisation being contracted to run some or all of the activities of another.

Manufacturing consortia type of joint venture market entry method involving two or more organisations agreeing to share in manufacturing for overseas markets.

Market entry see 'International market entry'.

Merger amalgamation of two or more organisations to create international market entry, growth, marketing or direct ownership.

Mixed venture type of joint venture market entry method involving different firms or products from different countries.

Multinational company or transnational company organisation conducting international trade in a number of countries and maintaining assets overseas.

OECD Organisation for Economic Co-operation and Development, comprising a number of member countries for the purposes of international trade development and research.

OPEC Organisation of the Petroleum Exporting Countries, set up and run by the oil-producing countries to regulate the supply and price of oil on the international market.

Overseas operations international market entry method involving an organisation setting up a subsidiary company, office or outlet abroad to sell its products or services.

Overseas sales agents method of international market entry whereby an individual or organisation abroad acts on behalf of the exporter to sell its products, but does not own the goods.

Overseas sales force method of direct exporting market entry involving an organisation's own field representatives operating across national boundaries.

'Piggy-back' schemes type of joint venture in which organisations use each other's resources to gain entry into international markets.

Quotas limitations on goods imported or exported, imposed on international trade organisations by countries or governments.

Spares and servicing agent intermediary working for an exporter by specialising in spares and servicing, usually in industrial markets.

Stocking agent intermediary working for an exporter by acting as a wholesaler and stocking the company's goods in warehouses.

Strategic alliance type of joint venture market entry method in which two or more organisations form a partnership with specific international marketing objectives.

Take-over acquisition of one company by another to create international market entry, growth, marketing or direct ownership.

Tariff tax imposed on imported or exported goods by countries as a means of controlling international trade.

Trade fairs or exhibitions direct exporting market entry method in which an organisation sends one or more representatives to secure overseas sales.

Trade mission direct exporting market entry method in which an organisation joins a delegation, often including political, economic and industrial representatives, from the home country to secure trade agreements with a country overseas.

Trading company overseas organisation set up by an exporting company as a subsidiary, in order to obtain direct representation in the target country.

Transnational company see 'Multinational company'.

UNCTAD United Nations Conference on Trade and Development, concerned with issues of international financing, development and commodity agreements.

Wholly-owned subsidiary method of direct owner-ship market entry in which a company is created by a merger, take-over or purchase and represents the parent company overseas, being completely owned by it but often acting independently.

WTO World Trade Organisation, set up to foster international trade worldwide.

SUGGESTED REFERENCES

VIDEO MATERIAL

International Marketing (series of five programmes), BBC, Open University, 1984.

Contemporary Marketing, Video Cases, No. 19 (Fluor Corp.), Boone, L. and Kurtz, D., Dryden Press, 1989.

The Europeans, 'European Advertising', BBC, 1989.

Strategy in Action, 'International strategies' (ICI); and 'Sustaining momentum' (BOC Group), Open College, Channel 4, 1990.

Business Studies, 'Telecommunications – 'phones and frontiers'; 'The Channel Tunnel – a missing link?'; and 'Marks and Spencer – Paris to Madrid', Thames TV, 1990.

Society and Social Sciences, 'The UK – continuity and change, regions apart?', BBC, Open University, 1990.

Business Matters, 'Mr Marita's mission'; 'A will to win'; 'A contract in Spain'; 'The big yellow elephant fights the green dragon'; and 'The borderless world', BBC, 1991.

Winning with Europe, 'Casting off the past', BBC, 1992.

Understanding Modern Societies, 'A global culture', BBC, Open University, 1992.

Germany Means Business series, 'The Frankfurt contenders', BBC, 1992.

France Means Business series, 'Birth of a Yogurt'; and 'Selling a City' (Lille), BBC, 1992.

Opening the Single Market, 'Trading to European Standards', BBC, Open University, 1992.

Business Matters, 'Going Solo'; and 'The giant has woken' (China), BBC, 1993.

Performance Measurement and Evaluation, 'Czech mates?', BBC, Open University, 1993.

MAGAZINE ARTICLES

Journal of Marketing Management, Vol. 1, No. 2, Winter 1985, p.145, 'Globalisation versus differentiation as international marketing strategies'; and p.201, 'Successful exporting to the Arabian Gulf region: a survey of Bahraini consumers'.

Journal of Marketing Management, Vol. 3, No. 2, Winter 1987, p.145, 'The influence of managerial characteristics on different measures of export success'.

Journal of Marketing Management, Vol. 9, No. 1, Jan. 1993, p.3, 'Developments in European business in the 1990's: the Single European Market in context'; p.65, 'The issue of import motivation in manufacturer–overseas distributor relationships: implications for exporters'; and p.79, 'Twenty years on – Europe after 2012'.

Journal of Marketing Management, Vol. 9, No. 4, Oct. 1993, p.383, 'International competition in the UK machine tool market'.

Marketing Business, April 1989, p.15, 'The Japanese art of marketing'.

Marketing Business, June 1989, p.16, 'Pathways and pitfalls of global marketing'.

Marketing Business, wFeb. 1990, p.12, 'The ultimate market?' (Japan).

Marketing Business, April 1990, p.16, 'Marketing to the USSR: perils and perestroika'.

Marketing Business, June 1990, p.8, 'Packaging Europe – and the globe?'; and p.16, 'Bigger Deutschland: bigger profits?'

Marketing Business, August 1990, p.16, 'Marketing to Spain – peseta power'.

Marketing Business, Oct. 1990, p.16, 'Poland – the opportunity'.

Marketing Business, Dec. 1990, p.12, 'BICC Cables – discovering Europe'; and p.14, 'France – une bonne marché?'.

Marketing Business, June 1991, p.18, 'Trading with Tiger' (Thailand).

Marketing Business, July/Aug. 1991, p.18, 'A nation of shopkeepers' (Italy).

Marketing Business, Sept. 1991, p.18, 'Eastern Enterprise' (Hungary).

...g Business, Oct. 1991, p.18, 'Play your cards right' (Japan).

Marketing Business, Nov. 1991, p.18, 'Swedish model'.

Marketing Business, Dec./Jan. 1991/92, p.18, 'Flying the flag'.

Marketing Business, Feb. 1992, p.19, 'British know-how'.

Marketing Business, March 1992, p.20, 'Building Blocks' (Kuwait).

Marketing Business, April 1992, p.19, 'Golden opportunity' (Spain); and p.24, 'Toshiba – made in the UK'.

Marketing Business, May 1992, p.19, 'Exchange and Mart' (Russia); and p.36, 'Marriage of convenience'.

Marketing Business, June 1992, p.20, 'Business with pleasure' (Portugal).

Marketing Business, July/Aug. 1992, p.10, 'Safe seat'; and p.20, 'Un*finn*ished business' (Finland).

Marketing Business, Sept. 1992, p.18, 'United we stand' (Germany).

Marketing Business, Oct. 1992, p.20, 'Behind the bamboo curtain' (China).

Marketing Business, Nov. 1992, p.20, 'Challenge Canada'.

Marketing Business, Dec./Jan. 1992/93, p.18, 'Made in Britain'; and p.28, 'Border crossing'.

Marketing Business, Feb. 1993, p.14, 'Two's company' (France and Germany).

Marketing Business, March 1993, p.15, 'Bill and Them' (USA); and p.30, 'An Englishman abroad' (language).

Marketing Business, April 1993, p.6, 'Swap shop'; and p.20, 'Lion's share' (Singapore).

Marketing Business, Oct. 1993, p.36, 'Brands across the border'.

Marketing Business, Dec./Jan. 1993/94, p.23, 'Japanese marketing – a review'.

Marketing Business, May 1994, p.30, 'After Apartheid' (South Africa).

Marketing Business, June 1994, p.30, 'All points east' (Japan).

Quarterly Review of Marketing, Vol. 11, No. 1, Autumn 1985, p.12, 'Marketing in lesser developed countries'.

Quarterly Review of Marketing, Vol. 13, No. 1, Autumn 1987, p.12, 'The selection of agents and distributors: a descriptive model'.

Quarterly Review of Marketing, Vol. 13, No. 4, Summer 1988, p.13, 'Multinational and international marketing in constraint economies'.

Quarterly Review of Marketing, Vol. 14, No. 3, Spring 1989, p.6, 'Managing design to improve international competitiveness'; and p.18, '1992: the realities of Single European Marketing'.

Quarterly Review of Marketing, Vol. 16, No. 1, Autumn 1990, p.1, 'Exporting to Japan – key factors for success'; and p.14, 'Eastern Europe: a dilemma for the strategic planner'.

FURTHER READING

Adcock, D., Bradfield, R., Halborg, A. and Ross, C., *Marketing Principles and Practice* (2nd edn), Pitman, 1995, ch. 24.

Albaum, G., Strandskov, J., Duerr, E. and Dowd, L., *International Marketing and Export Management*, Addison-Wesley, 1989.

Baker, M. (Ed.), *The Marketing Book*, Heinemann/ C.I.M., 1990, ch. 20.

Boone, L. and Kurtz, D., *Contemporary Marketing*, Dryden, 1989, ch. 19.

Booth, Don, *Principles of Strategic Marketing*, Tudor Publishing, 1990, chs 12 and 13.

Bradley, Frank, *International Marketing Strategy*, Prentice Hall, 1991.

Cannon, Tom, *Basic Marketing*, Holt Business Texts, 1980, ch. 10.

Cateora, Philip, *International Marketing*, Irwin, 1993.

Dibb, S., Simkin, L., Pride, W. and Ferrell, O., *Marketing*, Houghton Mifflin, 1994, ch. 25.

Foster, D., *Mastering Marketing*, Macmillan, 1982, ch. 9.

Giles, G., *Marketing*, MacDonald and Evans, 1985, ch. 12.

Jeannet, J. and Hennessey, H., *Global Marketing Strategies*, Houghton Mifflin, 1992.

Kotler, P. and Armstrong, G., *Marketing*, Prentice Hall, 1993, ch. 17.

McCarthy, J. and Perreault, W., *Basic Marketing*, Irwin, 1987, ch. 22.

Mercer, D., *Marketing*, Blackwell, 1992, ch. 14.

Oliver, G., *Marketing Today*, Prentice Hall, 1990, ch. 23.

Paliwoda, S., *International Marketing*, Heinemann, 1992.

Terpstra, V. and Sarathy, R., *International Marketing*, Dryden Press, 1990.

Walsh, L.S., *International Marketing*, MacDonald and Evans, 1993.

West, Alan, *Marketing Overseas*, MacDonald and Evans, 1987.

Acknowledgements

The Independent on Sunday.
The Northern Echo.
The Singapore Business Times and *Bloomberg Business News.*
The Yorkshire on Sunday.

16

MARKETING AND SOCIETY

DEFINITIONS

Non-profit marketing is the application of marketing concepts and activities to achieve some goal other than normal business goals of profit, market share or return on investment.

DIBB, SIMKIN, PRIDE AND FERRELL

Consumerism is a social movement seeking to augment the rights and power of buyers in relation to sellers to the point where the consumer is able to defend his/her interests. TOM CANNON

The Societal Marketing concept satisfies the needs, wants and interests of target markets . . . in a way that preserves or enhances the consumer's and the society's well-being. PHILIP KOTLER

INTRODUCTION

As we have seen, marketing affects everybody and everything, from individuals to ideas and geographical places to global corporations. Even sectors of society previously untouched by the world of business, such as religion and charities, are now discovering that the marketing concept can play an active, integral part in their existence and development.

However, with its boundaries now seemingly limitless and its influence spreading, there has inevitably been an increasing tendency towards abuse or misuse of the marketing philosophy in some quarters. This has led to a closer examination of the moral and legal issues surrounding the subject in many countries, together with a concern as to the role it should be playing in society as a whole.

Figure 16.1 highlights some of the central debates surrounding marketing. As we approach

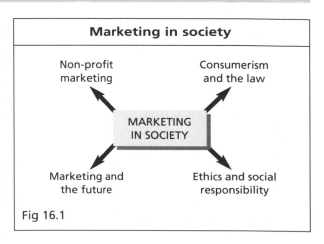

Fig 16.1

the turn of the century, these issues will undoubtedly keep surfacing and new ones arise as the subject itself continues to evolve within society.

KEY CONCEPTS

NON-PROFIT MARKETING

The rapid growth of marketing for reasons other than financial profit has been one of the most notable features of business development in recent times but, as a result of its strong links with some of society's contemporary issues, it is not without controversy.

Non-profit business has traditionally been classified into three main groups – the public sector, the voluntary sector and other organisations for which the primary objective is not expressed or measured in financial terms.

The public sector covers organisations within the scope of central government, including nationalised industries and other public corporations, local authority bodies and government departments such as Energy, Education and Health. However, with monetarist 'bottom-line' considerations increasingly the priority and privatisation prevalent, many of these organisations or the ones replacing them are now required to make a profit and as such, the fundamental principles of marketing are no different for them than for the consumer, service or industrial sectors.

So genuine non-profit marketing now tends to be confined to public service announcements and those public institutions which are still non-commercial in nature, together with organisations that require voluntary aid or membership to function, and any other business not clearly fitting into either of these two categories, as indicated in Figure 16.2.

Voluntary organisations include those that provide services for the benefit of clients, members or the public at large, rather than for shareholders, and which are not established by statute or under statutory control. Nevertheless they are not simply informal groups as they generally exhibit a formal structure of responsibility and authority.

The miscellaneous category incorporates all the other organisations for which profit is not para-

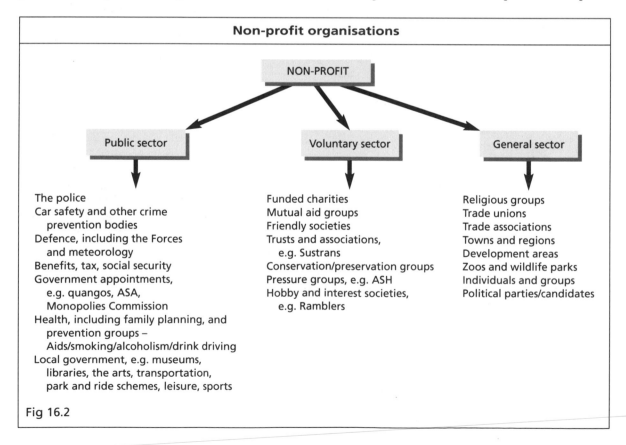

Non-profit organisations

NON-PROFIT

Public sector | Voluntary sector | General sector

The police	Funded charities	Religious groups
Car safety and other crime prevention bodies	Mutual aid groups	Trade unions
Friendly societies	Trade associations	
Defence, including the Forces and meteorology	Trusts and associations, e.g. Sustrans	Towns and regions
Development areas		
Benefits, tax, social security	Conservation/preservation groups	Zoos and wildlife parks
Government appointments, e.g. quangos, ASA, Monopolies Commission	Pressure groups, e.g. ASH	Individuals and groups
Hobby and interest societies, e.g. Ramblers	Political parties/candidates	
Health, including family planning, and prevention groups – Aids/smoking/alcoholism/drink driving		
Local government, e.g. museums, libraries, the arts, transportation, park and ride schemes, leisure, sports		

Fig 16.2

mount and this can involve the marketing of ideas, events, causes, people and places, as mentioned in Chapter 14.

All non-profit organisations possess certain characteristics differentiating them from commercial enterprises, the most important of which are:

- clear organisational structure often lacking;
- marketing effort rewarded by increased membership, donations, votes, event attendance, fewer deaths on the road or smoking-related cancer deaths, and so on, as opposed to the payment of money;
- planning and implementation of strategies incorporating social objectives;
- the need to serve two or more publics often on a non-discriminatory basis;
- lack of continuity of policies owing to changing social and political environments;
- the nebulous nature of benefits to subscribers, donors, or others directly or indirectly involved;
- organisational, financial and other resource matters usually conducted or strongly influenced by members of the public in general.

These differences mean that conventional marketing theory and practice applicable to commercial organisations are not always transferable to the non-profit sector, which thus requires a re-examination and separate treatment of the main principles. The areas where these differences are most pronounced, and where most adjustment is necessary, are outlined in Table 16.1.

Of course, the scale of adaptation necessary will vary according to the organisation involved, the nature of its business and the degree to which it can be labelled as non-profit. The situation also differs from country to country, and in the USA, for example, the commercial and non-business sectors are far more similar. This trend shows every sign of being repeated elsewhere as, despite its intangible objectives, products and services, non-profit marketing becomes more professionally organised, evaluated and subjected to the statutory and non-statutory controls of the commercial marketing world.

CONSUMERISM AND THE LAW

As we have seen throughout this book, many aspects of marketing are contentious and can arouse much controversy, often with far-reaching implications for both customers and organisations. The situations that arise can be dealt with by the

"We've made the box bigger, the contents smaller, increased the price and called it 'Improved'. Have we overlooked anything?"

Fig 16.3

Source: By courtesy of *The Yorkshire Post* and John Morris (cartoonist)

use of non-statutory pressures or recommendations, but can spill over into the legal environment if a party feels sufficiently aggrieved and if statutes exist to cover the particular circumstances.

Traditionally, there has been little come-back for the consumer in many exchange situations, and until recently the fundamental common-law maxim of *caveat emptor* ('let the buyer beware') was the rule. In other words, if buyers were not shrewd enough to assess the condition or value of the product or the integrity of the seller, then they only had themselves to blame and the law could not help to combat the type of unscrupulous dealer portrayed by the cartoon in Figure 16.3.

However, this essentially production-led doctrine clearly did not provide adequate protection for consumers or secure their four basic rights – to safety, to be informed, to choose and to be heard – as identified by John F. Kennedy in his 1962 Consumer Bill of Rights and widely established thereafter. In addition, the rights to service and to redress are often now included in this list to take account of current trends. As a result, the philosophy of *consumerism* emerged to ensure that a balance was achieved. This holds that the customer is at a basic disadvantage when purchasing and therefore has a right to advice and protection across a wide range of activities encompassed by the marketing process, including:

6.1 Variations in marketing principles and practice applicable to the non-profit sector

Area of conventional marketing theory	Main differences for practical adaptation in non-profit organisations
Marketing – definition	Difficult to identify the value of the exchange process where there is a separation between financial providers and beneficiaries (voluntary organisations) Consumer's perceptions of value vary if the product is compulsory (some education sectors), indirect (National Health Service) or a monopoly (the Police)
Marketing research	Traditional lack of commitment to information gathering and R and D Resistance to information gathering by consumers (suspicion as to its use, and accusations of wasting donors' or government's money) and organisations (often think they know best and don't need it) Small scale interviewing rather than mass questionnaire techniques used – a more sensitive way to gather important information on the market, resources, etc., as long as management and consumers are convinced of the need
Market selection	Market segmentation can be difficult as production, consumption and attraction of resources are spread widely across the population Restriction to niche markets not acceptable or viable Economically unfeasible market segments often targeted Markets tend to segment broadly into users and non-users, with strategies developed to target non-participants Voluntary segments often more identifiable, e.g. certain disease sufferers, but potential donor segments difficult to establish – psychographic variables often more relevant than traditional methods
Product	Intangibility of products/services Emphasis often on the nature of the 'cause' rather than the value of the offering Onus on the 'product' to provide a service and meet a need without price rises or other 'bottom-line' interference Benefits often spread unequally Consumer has less control of the product or service Difficult to quantify benefits for donors/members, e.g. satisfaction and public duty involvement
Place	No retail distribution structure often because of cost, so organisational access often poor Non-profit bodies are often themselves the intermediaries between 'buyer' and 'seller', e.g. charities co-ordinating the raising of funds and the operation of relieving famine Location determined by ease of access for the whole community rather than for individual consumers Methods used are job specific, e.g. charity donors recruited by street collectors, house to house, public tins, direct addresses, bank covenants, and so on (use of voluntary personnel important but can produce problems of control, compensation and acceptance)

Promotion	Mainly used in public sector for mass awareness, information giving (e.g. on price) and image building, by means of mass media advertising, PR and occasionally sales promotion Used in voluntary sector for education (e.g. Aids) and persuasion (for attracting resources), by means of personal selling, leaflets and other literature, advertising and PR. But requires sensitivity in handling and simplicity/convenience for contributions and general response Media selection can be difficult (e.g. for some under-privileged segments) so new communication channels desirable Criticisms of high-profile commercial techniques, e.g. TV advertising, particularly where little competition exists or is welcome Corporate promotions common (e.g. Oxfam) and use of celebrities to raise funds in the voluntary sector
Price	Difficult to put a price on 'essential' public services, or intangible voluntary products (where donations are at the discretion of individuals who receive certain benefits for levels of support, e.g. PR, relief activity involvement, research, etc) Inessentials can be more commercially priced, e.g. zoos Pricing required to provide a service (generally non-discriminatory), cover costs and allow something for re-investment Pricing aims difficult to achieve, even with government subsidies, gifts, etc, especially if free or token low price affordable to all Flexibility of pricing, justification of expenditure and publication of results often required
Marketing	Social objectives difficult to recognise, define or quantify, and can conflict Non-profit marketing plans hard to implement, control and evaluate Flexible strategies necessary to cope with environmental changes and multiple objectives Levels of effectiveness require constant monitoring

- complete information on product contents, ingredients, performance quality and methods of manufacture;
- accuracy of disclosure in terms of weight, dimensions, safety, durability and availability;
- security of money paid for goods and full details of price, credit and hire purchase arrangements;
- morality and truth in all forms of promotion and selling;
- control of the adverse effects of price changes, mergers and restrictive practices;
- safeguards against defective goods, shoddy workmanship and sharp practices in all other areas of marketing.

To be effective, these rights should be enforceable quickly, easily and cheaply, by recompense, restitution or damages, with support from the law if appropriate. As these guidelines have been introduced, so consumers have begun to express grievances directly to the offending party or indirectly to an intermediary, to vote with their feet by switching to alternative brands or organisations rather than suffering poor products or services, and to obtain greater access to legal advice and protection.

Thus consumerism has become widespread. At its heart is the notion of *consumer protection*, an umbrella term which covers the collection of laws, regulations, codes and information sources set up by government, industry and consumer groups to try to enforce the rights of customers in the market-place. However, there is some debate as to what exactly constitutes consumer protection and how much is socially, economically and legally desirable. Some degree of control and measurement of standards is certainly necessary, as *caveat emptor* is clearly unrealistic in this day and age.

y and non-statutory pressures are therefore generally accompanied by educational methods, such as the provision of literature and general advice, to enable consumers to be better equipped to protect themselves.

Many of the checks putting pressure on organisations to conform to minimum standards of practice are *non-statutory*, meaning that they influence marketers to behave in a certain way but are not legally binding or covered by a legal act. The main controls on marketing activities in this category are listed in Figure 16.4.

On the other hand, consumers do have recourse to many legal channels through the assortment of statutory acts which have come into being over the years, associated with various aspects of marketing and backed up by the relevant legal framework of the country concerned. The most important of these laws in the UK are described in Table 16.2, in relation to the particular element of marketing activity with which they are connected.

In addition to all the statutory methods of consumer protection, there are certain voluntary codes of practice and conduct which cover different sectors of the industry, some of which have already been referred to in previous chapters. These codes are voluntary in that it is left to the discretion of the organisation whether or not to follow them, and they are designed to extend professional stan-dards beyond legal minima or to provide guidance on standards where no legal framework exists. The most important of these codes are:

- the Code of Advertising Practice, which requires advertisements to be 'legal, decent, honest and truthful' and is monitored by the Advertising Standards Authority (see Chapter 11);
- the Code of Sales Promotion Practice (1982);
- the Direct Mail Association Code of Practice;
- the Independent Television Commission Code of Advertising Standards and Practice.

The presence of increasing numbers of statutory and non-statutory controls relating to marketing, along with professional codes of practice and the advance of the consumerism movement, has not prevented fraud or illegal operations. However, it has had the effect of exposing these practices to large mass media audiences and generally leading to tighter pressures on organisations to conform to acceptable standards, while increasing the credibility of the role of marketing in society.

The focus of consumerism has thus shifted to a number of areas where marketing and society interface, which are far more hazy and debatable in nature and therefore very difficult to regulate adequately. These are the issues covered by marketing's relationships with ethics and social responsibility.

Non-statutory and voluntary marketing controls

Fig 16.4

Table 16.2 Statutory controls in marketing

Marketing activity	Legal coverage
Marketing research/ market selection	Data Protection Act 1984 – data protection principles
Product	Trade Marks Act 1994, and 'passing off' imitation laws Food and Drug Act 1955 Copyright, Design and Patents Act 1988 Consumer Protection Act 1987, Parts 1 and 2 – liability and criminal proceedings for product defects
Place	Legislation on Agents and Third Parties Town and Country Planning Act 1962 Town and Country Amenities Act 1974 Supply of Goods and Services Acts 1971, 1973, 1982
Selling	Contract – offer, acceptance and consideration Sale of Goods Act 1979 – merchantable quality and fitness for purpose 'Cooling-off' period legislation Fair Trading Act 1973 – misinformation, confusion, pressure Unfair Contract Terms Act 1977 – exclusion clauses Consumer Credit Act 1974 – agreements, obligations, liabilities Sunday Trading Act 1994
Promotion	Weights and Measures Acts 1963, 1976, 1979 Advertisements (Hire-Purchase) Act 1967 Misrepresentation Act 1967 Control of Advertisements Regulations 1969 Trade Descriptions Act 1968 and 1972 – false or misleading descriptions in advertising and supplying such goods Sale of Goods Acts 1979 – sale by description Consumer Protection Act 1987, Part 3 – criminal liability for misleading
Price	Price Marking (Bargain Offers) Order 1979 Resale Price Maintenance
Management	Monopolies and Mergers, anti-competitive and restrictive trade practices legislation, plus EU Competition Law, etc

ETHICS AND SOCIAL RESPONSIBILITY

As discussed in Chapter 1, marketing focuses on the unpredictable human being as a consumer and is thus a business discipline which has more to do with social science than with economics. There is no one right answer in marketing, only preferred options based on sound theoretical considerations which can be tried, tested and revised where necessary.

For this reason organisations vary greatly in the ways in which they approach and implement marketing activities and in the manner in which they interpret different situations. This often leads to difficulties and controversies over issues of business ethics and social responsibility instigated by marketing or in which marketing plays a part, but which are not covered by any form of statutory or non-statutory control. Most would agree that marketers have a moral duty to abide by common acceptance of good practice, honesty and social

n, but there are often only hazy official guidelines or suggestions to follow, or none at all; and what is ethical and socially responsible to some organisations or customers is not to others.

Ethics can be defined as a set of moral principles or learned standards, open to adjustment in the light of experience and emanating from organisations, in the form of reinforcement of positive or negative statements on corporate policy, industrial codes of practice or Trade Associations, the morals and values of society, the demands and expectations of individual consumers, or a combination of all these sources.

Marketing has developed a reputation for being involved in ethical issues and many of these have been referred to previously within the chapter relevant to the particular aspect of marketing practice concerned. These, and others not mentioned before, are listed in Table 16.3 under the main subheadings of the marketing mix.

Table 16.3 Ethical issues in marketing

Marketing activity	Associated ethical issues
Marketing research	Invasion of privacy Product testing on animals Commercial and industrial espionage, gifts, bribes
Market selection	Targeting the susceptible, e.g. elderly markets – shock tactics; children's markets – pressure on parents
Product	Planned obsolescence Accuracy/honesty of product description/labelling Copying in new product development Dangerous packaging or contents, e.g. toys, drugs Other quality issues
Place	Channel control/selective distribution Elimination of small retailers and low coverage in marginally profitable results Anti-competition pressures Transportation monopolies
Promotion	Tobacco and alcohol promotion Pressure and pyramid selling Misleading or deceptive advertising/sales promotion Sexism and discrimination in promotion Knocking copy in advertising Subliminal advertising Aspirational advertising Fear-based messages Shock/offensive advertising, e.g. Benetton Excessive advertising e.g. detergent companies
Price	Loss leaders Price collusion Price discrimination Unfair pricing Excessive profits, e.g. from skim-pricing

In all these areas, the onus is on the organisation to fulfil its marketing objectives without causing offence to the consumer or public at large, infringing their rights or otherwise taking unfair advantage.

, However, in a broader context than that encompassed by issues of ethics, companies are now being urged to acknowledge that marketing also has certain social responsibilities to fulfil and it is these concerns which are at the forefront of many current developments in marketing. The *social responsibility* of marketing covers a range of issues, the most important of which can be categorised in three main areas.

1 Community relations

As the world of business is projected as an affluent sector of society and the possessor of considerable human and financial resources, so it is now also expected to contribute to society's overall well-being by assessing and understanding local and national issues or grievances and helping to solve social problems. This essentially public relations role involves organisations taking a positive, appropriate and visible stance on broad policy matters ranging from equality, discrimination, the disadvantaged and health (e.g. family planning, Aids, alcohol and anti-smoking campaigns) to education, the provision of leisure facilities, crime, safety and general welfare.

If the issue were connected more specifically with the nature of their business or geographic surroundings, organisations might also take a lead in more specific issues such as intensive farming, famine, disarmament or the nuclear problem, which might in turn lead to hitherto unexplored marketing opportunities.

2 Green or environmental marketing

As growing concern for the global environment in which we all live, expressed through phenomena such as the greenhouse effect, ozone depletion and acid rain, gave rise to the 'green' movement at both a social and political level, so the same concerns are gradually being manifested within business as a whole and marketing in particular. Consumers are increasingly insisting on a healthy environment in which to maintain a high standard of living and quality of life, for which they are now willing to pay extra. Thus there is constant pressure on organisations to conform to environmental stan-

dards in many areas, particularly relating to the pharmaceutical, chemical and oil industries. The main concerns have included air, land and water pollutants, such as pesticides, chlorinated fluorocarbons (or CFCs) and leaded petrol, cruelty to animals (fishing methods, animal research and use in product manufacture, e.g. furs and cosmetics), packaging wastage, and destruction of nature and heritage. As a result, marketing has been directed towards the search for products perceived as natural or green and therefore containing added value, such as homeopathic medicines, free-range eggs, aerosol alternatives (e.g. roll-on deodorants), recyclable materials and organic foods, as well as general movements towards conservation, regulation of car emissions, and so on.

Some organisations have taken a lead in propagating the green message, either to use as a USP or a public relations tool, while for others it is their main *raison d'être*. The Body Shop, for example, has specialised in environmentally friendly products, and it is its declared intention to generate 'a vision of a better world'.

To reflect this contemporary emphasis on green issues, the Chartered Institute of Marketing's definition of marketing (see Chapter 1) might thus be adjusted to 'the management process responsible for identifying, anticipating and satisfying the requirements of customers *and society* in a profitable *and sustainable* way.

3 Societal marketing

Philip Kotler first coined this expression when talking about the need for marketing to address all the wider ethical and environmental issues affecting the business world and society in general, and to repair the damage done by unethical practices. Kotler's view of societal marketing envisages the organisation and the consumer working together to forge a business relationship based on mutual respect and honesty, in which all parties will benefit in the short term and continue to thrive in the long term.

Societal marketing contains a number of major implications, however. It involves more than just the incorporation of a sense of social responsibility and, in its complete form, it requires a company to give up the opportunity for short-term gains if these will cause long-term harm. Again, it insists that a central objective of new product development is the well-being of both the individual and

nd it requires a company to educate its ..rget markets and recognise what are genuinely their best interests, whilst dealing justly at all times with its customers and maintaining a position of 'corporate accountability'.

So ethics and social responsibility are therefore important issues for organisations to address within their marketing activities, and instrumental factors in determining the direction which marketing will take in the future.

MARKETING IN THE FUTURE

As marketing in all its forms becomes interwoven with the fabric of contemporary society, so it has to monitor, react and adapt to society's changes or itself be forced to change by them. In recent times both business and social life has been evolving in many ways which have had and will continue to have a profound impact on how marketing is perceived, planned and implemented.

These evolutionary changes can be classified into two main groups, depending on whether the prime mover has tended to be the company or the consumer, as indicated in Figure 16.5.

Where the customer is the central catalyst for change, the main influencing factors have been shifting social structures, conditions and expecta-

tions. The old orders are changing – single people form a significant proportion of all households, while at 28 per cent the largest family unit is now the 'married – no children' sector, all of which has many obvious implications for marketing. Again, consumers are taking more risks but exercising more control, and making more social contacts but expecting more emotional experiences and pleasure as a right rather than a reward.

People thus exhibit more individuality now and have a greater variety of choice, meaning less brand loyalty and more emphasis on value for money. As a result, several movements are having a considerable effect on marketing and will continue to do so for the foreseeable future, notably:

* *The buyer's mix* – traditional marketing has centred around the Four Ps, which encompass all the key components of the marketing mix from the company's or the seller's point of view. But all the changes outlined previously have started to demand a re-organisation of the main elements of marketing focusing on the customer's perspective. Many suggestions have been put forward for this new 'buyer's mix', including the Four Cs of Customer care, Cost and value, Convenience and Communication.

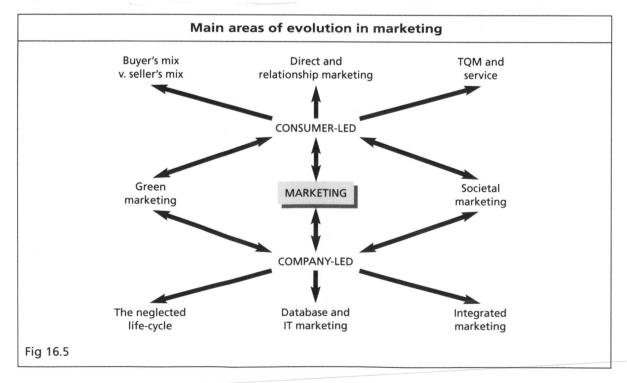

Main areas of evolution in marketing

Buyer's mix v. seller's mix — Direct and relationship marketing — TQM and service

CONSUMER-LED

Green marketing — MARKETING — Societal marketing

COMPANY-LED

The neglected life-cycle — Database and IT marketing — Integrated marketing

Fig 16.5

- *Direct and relationship marketing* – as referred to in Chapters 9 and 12, organisations are increasingly seeking to meet consumers' demands by building long-lasting relationships with their customers, as marketing is viewed more as a 'longitudinal', interactive exercise over time rather than a 'vertical', short-term, distance activity. The detailed and precise information now available will enable organisations to analyse consumer loyalty, worth and retention value, and to focus on the customer as a friend rather than an acquisition. This will complete the historical sequence from mass marketing to segmentation to niche marketing to one-to-one relationships, as the emphasis moves more and more towards direct response and personalised service. The main components in this fully integrated system are targeting strategy, interaction development and relationship building, with the management element of control to bind them all together and ensure a successful outcome.
- *TQM and service* – the interface between marketing and quality has been discussed in Chapter 6 and is becoming a vital and indispensable indicator of organisational ability and success. Associated with this is the increasing importance of the service element and the service marketing sector as a whole, outlined in Chapter 8, as the organisation is expected to provide extra added value for the ever more discerning and demanding public, and to 'get it right every time' by meeting customer requirements in areas such as 'user-friendly' products (video technology has become progressively simpler, for example).

Where the organisation has been taking the lead in developments, the main causes have tended to be environmental, in particular the changes in technology, demographic patterns and market demands which are described in earlier chapters and which have resulted in the following:

- *The neglected life cycle* – many organisations are now starting to accept the wider, long-term implications of making progress through marketing rather than looking purely at the more limited tactical considerations. In other words,

no company can survive on new business alone, and marketing is thus now increasingly seen as encompassing not just concepts such as the product life cycle but also the 'business life cycle' of customer orientation, product development, brand awareness, company growth and industrial success.
- *Database and IT marketing* – continued advances in information technology have enabled marketers to locate quickly almost any sort of marketing research information, segment their markets accurately and complete tasks efficiently over the whole spectrum of marketing activities. These developments will undoubtedly become global as companies take advantage of the establishment of the 'information super-highway', and the growth of database methods will lead to further expansion in direct and relationship marketing.
- *Integrated marketing* – the ultimate goal for a marketing orientated company is to combine all its marketing functions and activities into a logical and united philosophy of business and customer focus. Such an integrated approach will become essential for organisations that want to maximise their effectiveness, and will require all components of the marketing system to reflect the same objectives and be consistent that each other, rather than being viewed as separate, temporary and isolated activities. This approach will demand a blend of theoretical expertise, practical creativity and marketing commitment, at all levels and in all situations.

In addition to these developments, the influential green and societal marketing movements mentioned before are gathering momentum, led by a combination of consumer and organisational stimuli, and social marketing campaigns of all types will become increasingly necessary and commonplace.

The use of and need for marketing in broader contexts is thus growing rapidly, and all of these movements will gradually change the face of the subject in every sector. An ever more professional, customer orientated approach, therefore, is required for business success at all levels towards and into the next century.

ARTICLES

A1

Boosting the congregation

CHURCHES in the North have been quick to take advantage of provisions in the new Broadcasting Bill allowing religious advertising on radio and television. The previous ban was a strange anomaly and in view of their declining congregations, churchmen are right to set aside traditional reserve and adopt the marketing strategies of the 20th century. Their problem, shared by a number of institutions today, is a failure to attract the interest of the 15–25 year-olds. Any advertising account executive will tell you that without a radio and television campaign, you don't stand a chance. But the clergy should beware of the 'quick-fix' promised by paid-for media campaigns. What is more important, of course, is what the persuaded find when they tentatively come through the church doors. Many will be bored by some of the traditional forms of worship practised in our parish pulpits, others will be offended by the stridency and zealotry of services found in some evangelical churches. There must be a middle way, an approach to God which strikes a chord with all age groups and classes. Perhaps before the advertising men are brought in, some market research would be in order.

Source: The Northern Echo, 30 March 1991

1 What are the main objectives of religious organisations? In what ways, if any, are they becoming more commercial?

2 Outline the religion 'product'. Suggest the most appropriate promotional methods by which it can be conveyed to potential customers, giving reasons.

3 What methods might church leaders use to conduct the market research suggested in the article?

4 Do you agree that 'churchmen are right to set aside traditional reserve and adopt the marketing strategies of the twentieth century'? What other alternatives are available to them?

A2

Too little fruit lands Kelloggs a £4,000 fine
By DENIS McLOUGHLIN

CEREAL giant Kelloggs was fined yesterday for putting too little fruit and too much fibre in its popular breakfast cereal.

Consumers were sold short by the company, which declared that 'Fruit and Fibre' contained 27.5 per cent fruit.

But samples of cartons from four different stores in Cleveland showed the content was not that high.

The phantom fruit proved a costly error for Kelloggs, which admitted four charges under the Food Safety Act at Teesside Magistrates Court.

In a case brought by the county council trading standards, the company was fined £4,000 with £1,200 costs for misleading labels on four sample cartons.

The company emphasised the fruit content on the front of the packet and declared the actual amount on the side at 27.5 per cent.

But Anne Silvester, prosecuting, told the bench that samples analysed from four stores in the county were found to have fruit contents as low as 13 per cent.

Simon James, for the company, said the 27.5 per cent marking was an average fruit content. In the spring of 1992, Kellogg decided to put an extra ten per cent of fruit into the packet and the packaging simply said 'more fruit', said Mr James.

He said the 27.5 per cent statement on the side was added following queries from North Yorkshire trading standards.

Mr James said that during production, samples were taken every hour to ensure the fruit content was within the guidelines. The court heard the company was under no obligation to indicate the percentage of fruit and it was not now included on the packaging.

Source: The Northern Echo, 9 February 1994

1 Describe the statutory legislation affecting the company in this case and explain how it has been administered. Are there any other legal controls which also could have been used?

2 What non-statutory controls might additionally be putting pressure on Kelloggs to conform to the law?

3 What part of the organisation do you think could be responsible for this situation? In what ways might it be costly for the company in the future?

4 Kelloggs is not legally obliged to indicate the percentage of fruit on its packaging and it does not now do so. Do you think it should, and if so, why?

A3

Stereo ad went too far

THE Advertising Standards Authority has ruled a poster campaign of a couple having an intimate cuddle in the front seat of a car was "offensive".

The car stereo ads had the caption: "Goodmans. Britain's second favourite in-car entertainment."

But 40 people nationwide objected to the "unnecessarily erotic" posters, designed by Saatchi and Saatchi.

Goodmans said the most common reaction to the posters had been humour and the joke had been "understood and appreciated", said the firm.

But the advertising watchdog said: "The illustrations showed a lack of social responsibility."

Source: *The Northern Echo*, 12 November 1991

1 Why do you think Saatchi and Saatchi created this style of advertisement for Goodmans car stereos?

2 From the description of the advert given in the article, why do you feel the 'joke' has misfired? Why do you think it shows 'a lack of social responsibility'?

3 Would you find such an advert 'offensive'? If not, describe an advertising or marketing campaign which you do consider comes into that category.

4 Describe the full role of the ASA in dealing with this advertisement and the resulting complaints. What options are now open to Goodmans in reacting to the ASA statement?

CONSUMERS

Nearly four in 10 green shoppers believe supermarkets selling environment-friendly products are exploiting the market.

They feel the companies are merely making a profit rather than genuinely trying to help to protect the earth, says a survey published today.

Only 10pc of shoppers believed campaigns were aimed at persuading them that shops were caring businesses.

Many thought the advertising and public relations was just a smokescreen, said the survey from market researchers Mintel. Its research suggested that those who went out of their way to buy environmentally friendly products: "Do so in spite of corporate public relations efforts, rather than because of them".

About 40pc of 'dark greens' actively sought green and ethical products and were especially choosy.

But supermarkets should look after them as they tended to be more affluent and shop for larger households than other customers, said the report.

"Supermarkets need to be aware their efforts to present themselves to the consumer in the best possible light are by no means accepted uncritically, especially among those at whom the publicity is most often directed – the green and ethical shoppers," the survey said.

"Perhaps companies should take a more open stance and explain the difficulties in taking into account both environmental and ethical considerations while still pleasing the cost and quality-conscious shopper."

The greenest and most ethical shoppers went to stores with the most upmarket customers. These included stores such as Marks and Spencer and Sainsbury's.

The Co-op has actively promoted environmental issues by measures such as switching some of its farmland to organic production.

But the Co-op has a relatively small number of green shoppers because of the store's elderly and downmarket customer profile, Mintel said.

The survey said women shoppers were most conscious of the environment.

A total of 46pc actively sought green products compared with 31pc of male shoppers.

The greenest consumers tended to be aged under 24 or between 35 and 44.

Source: The Northern Echo

1 Summarise the main findings of the Mintel report on 'green' and 'ethical' products. Describe how the Co-op has become involved in this area. How successful do you think it might be in the future?

2 Do you believe that organisations are 'exploiting the market' when selling environmentally friendly products, or are they mainly genuine? Discuss reasons and examples.

3 How do you think a free, meaningful dialogue on environmental and ethical matters might be achieved between the organisation and its publics? The article suggests that most purchasers of green products would buy them anyway whether they were marketed or not. Do you agree? How might an organisation go about promoting its environmentally friendly products?

4 Describe your own 'green' product purchasing habits, if any. Do you think environmental marketing will be an important part of the whole marketing package in the future, and if so, why?

A5

Ethics audited at Traidcraft

By IAN GREEN

TRAIDCRAFT the Gateshead-based ethical trading company has published what it claims is the first full social audit carried out by a public company.

The report examines the Christian organisation's operations from the viewpoint of suppliers, staff, and agents as well as shareholders.

It reveals that a shared vision of fairer trade is important for them all, but emphasises the difficulty of assessing the company's progress.

Richard Evans, external affairs director at the company, said: "As Traidcraft has felt more keenly the financial pressure of trying to run an effective business it seemed right to the directors, to measure our social and ethical performance, as well as measuring and reporting upon our financial performance. Hence the notion of a social audit."

The company, which operates throughout the Third World, committed itself to the process last year.

The cost of the audit, which defines Traidcraft's impeccable credentials as an ethically-led business, came in at £20,000 compared to £18,000 for a statutory financial audit.

The financial accounts show that Traidcraft returned to profit in the year to March 1993, with pre-tax profits of £74,000 compared to a £23,000 loss last time. During the period under review turnover rose 8pc to £5.8m.

The social auditor, Ed Mayo, director of the New Economics Foundation, says in his report that Traidcraft needs to develop the audit to make it more useful.

Traidcraft was founded in 1979 and imports and distributes handicrafts, fashion goods, beverages and foods sourced in the Third World. It employs about 123 staff at Gateshead and markets its products through mail order catalogues.

Professor Rob Gray of Dundee University, a member of the audit advisory group, praised Traidcraft's initiative.

He said: "It is a massive undertaking, but you can see little bits of it in disclosure about companies' community involvement, employee and pension affairs. It's do-able.

"The question is whether there's a will to do it."

Source: The Northern Echo

1 Describe what is meant by a 'full social audit'. Do you believe 'social and ethical performance' can be accurately measured, and if so, how?

2 How do you think Traidcraft might have initially created the 'will' to pursue this concept within the organisation?

3 Explain how disclosures about 'companies' community involvement, employee and pension affairs' could help to establish this societal marketing approach. Can you suggest any additional ways of supporting this philosophy?

4 Do you think Traidcraft is adopting a viable marketing model for organisations to follow in the future, and if so, why?

ISSUES

NON-PROFIT MARKETING

Public sector and voluntary organisations have no profit motive, therefore no need to commit resources to marketing.

1 Discuss the validity of this statement. Are there any situations in which it might be true?

2 Select a charity or other non-profit organisation with which you have been personally involved or are familiar, and discuss the main focal points of its marketing effort.

3 Prepare an outline plan for the marketing of either (a) police activities in a major city, (b) a regional weather service or (c) a canal or railway preservation society. Discuss the organisation's objectives, where the marketing emphases will be placed and how the plan might be evaluated.

CONSUMERISM

The consumer movement is a laudable control mechanism in theory but a 'paper tiger' in practice.

1 What is meant by this statement? Discuss whether it is accurate, citing examples from the broadcast or print media. Do you view consumerism as an opportunity or a threat? Could it get out of hand?

2 Recount any experience where you have had cause to complain about a product or a service. Were you satisfied with the outcome and what other consumer channels might you have used?

3 Debate (a) whether the consumer movement will grow in size and importance in the future, and if so, in what ways; and (b) what is likely to be the response of organisations and business in general to the increasing influence of consumer pressure groups.

THE LAW RELATING TO MARKETING

Marketing laws do not go far enough, either in scope or enforcement, to be truly effective.

1 Briefly describe the main statutory laws relating to marketing. Do you think that they are enforced widely enough? Do the punishments tend to fit the crime?

2 List and debate the marketing activities you consider are not well served by legal controls. What laws would you consider introducing and why?

3 Research, explain and discuss a marketing-related situation dealt with recently in a court of law. Was the law effective? Why or why not?

ETHICS IN MARKETING

Moral issues are really social rather than business considerations and not the concerns of marketing people.

1 Do you agree with the viewpoint expressed above? Discuss the main areas where marketing and ethics interface and in what circumstances, if any, an organisation can afford to ignore the moral environment. Do you believe ethics can be taught?

2 Outline and compare the cases for and against advertising (a) tobacco and (b) alcohol products. Discuss the ethical and economic issues involved. Do you feel organisations providing these products should be able to use sponsorship as a promotional tool when they are banned from mass media advertising?

3 Describe an issue of marketing morals which has affected you personally or concerns you generally, and discuss how you think it should be resolved, e.g. should marketers directly target children?

SOCIAL RESPONSIBILITY IN MARKETING

All organisations have a duty to be socially responsible in their marketing activities.

1 Do you believe Benetton has been practising social responsibility in drawing the public's attention to global issues by shock advertising tactics?

2 Discuss the differences between social responsibility in (a) consumer, (b) service and (c) industrial marketing, giving examples.

3 How much say do you consider organisations should have in the running of a local community and its resultant issues?

MARKETING IN THE FUTURE

Marketing cannot become more of an exact, accountable science, whilst also meeting the needs of individuals and society at the same time.

1 Discuss whether the aims of relationship, green and societal marketing are compatible with a business world increasingly led by technology and finance. Do they possess realistic and attainable goals?

2 Debate what you believe will be the most important challenges which the discipline of marketing will have to face and/or the changes it will have to undergo as we approach the 21st century.

3 Suggest a definition of 'marketing' appropriate for theoretical and practical use in the next decade. Explain and discuss the differences in emphasis from current definitions.

4 Do you believe local and national governments should have a greater say in the future direction of marketing? If so, in what specific areas and how might this involvement be manifested?

QUESTIONS

1 Give a definition of non-profit marketing.

2 List five examples of non-profit marketing in the public sector.

3 List three examples of non-profit marketing in the voluntary sector.

4 Give three other examples of non-profit marketing.

5 List ten ways in which the marketing of non-profit organisations differs from the marketing of commercial enterprises, in any of the marketing mix categories.

6 Define the term 'consumerism'.

7 List four major rights of consumers.

8 What is consumer protection?

9 What is meant by non-statutory and voluntary controls?

10 Give five different types of non-statutory and voluntary controls in marketing.

11 What is meant by statutory controls?

12 List six different laws regulating marketing and relate them to their particular area of marketing activity.

13 Give two examples of voluntary codes of marketing practice.

14 What is meant by ethics in marketing?

15 List ten examples of ethical issues in marketing and relate them to their particular area of marketing activity.

16 What is meant by social responsibility in marketing?

17 Give two examples of organisations involving themselves in community relations matters.

18 Define green or environmental marketing.

19 Give four examples of green or environmental marketing.

20 What is meant by societal marketing?

21 Give two examples of current and future changes in marketing which are consumer led.

22 Give two examples of current and future changes in marketing which are led by the organisation.

23 What is integrated marketing?

PROJECTS

1 'It is a fact that donors to charitable organisations receive few, if any, tangible rewards; donor rewards are primarily psychological and spiritual in nature' (Yavas *et al.*). What effect does this have on marketing in the voluntary sector?

2 Consider the contention that genuine non-profit marketing is a contradiction in terms and thus does not really exist, giving examples.

3 'If customers perceive themselves not as patrons to be served but as resources to be manipulated they will express their resentment both in their purchasing and in their voting behaviour' (Peter Drucker). Discuss this viewpoint and explain the role of the individual in the consumerism movement.

4 'Nine out of ten dissatisfied customers don't complain, they just go elsewhere' (Institute of Customer Care). How might the consumer movement encourage people to complain through official channels rather than not bothering, and what effect could this have?

5 How effective are statutory controls relating to marketing? Give examples and discuss the current role of non-statutory bodies in helping to enforce the law.

6 'Sound marketing ethics are essential for success in contemporary business.' Use examples of contemporary organisations to discuss whether this is so.

7 What practices have led to marketing gaining a bad press in the past, and how have organisations gone about changing this image?

8 'If it's legal to sell, then it's permissible to sell it' (Advertising Association). Discuss this statement with relation to the marketing of tobacco.

9 How realistic do you consider the application of societal marketing and social responsibility by organisations to be in business today?

10 'The consumer is willing to pay an organisation more for its use of environmentally friendly products and its adherence to policies benefiting local and national society.' Explain this statement with reference to specific examples.

11 'Marketing is an evolving discipline that must develop new answers as new problems arise'. (Philip Kotler). What are these 'new problems' likely to be and what 'new answers' might be developed to cope with them?

12 Describe the main ways in which you believe marketing might evolve as a business discipline in the future.

13 In what ways do you feel organisations have failed to fulfil the true spirit of the marketing concept in contemporary society?

GLOSSARY

Advertisements Act law relating to marketing used as a statutory control mechanism.

Aspirational advertising unethical form of advertising encouraging consumers to purchase products or services in the unrealistic belief that they will attain the 'good life' as a result.

Buyer's mix new philosophy of marketing which considers the mix from the consumer's rather than the seller's perspective.

Caveat Emptor Latin legal expression meaning 'let the buyer beware', implying consumer common sense is necessary and no legal backing or obligation exists.

Citizens Advice Bureau non-statutory control method used by consumers when seeking help in problems relating to marketing.

Code of ethics voluntary control method recommending certain ethical standards for employees to observe in different aspects of marketing and organisational practice.

Code of practice voluntary control code laid down in certain areas of marketing and adhered to by organisations.

Code of sales promotion practice specific voluntary code of practice relating to the sales promotion industry.

Community relations awareness aspect of social responsibility in marketing whereby the organisation involves itself positively with local and national issues, grievances and problems.

Consumer Credit Act law relating to marketing used as a statutory control mechanism.

Consumerism movement by individuals and pressure groups designed to ensure that the consumers' best interests are safeguarded.

Consumer protection statutory and non-statutory controls designed to safeguard consumers, increase the information available to them and provide warnings on misleading and deceptive techniques.

Consumer Protection Act law relating to marketing used as a statutory control mechanism.

Cooling-off period a stipulated time period and ethical non-statutory control written into some sales contracts to give consumers thinking time, after a purchase, in which they might change their mind.

Corporate accountability organisational identification with societal marketing and thus with the moral standpoint that a company should be accountable for all its actions that involve wider issues affecting society.

Data Protection Act law relating to marketing research used as a statutory control mechanism.

Direct Mail Association Code of Practice specific voluntary code of practice relating to the direct mail industry.

Environmental marketing see 'Green marketing'.

Ethics appropriate policies formulated by organisations concerning problems, situations or other controversial issues in which the company is involved.

Fair Trading Act law relating to marketing used as a statutory control mechanism.

Fitness for purpose fundamental basis of the statutory Sale of Goods Act.

Food and Drug Act law relating to marketing used as a statutory control mechanism.

Green marketing or environmental marketing development of marketing mixes for products which are sustainable and do not harm the environment, reflecting society's concern about such matters as expressed by the green movement.

Information super-highway the development of a global electronic communications network which is revolutionising the practice of marketing.

Integrated marketing the combination of all the functions and activities of a marketing orientated organisation into one central philosophy of business.

ITC Code of Advertising Standards and Practice voluntary code of practice relating to TV advertising and formulated by the Independent Television Commission.

Laws relating to marketing all those legal statutes covering the activities of marketing.

Merchantable quality fundamental basis of the statutory Sale of Goods Act.

Misrepresentation Act law relating to marketing used as a statutory control mechanism.

Neglected life cycle the wider perspective of marketing whereby the organisation aims for a customer orientation, product development, brand awareness, company growth and industrial success.

Non-profit marketing marketing performed by organisations in the public and voluntary sectors, where profit is not the primary objective.

tutory controls all the non-legal influences and pressures on companies, relating to marketing, which are not enforceable in a court of law.

Office of Fair Trading non-statutory control method used by consumers when seeking help in problems relating to marketing.

Patent Act law relating to marketing used as a statutory control mechanism.

Public sector marketing marketing performed by non-profit organisations such as government.

Rights the four basic areas to which consumers should have access – the rights to safety, to be informed, to choose and to be heard, as identified by John F. Kennedy.

Sale of Goods Act law relating to marketing used as a statutory control mechanism.

Social marketing the design, implementation and control of programmes calculated to influence the acceptability of social ideas or causes and involving all aspects of marketing activities.

Social responsibility the orientation of marketing organisations towards dealing positively with important issues affecting society as a whole.

Societal marketing an organisational philosophy whereby marketing decisions are made after consideration of consumers' and society's short- and long-term needs, wants and interests.

Statutory controls all the legal controls relating to marketing which are enforceable in a court of law.

Sunday Trading Act law relating to marketing used as a statutory control mechanism.

Supply of Goods and Services Act law relating to marketing used as a statutory control mechanism.

Trade Descriptions Act law relating to marketing used as a statutory control mechanism.

Trade Marks Act law relating to marketing used as a statutory central mechanism.

Trading Standards Department non-statutory control method used to monitor accuracy and ethics in marketing.

Unfair Contract Terms Act law relating to marketing used as a statutory control mechanism.

Voluntary controls system of self-control adopted by advertising, for example, whereby organisations conform to a defined code of practice.

Voluntary sector marketing marketing by non-profit organisations such as charities.

Weights and Measures Act law relating to marketing used as a statutory control mechanism

'Which?' magazine conveyor of consumer watchdog reports and surveys and thus a non-statutory marketing control mechanism.

SUGGESTED REFERENCES

VIDEO MATERIAL

Marketing in Action, 'Launching Neptune', BBC, Open University, 1985.

It's a Deal (consumer legislation), Distributive Industry Training Board, 1985.

The Marketing Mix, 'Social Variety', No. 3, 'Fundraising for Charity', Yorkshire Television, 1988.

Contemporary Marketing, Video Cases, No. 1, 'The US Army', Boone, L. and Kurtz, D., Dryden Press, 1989.

Business Studies, 'Going Green – threat or opportunity?', Thames TV, 1989.

Business Matters, 'The Giving Business' (charities), BBC, 1990.

Business Matters, 'Managing to be Green', and 'The Saints and the profits', BBC, 1991.

Walk the Talk, No. 3, 'Dinosaurs and sacred cows' (museums), BBC, 1991.

Good housekeeping – decade of decency, Marketing Videotape, Dibb, S., Simkin, L., Pride, W., and Ferrell, O., Houghton Mifflin, 1991.

Nature, 'Close encounters of the European kind – lies, damned lies and labels', BBC, 1992.

This Week, 'Violating Virgin', ITV, 1992.

First Tuesday, 'Tobacco Wars', Yorkshire Television, 1992.

Dispatches, 'Body Search' (Body Shop), Channel 4, 1992.

One World, 'Greenbucks – the challenge of sustainable development', Australian Film Finance Corporation, 1992.

We have ways of making you think, 'Selling politics – American style', BBC, 1992.

Off the back of a lorry, 'Waste wars', BBC, 1992.

Winning resources and support, 'Strategies for survival' (non-profit), BBC, Open University, 1993.

Eat up, 'Sweet Persuasion', Channel 4, 1993.

The God tapes, 'Selling God' (religion), Channel 4, 1994.

Forty Minutes, 'A case of corporate murder' (Laker Airways), BBC, 1994.

Poor Dear, No. 1, 'Advertising in the Disability Charity Industry', BBC, 1994.

The Business, 'From food to fashion accessory' (Häagen Dazs), BBC, 1994.

RADIO MATERIAL

Market Forces 'Packaging the professionals', and 'Marketing the unmarketable', BBC Radio, 1985.

MAGAZINE ARTICLES

Business Magazine, Vol. 30, No. 5, 1980, pp. 41–5. Yaras, U., Rieken, G., and Parameswaran, R., 'Using psychographics to profile potential donors'.

European Journal of Marketing, Vol. 17, No. 5, 1983, pp.33–43. 'A re-examination of marketing for British non-profit organisations', Octon, C. M.

Journal of Marketing Management, Vol. 8, No. 2, April 1992, p.147, 'Producing environmentally acceptable cosmetics? The impact of environmentalism on the UK cosmetics and toiletries industry'.

Journal of Marketing Management, Vol. 9, No. 3, July 1993, p.301, 'Charity affinity credit cards – marketing synergy for both card issuers and charities?'

Marketing Business, Oct. 1988, p.6, 'Elements of nuclear marketing'.

Marketing Business, Dec. 1989, p.18, 'Putting a price on being green'.

Marketing Business, Feb. 1990, p.8, 'The unconscious marketer'.

Marketing Business, Oct. 1990, p.2, 'Green marketing: a passing fad?' and p.18, 'Recruit-ment – marketing ethics'.

Marketing Business, Jul./Aug. 1991, p.14, 'Adam's ethics'; p.32, 'Please give generously'; and p.37, 'The appliance of green science'.

Marketing Business, Sept. 1991, p.32, 'On the front line'.

Marketing Business, Nov. 1991, p.8, 'Money to burn' (tobacco); p.24, 'The body and soul of marketing' (Body Shop); and p.29, 'Consumer Speak' (Benetton).

Marketing Business, Dec./Jan. 1991/92, p.8, 'Present Tense' (children and toys).

Marketing Business, March 1992, p.24, 'Political packaging'; and p.30, 'Product liability' (law).

Marketing Business, April 1992, p.10, 'Greener than thou'.

Marketing Business, May 1992, p.24, 'Face value'; and p.30, 'Data protection'.

Marketing Business, July/Aug. 1992, p.30, 'Bridgework' and p.41, 'Duty Calls'.

Marketing Business, Sept. 1992, p.22, 'Advertising credit' (law).

Marketing Business, Oct. 1992, p.31, 'CIM Forum' (ethics).

Marketing Business, Nov. 1992, p.8, 'Standard Practice' and p.18, 'Controlling product descriptions'.

Marketing Business, Feb. 1993, p.29, 'Consumer Speak' (condoms); and p.30, 'The cost of giving it away' (sales promotion law).

Marketing Business, April 1993, p.28, 'Price Promises' (sales promotion law).

Marketing Business, June 1993, p.18, 'Protection Racket'.

Marketing Business, Sept. 1993, p.22, 'Can marketing save the unions?' and p.40, 'Putting your house in order'.

Marketing Business, Oct. 1993, p.8, 'Ministries, missions and markets' (the church).

Marketing Business, Nov. 1993, p.42, 'Legal make-up' (cosmetics).

Marketing Business, Dec./Jan. 1993/94, p.12, 'The transformation of marketing – new marketing vision'; p.28, 'Election promises' (politics); and p.36, 'Childish things'.

Marketing Business, Feb. 1994, p.34, 'Marketing laws – a European flavour'.

Marketing Business, April 1994, p.33, 'Bill of Fare' (food labelling laws).

Marketing Business, June 1994, p.24, 'The marketing prescription' (National Health Service).

FURTHER READING

Adcock, D., Bradfield, R., Halborg, A., and Ross, C., *Marketing Principles and Practice* (2nd edn), Pitman, 1995, chs 23 and 24.

Baker, M. (Ed.), *The Marketing Book*, Heinemann C.I.M., 1990, chs 22–24.

Boone, L., and Kurtz, D., *Contemporary Marketing*, Dryden, 1989, chs 1 and 2.

Cannon, Tom, *Basic Marketing*, Holt Business Texts, 1980, chs 1, 19 and 20.

Dibb, S. Simkin, L., Price, W. and Ferrell, O., *Marketing*, Houghton Mifflin, 1994, ch. 22.

., and Fraedrich, John, *Business Ethics*, ⌐ton Mifflin, 1994.

Eureka, W., and Ryan, N., *The Customer-driven Company: Managerial perspective on quality function deployment*, Irwin, 1994.

Foster, D., *Mastering Marketing*, Macmillan, 1982, ch. 9.

Giles, G., *Marketing*, MacDonald and Evans, 1985, ch. 1.

Kotler, P. and Armstrong, G., *Marketing*, Prentice Hall, 1993, chs 1, 18 and 19.

McCarthy, J. and Perreault, W., *Basic Marketing*, Irwin, 1987, chs 1 and 23.

Oliver, G., *Marketing Today*, Prentice Hall, 1990, ch. 25.

Peattie, Ken, *Green Marketing*, MacDonald and Evans, 1992.

Smith, N. Craig and Quelch, John A., *Ethics in Marketing*, Irwin, 1992.

Acknowledgements

The Northern Echo.

MARKETING: PRINCIPLES AND PRACTICE
2nd Edition

The first edition of *Marketing: Principles and Practice* was well received by lecturers everywhere.

'A first class text bringing the subject to life with varied excellent examples.'

'Clearly written with good coverage of, and effective comment on, recent developments in marketing.'

'It is a good comprehensive marketing text and a useful Instructor's Manual.'

'An excellent introductory text for multi-disciplinary undergraduates for whom marketing is a unitary module.'

In producing the second edition, we have taken account of the thousands of comments that we received to produce a core textbook that we think is exactly what marketing lecturers have been waiting for.

The second edition of this best-selling text has been revised and up-dated to provide an even more student-friendly guide to the whole of the marketing process. Now printed in two colours and with a greater number of illustrations and diagrams, *Marketing: Principles and Practice* is the perfect text for use on introductory and modular marketing courses.

The new edition contains additional material on direct marketing, advertising and PR and includes questions, exercises and European mini-cases throughout.

Marketing: Principles and Practice
- is presented in a highly accessible and student-friendly style
- is perfect for use on modular and introductory marketing courses
- is ideal for non-specialists

Dennis Adcock, Coventry Business School, **Ray Bradfield**, Southampton Institute of HE, **Al Halborg**, Coventry Business School and **Caroline Ross**, Coventry Business School

0 273 60734 0

MARKETING
A Multiple Choice Study Guide

Multiple choice questions are used increasingly by students on a wide range of courses, as a revision aid and by lecturers as a supplementary test bank to the recommended text. This new book of self-testing, multiple choice questions is conveniently arranged under the principal marketing subject headings and the questions are graded in order of difficulty. Complete with answers and an introduction on the best use of the book, it will be invaluable to students in their preparations for the increasing numbers of examinations which make use of multiple choice questions.

Every fifth question is left unanswered for use in seminars or course preparation.

Marketing: A Multiple Choice Study Guide
- covers a broad range of marketing subjects
- contains questions of varying difficulty
- arranges multiple choice questions distinctly under key marketing headings
- is an ideal study guide and revision aid

Dr Everett Jacobs, Senior Lecturer in Business Studies and former Chairman, Business Studies Board of Study, Sheffield University Management School

0 273 60280 2

MARKETING INTERFACES
Exploring the Marketing and Business Relationship

The exciting text is the first of its kind which seeks to explore and clarify the relationship between marketing and the other functional areas of business. It enables both marketing specialists and non-marketers to better understand the nature of marketing and its interdependencies with Corporate Strategy, Finance, Manufacturing, Research and Development, Design, Information Technology and Human Resource Management. Each section is written by a specialist in that particular functional area and is illustrated with mini-cases and two major case studies.

Marketing Interfaces
- provides marketers with a necessary and clear view of the operations and capabilities of the other main business areas and how they impact upon marketing strategy and operations
- provides non-marketers with an up-to-date perspective of marketing and their own role in contributing towards the development of marketing orientation and the implementation of marketing strategy
- recognises the importance of improved inter-functional communications and understanding in achieving organisational success
- illustrates each chapter with mini-cases and two major case studies written to provide integrated cross-functional analysis
- is ideally suited to marketing and general management courses

Ian Wilson, Senior Lecturer, The Business School, Staffordshire University

0 273 60286 1